Alcoholism and Treatment *by David J. Armor, J. Michael Polich, and Harriet B. Stambul*

A Biodevelopmental Approach to Clinical Child Psychology: Cognitive Controls and Cognitive Control Theory *by Sebastiano Santostefano*

Handbok of Infant Development *edited by Joy D. Osofsky*

Understanding the Rape Victim: A Synthesis of Research Findings *by Sedelle Katz and Mary Ann Mazur*

Childhood Pathology and Later Adjustment: The Question of Prediction *by Loretta K. Cass and Carolyn B. Thomas*

Intelligent Testing with WISC-R *by Alan S. Kaufman*

Adaptation in Schizophrenia: The Theory of Segmental Set *by David Shakow*

Psychotherapy: An Eclectic Approach *by Sol L. Garfield*

Handbook of Minimal Brain Dysfunctions *edited by Herbert E. Rie and Ellen D. Rie*

Handbook of Behavioral Interventions: A Clinical Guide *edited by Alan Goldstein and Edna B. Foa*

Art Psychotherapy *by Harriet Wadeson*

Handbook of Adolescent Psychology *edited by Joseph Adelson*

Psychotherapy Supervision: Theory, Research and Practice *edited by Allen K. Hess*

Psychology and Psychiatry in Courts and Corrections: Controversy and Change *by Ellsworth A. Fersch, Jr.*

Restricted Environmental Stimulation: Research and Clinical Applications *by Peter Suedfeld*

Personal Construct Psychology: Psychotherapy and Personality *edited by Alvin W. Landfield and Larry M. Leitner*

Mothers, Grandmothers, and Daughters: Personality and Child Care in Three-Generation Families *by Bertram J. Cohler and Henry U. Grunebaum*

Further Explorations in Personality *edited by A.I. Rabin, Joel Aronoff, Andrew M. Barclay, and Robert A. Zucker*

Hypnosis and Relaxation: Modern Verification of an Old Equation *by William E. Edmonston, Jr.*

Handbook of Clinical Behavior Therapy *edited by Samuel M. Turner, Karen S. Calhoun, and Henry E. Adams*

Handbook of Clinical Neuropsychology *edited by Susan B. Filskov and Thomas J. Boll*

The Course of Alcoholism: Four Years After Treatment *by J. Michael Polich, David J. Armor, and Harriet B. Braiker*

Handbook of Innovative Psychotherapies *edited by Raymond J. Corsini*

The Role of the Father in Child Development (Second Edition) *edited by Michael E. Lamb*

Behavioral Medicine: Clinical Applications *by Susan S. Pinkerton, Howard Hughes, and W.W. Wenrich*

Handbook for the Practice of Pediatric Psychology *edited by June M. Tuma*

Change Through Interaction: Social Psychological Processes of Counseling and Psychotherapy *by Stanley R. Strong and Charles D. Claiborn*

Drugs and Behavior (Second Edition) *by Fred Leavitt*

Handbook of Research Methods in Clinical Psychology *edited by Philip C. Kendall and James N. Butcher*

A Social Psychology of Developing Adults *by Thomas O. Blank*

Women in the Middle Years: Current Knowledge and Directions for Research and Policy *edited by Janet Zollinger Giele*

Loneliness: A Sourcebook of Current Theory, Research and Therapy *edited by Letitia Anne Peplau and Daniel Perlman*

Hyperactivity: Current Issues, Research, and Theory (Second Edition) *by Dorothea M. Ross and Sheila A. Ross*

Review of Human Development *edited by Tiffany M. Field, Aletha Huston, Herbert C. Quay, Lillian Troll, and Gordon E. Finley*

Agoraphobia: Multiple Perspectives on Theory and Treatment *edited by Dianne L. Chambless and Alan J. Goldstein*

The Rorschach: A Comprehensive System, Volume III: Assessment of Children and Adolescents *by John E. Exner, Jr. and Irving B. Weiner*

Handbook of Play Therapy *edited by Charles E. Schaefer and Kevin J. O'Connor*

Adolescent Sexuality in a Changing American Society: Social and Psych Perspectives for the Human Service Professions (Second Edition) *by Catherine S. Chilman*

Failures in Behavior Therapy *edited by Edna B. Foa and Paul M.G. Emi*

Fatherhood Today

MEN'S CHANGING ROLE IN THE FAMILY

Edited by

Phyllis Bronstein
Department of Psychology
University of Vermont
Burlington, Vermont

Carolyn Pape Cowan
Department of Psychology
University of California, Berkeley
Berkeley, California

A WILEY-INTERSCIENCE PUBLICATION

JOHN WILEY & SONS

New York • Chichester • Brisbane • Toronto • Singapore

ISBN 0-471-83627-3

Printed in the United States of America

10 9 8 7 6 5 4 3 2 1

To my father, Burke Bronstein,
To Robert Rossel,
And to the memory of my grandfather, Oswald M. Karpf.
PHYLLIS BRONSTEIN

To Ben Pape, Norman Cowan, and Phil Cowan,
Who have taught me most about fathering.
CAROLYN PAPE COWAN

Contributors

Rosalind C. Barnett, Ph.D.
Research Associate
Center for Research on Women
Wellesley College
Wellesley, Massachusetts

Grace K. Baruch, Ph.D.
Research Associate
Center for Research on Women
Wellesley College
Wellesley, Massachusetts

Frederick W. Bozett, R.N., D.N.S.
Professor
College of Nursing
University of Oklahoma Health
    Sciences Center
Oklahoma City, Oklahoma

Phyllis Bronstein, Ph.D.
Associate Professor
Department of Psychology
University of Vermont
Burlington, Vermont

Catalyst Staff
Margaret Meiers
Senior Associate, Career and Family
    Programs
New York, New York

James Cooley, M.D.
Pediatrician
Wellesley Center, Harvard
    Community Health Plan
Wellesley, Massachusetts

Carolyn Pape Cowan, Ph.D.
Research Psychologist
Department of Psychology
University of California
Berkeley, California

Philip A. Cowan, Ph.D.
Professor
Department of Psychology
University of California
Berkeley, California

Pamela Daniels, M.A.
Dean of the Class of 1988
Lecturer in Psychology
Wellesley College
Wellesley, Massachusetts

Mark Fine, Ph.D.
Assistant Professor
Department of Psychology
The University of Dayton
Dayton, Ohio

Shirley M. H. Hanson, R.N., Ph.D.,
    FAAN
Professor
Department of Family Nursing
The Oregon Health Sciences
    University
Portland, Oregon

v

Daniel H. Kindlon, Ph.D.
Assistant Site Director
Infant Health & Development Program
The Children's Hospital
Instructor in Psychology
Harvard Medical School
Boston, Massachusetts

Ronald F. Levant, Ed.D.
Director, Fatherhood Project
Associate Clinical Professor of
   Counseling Psychology
Boston University
Boston, Massachusetts

James W. Loewen, Ph.D.
Professor
Department of Sociology
University of Vermont
Burlington, Vermont

John Lewis McAdoo, M.S.W., Ph.D.
Associate Professor
School of Social Work & Community
   Planning
University of Maryland at Baltimore
Baltimore, Maryland

Alfredo Mirandé, Ph.D.
Professor
Department of Sociology
University of California, Riverside
Riverside, California

John R. Moreland, Ph.D.
Affiliated Health Psychologists
Jacksonville, Florida

Patrick Prindle, Ph.D.
Associate Professor
Department of Psychology
Urbana University
Urbana, Ohio

Ross D. Parke, Ph.D.
Professor
Department of Psychology
University of Illinois at Urbana-
   Champaign
Champaign, Illinois

Norma Radin, Ph.D.
Professor
School of Social Work
University of Michigan
Ann Arbor, Michigan

John W. Santrock, Ph.D.
Professor
Program in Psychology & Human
   Development
University of Texas at Dallas
Richardson, Texas

Andrew I. Schwebel, Ph.D.
Professor
Department of Psychology
The Ohio State University
Columbus, Ohio

Karen A. Sitterle, Ph.D.
Department of Psychology
Timberlawn Psychiatric Hospital
Dallas, Texas

Barbara J. Tinsley, Ph.D.
Assistant Professor
Department of Speech Communication
University of Illinois at Urbana-
   Champaign
Champaign, Illinois

Richard A. Warshak, Ph.D.
Clinical Assistant Professor of
   Psychology
University of Texas Health Science
   Center at Dallas
Dallas, Texas

Kathy Weingarten, Ph.D.
Director, Family Systems Therapy
    Training Program
Department of Psychiatry
Children's Hospital and Judge Baker
    Guidance Center
Boston, Massachusetts

Michael W. Yogman, M.D.
Site Director
Infant Health & Development Program
The Children's Hospital
Assistant Professor of Pediatrics
Harvard Medical School
Boston, Massachusetts

Foreword

ROSS D. PARKE

University of Illinois

This is more than a volume about fathers. It is a book about how social science and culture interact, mutually influencing social roles in modern society. It is not clear whether the rediscovery of fathers in the 1970s by social scientists encouraged us to notice fathers' active participation in families or whether the cultural shifts in womens' work roles and alterations in mens' awareness of their emotional and expressive capacities led to an awakening of interest among social researchers. In either case, this volume is a marvelous testimony to the clear interdependence of science and society.

There have been many books about fathers, but this volume goes well beyond waving the banner of rediscovery. The field is now well aware of fathers as an object of scientific scrutiny and study. However, much of the early work on fathering was devoted to demonstrating that fathers are capable of many of the activities that mothers had been depicted as being routinely engaged in for centuries. While important, this pioneering work portrayed a very narrow view of fathers—Caucasian, middle class, and married. One of the primary contributions of this volume is a reminder that the father role is multifaceted, complex, and changing. No single portrait adequately captures the nature of fatherhood in the 1980s. Instead, as this volume vividly illustrates, there are many different kinds of fathers. This volume provides a corrective to our earlier and oversimplified views of fathering and opens a needed window on how fathers have changed. You'd never recognize dear old dad!

One of the major contributions of this volume is the articulation of the forms that fatherhood can assume and the determinants of the multiplicity of forms. One of the least understood aspects of fathering is the impact of cultural background. The ethnocentricism that has characterized research in social science generally, and in the area of fatherhood in particular, is finally beginning to disappear. As McAdoo and Mirandé illustrate in their chapters, there are circumstances as well as unique characteristics of fathers of differing cultural heritages that need to be described and understood. Moreover, understanding of the uniqueness of the cultural backgrounds may provide useful insights into both the range of behaviors subsumed by the fathering role as well as the strategies that are most effective for intervention.

Second, families are not static entities, and as the rate of divorce continues to increase, the father's role in these changing circumstances requires attention. Fathers vary considerably in their behavior during these increasingly common transitions. Maternal custody is still the principal outcome and under these conditions, some fathers disappear while others continue to have regular and sustained contact with their former spouse and children. Each of these choices yields very different effects not only for children and mothers but for fathers themselves. However, maternal custody is no longer the only outcome following divorce. As the courts and the culture recognize the competence of fathers, joint custody and paternal custody are increasingly popular arrangements. As Hanson notes, single custodial fathers, just as single custodial mothers, may have problems, but the problems may be unique to each.

One further social trend that accompanies the rise in divorce is the increase in remarriage which ushers in a new role for the father—as stepfather. As Santrock and his colleagues note, this role is undergoing closer scrutiny from researchers, and the benefits and difficulties of this role for children, mothers, and fathers are becoming clearer.

Even within two-parent families, there is good cause for recognizing a wide variety of fathering styles and family arrangements. Father involvement may be very low in traditional families in which the mother assumes a major share of the caregiving burden. In other families it may be more equal, and in some families role reversal is explored. Each of these arrangements have clear consequences for the fathers, their wives, and their offspring. The chapters by Barnett and Baruch and by Radin illustrate this diversity.

At the same time that it is clear that diversity is evident, there remain clear vestiges of earlier eras of father study. The earlier competence-performance distinction still has utility, since fathers' performance is still lagging behind their ability to execute many caregiving roles. As a number of contributors have demonstrated, women still assume more of the daily responsibilities for child care than men—in spite of ideological commitments to role equality between the spouses. Nor are nontraditional roles easy to maintain—as both cross-cultural and American investigations have shown. This volume offers some additional clues to this puzzle. The cultural code changes slowly, and current attitudes still offer men more latitude in the definition of family roles than women. Motherhood may be mandated; fatherhood may be discretionary. The contributors raise a cautionary flag; by warning us that the degree of social change is still lagging behind social expectations.

A recurring theme of this volume is the importance of a developmental perspective on fathering. As the contributors illustrate, this perspective has multiple meanings. Fathering behaviors shift as the child develops—a common but still infrequently studied determinant of fathering. Moreover, as Daniels and Weingarten suggest, fathers show a wide range of patterns of involvement across the span of childhood—some steadily increase, others linearly decrease, while others show fluctuations in their involvement. Consistent with a life span perspective, fathers' own developmental trajectory is another aspect of development that is highlighted by a number of the authors in this volume. The loction of the father in terms of his age, life style, occupation, and education are important determinants of his involvement. Even in the case of grandfathers, timing of the attainment of this role will shape the form and amount of his involvement with his grandchildren.

Finally, there is a further face of development that is rarely seen—the impact of fatherhood on men themselves. As Philip Cowan argues, becoming a father may change men in a variety of ways. Some are challenged and develop further, others are overcome by the demands of their new role. At the same time the field is challenged to recognize more fully fatherhood as an important developmental transition in the lives of adult men.This recognition will also serve as a corrective to a long-held view that fatherhood was primarily of interest because of the possible impact of fathers on childrens' development. This volume is a cogent reminder that the developmental trajectories of all family members—children, fathers, mothers—merit consideration if the richness of fatherhood is to be fully appreciated.

A closely related perspective on fatherhood that this volume offers is an intergenerational one. This is reflected in several ways. First, it is becoming clear that the earlier relationships with one's own parents influence the ways in which men enact their fathering role, although the relative influence of one's mother and father is far from clear at present. In addition to the long-term influence of fathers' relationships with their own parents as a shaper of current parenting practices, grandparents are important as providers of support and advice to fathers in their struggle to define their new roles. This underscores the need to view fathers and families within a larger network of informal and formal systems, including the extended family.

Research and clinical work are often seen as separate entities. One of the contributions of this volume is the demonstration that these distinctions are often artificial and unnecessary. Many of the authors creatively move across these boundaries to illuminate our understanding of fatherhood. There has been a long and venerable tradition, most notably the Freudian legacy, which has shown us repeatedly how clinical material can generate hypotheses and provide opportunities to test our theories. Understanding deviations in a system, as well as the insights associated with trying to correct the problems are legitimate ways to gain new knowledge about underlying processes. Interventions in the best sense are, of course, ways not only of modifying a relationship or condition; they are tools for theory testing and evaluation. Interventions can be viewed as another type of field experiment—one that can yield new clues about the nature of fatherhood.

As fathers change, their needs change as well. Just as mothers have received educational and supportive interventions, fathers can benefit from these types of assistance. Educational programs for fathers are a new growth industry and as this volume illustrates, their timing and form are wide-ranging and ingenious. Children can learn early about parenting, just as expectant parents can profit from well-designed interventions. But educational programs are not the only form of support. To increase competence and expand knowledge alone is insufficient if fathers are going to realize their full potential. Government and corporate policies need to change as well to provide fathers with expanded opportunities to combine work and fathering activities effectively. Paternity leaves, time flexibility, and work-centered child care programs are innovative and pioneering ways of increasing options for fathers.

Consistent with the theme of this volume, the editors provide a helpful agenda for future research. Raising unanswered questions is just as critical as the assessment of our current knowledge. This book is an invitation to join the search for better answers and to help understand how fathers and families have changed and how they will change.

ROSS D. PARKE

Urbana, Illinois
May 1987

Series Preface

This series of books is addressed to behavioral scientists interested in the nature of human personality. Its scope should prove pertinent to personality theorists and researchers as well as to clinicians concerned with applying an understanding of personality processes to the amelioration of emotional difficulties in living. To this end, the series provides a scholarly integration of theoretical formulations, empirical data, and practical recommendations.

Six major aspects of studying and learning about human personality can be designated: personality theory, personality, structure and dynamics, personality development, personality assessment, personality change, and personality adjustment. In exploring these aspects of personality, the books in the series discuss a number of distinct but related subject areas: the nature and implications of various theories of personality; personality characteristics that account for consistencies and variations in human behavior; the emergence of personality processes in children and adolescents; the use of interviewing and testing procedures to evaluate individual differences in personality; efforts to modify personality styles through psychotherapy, counseling, behavior, therapy, and other methods of influence; and patterns of abnormal personality functioning that impair individual competence.

Irving B. Weiner

Fairleigh Dickinson University
Rutherford, New Jersey

xiii

Preface

In 1981, one of us (Phyllis Bronstein) was invited with Robert Rossel to co-chair a task force on Men and Family Work, for Division 35 (The Psychology of Women) of the American Psychological Association. Since we were given no charge or directions on how to proceed, we realized that our first task was to come up with a task, and that it would be helpful to have other people involved in the process. Over that year we acquired a list of potential participants, and, at the APA convention in the summer of 1982, we held an open meeting for anyone interested in joining the task force. From that meeting, and from our initial list, came a group of researchers and clinicians interested in sharing information and ideas about the father's role in the family with one another, and with practitioners and researchers in the field. In addition, at that meeting, which started over breakfast and ended up lasting until lunch time, we began to plan two programs to be presented at the APA convention the following year: one, a workshop for clinicians working with fathers on issues concerning their family role, and the other, a symposium which would present current research related to the changing role of the father.

The workshop, at the convention in Anaheim the following summer (1983), conducted by Robert Rossel, Nancy F. Young, Dona Alpert, Kent Louscher, and Judson Reese-Dukes, was well-attended and well-received. The symposium, on the other hand, which was presented by Phyllis Bronstein, Carolyn and Phil Cowan, Rosalind Barnett, and John Moreland, became something of a media event. Not only were we given a full page spread (with pictures) in the *Los Angeles Times*, but the information we presented in the symposium and in the press conference afterwards was picked up by at least a dozen newspapers across the country. After those initial articles appeared, we continued to receive requests for interviews and information, from sources as diverse as *U.S. News and World Report*, *Seventeen*, and the *National Enquirer*. At this point, it became apparent to us that there was a real need for more widely disseminated information about fathers. In response to this need, the present volume was conceived.

Many people have contributed to the final product, in addition to the scholars who shared their research and their ideas in each of the chapters. We are grateful to Joe Pleck, who initially proposed the task force, and suggested potential contributors when the book was first taking shape. For providing thoughtful, critical commentary on some of the Chapters, we thank Phil Cowan, Robert Rossel, Trudie Heming, Sam Picciotto, Lonnie Snowden, Don McKillop, Lynda Siegal, and Laura

Fishman. In addition, we thank Ruth Landé and Jennifer Walmsley Cowan for their verification and editing of references, the staff of Catalyst and Jim Loewen for providing resource material, and Jennie Marcotte, Hillie Bosterle, and Kelly Allen for their assistance in typing the manuscript. Finally, we appreciate Herb Reich at Wiley, for his encouragement, patience, and humor in seeing us through this process.

PHYLLIS BRONSTEIN
CAROLYN PAPE COWAN

Burlington, Vermont
Berkeley, California
January 1988

Contents

PART THREE   FATHERS AND FAMILY RELATIONSHIPS: VARIATIONS AND CHANGE

PART FOUR   PREVENTION AND INTERVENTION PROGRAMS FOR MEN AND BOYS

PART FIVE   MEN'S CHANGING ROLE IN THE FAMILY: DIRECTIONS FOR RESEARCH AND SOCIAL CHANGE

PART 1

Introduction

CHAPTER 1

Marital and Parenting Roles in Transition

An Overview

PHYLLIS BRONSTEIN

[He] is one of the thousands of working fathers across the USA today who are getting more actively involved with the nurturance of their children than any other generation in history. They are staying at home with their kids, taking them to school, changing their diapers, and picking them up at the play group.

FROM AN ARTICLE ON "SUPERDADS" IN *USA TODAY* (Meyers, 1984)

More men are taking classes in fathering and working as volunteers in their children's day-care centers. Women's work? There's no such thing for [this] suburban "house daddy" . . . , who watches over his four children.

PICTURE CAPTIONS FROM A FEATURE ARTICLE ON THE AMERICAN MALE, IN *U.S. NEWS & WORLD REPORT* (1985)

Judging from the flurry of articles in the popular media over the past five years on "the new father," it appears that new roles and options for parents have become a fact of modern-day life. These articles present examples of men and women sharing in housework and child care—sometimes with the men taking over the larger share—in homes where both parents are in the labor force, and moving forward in the career of their choice. Thus the message seems to be that with some careful arranging of schedules, and some initial effort in the early years to find good day care for their children, both fathers and mothers can experience satisfaction in their worklife *and* a rich and rewarding family life. This family life is seen as one in which fathers are just as likely as mothers to stay home when their infant is sick, or go to a teacher conference, or take their 12-year-old to the orthodontist, and in which spouses experience a deepened sense of respect, equality, and cooperation with one another.

Another option that the media have frequently described is that of the single parent, who balances a career, a close parent–child relationship, and an active social life. A number of recent television series have included at least one character representing that life-style (e.g., "Kate and Allie," "St. Elsewhere," "Cheers," "Hill Street Blues," and "L.A. Law"). The traditional rule for families used to be that incompatible couples stayed together "for the sake of the children," until the children were grown. The present view seems to be that incompatible spouses deserve an op-

3

portunity to find compatibility and emotional fulfillment elsewhere, and that divorce and single parenthood may be a creative solution, freeing each partner from dysfunctional dependencies and conflicts, and allowing for growth and ultimate self-actualization.

Are these media images accurate representations of the ways roles and families are changing in today's society? Is the quality of family life for parents and children improved by the fact that men are becoming more involved in child care, while women are becoming more involved in the workplace? Are well-being and life satisfaction enhanced for all involved by the dissolution of unsuccessful marriages and the forming of alternative family structures? If we look at available data, the answers at present seem to be both yes and no.

FAMILY-RELATED SOCIAL CHANGES IN THE PAST 15 YEARS

In order to understand the ways in which family roles are changing, it is helpful to consider recent social trends and their possible effects on family arrangements and family stability. The Women's Movement, which began in the 1960s and took hold in the 1970s, has probably been the most powerful force for family change in this country, with the most striking change being the movement of mothers into the workforce. As of 1985, 71% of all women of childbearing age were in the labor force, and 62% of all women who already had children were working or looking for work outside the home. These figures, which have been climbing steadily for a long period of time, have increased substantially in the last 15 years, due to the growing number of mothers with preschool children who no longer devote full time to child care. In fact, married women with children under six represent the fastest growing segment of the labor force in this country. Mothers of infants and toddlers are also working in record numbers, with 50% of married women with children under the age of three in the labor force in 1985, compared with only 24% in 1970 ("Labor Force," 1985).[1]

Yet the meaning of these statistics is not entirely clear. It has become much more acceptable for married women with children to work outside the home, but this does not necessarily mean that mothers are doing it mainly because of intrinsic career interests. Most employed women in this country in fact hold jobs in low status fields that provide low wages, little stimulation, and little (if any) opportunity for advancement. In 1983, almost 80% of employed women were in clerical, service, sales, or factory jobs (National Commission on Working Women, 1983). In almost all areas, women's careers tend to be at a lower level than men's, in terms of both salary and status (Lott, 1987). Thus, though there are a number of different reasons why women seek employment outside the home, the primary one seems to be financial need.

Does the fact that more married women with children are working outside the home and sharing the responsibility as breadwinner mean that their husbands are

[1] I am grateful to Catalyst for providing some of the information reported here.

reciprocating, by participating more in child care and household work? The answer seems to be yes—somewhat. According to one survey (Radin & Goldsmith, 1983), between 1975 and 1981 the amount of time fathers spent in child care and household work increased 20–30%. On the other hand, the amount of time fathers were spending on child care in 1981 was still only about one-third that of mothers. The facts remain that men's jobs generally can bring more income into the family, that the workplace is less tolerant of men than of women taking time off from work for child care, and that society still does not sanction men's putting their family equal to or ahead of their career. These issues are discussed in length in Chapter 18 of this volume.

The final question about dual career families is, do the spouses experience greater satisfaction with each other, their marriage, and their life in general, as a result of this greater degree of role sharing? Recent research by Baruch and Barnett (Chapter 5, this volume), and by Cowan and Cowan and their colleagues (Chapters 2, 16, and 19, this volume) suggest that the picture is quite complex, and that while there are certainly benefits, there are also drawbacks and difficulties.

Between 1970 and 1984, the divorce rate increased from 47 to 121 per 1000 married persons (Statistical Abstract of the United States, 1986); according to the projections of the National Center for Health Statistics, one out of two marriages will end in divorce (Berman, 1987). This radical change in traditional family structure leads to a number of different alternatives, all of which have implications for fathers and their relationships with their children. The most common family arrangement following divorce is maternal custody, with the father given visitation rights. Occasionally, fathers seek and are awarded custody; approximately 11% of single custodial parents are fathers ("Household and Family," 1985). Joint custody, which is becoming a more available option in many states, is viewed by many as an ideal solution, in which the ex-spouses maintain a cooperative co-parenting relationship, and children are assured frequent access to both parents. In addition, four out of five divorced adults remarry within three years (Glick, 1980) and, if their new spouse has children, assume a stepparenting role; it is estimated that by 1990, one-fourth to one-third of children under the age of 18 will have spent part of their lives as a member of a stepfamily (Glick, 1984). Thus there are currently a number of different kinds of fathering roles outside the traditional intact family structure.

Research on these postdivorce family arrangements reveals that they are not always the stuff of which television situation comedies are made. In the majority of instances in which the mother gets custody and the father visitation, visitation becomes very infrequent, and more often than not, stops altogether. Father custody became a legal possibility in the 1950s, when the states replaced the "young and tender years" doctrine, which had explicitly presumed mother custody, with a "best interest of the child" doctrine, which had no such explicit presumption (Loewen, Chapter 12, this volume). However, few fathers end up with custody, because they or their lawyers have limited knowledge of their options, because judges often implicitly presume mother custody, and because society neither encourages fathers to assume the primary parenting role, nor prepares them for it. Joint custody has been heralded as a way to meet equitably the needs of both parents and children, yet it too has its drawbacks. It is difficult for many divorced couples to overcome feelings of bitterness, rancor, and guilt, which may exist as residue from marital conflict and the divorce itself, so that cooperative co-parenting may be, to all extents, impossible. In addition, joint *legal* custody does not necessarily mean joint *residential* custody, and in practice, joint custody often turns out to be a version of mother custody with father visitation. Noncustodial fathers have been found to undergo major changes in self-esteem, and to experience guilt and depression to the extent that their job performance is adversely affected (Hetherington, Cox, & Cox, 1976). Chapter 12 in this volume provides a full discussion of custody and visitation issues.

Unlike noncustodial fathers, single custodial mothers often encounter economic insufficiency (Weitzman, 1985). Of the families classified as below the poverty line in this country in 1984, 34% were single mother-headed families (Statistical Abstract of the United States, 1986). A custodial mother's remarriage becomes an opportunity to compensate for the absence of a biological father, and to provide financial and emotional support for the mother and for her children; yet becoming a stepfamily is a complex and often difficult transition, and accepting and being accepted in a stepparent role often takes years to accomplish. Chapter 10, by Santrock and colleagues, discusses this process at length, and presents their own findings on the benefits and limitations of the stepfather–child relationship.

RESEARCH ON FATHERS: PAST AND PRESENT

Early research on parenting, in both the child development and family sociology literature, tended to view the mother not only as the primary caregiver, but also as the main agent of socialization, and the most dependable source of information about parenting and child development within the family. Since it was believed that nurturant and competent mothering was the key to children's successful social, emotional, and cognitive development, it was not necessary to examine the quality of fathering children might be receiving; thus fathers were generally considered only through mothers' reports of their behaviors or attitudes (e.g., Newson & Newson, 1963, 1968; Pederson & Robson, 1969; Schaffer & Emerson, 1964). Sometimes, too, children were asked about their parents' behaviors (Armentrout & Berger, 1972; Bronfenbrenner, 1961; Droppelman & Schaeffer, 1963; Kagan & Lemkin, 1960). Rarely, however, were fathers asked about their *own* behaviors or, in the beginning years of laboratory observation of parent–child behavior, observed in interaction with their child. Ironically, however, though the father's impact on the child's development was apparently presumed to be minor, his absence was felt by researchers to be detrimental, and many studies were conducted to examine the effect of father absence on such things as gender role development ("masculinity" and "femininity"), IQ, scholastic achievement, moral development, and peer relations (see Biller, 1976, 1981, for extensive reviews).

Beginning in the mid-1970s, as a reflection of the social changes that were occurring in this country, researchers began to give much more direct attention to the role of the father in the family. Fathers were now included in interviews about the parenting experience, including household work allocation and child care (Baruch & Barnett, 1981; Daniels & Weingarten, 1982). They were observed in the laboratory (and sometimes in the home) interacting with their infants or preschoolers (Clarke-Stewart, 1978, 1980; Lamb, 1976, 1977; Parke & Sawin, 1975; Power & Parke, 1982). They were asked about their experiences during and after divorce (Hetherington, et al., 1976; Keshet & Rosenthal, 1978), and as a member of a remarried family (Hess & Camara, 1979; Santrock & Warshak, 1979). The results from these studies clearly indicated that fathers were important agents in their children's development, that they had the potential to be involved, competent parents with infants as well as with older children, and that many wished for or were actively seeking greater involvement in the child rearing process than had been modeled by their own fathers.

This volume covers that range of recent research on fathers. Part 2, "The Father in the Developing Two-Parent Family," includes chapters that focus on men's experiencing of fatherhood, on changing perceptions of fathers, and on fathers' effects on their families and their children. The section begins with Philip Cowan's consideration of fatherhood within a framework of adult development—the changes in perspective, personality, and maturity brought about by the experience of becoming a father. Chapter 3, by Pamela Daniels and Kathy Weingarten, examines the differences in the experiencing of fatherhood for men who became fathers earlier versus later in their lives, during the 1950s and the 1970s. The authors focus on the special moment or period in time when fatherhood "clicks"—when a man fully owns his identity as a father on a psychological and emotional level, and comes to take deep pleasure from it. John McAdoo and Alfredo Mirandé (in Chapters 6 and 7, respectively) provide contemporary views of Black and Chicano fathers, contrasting those views with the stereotypes that have long existed in the literature. My chapter (Chapter 8) and those by Michael Yogman, James Cooley, and Daniel Kindlon (Chapter 4), Rosalind Barnett and Grace Baruch (Chapter 5), and John McAdoo (Chapter 6) consider fathers' behaviors in the context of the developing two-parent family. These chapters examine fathers' degree of involvement in family work and child care, the kinds of interactions they have with their children, and the implications of their involvement and interactions for children's development as well as (in Chapter 5) parents' individual well-being and marital satisfaction.

In Part 3 we consider variations in the fathering role. Norma Radin (Chapter 9) examines the still rare role arrangement in which the father rather than the mother in a two-parent family is the primary caregiver for the children. She reviews existing findings about such arrangements, and presents her own data highlighting the differences between families who have persisted with that alternative, and families who initially chose it, but later reverted to a more traditional arrangement. Shirley Hanson, James Loewen, Frederick Bozett (Chapters 11, 12, and 13) and John Santrock, Karen Sitterle, and Richard Warshak (Chapter 10) look at variations of the posttraditional-family father, examining the lives fathers make for themselves and their children after the ending of their initial marriage. Loewen presents an informative and moving account of the plight of visitation fathers, from the men who absent themselves totally from their former families, to the "Disneyland Daddies" who fill their visits with their children with frenetic activities and special treats, to the noncustodial fathers who manage to establish a true second home for their children. Bozett examines the special issues faced by gay fathers, including the process of accepting their dual identites as gay men and fathers, dealing with prejudices in both the heterosexual community and in the singles-oriented gay community as they move their lives from the former domain to the latter, and finding ways to maintain close and open relationships with their children. Hanson tells us what is known about the 11% of divorced fathers who become the single-parent custodians of their children—the struggles and rewards these men experience, and the outcomes for their children. Santrock, Sitterle, and Warshak consider the role of the stepfather, and parent–child relationships that evolve in stepfather families. They compare stepfathers to stepmothers and to biological fathers in intact families, and find that stepfathers have the most difficulty in carrying out a parenting role and establishing a close relationship with the children. Finally, Barbara Tinsley and Ross Parke (Chapter 14) consider the role of grandfathers in their grandchildren's lives, reviewing the little that is known at this time, and presenting their own research on grandfathers' play with their infant grandchildren.

Part 4 of this volume examines current programs that have been created to help fathers move in new directions, initiating changes in their family role, or adjusting to changes that have occurred in their family arrangement or structure. Ronald Levant (Chapter 15) reviews and considers the effectiveness of existing models of parent training that are available to fathers at different phases of their lives, as well as programs offered for the fathers of tomorrow. In addition, he describes in detail one of the fatherhood education courses that he conducts for men who want to become more competent, involved parents. Carolyn Cowan (Chapter 16) describes a preventive intervention program for couples becoming first-time parents, which involved six months' participation in a couples group led by mental health professionals. Outcomes for fathers in these groups, which focused on marital and family issues and adjustments related to the transition to parenthood, were found to be more positive than those for a matched control sample of fathers who had not participated in such groups. Andrew Schwebel, Mark Fine, John Moreland, and Patrick Prindle (Chapter 17) describe their work helping divorced and widowed fathers adjust to the drastic changes in their family structure, develop their parenting skills, and establish close and supportive relationships with their children.

Part 5 considers the father's role in the wider social context. Chapter 18 describes changes that are occurring in the workplace which support fathers' greater participation in child care and family life. In addition, it examines workplace attitudes and structures that inhibit such changes, and indicates the direction in which we need to move to maximize the possibilities for compatibility between career and family roles for both parents. Chapter 19 summarizes some of the major findings presented in this volume, highlighting the variations and changes that have been documented, and pointing to unresolved issues, areas where further change is needed, and directions for future research.

In presenting our picture of fatherhood today, we have chosen a broad approach from a variety of perspectives. Our contributors include scholars from diverse fields: psychology, sociology, psychiatry, pediatrics, social work, and nursing. Some have presented intensive reviews of the research literature, while others have placed their topic within a historical perspective, and still others have reported mainly on their own research. Research methods have included in-depth clinical interviews, surveys, laboratory experiments, home observations, questionnaires, and participant observation; studies have looked at developmental change, structural change, and cross-cultural variation, some at one point in time, and others longitudinally. It is our hope that this broad-spectrum approach will enable the book to be a resource for researchers, teachers, and students interested in men's changing role in the family. In addition, we hope that it will be of use to those in the mental health, social service, health, and legal fields, whose work involves helping men discover and adjust to new family roles and options.

REFERENCES

American male. (1985, June 3). *U.S. News & World Report*, pp. 44-51.

Armentrout, J.A., & Burger, G.E. (1972). Children's reports of parental child-rearing behavior at five grade levels. *Developmental Psychology, 7*(1), 44–48.

Baruch, G., & Barnett, R.C. (1981). Fathers' participation in the care of their preschool children. *Sex Roles, 7*, 1043–1054.

Berman, C. (1987). *Preparing to remarry*. New York: Public Affairs Pamphlets.

Biller, H.B. (1976). The father and personality development: Paternal deprivation and sex role development. In M.E. Lamb (Ed.), *The role of the father in child development*. New York: Wiley.

Biller, H.B. (1981). Father absence, divorce, and personality development. In M.E. Lamb (Ed.), *The role of the father in child development* (2nd ed.). New York: Wiley.

Bronfenbrenner, U. (1961). some familial antecedents of responsibility and leadership in adolescents. In L. Petrullo & B.M. Bass (Eds.), *Leadership and interpersonal behavior*. New York: Holt.

Clarke-Stewart, K.A. (1978). And daddy makes three: The father's impact on mother and child. *Child Development, 49*, 466–468.

Clarke-Stewart, K.A. (1980). The father's contribution to children's cognitive and social development in early childhood. In F.A. Pedersen (Ed.), *The father-infant relationship: Observational studies in the family setting*. New York: Praeger.

Daniels, P., & Weingarten, K. (1982). *Sooner or later: The timing of parenthood in adult lives*. New York: Norton.

Doppelman, L.F., & Schaeffer, E.S. (1963). Boys' and girls' reports of maternal and paternal behavior. *Journal of Abnormal and Social Psychology, 67*(6), 648–654.

Glick, P.C. (1980). Remarried: Some recent changes and variations. *Journal of Family Issues, 1*, 455–478.

Glick, P.C. (1984). Prospective changes in marriage, divorce, and living arrangements. *Journal of Family Issues, 5*, 7–26.

Hess, R.D., & Camara, K.A. (1979). Post-divorce family relationships as mediating factors in the consequences of divorce for children. *Journal of Social Issues, 35*(4), 79–96.

Hetherington, E.M., Cox, M., & Cox, R. (1976). Divorced fathers. *The Family Coordinator, 25*, 417–428.

Household and family characteristics: March, 1984. (1985). (Current Population Reports, Series P-20, No. 398, U.S. Bureau of the Census). Washington, DC: U.S. Government Printing Office.

Kagan, J., & Lemkin, J. (1960). The child's differential perceptions of parental attributes. *Journal of Abnormal and Social Psychology, 61*(3); 440–447.

Keshet, H., & Rosenthal, K. (1978). Fathering after marital separation. *Social Work, 23*, 11–18.

Labor force activity of mothers of young children continues at record pace. (Sept. 19, 1985). *Bureau of Labor Statistics News.*

Lamb, M.E. (1976). Interactions between eight-month-old children and their fathers and mothers. In M.E. Lamb (Ed.), *The role of the father in child development*. New York: Wiley.

Lamb, M.E. (1977). Father-infant and mother-infant interaction in the first year of life. *Child Development, 48*, 167–181.

Lott, B. (1987). *Women's lives: Themes and variations in gender learning*. Monterey, CA: Brooks/Cole.

Meyers, R. (1984, August 9). Close-up: The superdad phenomenon. The tensions of 2-parent child care. *USA Today*, p. 4D.

National Commission on Working Women. (1983). *Women's Work: Undervalued, underpaid*. Washington, DC: Center for Women and Work.

Newson, J., & Newson, E. (1963). *Infant care in an urban community*. London: Allen & Unwin.

Newson, J., & Newson, E. (1968). *Four years old in an urban community*. London: Allen & Unwin.

Parke, R.D., & Sawin, D.B. (1975). *Infant characteristics and behavior as elicitors of maternal and paternal responsivity in the newborn period*. Paper presented at the Society for Research in Child Development, Denver.

Pedersen, F.A., & Robson, K.S. (1969). Father participation in infancy. *American Journal of Orthopsychiatry, 39*, 466–472.

Power, T.G., & Parke, R.D. (1982). Play as a context for early learning: Lab and home analyses. In L.M. Laosa & I.E. Sigel (Eds.), *The family as a learning environment*. New York: Plenum.

Radin, N., & Goldsmith, R. (1983). *Predictors of father involvement in childcare*. Paper presented at the biennial meeting of the Society for Research in Child Development, Detroit.

Santrock, J., & Warshak, R. (1979). Father custody and social development in boys and girls. *Journal of Social Issues, 35*(4), 112–125.

Schaffer, H.R., & Emerson, P.E. (1964). The development of social attachment in infancy. *Monographs of the Society for Research in Child Development, 29* (Serial No. 94).

Statistical Abstract of the United States. (1986). U.S. Department of Commerce, Bureau of the Census.

Weitzman, L.J. (1985). *The divorce revolution*. New York: Free Press.

PART 2

The Father in the Developing Two-Parent Family

CHAPTER 2

Becoming a Father

A Time of Change, An Opportunity for Development

PHILIP A. COWAN

This chapter attempts to resolve a professional and personal dilemma associated with understanding the impact of becoming a father. As a researcher studying the early years of family formation, and as a father of three children now grown and out of the nest, I am acutely aware of two conflicting views of what happens to men, women, and marriage as partners become parents. It feels as if I am watching an out-of-synch 3-D movie with the picture on the left representing the transition to parenthood as a time of disequilibrium, stress, and crisis, while the picture on the right portrays becoming a father as a time of joy, with a potential for significant individual and marital growth. My dilemma is not that these views are mutually exclusive. There are theoretical glasses capable of resolving the two pictures into a single three-dimensional image. Following Rapoport (1963), Osofsky (1982) states the potential synthesis quite simply: "Consistent with Bibring's (1959, p. 226) broad definition of the woman's pregnancy experience, my hypothesis is that expectant and new fatherhood is both a crisis and a developmental opportunity for maturation and new growth."

My dilemma stems from the realization that my colleagues and I have been participating in research that provides extensive documentation of parents' negative changes and distress during the transition to parenthood (e.g., Cowan, Cowan, Heming, Garrett, Coysh, Curtis-Boles, & Boles, 1985), but which has not yet systematically investigated *development* in new fathers and mothers. This omission does not stem from deliberate oversight. It follows from the fact that there are reasonably good instruments for assessing problems and stress, but we lack clear concepts of what developmental change should look like, and we lack instruments for assessing when that change has occurred. Consider the following statements made by fathers in interviews when their first children were six months old:

Preparation of this chapter was supported in part by NIMH grant RO1 MH-31109. The author recognizes with gratitude the collaboration of Carolyn Pape Cowan, the co-principal investigator of the Becoming a Family Project, and major contributions to the data analysis by Gertrude Heming, data manager, and Dena Cowan, data processor. The final version of this chapter has benefited greatly from discussions with Naomi Lowinsky, Ravenna Helson, Dan Wile, and John Coie.

I said then [in pregnancy], "This baby isn't gonna change *my* life," but I just didn't know what I was talking about.

It opens up a whole new world, just to see her looking out the window at the rain making puddles on the sidewalk.

Well, I wouldn't give her back, but we don't have any spontaneity any more. To go down the street for an ice cream cone requires an hour of planning to get a babysitter or packing what we need to take her with us. And we still haven't slept all the way through the night. Partly I'm lying awake worrying about how I'm gonna get everything done at work the next day and still have some time left to play with her when I get home. [Then, as if it were somehow unrelated to what he has been saying] And, uh, Helen and I, uh, haven't made love since I can't remember when. . . .

It's the hardest thing I've ever done, but there's just nothing like having him around. He's more entertainment than the TV. And, since I've become a father I just feel more grown up. My parents are finally letting me in on family secrets they thought I was too young to know before. And on the job, I've become more serious. I've really had to get my act together. It's not just me and Barbara now. I've got a family to provide for.

These quotes from four different men capture the fact that becoming a father is both wonderful and stressful. The central task of this chapter is to find a way to integrate both positive and negative views of this important life transition into a more coherent picture that fits the facts of new parents' experience.

In the first part of this chapter, I summarize data from the Becoming a Family Project, a longitudinal research and intervention study in which Carolyn Pape Cowan and I followed 72 couples becoming parents and 24 couples not yet decided about having a baby (Cowan, et al., 1985; Cowan & Cowan, 1987a, b, in press). Consistent with other longitudinal studies of the transition to parenthood (e.g., Belsky & Pensky, in press; Feldman & Nash, 1984; Grossman, Eichler & Winickoff, 1980; Shereshefsky & Yarrow, 1973), the findings document a number of negative changes that occur in men's lives as they become fathers for the first time.

In the next section of this chapter, I present a more speculative analysis—of the transition to fatherhood as an opportunity for adult development. I suggest that development during this transition cannot be described as a *stage* change in the same way that Freud and Piaget have described universal, necessary, qualitative reorganizations from birth through adolescence. However, I believe that there is merit to considering fatherhood as an opportunity for increased differentiation and integration, a qualitative change that can be summarized using the multidimensional developmental concept of "maturity" (Allport, 1961). As a step toward defining and assessing development in new fathers, I then propose a set of markers that can be used to assess maturity in men's individual development and in their relationships.

The final section of this chapter represents a beginning attempt to integrate actual data from existing longitudinal studies of the transition to parenthood with the conceptual framework derived from theories of adult development. Consistent with Erikson's view and other formulations of "crisis theory" (e.g., Caplan, 1964; Hill, 1949), an adult developmental perspective may help us to remember that stress and disequilibrium are not always detrimental to growth and adaptation. Some of what we tend to characterize as negative change may in fact be necessary for individual and family development to occur.

CHANGE AND CONSISTENCY: PREGNANCY TO 18 MONTHS POSTPARTUM

Carolyn Pape Cowan and I have summarized previous research on becoming a father (1987b), making three central points:

1. There has been some debate about whether the transition to parenthood generates a crisis in individuals' and couples' lives (Hobbs, 1968; Hobbs & Cole, 1977; LeMasters, 1957). It has been clear for some time that motherhood is accompanied by substantial, stressful changes for many women (e.g., Rossi, 1968). Although there have been alarming articles based on case studies of male psychiatric patients who were new fathers (e.g., Wainwright, 1966), men's transition to parenthood did not become a subject for systematic research until Fein's groundbreaking study just over a decade ago (1976). In recent research, expectant and new fathers have been described as "at risk" for intrapsychic stress (May, 1982; Osofsky & Osofsky, 1985), symptoms of depression, and the blues (Ventura & Stevenson, 1986; Zaslow, Pedersen, Kramer, Cain, Suwalsky, & Fivel, 1981). In addition, if men have had previous psychiatric histories, fatherhood increases the risk of unipolar or bipolar affective disorders (Weiner, 1982).

2. The weight of recent evidence suggests that the state of the *couple relationship* is a central ingredient of both men's and women's adaptation to parenthood (Belsky & Pensky, in press; Cowan, et al., 1985; Feldman & Nash, 1984; Grossman, et al., 1980; Rapoport, Rapoport, & Streilitz, 1977; Russell, 1974; Shereshefsky & Yarrow, 1973; Wente & Crockenberg, 1976).

3. There has been little theoretical rationale for the choice of variables or domains to be assessed in understanding how men and women cope with becoming a family. Attempting to synthesize previous schemes (e.g., Belsky, 1984; Heinicke, 1984; Parke & Tinsley, 1982), we have developed a five-domain model of family structure to examine interrelated aspects of new parents' adaptation:

   a. The characteristics of each individual in the family, with special emphasis on self-concept and self-esteem
   b. The husband–wife relationship, with special emphasis on division of labor and patterns of communication
   c. The relationship between each parent and his or her child
   d. The intergenerational relationships among grandparents, parents, and grandchildren

e. The relationship between nuclear family members and individuals or institutions outside the family, with special emphasis on the balance between life stress and social support

To understand what happens to family members and relationships during major life transitions, it is necessary to examine the interconnections among all five domains. For example, it seems reasonable to assume that a man whose self-esteem is in a precarious state may have difficulty negotiating new household tasks and family decisions around the birth of a baby. Wanting things to be different from the family he grew up in, and pressured by demands from his job, he may begin to attribute the distress he feels at home to difficulties in the marriage. Under these circumstances, it seems inevitable that both partners will begin to experience tensions in their relationship. It also seems reasonable to assume that the road to marital satisfaction and dissatisfaction may begin in any domain of the family system. Difficulties in the partners' relationship with in-laws or with the child can affect their self-esteem and reduce their intimacy. In contrast to family research focusing either on individuals or on the system as a whole, the Becoming a Family Project assumed that individual, dyadic, triadic, three-generational, and extra-family domains each contribute unique information to our understanding of marital quality in the early years of family life.

After two years of pilot work with a small number of couples (Cowan, Cowan, Coie, & Coie, 1978), we recruited 72 couples who were expecting their first child. Participants were obtained through obstetrician–gynecologists in the greater San Francisco Bay Area, through a health maintenance organization, and through notices in community newsletters. We contacted couples in the late months of pregnancy and invited them to participate in a study of how marital relationships change during the transition to parenthood. After an initial two-hour interview, we assigned them randomly to one of three conditions:

1. A weekly group of 24 couples met for six months during the last trimester of pregnancy and the first three months postpartum. Each partner participated in a two-to-three-hour couple interview and then filled out an extensive set of questionnaires before the groups began. Spouses were then interviewed and assessed after the groups ended, when the children were 6 and 18 months old (see C. Cowan, Chapter 16, this volume, for a discussion of the couples group intervention).

2. Another 24 couples were assessed at the same times, but did not participate in a couples group.

3. A third sample of 24 couples was interviewed but not assessed initially so that we could examine the impact of the assessment on the other two samples. However, we did assess them fully at 6 and 18 months postpartum.

Most previous studies of the transition to parenthood have not included a comparison sample of childless couples in order to separate normal marital change over time from change attributable to becoming a family. For this purpose we recruited

24 couples who had not yet decided about whether to have a first child and who were not have fertility problems.

The couples ranged in age from 20 to 49 with a mean age at the beginning of the study of 30 for the men and 29 for the women. They lived in 28 different communities within a 40-mile radius of Berkeley and Oakland, California. In terms of racial makeup, 85% of the participants were Caucasian, and 15% were Black, Asian, or Hispanic.

Changes in Individual and Family Life Associated with Becoming a Father

From late pregnancy to 18 months postpartum, new fathers described significant changes in each of the five domains of family life that we assessed. The meaning of these changes can best be evaluated by viewing them in comparative perspective. Men becoming fathers for the first time reported significantly more change over a 21-month period than childless men, but they changed much less, and in different directions, than their wives. Jessie Bernard observed that there are "his" and "her" marriages (1974); we are finding "his," "her," and "their" transitions to parenthood (Cowan, et al., 1985).

Individual Self-Concept and Self-Esteem.

On an instrument we call The Pie, each partner listed the main roles in his or her life and then divided a 4-inch circle into sections reflecting how salient or important each aspect of the self felt, not the amount of time spent in the role. Men who remained childless showed a significant increase in the "partner/lover" aspect of the self over 21 months, while new fathers were squeezing partner/lover into a smaller space to accommodate the significant increase in the "parent" piece of the pie. In comparison with their wives, however, new fathers showed a smaller increase in the "parent" aspect of self and a smaller decrease in their psychological involvement in the marital role. The reallocation of these aspects of self appears to be greater for new mothers than for their partners, and much greater for new mothers than for women of comparable age who were not having children.

These changes, and the fact that they are of different magnitude for men and women, may have had consequences for couples' evaluation of their marriage, but they did not seem to affect how men evaluated themselves. Contrary to the findings in some previous studies (e.g., Rossi, 1968), self-esteem as assessed by the Adjective Check List (Gough & Heilbrun, 1980) remained stable over time for both the new parents and the childless couples in our sample.

Marital roles and communication.

Our "who does what?" assessment of actual and ideal divisions of household tasks, decision making, and child care revealed that after childbirth, men and women were less likely to share participation in household tasks and decision making than they were before becoming parents. Instead, they adopted a more specialized division of labor, with each partner taking responsibility for specific aspects of running the household. In the short term (at six months postpartum), couples made some changes usually described as traditional; men did less of the laundry than they had during pregnancy, and they began to provide more of the family income. However, men also increased their involvement in meal preparation, housecleaning, and food shopping during the early postpartum months (Cowan & Cowan, in press).

What seems like a trade-off occurred during the next year. Men's participation in household tasks decreased, but they became more involved in the daily care of their children. This change must be interpreted in light of the fact that women retained most of the responsibility for child care even if they were working full time outside the home. In addition, despite significant increases in fathers' involvement with their children, that involvement was much lower than either spouse predicted during pregnancy.

Given the discrepancy between prediction and actuality, it is not surprising that both men's and women's satisfaction with their role arrangements tended to decline during the transition to parenthood. Even when they changed in the same direction, however, men and women differed in the *timing* of their decline in role satisfaction. Women showed a large decline in satisfaction with the "who does what?" of family life in the early months of parenthood, while men showed more of a decline in the next year, from 6 to 18 months after they became fathers. I will discuss how these changes in roles and communication were connected with each partner's view of their marriage after presenting data from the remaining three family domains.

Parenting Attitudes and Stress.

We know from discussions with men that there were changes in many of their ideas about how to care for children once they actually became fathers. Although our Ideas About Parenting inventory revealed no changes in parents' child-centered or permissive attitudes, the fathers in our sample did become more controlling in their attitudes between pregnancy and 18 months after birth. They were more likely to endorse items calling for limits and direct intervention, especially when their children did not do what was expected of them. In this change they were similar to their wives, but different from childless men and women whose parenting attitudes showed no systematic changes over a comparable two-year period. On a measure of Parenting Stress (Abidin, 1980), men described their children as more demanding and difficult during toddlerhood than they had been in infancy, although there was no change in total amount of stress experienced in the parent role from 6 to 18 months after the birth of their first child.

The Three-Generational View.

In interviews and group sessions with the couples, we found that as men became fathers, their relationships with their parents changed markedly. One man who had not talked with either parent in seven years, phoned to announce that he and his wife were expecting a baby, and he then resumed regular telephone contact. Most of the changes were less profound, but it appeared that most men became more involved with their parents, especially with their fathers. Some reported that they finally felt like a grown-up, and were treated more as adults once they became parents. Others renewed their resolve to know their children better than their fathers knew them.

We found some support for the notion that fatherhood strengthens the connections between men's growing up years and their current level of adaptation. Men's marital satisfaction *before* the birth of their first child was not linked with their perceptions of relationships in their family of origin, either on the Family Environment Scale (Moos, 1974) or on our Family Relationship Questionnaire (adapted from Grossman, et al., 1980). However, *after* the baby came along, the more positively men described their early relationship with their mothers, the greater their satisfaction with their own marriage. It may be that caring for their babies resurrected men's memories of securities and insecurities in their relationship with their mothers, which, if the early relationship was stressful, may in turn have colored their feelings about the mother of their child (Clulow, 1985).

Life Outside the Nuclear Family: Support and Stress.

The most notable difference between husbands and wives occurred in their patterns of working outside the home. During the period of family formation, men's work outside the family increased, while women's markedly decreased. All the women in our sample took at least several months off work. A slight majority were still at home full time at 18 months postpartum with primary responsibility for the care of the household and the baby. Of those who returned to work by 18 months, only a few were employed full time. As we shall see, these differences between husbands and wives were associated with their feelings about the quality of their marriage.

We found no statistically significant changes from pregnancy to 18 months after birth in men's overall description of stressful life events. However, we did find an initial increase in perceived social support from pregnancy to 6 months postpartum, followed by a decrease from 6 to 18 months after birth. The increased social support, even though temporary, was one of the few examples where new fathers appeared to be at an advantage compared with men who had not yet decided to have children.

Summary: What Happens to Satisfaction with Marriage?

I have shown that, with the exception of self-esteem and life stress events, new fathers and mothers showed significant changes in most of the major measures of our study. They changed more, often in more negative directions, than partners not yet decided about having children who were assessed over the same period of time. In the context of these findings, it makes sense that on the average, satisfaction with the marriage declined for both spouses from pregnancy to 18 months after they became parents. The greatest decline in marital satisfaction occurred for women from pregnancy to 6 months after birth, while men remained relatively stable during that period. Over the next year women showed a small further decline while men reported a much larger drop in satisfaction with their marriage.

In several of the family domains, then, men were slower to experience the impact of becoming a parent than women. The timing of assessment may account for some of the discrepancies in findings between studies of the impact of a first child on men, women, and marriage. Fein (1976), for example, found very few negative effects on men becoming parents, but his assessments, like those in most pre- to postbirth studies of parents, ended before the child's first birthday. Our findings suggest that later assessments may provide a more accurate gauge of both positive and negative outcomes of men's transition to parenthood.

The fact that men change at different rates and in different directions than their wives appears to have important consequences for their couple relationships. We have hypothesized (Cowan, et al., 1985) that differences between partners lead to feeling distant, that feeling distant tends to stimulate conflict, and that increased conflict, in turn, affects both partners' feelings about their marriage. We constructed an index based on absolute differences between partners' perceptions of (1) themselves, (2) their relationships, (3) their families of origin, (4) their ideas about parenting, and (5) their balance between life stress and social support. Using multiple regression analyses, we found that the more different partners became between pregnancy and six months postpartum, and the greater their increase in conflict during that same period of time, the more decline they described in marital satisfaction from pregnancy to 18 months after birth ($R = .64$).

Between-partner differences were not the only factor associated with negative changes in satisfaction with marriage. Belsky, Ward, and Rovine (in press) and Garrett (1983) note that unfulfilled expectations may have a negative impact on marital quality. In our sample, when there was a larger discrepancy between women's predicted and actual involvement of their husbands in the care of their children, their wives showed a greater decline in marital satisfaction from pregnancy to 18 months postpartum ($r = .65$).

Continuity Over Time

Despite statistically significant shifts in average scores, both parents and non-parents showed remarkable correlational consistency across time. As Belsky, Spanier, and Rovine (1983), Belsky, Lang, and Rovine (1985), and Feldman and Nash (1984) also note, the focus on change during the transition to parenthood often masks an essential stability of relative ranking. Men and women with the highest self-esteem and marital satisfaction after having a baby also tended to have the highest self-esteem and marital satisfaction in late pregnancy. Symptoms of depression and level of marital satisfaction at 18 months after birth were predictable from a combination of measures obtained two years earlier (Heming, 1985, 1987).

We could also make statistically significant predictions about men's behavior and experience in the father role from data obtained before their children were born (Cowan & Cowan, 1987b; Coysh, 1984). Based on correlations and multiple regressions predicting 18-month postpartum outcomes from data obtained in pregnancy, it appears that a combination of individual and relational factors in evidence before men become fathers leads some to become more involved with their children, to be more satisfied with that involvement, and to be less stressed than other fathers. The kind of role a man plays in the care of his child, and how he feels about it, follows from the family he grew up in, his feelings about himself, his perception of the quality of his marriage, his ideas about child rearing, and his plans for involvement before the child is born. Multiple regressions using data from both fathers and nonfathers indicate that having a baby accounts for a statistically significant but small amount of variance (7%) in men's responses to our questionnaires at 18 months postpartum, while combinations of variables from the pregnancy assessment account for from 36–55% of the variance in men's depression, parenting stress, and marital satisfaction almost two years later (Heming, 1985). The point here is that there is consistency and predictability during the early years of family formation despite the disequilibrium, stress, and change accompanying parenthood. Men adapting well to having a first child are likely to be those who were adapting well before the child arrived.

Thus far, I have focused on quantitative results, with the emphasis on difficulty and stress. But almost all of the men and women in our study felt that having a child was one of the most positive aspects of their lives. In part, that feeling came from the sense that the experience of child rearing had contributed to their growth as individuals and as a family. This brings us to the question of how to conceptualize and measure the more positive, developmental aspects of becoming a father.

FATHERHOOD AS AN OPPORTUNITY FOR ADULT DEVELOPMENT

The idea that development continues after adolescence has gathered increasing support over the last four decades. However, there is no consensus about the markers that signal developmental progress as distinct from simple change in life circumstances. Does a new father's increased involvement with his parents signify a developmental change? Is the reorganization of the pie indicative of a developmental restructuring of the self? Four very different types of markers have been used to answer these questions, each implying a different conceptualization of adult development.

Age as a Marker

The first and simplest marker of development is age. We tend to expect that increasing age brings with it systematic changes in experience, understanding, and behavior. But except for the fact that there are biologically linked age limitations on becoming a father, and that the age at which men become fathers may affect the quality of their experience (Daniels & Weingarten, Chapter 3, this volume), age has little relevance in describing developmental changes associated with parenthood.

Life Cycle and Developmental Task Markers

Long before Shakespeare's eloquent description of the seven ages of man, it had been assumed that there is a sequence defined by a set of life cycle markers beginning with birth and ending with death. In the simple life-cycle model, the mere fact of becoming a parent advances men to a new developmental phase. A more complex set of life-cycle theories have been advanced by Erikson (1950, 1959), Jung (1964), and Havighurst (1953), who have described psychological and interpersonal *developmental tasks* associated with each individual life milestone. Duvall (1975), Hill (1949), and others have extended this individual focus to create a picture of the *family* life cycle (Hill & Rodgers, 1964). In the life cycle/developmental task view, development occurs when individuals and families master a given set of challenges. Failure to do so in any period at best may make the next developmental tasks more difficult, and at worst may lead to regression and psychological dysfunction. While there is recognition that there may be "on-time" and "off-time" variations in the rate of progression through the life cycle (Helson, Mitchell & Moane, 1984; Lowenthal, Thurner & Chiriboga, 1976; Neugarten, 1968), there is the expectation of a well-defined normative sequence from which individual departures are evaluated (Gould, 1978; Levenson, 1978).

In my view, there are four fundamental problems with life-cycle or task mastery markers as indexes of development during the transition to parenthool. First, parenthood is not universal within this culture: growing numbers of couples are choosing to remain child-free (Bram, 1978). Second, there is tremendous variability in the age of men becoming fathers; some begin in their early teenage years while others begin very late in their lives. Third, fatherhood no longer fits comfortably into a well-defined individual or family life cycle (if it ever did). In many couples, pregnancy occurs before marriage and even before courtship, while other couples wait to begin their families until they have finished their education and launched their careers (Daniels & Weingarten, 1982, and Chapter 3, this volume). Fourth, there are no widely accepted definitions of the central tasks of parenthood, and no empirical evaluations of what would constitute task mastery. Outside of the simple fact that many men become fathers at some time in their lives, life-cycle markers cannot help us understand or assess whether becoming a father represents developmental progress.

Structural Markers and the Definition of Stages

Hill (1949) and Benedek (1959, 1970) appear to be the first to propose the intriguing possibility that parenthood could mark a new stage of development, but Benedek later regretted having used the term "stage" (Parens, 1975). Hill and Mattesich (1979) note the tendency of most family life-cycle theorists to use stage language to describe major life changes, even though the formal defining criteria for stage changes have not been met. Stage changes occur (1) in an invariant sequence, with (2) qualitative differences between successive periods, such that (3) each period constitutes a "structured whole" that (4) hierarchically integrates rather than replaces previous stages. A good example can be found in Piaget's description of the changing set of logical rules used by infants, children, and adolescents as they come closer to the structure of adult scientific reasoning (Inhelder & Piaget, 1958).

Is it possible that becoming a father marks a change in stage? I believe that fatherhood can signal a marked, qualitative life change, but I have already indicated that there are no invariant sequences in parenthood. While structural stage models may be adequate to describe major changes from infancy through adolescence, there is no convincing body of theory or research to suggest that they apply to development during adulthood (with the possible exception of Loevinger's theory of ego development, 1976; Kegan's theory of the development of self, 1982; and Noam, 1985). Let us examine a fourth, less restrictive type of marker, one that retains some essential features of prevailing definitions of development, yet is flexible enough to deal with the variability and lack of sequence in men's transition to parenthood.

Functional Markers

A number of cognitive, personality, and family theorists interested in development tend to focus on levels of *differentiation* and *integration* in individuals, relationships, and social systems. Differentiation within a person refers to increasing ability to analyze a whole into parts, to discriminate rather than generalize, and to make specific and appropriate responses to each new situation. Integration refers to a coordination of separate parts of the person or system. More differentiated and integrated individuals or families are regarded as more highly developed, according to the functional criterion of *adaptation* defined in terms of mental health or maturity. The criterion of how well an individual functions can provide a yardstick for assessing the impact of life events occurring in any sequence at any age. Instead of trying to delineate whether fatherhood leads to a qualitative shift in structure or organization of the person, we can evaluate whether new fathers display greater maturity—differentiation, integration, and adaptation— in their ability to cope with internal and external challenges.

Maturity as a Developmental Concept

About 25 years ago, Allport's functional theory of personality (1961) provided a description of maturity as a general criterion of personality development. According to Allport, maturity can be defined in terms of six characteristics: (1) extension of the sense of self, (2) warmth in relating to others, (3) emotional security/self-acceptance, (4) realistic perceptions and skills, (5) self-insight and humor, and (6) the establishment of a unifying philosophy of life. These criteria of maturity focus on individual personality and on relationships with others. They evaluate maturity from the perspective of both the subject and the researcher. The subject provides statements concerning his or her self-concept and self-evaluation. The researcher provides assessments of the individual's competence in coping with intrapsychic and interpersonal events. A change in self-concept or competence is judged to be *developmental* when a person's level of functioning after a change can be described as more differentiated, integrated, and adaptive than before.

I have chosen a different organization of Allport's characteristics to make them specifically relevant to the transition to parenthood, but I intend to cover very similar conceptual ground. When we began our longitudinal study of men and women becoming parents, we were interested in change, but we did not plan to assess their development. What follows is a speculative reexamination of our quantitative and qualitative findings, to identify markers of individual and relationship development.

This, then, is the counterweight to the emphasis on the negative changes during the transition described in the previous section.

First, I will describe maturity from the vantage point of the new father, showing that three aspects of his self-concept can change in the direction of increased maturity—his identity, locus of control, and self-esteem. Then, I will shift to the viewpoint of the observer of new fathers, showing that developmental changes in maturity can be marked by increased personal competence in problem solving, perspective-taking, flexibility, regulation of emotion, and vital commitment (cf., Galinsky, 1980). I will also provide a brief description of developmental maturity in relationships. Because I am attempting to provide concrete referents for the meaning of maturity in the context of fatherhood, the examples in the following sections are very positive and optimistic; they reflect the experience of some men in our study, but certainly not all of them.

Individual Development: Self-Concept

Identity.

Most of the men in our study intimated that their sense of themselves changed profoundly when they became fathers. In the metaphor of the pie, men added a significant new piece to their identities when they became fathers, a change that appeared to be a sign of increased differentiation. The data show that this new aspect of self increased markedly in size from expectant fatherhood to two years postpartum. The nonparents we followed did not tend to divide their pie much differently over time.

Developmental change is not simply a matter of adding one new aspect of identity to an array, but requires some integration of "father" with already-established aspects of one's self-concept. This integration is achieved only by grappling with conflicting sets of demands. Before they became fathers, the men did not appear to be conscious of the fact that home and work life often require different personal qualities. In their work lives, men tend to believe that they should be independent, aggressive, and self-focused; the men in our study who were not becoming parents tended to bring this persona home. By contrast, new fathers were usually painfully aware of the needs of others, experiencing a pull to be caring and empathic even when their own resources were depleted. Over time, some were able to establish a more differentiated sense of themselves by changing gears appropriately in different settings, and began to establish a more coherent self in different roles: they described themselves as more aware of their personal relationships on the job, and more able to use some of their managerial skills in the solution of family problems. These struggles with issues of personal identity were not as marked in the men who remained childless during this phase of our study.

I should note that the process of redefining oneself and one's identity begins before the actual birth of the child. May's (1982) detailed qualitative analysis of interviews with 20 expectant fathers over the course of pregnancy suggests that the reality of impending fatherhood begins to sink in around the 25th to 30th weeks. Before that time, there is often a moratorium—a postponement of emotional investment and involvement—after which the expectant father tends to give increasing thought to his future status as a father and family provider.

Locus of Control.

As originally described by Rotter (1966), there is a continuum extending from those who assume that the successful resolution of problems is largely a matter of chance or luck (external control) to those who assume that personal efforts can lead to increased adaptation (internal control). The newness of parenthood, the changes in self-concept and relationships that parenthood brings, and the sheer fatigue associated with interruptions in sleep, often combined to give new fathers a sense that they were losing control of their lives. However, for some, the fact that they *became* fathers constituted proof of an almost mystical degree of control, by sharing in the power to create a new life, and often a new generation in their family line.

Locus of control as an indicator of maturity is not merely an increased feeling of being able to affect events, but the ability to discriminate between events that are inside and outside one's control. For new fathers, this balance may take months or even years to emerge. We heard men working on it when they discussed their struggles with wanting it all—job advancement, involved relationships with their wives and children, time for themselves—while accepting the fact that no matter how hard they tried, some things had to be put aside for the time being. It is our impression that as a group, men who were not parents had fewer competing demands to balance, were less aware of their limitations, and more invested in maintaining at least the illusion of personal control.

Self-Esteem.

Issues of identity formation and locus of control are concerned with the *descriptive* aspect of the self: "What kind of person am I and how do I relate to the world?" The *evaluative* aspect of the self-concept is summarized under the general heading of self-esteem (Harter, 1985; Rosenberg, 1979; Wylie, 1979). It is not entirely clear what "should" happen to self-esteem in the course of development. If a man begins to resolve the tasks and challenges posed by major life transitions, he might evaluate himself more positively. On the other hand, men's aspirations for themselves tend to grow exponentially once they become fathers. What was once an acceptable way of life or level of achievement can now become cause for self-recrimination.

In our study, the self-esteem of both men and women was remarkably stable from pregnancy to 18 months postpartum. Despite many of the negative shifts we have reported in new parents, there were no differences between new fathers and childless men in their average level of self-esteem. It may be that the positive aspects of becoming a father were sufficient to balance out the difficulties. Repeatedly in interviews fathers reported not only surviving but thriving in response to challenges that were unexpectedly stressful. In line with Allport's criteria, it seems to me that mature self-esteem in adulthood is not a global capacity to feel good about oneself regardless of what transpires, but an ability to arrive at a realistic evaluation of the self after considering one's strengths, weaknesses, and life circumstances. A high level of self-esteem, then, should not be regarded as mature unless it is based in part on demonstrable psychological and social competence.

Individual Development: Competence

In our quest for a definition of maturity we now shift from the point of view of fathers themselves to the perspective of the observer or researcher.

Problem Solving.

When new tasks and new circumstances require skills not previously in one's repertoire, the immediate result may be stressful (Lazarus & Folkman, 1984). A normal crisis may follow as people try to meet new challenges and mobilize appropriate resources (Caplan, 1964; Hansen & Johnson, 1979; Hill, 1949). Rising to the challenge of this stressful life transition, many of the men in our study described new abilities to juggle conflicting demands, make decisions, and communicate quickly and clearly both at home and at work.

Perspective-Taking.

As some men became fathers, especially after the first few months, they were able to step back from their involvement in day-to-day events to take a broader view of their life. In the cognitive realm, this perspective-taking ability (Piaget & Inhelder, 1967) sometimes led to significant revisions in their philosophy of life, new ways of making sense of where they had come from and where they were heading. In the affective realm, a broader perspective sometimes helped men to avoid marital tensions when new family demands seemed endless. Some said, for instance, that their lives were difficult at the moment, but that they had once been more serene and probably would be again. Achievement of such a perspective, which is difficult in the press of daily concerns, seemed to be facilitated by participation in one of our intervention groups (see C. Cowan, Chapter 16, this volume).

Regulation of Emotion.

The ability to control one's own impulses in the service of caring for one's children and emotionally supporting one's spouse would seem to be an important marker of maturity. However, control is only one side of the coin in coping with the strong emotions evoked by becoming a father. New fathers are often anxious, yet traditionally men have few places where they feel safe to express their vulnerability. Society expects them to be the strong ones, and they worry that talking about their doubts and fears would only upset their wives. Some fathers in our study went against stereotype and reported that having a child brought them more in touch with their feelings, and helped them learn how to be more comfortable with self-disclosure. In some cases, too, the pride of fatherhood seemed to enable some men to subordinate their own needs and feelings in the service of their family.

Vitality/Commitment.

In our interviews and weekly meetings with couples, we saw many men becoming more actively engaged in both their inner and outer world after becoming fathers.

Some redoubled their efforts to be caring and supportive husbands ("I'm just so proud of her and she's such a terrific mom"), and to succeed on the job ("I've got a kid to provide for"). Others became more introspective about what kind of people they were, questioning whether they were on the right life path, and whether they could overcome some of the internal conflicts that seemed to be interfering in their day-to-day functioning. Many of the new fathers seemed to be more vital, committed, and involved in each of the domains of life inside and outside the family.

Developmental changes in new fathers' functioning would not simply mean specific changes within one of the four aspects previously described. For example, the learning of new problem-solving skills in itself would not mark a developmental advance. It would have to be demonstrated that over the transition to parenthood fathers show new levels of differentiation and integration in their ability to solve problems. Similarly, perspective-taking requires a coordination of information from two or more frames of reference into a single and more comprehensive system. Differentiation and integration can also be seen in the changing balance between expressing and containing emotion, and the establishment of a vital, positive approach to life, despite a myriad of frustrating and stressful experiences. That is, markers of maturity are not to be found in isolated advances on single tasks, but rather a qualitative, generalized increase in men's view of themselves and in their ability to adapt flexibly to a changing world.

In describing these positive developments in new fathers, I am not intending to portray the world only in rose-colored glasses. Fatherhood left some men feeling fragmented in their identities, powerless, and low in self-esteem. There were new fathers who seemed unable to solve problems, take perspective, and regulate their emotions. Some seemed listless and only tentatively committed to their wives and children. What I am intending to convey here is that we were impressed with increased maturity in many men that appeared to be a direct outcome of their transition to parenthood.

Maturity in the Couple Relationship

Thus far, consistent with most current theories of adult development, the focus of this discussion has remained on the individual, the first of the five family domains in our model. However, the working hypothesis of the Becoming a Family Project posits an intimate, circular connection between individual adaptation and the state of the individual's relationships with spouse, children, parents, co-workers, and friends.

Psychology does not yet have a specialized language to describe the development of relationships. Yet, it seems perfectly appropriate to describe a mature couple, or even a competent parent–child dyad in much the same terms we would use to describe an individual. Couples, too, develop levels of competence in problem solving, perspective-taking, and regulation of emotion; they show varying levels of vitality and commitment to the relationship. Measurement of relationship development is, of course, a difficult problem. At this point my goal is simply to illustrate dimensions along which measures of relationship development in adulthood might be created.

Several different theorists have described relationship styles in terms of a recurring polarity, with one end representing a traditionally "masculine" style and the other representing a "feminine" style. From different theoretical perspectives, Chodorow (1978), Grossman (in press), and Helson and colleagues (1984) have focused on two contrasting pathways of development: growth through separation/individuation versus growth through attachment. The first, more often applied to males, is the process by which a child becomes increasingly autonomous in his or her relationship with the primary caregiver. The second emphasizes attachment and connectedness, a route to development more characteristic of females.

A similar polarity in describing relationship orientations is the contrast between self-focus versus commitment/obligation. Though neither side is an exclusive property of men or women, men are more often described as focusing on their own needs, while women are expected to pay more attention to the needs of children, spouses, and parents (Gilligan, 1982; Miller, 1975).

A third description of the tension between individual and relationship development focuses on agency versus communion (Bakan, 1966; Baumrind, 1982). This contrast is similar to Parsons' (1951) original description of instrumental and expressive family roles. Men are described as developing active, independent roles as agents in their own lives, while women are described as focusing on the process of communion between individuals.

A common theme unifies these three sets of polarities: The overarching issue for couples, and indeed for all intimate relationships, is the challenge of coordinating individuality and mutuality (cf., Walsh, 1983). How can each person satisfy individual needs and develop independence and autonomy, while avoiding separation and isolation from one's partner? How can two people establish mutuality, interdependence, and intimacy while allowing each person to maintain a sense of uniqueness? To the extent that men and women differ in their orientations to self and relationships, the task of answering these questions satisfactorily for both partners becomes even more difficult.

Although individuality and connectedness can be considered as equally desirable goals, the extremes of either end of the polarity may be dysfunctional for the development of the individual or the relationship. It is obvious that if one or both partners is devoted to fostering only individuality, the relationship can be severely strained. It is, perhaps, less obvious that emphasis only on the relationship may lead to a state of fusion that could interfere with the individual growth of the partners. Thus the *balance* between the two orientations, rather than the adoption of either one, would constitute relationship development.

Despite the fact that a majority of the couples in our study experienced a decline in marital satisfaction after the birth of a first child, there is evidence that the outlook for relationship development during this transition was not unrelentingly bleak. A sizable minority of the couples (about 32%) showed an increase in satisfaction with their marriage, especially if they had been in one of our intervention groups. But beyond the quantitative measure of satisfaction, some couples both reported and demonstrated a shift in the polarities I have described. They said that the new baby had both brought them closer together *and* moved them farther apart. Being parents enhanced their sense of themselves and gave them a new, more solid identity as a couple. A number of men and women indicated that the arrival of a baby had nudged them away from a focus on themselves and their satisfactions to a greater concern with others in the family, the community, and even the world, because issues such as peace and nuclear policy took on new urgency. Babies opened up men to a concern with intimate relationships, and the demands of juggling work and families roles stimulated women's investment in managing family tasks efficiently and paying attention to their own personal growth. In the first 18 months after birth we observed in most couples a greater sense of differentiation than integration, but we did see partners whose transition to parenthood appeared to lead them to a better balance of individuality and mutuality in their marriage.

INTEGRATING POSITIVE AND NEGATIVE VIEWS OF THE TRANSITION

Models of development in a family context must be interactive and circular to allow for the possibility that individual and relationship development are in a continual process of interaction and mutual influence. What happens in the couple relationship should affect the quality of the parent–child relationship, and both of these relationships should affect the development of family members as individuals.

We know now, from preliminary analyses of data when the children were 3½ (Cowan & Cowan, 1987c), that the quality of a marriage can generalize to the quality of interactions between parents and children. We also know that the parent–child relationship may have a decided influence on the child's present and future level of individual development. In our study, fathers who displayed more warmth and less anger in interaction with their preschoolers tended to have sons and daughters with higher academic achievement scores when they entered first grade. Parke (1981) underlines the importance of the father's contribution to the development of the child. Summarizing current research, Lamb (1981) and his colleagues (Lamb, Pleck, Charnov & Levine, in press) also suggest that "nurturant and at least somewhat involved fathers, as well as fathers who are emotionally and materially supportive of their wives, tend to facilitate the development of achievement motivation, cognitive and social competence, psychological adjustment, and sex-stereotyped sex-role attitudes and attributions, particularly in sons."

Family system theories would also lead us to expect that a man's relationship with his child could affect his level of individual adaptation and his relationship with his wife. In the Becoming a Family Project, men who were more involved in the day-to-day care of their young children appeared to be less involved in their work lives and to report fewer symptoms on the Hopkins Symptom Checklist (Derogatis, Lipman & Covi, 1973). These involved fathers also experienced more satisfaction with their marriage.

In general, then, while the transition to parenthood is a time of negative changes for many men, there are marked individual differences between fathers of young children in their level of maturity and satisfaction with themselves and their relationships. This brings us back to the dilemma with which we began—how to integrate the existing research focus on negative change with the theoretical possibility that becoming a father provides a unique developmental opportunity. It appears that both pictures represent aspects of the reality of early family life. What I have been describing is consistent with the view that major life changes, even those we view most positively, bring with them the potential for individual and relationship disequilibrium and distress (Dohrenwend & Dohrenwend, 1974). In the process, they have the potential for stimulating new coping skills. Following Erikson, a number of theorists have characterized these life changes as crises (Caplan, 1964; Felner, Farber, & Primavera, 1983; Hill & Hansen, 1960; Moos, 1986), with the assumption that disequilibrium may provoke distress in the short run, but can promote the development of new skills in the long run, especially if family members have help in mobilizing the strengths and coping skills they already possess.

Crisis theory presents developmental progress as a *possible* outcome of stress and distress. In Werner's (1942) and Piaget's (1967) organismic theories of development, on the other hand, disequilibration and the reorganization of old patterns are *necessary* if developmental change is to occur. If we accept this more sweeping view, we may be forced to reevaluate what are usually described as negative changes. Although we tend to assume that even short-term increases in internal or interpersonal conflict are undesirable, perhaps these conflicts serve a function of helping to reorganize the family to cope with the needs of both children and parents. In our study, disagreements about "who does what?" in housework and child care were at the top of the list of issues leading to conflict during pregnancy, and again at 6 and 18 months postpartum. Some couples described ongoing struggles to modify their role arrangements; those who made headway in this process were more encouraged about their problem-solving ability and more positive about the quality of their overall marriage (Ball, 1984).

In addition, the decline in satisfaction with marriage is not *necessarily* a negative change. Given that men's and women's energies are not infinitely expandable, it may be adaptive for some energy to be diverted from the couple relationship in the service of attending to the needs of the infant or young child. This change may lead to increased tension in the couple relationship, but may also lead to both individual and relationship development in other family domains. Those who can adopt the perspective that placing the marriage on the back burner is a regrettable but temporary state of affairs may be able to return to enhanced relationship satisfaction and quality in the future. In part, their perspective-taking may lead to a change in their expectations and a redefinition of what is necessary for a satisfying marriage at this time of life.

I am not trying here to turn every disaster into a triumph. Certainly if conflict increases and satisfaction with marriage decreases in the long run, the marriage may be in jeopardy. In fact one in eight of the new parents in our study separated or divorced by the time the children were 18 months old. Furthermore, children are placed at risk whether or not marital distress ends in divorce (Hetherington & Camara, 1984; Wallerstein & Kelley, 1980). I am suggesting that if new fathers and mothers can manage to create their own versions of crisis or organismic theories with the built-in assumption that stress can lead to growth, they may be better able to avoid family dissolution by using the disequilibration of the transition as an opportunity for development.

Further research on maturity and development in father's perspective should be addressed to three main tasks. First, it will be necessary to create some systematic measures of developmental maturity that can be used to assess change in men and their relationships as they become fathers. The picture of distress emerging from previous transition-to-parenthood research tends to be based on quantitative data, while development has been described more qualitatively and anecdotally. It should be possible, from existing personality tests, observations, and interviews, to create indices of differentiation and integration of men's sense of themselves, their competence, and the balance between individuality and mutuality in each of their central relationships. These data would make it possible for us to understand the connections between negative changes and individual growth.

Second, in collaboration with obstetricians and pediatricians, it should be possible to identify men whose reactions to the demands of new parenthood may make their progress toward maturity problematic. Early identification of men at risk would enable health professionals to offer interventions to help them use the challenges of new parenthood as an opportunity for their own growth and development, and for development of their relationships inside and outside the family.

Finally, as Hanson and Bozett (1987) point out in their discussion of fatherhood along the family life span, most of the empirical research on fatherhood focuses on men's transition to parenthood. Surely, men face new challenges and opportunities for development as their children proceed through the explorations of toddlerhood, the anxieties of entering school, the agonies of adolescence, and the uncertainties of beginning families of their own. We need new studies, then, examining the links between men and their children as each provides challenges and opportunities for the other to become more differentiated and integrated. The functional view of maturity and adaptation implies that development does not simply follow from the fact that men become fathers, but is a reflection of the kind of fathers that men ultimately become.

REFERENCES

Abidin, R. (1980). *Parent education and intervention handbook*. Springfield, IL: Thomas.

Allport, G. (1961). *Pattern and growth in personality*. New York: Holt, Rinehart & Winston.

Bakan, D. (1966). *The duality of existence: Isolation and communion in Western man*. Boston: Beacon Press.

Ball, F.L.J. (1984). *Understanding and satisfaction in marital problem solving: A hermeneutic inquiry*. Doctoral dissertation, University of California, Berkeley.

Baumrind, D. (1982). Are androgynous individuals more effective persons and parents? *Child Development, 53*, 44–75.

Belsky, J., & Pensky, E. (in press). Marital change across the transition to parenthood. *Marriage and Family Review*.

Belsky, J., Spanier, G.B., & Rovine, M. (1983). Stability and change in marriage across the transition to parenthood. *Journal of Marriage and the Family, 45*, 567–577.

Belsky, J., Lang, M.E., & Rovine, M. (1985). Stability and change in marriage across the transition to parenthood: A second study. *Journal of Marriage and the Family, 47*, 855–865.

Belsky, J., Ward, H., & Rovine, M. (in press). Prenatal expectations, postnatal experiences and the transition to parenthood. In R. Ashmore & D. Brodzinsky (Eds.), *Perspectives on the family*. Hillsdale, NJ: Erlbaum.

Benedek, T. (1959). Parenthood as a developmental phase: A contribution to libido theory. *Journal of the American Psychoanalytic Association, 7*, 389–417.

Benedek, T. (1970). Parenthood during the life cycle. In E.J. Anthony & T. Benedek (Eds.), *Parenthood: Its psychology and psychopathology*. Boston: Little, Brown.

Bernard, J. (1974). *The future of marriage*. New York: World.

Bibring, G.L. (1959). Some considerations of the psychological processes in pregnancy. *Psychoanalytic Study of the Child, 14*, 113–121.

Bram, S. (1978). Through the looking glass: Voluntary childlessness as a mirror for contemporary changes in the meaning of parenthood. In W. Miller & L. Newman (Eds.), *The first child and family formation*. Chapel Hill, NC: Carolina Population Center.

Caplan, G. (1964). *Principles of preventive psychiatry*. New York: Basic Books.

Chodorow, N. (1978). *The reproduction of mothering: Psychoanalysis and the sociology of gender*. Berkeley: University of California Press.

Clulow, C. (1985). *Marital therapy: An inside view*. Aberdeen, Scotland: Aberdeen University Press.

Cowan, C.P., & Cowan, P.A. (1987a). A preventive intervention for couples becoming parents. In C.F.Z. Boukydis (Ed.). *Research on support for parents and infants in the postnatal period*. New Jersey: Ablex.

Cowan, C.P., & Cowan, P.A. (1987b). Men's involvement in parenthood: Identifying the antecedents and understanding the barriers. In P. Berman & F. Pedersen (Eds.), *Men's transitions to parenthood*. Hillsdale, NJ: Erlbaum.

Cowan, C.P., & Cowan, P.A. (1987c, April). *Couple relationships, parenting styles, and the child's development at three*. Paper presented at the Society for Research in Child Development, Baltimore.

Cowan, C.P., & Cowan, P.A. (in press). Who does what when partners become parents: Implications for the marriage. *Marriage and Family Review*.

Cowan, C.P., & Cowan, P.A, Coie, L., & Coie, J.D. (1978). Becoming a family: The impact of a first child's birth on the couple's relationship. In W.B. Miller & L.F. Newman (Eds.), *The first child and family formation*. Chapel Hill, NC: Carolina Population Center.

Cowan, C.P., Cowan, P.A., Heming, G., Garrett, E., Coysh, W.S., Curtis-Boles, H., & Boles, A.J. (1985). Transitions to parenthood: His, hers, and theirs. *Journal of Family Issues, 6*, 451–481.

Coysh, W.S. (1984). *Factors influencing men's roles in caring for their children and the effects of father involvement*. Doctoral dissertation, University of California, Berkeley.

Daniels, P., & Weingarten, K. (1982). *Sooner or later: The timing of parenthood in adult lives*. New York: Norton.

Derogatis, L.R., Lipman, R.S., & Covi. L. (1973). SCL-90: An outpatient psychiatric rating scale—preliminary report. *Psychopharmacology Bulletin, 9*, 13–28.

Dohrenwend, B., & Dohrenwend, B. (1974). *Stressful life events: Their nature and effects*. New York: Wiley.

Duvall, E.M (1975). *Marriage and family development* (5th ed.). Philadelphia: Lippincott.

Erikson, E. (1950). *Childhood and society*. New York: Norton.

Erikson, E. (1959). Identity and the life cycle. *Psychological Issues, 1*, 1–171.

Fein, R. (1976). Men's entrance to parenthood. *Family Coordinator, 25*, 341–348.

Feldman, S.S., & Nash, S.C. (1984). The transition from expectancy to parenthood: Impact of the firstborn child on men and women. *Sex Roles 11*, 61–78.

Felner, R.D., Farber, S.S., & Primavera, J. (1983). Transitions and stressful life events: A model for primary prevention. In R.D. Felner, L.A. Jason, J.N. Moritsugu, & S.S. Farber (Eds.), *Preventive psychology: Theory, research, and practice*. New York: Pergamon.

Galinsky, E. (1980). *The six stages of parenthood: Between generations*. New York: Times Books.

Garrett, E. (1983, August). *Women's experience of early parenthood: Expectations vs. reality*. Paper presented at the American Psychological Association, Anaheim.

Gilligan, C. (1982). *In a different voice: Psychological theory and women's development*. Cambridge, MA: Harvard University Press.

Gough, H.G., & Heilbrun, A.B., Jr. (1980). *The Adjective Check List manual*. Palo Alto, CA: Consulting Psychologists Press.

Gould, R. (1978). *Transformations: Growth and change in adult life*. New York: Simon & Schuster.

Grossman, F.K. (1987). Separate and together: Men's autonomy and affiliation in the transition to parenthood. In P. Berman & F.A. Pedersen, (Eds.), *Men's transitions to parenthood*. Hillsdale, NJ: Erlbaum.

Grossman, F., Eichler, L., & Winickoff, S. (1980). *Pregnancy, birth, and parenthood*. San Francisco: Jossey-Bass.

Hansen, D., & Johnson, V. (1979). Rethinking family stress theory: definitional aspects. In W.R. Burr, R. Hill, F.I. Nye, & I.L. Reiss (Eds.), *Contemporary theories about the family: Research-based theories: Vol. I*. New York: Free Press.

Hanson, S.M.H., & Bozett, F. (1987). Fatherhood and changing family roles. *Family and Community Health, 9*, 9–21.

Harter, S. (1985). Developmental perspectives on self-esteem. In P. Mussen, (Gen. Ed.), & E.M. Hetherington (Vol. Ed.), *Handbook of child psychology, Vol. 4*, 275–386.

Havighurst, R.J. (1953). *Human development and education*. New York: Longmans, Green.

Heinicke, C. (1984). Impact of prebirth parent personality and marital functioning on family development: A framework and suggestions for further study. *Developmental Psychology, 20*, 1044–1053.

Helson, R., Mitchell, V., & Moane, G. (1984). Personality patterns of adherence and non-adherence to the social clock. *Journal of Personality and Social Psychology, 46*, 1078–1096.

Heming, G. (1985). *Predicting adaptation during the transition to parenthood*. Unpublished doctoral dissertation, University of California, Berkeley.

Heming, G. (1987, April). *Predicting adaptation during the transition to parenthood*. Paper presented at the Society for Research in Child Development, Baltimore.

Hetherington, E.M., & Camara, K.A. (1984). Families in transition: the process of dissolution and reconstitution. In R.D. Parke (Ed.), *Review of child development research: The family* (Vol. 7). Chicago: University of Chicago Press.

Hill, R. (Ed.). (1949). *Families under stress*. New York: Harper.

Hill, R., & Hansen, D.A. (1960). The identification of conceptual frameworks utilized in family study. *Marriage and Family Living, 22*, 299–311.

Hill, R., & Mattesich, P. (1979). Family development theory and life-span development. In P. Baltes, (Ed.), *Life-span development and behavior: Vol. 2*. New York: Academic.

Hill, R., & Rodgers, R.H. (1964). The developmental approach. In H. Christensen (Ed.), *Handbook of marriage and the family*. Chicago: Rand McNally.

Hobbs, D.F., Jr. (1968). Transition to parenthood: A replication and an extension. *Journal of Marriage and the Family, 30*, 413–417.

Hobbs, D., & Cole, S. (1977). Transition to parenthood: A decade replication. *Journal of Marriage and the Family, 38*, 723–731.

Inhelder, B., & Piaget, J. (1958). *The growth of logical thinking from childhood to adolescence*. New York: Basic Books.

Jung, C. (1964). *Man and his symbols*. New York: Doubleday.

Kegan, R. (1982). *The evolving self*. Cambridge, MA: Harvard University Press.

Lamb, M.E. (1981). *The role of the father in child development* (rev. ed.). New York: Wiley.

Lamb, M.E., Pleck, J.H., Charnov, E.L., & Levine, J.A. (in press). A biosocial perspective on paternal behavior and involvement. In J.B. Lancaster, J. Altmann, A. Rossi, & L. Sherrod (Eds.), *Parenting across the lifespan: Biosocial perspectives*. Chicago: Aldine.

Lazarus, R., & Folkman, S. (1984). *Stress, appraisal, and coping*. New York: Springer.

LeMasters, E.E. (1957). Parenthood as crisis. *Marriage and Family Living, 19*, 352–355.

Levenson, D.J. (1978). *The seasons of a man's life*. New York: Knopf.

Loevinger, J. (1976). *Ego development*. San Francisco: Jossey-Bass.

Lowenthal, M.F., Thurner, M, & Chiriboga, D. (1976). *Four stages of life*. San Francisco: Jossey-Bass.

May, K.A. (1982). Three phases of father involvement in pregnancy. *Nursing Research, 31*, 337–342.

Miller, J.B. (1975). *Toward a new psychology of women*. Boston: Beacon Press.

Moos, R.H. (1974). *Family Environment Scale*. Palo Alto, CA: Consulting Psychologists Press.

Moos, R. (Ed.). (1986). *Coping with life crises: An integrated approach*.

Neugarten, B.L. (1968). Adult personality: Toward a psychology of the life cycle. In B.L. Neugarten (Ed.), *Middle age and aging: A reader in social psychology*. Chicago: University of Chicago Press.

Noam, G. (1985). Stage, phase, and style: The developmental dynamics of the self. In M. Berkowitz & F. Oser (Eds.), *Moral education: Theory and application*. Hillsdale, NJ: Erlbaum.

Osofsky, H. (1982). Expectant and new fatherhood as a developmental crisis. *Bulletin of the Menninger Clinic, 46*, 209–230.

Osofsky, J.D., & Osofsky, H.J. (1985). Psychological and developmental perspectives on expectant and new parenthood. In R.D. Parke (Ed.), *Review of child development research: The family* (vol. 7). Chicago: University of Chicago Press.

Parens, H. (1975). Parenthood as a developmental phase. *Journal of the American Psychoanalytic Association, 23*, 154–165.

Parke, R. (1981). *Fathering*. Cambridge, MA: Fontana Paperbacks.

Parke, R.D., & Tinsley, B.R. (1982). The early environment of the at-risk infant: Expanding the social context. In D. Bricker (Ed.), *Intervention with at-risk and handicapped infants: From research to application*. Baltimore: University Park.

Parsons, T. (1951). *The social system*. New York: Free Press of Glencoe.

Piaget, J. (1967). *Six psychological studies* (D. Elkind, Ed.). New York: Random House.

Piaget, J., & Inhelder, B. (1967). *The child's conception of space*. New York: Norton.

Rapoport, R. (1963). Normal crises, family structure, and mental health. *Family Process, 2*, 68–80.

Rapoport, R., Rapoport, R.N., & Streilitz, A., with Kew, S. (1977). *Fathers, mothers and society: Towards new alliances*. New York: Basic Books.

Rosenberg, M. (1979). *Conceiving the self*. New York: Basic Books.

Rossi, A. (1968). Transition to parenthood. *Journal of Marriage and the Family, 30*, 26–39.

Rotter, J. (1966). Generalized expectancies for internal versus external control of reinforcement. *Psychological Monographs, 80* (1, Whole No. 609).

Russell, C. (1974). Transition to parenthood: Problems and gratifications. *Journal of Marriage and the Family, 36*, 294–302.

Shereshefsky, P.M., & Yarrow, L.J. (1973). *Psychological aspects of a first pregnancy*. New York: Raven.

Ventura, J.N., & Stevenson, M.B. (1986). Relations of mothers' and fathers' reports of infant temperament, parents' psychological functioning, and family characteristics. *Merrill-Palmer Quarterly, 32*, 275–289.

Wallerstein, J., & Kelly, J. (1980). *Surviving the breakup*. New York: Basic Books.

Walsh, F. (Ed.). (1983). *Normal family processes*. New York: Guilford.

Wainwright, W.H. (1966). Fatherhood as a precipitant of mental illness. *American Journal of Psychiatry, 123*, 40–44.

Weiner, A. (1982). Childbirth-related psychiatric illness. *Comprehensive psychiatry, 23*, 143–154.

Wente, A.S., & Crockenberg, S.B. (1976). Transition to fatherhood: Lamaze preparation, adjustment difficulty and the husband-wife relationship. *The Family Coordinator, 25*, 351–357.

Werner, H. (1942). *The comparative psychology of mental development*. New York: Follett.

Wylie, R. (1979). *The self-concept. Volume 2. Theory and research on selected topics*. Lincoln, NE: University of Nebraska Press.

Zaslow, M., Pedersen, F., Kramer, E., Cain, R., Suwalsky, J., & Fivel, M. (1981, April). *Depressed mood in new fathers: Interview and behavioral correlates*. Paper presented at the Society for Research in Child Development, Boston.

CHAPTER 3

The Fatherhood Click

The Timing of Parenthood in Men's Lives

PAMELA DANIELS and KATHY WEINGARTEN

Becoming a father still seems to me about the most dramatic event and psychological change in my life. Everything seemed different and very wonderful. Having Ted changed my attitude and my perspective. But thanks to my wife, I don't believe it ever made a difference in what I did.
                    A 45-YEAR-OLD EARLY-TIMING FATHER WHOSE FIRST CHILD WAS BORN IN 1956.

My preoccupation with competence helped me get through the first few months. I like doing things well, and right. When I realized that there was a whole new set of tasks—changing diapers, washing diapers, taking a screaming infant and making him feel placid and sleepy, feeding him—when I realized all those things were new areas to master I felt better.
                    A 34-YEAR-OLD LATE-TIMING FATHER WHOSE FIRST CHILD WAS BORN IN 1976.

Parenthood is a powerful generator of development. It affects those who become engaged in it in profound and particular ways. Do the ways in which parenthood affects people differ systematically depending on *when* in the life cycle the transition to parenthood occurs? In order to identify some of the consequences of the timing of parenthood, in the late 1970s we decided to explore family timing patterns by means of intensive interviews with parents who had had their first child "early" or "late" in the life cycle (Daniels & Weingarten, 1982).

We interviewed a sample of 72 couples (husbands and wives together) representing three minigenerations a decade apart. When we interviewed them, these parents were living in the cities and suburbs along the Northeast Corridor from Portland, Maine to Washington, DC, and in the farms, mountains, and seacoast towns of New England. One third of the sample (24 couples) were in their late twenties/early thirties, one third in their late thirties/early forties, and one third in their late forties/early fifties (see Table 3.1). The large majority (78%) of the couples we interviewed were no more than three years apart in age, in accord with the national statistical picture of age differences between husbands and wives.

TABLE 3.1   Family-Timing Patterns

	Age of Mother in January 1980		
Average age of mother at birth of first child	Early thirties	Early forties	Early fifties
Early timing 21½ years	A 12 couples	C 12 couples	E 12 couples
Late timing 30½ years	B 12 couples	D 12 couples	F 12 couples

n = 72 couples

In each group, half of the couples had their first child when the wife was 22 years or younger—*early first-time parents*.[1] Half of the couples in each age group had their first child when the wife was between the ages of 28 and 33—*late first-time parents*. When we met them, all 144 mothers and fathers in our sample were still married to the person with whom they had had their first child.

The parents in our sample represented the ethnic and religious diversity of white Americans, as well as a wide range of socioeconomic circumstance, education, and employment. Most parents had finished high school; some had advanced degrees. Women's nonparental occupations ranged from school traffic safety supervisor to psychiatrist, men's from rural sawyer to college professor and urban lawyer.

In gathering these parents' stories, we used a method of intensive, unstructured interviewing that we call the *psychological research interview*, a technique intended for small samples, which emphasizes the descriptive and reflective rather than the codable and measurable. It is a means of generating subjective data—the rich, complex, not always conscious personal particulars of people's lives.

The interviews lasted from two to three hours, and covered three broad topics: how the partners arrived at the decision to become parents at a particular time in their lives; the impact of the first birth and its timing on other spheres of their lives as individuals and as a couple; and the pluses and minuses of becoming parents when they did.

With respect to men, we were interested in the difference between the identity and the hands-on experience of fatherhood. As we read and reread the interview transcripts, we discovered that men become fathers at different times of the life cycle, not only literally but experientially. That is, as a central, fully realized developmental experience,[2] fatherhood "clicked" at different times for different fathers, and at a time distinct from the timing of the birth of their first child.

In reading through the transcripts, we also gained a vivid sense of each man's story. In some instances, when a particular father's account crystallized a point for us, we have used part of his story to make that point. In other instances, when the conjunction of evidence in many transcripts illuminated a point or yielded insight,

[1]At the time of our study, the early thirties was still considered a late age to be having a first child.
[2]See P. Cowan, Chapter 2, this volume, for a discussion of fatherhood as a generator of men's development.

we have tried to find the case that best exemplifies the point we want to make. We have written about both parents' experiences elsewhere (Daniels & Weingarten, 1982); in this chapter, we will focus on the experience of the fathers in our study, drawing on our case material and summarizing our findings on the timing of the fatherhood "click."

Traditionally, becoming a father may have meant a shift in a man's inner world and/or a heightened sense of responsibility to provide for his family's livelihood, but fatherhood has not usually included regular, routine participation in the hands-on work of parenthood. Most men work full time away from home and have been largely absent from domestic life (Lerner, 1965). Moreover, until recently, most men have not looked to parenthood or sustained relationships with their children as a source of their own development, except perhaps belatedly, when children break away and leave home, generating in their fathers a mid-life crisis of nostalgia and regret as they realize what they have missed (Levinson, 1978; Vaillant & McArthur, 1972). Today, however, more fathers are becoming more involved in the day-to-day care of their children (Barnett & Baruch, Chapter 5, this volume; Blum, 1980; C. Cowan, Chapter 16, this volume; Levine, 1978; Schwebel, Fine, Moreland & Prindle, Chapter 17 this volume). Both parents and researchers are asking questions about the importance of fathers to families and the importance of family to fathers. In our study we wanted to see whether these changing conceptions of men's work and family roles were reflected in the experiences of early- and late-timing fathers.

THE IMPLICATIONS OF FATHERHOOD FOR MEN'S WORK IN THE WORLD

Male Versus Female Career Choices

As we have suggested, the impact of new parenthood in the sphere of work is different for women and men. Women have had to accommodate their work lives to the demands of parenthood in ways men have not had to contemplate. All of the women we interviewed readjusted their life structure to make room for motherhood and for its occupational consequences. For all but six women this meant drastically cutting back or giving up nonfamily work. By contrast, only one of the 72 men in our study made a comparable adjustment in his educational plans, career ambition, or employment goals. Louis Edelman,[3] a 53-year-old early-timing father of five grown children, gave up a scholarship for advanced study at a prestigious university when his wife became pregnant early in their marriage. Instead, he settled in his home town and joined the family business in order to support his young family. "In our day," he said, "if you were a husband and a father, and you took those things seriously, you didn't go to school. You went to work."

Many men described the incremental impact of their responsibilities as breadwinners and family providers. But no one, with the exception of Louis Edelman,

[3]The names of all the fathers quoted here are pseudonyms.

changed his plans or deferred a career dream on account of becoming a parent. New parenthood did not disrupt men's work trajectories. Rather, men's work seemed to accelerate along that trajectory. In all three minigenerations in our sample, regardless of whether the men became fathers early or late, their work commitments, while responsive to needs set in motion by the birth of the first child, were insulated from the daily cares of hands-on parenting.

For a number of men, first-time fatherhood meant spending extra hours away from home, working longer hours at the jobs they had, going to school, or moonlighting in order to accommodate the new pressures to generate income, acquire some security, and make a success of themselves. Joe Alonso graduated from high school in 1966, served in Vietnam, came home, and got a job in an electronics plant. Six months on the job, he got his first raise and married his high school sweetheart. "All the guys at work were supporting families," he said, "and I thought, why not me and Angie?" Fifteen months later, the first of their two children was born. "The baby's coming was a good thing," Joe went on, "because it drove home to me that I had to have a better job. And I knew I'd need an education to get one. I transferred to the evening shift so I could go to college during the day. The hours were hard, I was under a lot of pressure, and I missed my family, but it was something I had to do." Joe earned a bachelor's degree in mathematics in record time, left the plant, and now works as a computer specialist for a large bank. His sense of family needs still governs his work choices, for he admits that he would actually love to teach high school, but can't afford the drop in pay that a starting teacher's salary would mean.

Only two men in our study suggested that fatherhood influenced the *type* of work they did, another way in which the work lives of mothers and fathers differ markedly. For these two men, the family budget took priority over job preference. On the other hand, the women we interviewed generally did not choose their type of work for financial reasons; they deliberately or intuitively chose careers or jobs that allowed them to arrange their work so that they could be with their families when they felt they should be. As documented elsewhere (Epstein, 1970), the structure of occupations that are sex-typed "male" differs from that of "female" occupations. "Female" occupations tend to permit (though they do not reward) flexible entry and reentry and a self-scheduled, seasonal time commitment that eases the accommodation of work and family life. Men do not choose their jobs and careers by these criteria.

Becoming parents changed women's and men's work *motivation*, in opposite ways. Women were less emotionally involved with their work for a while; they drew back temporarily from the outside work world into the domestic one. By contrast, many fathers felt an additional impetus to make it in their jobs—the need to work more, to be an especially good provider.

Economic Factors in the Timing of Fatherhood

Since the fathers were the principal breadwinners for all but one of the couples we interviewed, it is not surprising that they were the ones to talk most about the economic pluses and minuses of early and late parenthood. The major disadvantage of early parenthood, according to fathers, was the financial strain of starting and raising a family at a time of minimum earning power. As one father said, "We lived on a deficit economy around here for 15 years. You have very young children when you have the least money you'll ever have, when you could really use a few hours away, but you can't afford a sitter. You feel the need then, and you don't feel it later."

The early-timing fathers, in their fifties at the time of our interview, emphasized the economic trade-off of early parenthood, and the subsequent advantage later on: "I was 48 when I paid my last college tuition," one man said. "We're young enough so that we can enjoy the money I'm making now, and I don't have to be worrying about retirement yet either. I'm glad we have the money now, rather than when we were 20, because we wouldn't have appreciated it half as much then. Now we know what we want to do with it."

The economic pluses and minuses of late parenthood are the reverse. Late-timing parents started their families and were able to support them at a higher and more secure financial level than early-timing parents. Late-timing couples could afford dinners out, vacation, travel, and countless other luxuries early-timing couples never could. Still, the longer the initial postponement, the greater the likelihood that the expenses of children's college education will coincide with the need to save toward retirement, with medical bills that begin to accumulate in middle age, or with increased financial responsibilities connected with the care of parents' own aging parents (Oppenheimer, 1974).

Fatherhood and Men's Work Identity

Parenthood does not usually provide men with a work identity. However, new fatherhood can and does serve to galvanize it, clarify it, or strengthen it. The birth of his first child brought occupational identity issues front and center for Stephen Anderson. Without a career dream or direction, Stephen was floundering in college. "I managed to graduate," he said, "for with the baby coming I felt I had to have some sort of work identity. It was no longer sufficient to be a student who wasn't taking what he was doing very seriously. I began to concentrate much more on what I was doing."

Bob Berger is a theatrical press agent. Unlike Stephen Anderson, during his twenties Bob had chosen a field he liked, and acquired experience and public respect in it. For him, imminent parenthood clarified and confirmed his work identity and gave him the courage to start his own press agency:

Sometime in the first trimester of Betsy's pregnancy, I started to panic. I wondered if maybe I shouldn't get into some more conventional line of work. We had always got by by the seat of our pants, and I began to worry about whether I would be able to support this kid. I had a major decision to make at that point—whether to get an office and start an agency of my own, whether to continue as we were, or whether to do something else. I finally decided that I wanted to have the agency, that I didn't want to work for anybody else, and that it was better to start now while we were still poor and didn't have anything to lose. . . . So having a baby had a very powerful effect. It mobilized me. I was much more of a dreamer than I am now. I think it gave me a dose of reality.

Only one man described feelings of conflict between work and family life similar to those expressed by the women we spoke to. George Crosby, an early first-time father in his forties at the time of the interview, whose work in a brokerage firm never engaged his special capacity to care or sustained his sensitive interest in people, told us: "The conflict I've had was having to go to work in the first place, because I would have enjoyed being at home with the kids and the family." Had Crosby's first child been born in 1978, not 1958, he might have become (for a while) a full-time father and house husband. His steady progress up the promotional ladder in his firm belies the fact that his heart was not fully in his work. For such men, research that focuses on work histories and career cycles misses the central phenomenon of their generative lives.

Recent research on men's development, which sets forth an age-based progression of occupational events in men's lives (Levinson, 1978), obscures the family drama as well as a fundamental difference in the unfolding of men's and women's generativity (Erikson, 1968). For it is often the presence of a wife—tending to home, tending to children, tending to men—that enables men to pursue their work and maintain their education and employment records in an unbroken sequence.

FATHERING: NATURE OR NURTURE?

We live in a culture that idealizes the mother as someone who intuitively knows what to do for a child, who is inherently calm and patient and responsive to the needs of others, and who takes care without awkwardness or ambivalence. This mythical ideal does a disservice to parents on two counts. It assumes that the ability and desire to nurture the growth of a child are inborn, and it suggests that these qualities are inborn exclusively in women. But nurturance is not a matter only of endowment. It calls for development—in both sexes. Nurturance refers to a range of feelings and skills that can and must be learned and practiced, and themselves nurtured (Ruddick, 1980). Some women seem to be "born mothers," but many more learn the practical business of caring for their children just as they learn the depth and limits of their maternal feelings—on the job. By the same token, a man's capacity for emotional involvement with his children and his ability to care for them in practical ways may come naturally or they may need to be developed (Pleck, 1981b).

The men in our study interpreted their role as fathers in a variety of ways. Virtually all of them believed that being a good father meant first and foremost being a good provider. However, only a few considered the provider function a sufficient expression of fatherliness; most felt that a father's responsibility went beyond funding their families. They valued their relationships with their children, and they considered themselves family men. Finally, a few men throughout their parenting years (and many men intermittently) looked after their families not only as income earners in the outside world, but as daily caregivers at home.

We did not meet many men who were primarily responsible for taking care of their children on a daily basis, nor did we expect to. Time budget studies conducted in the 1960s and early 1970s, in which people were asked to keep daily diaries of how they spent their time, found that men did about 1.6 hours of family work per day, of which 12 minutes were spent in primary child care (Pleck, 1981a). However, the experience of the men in our study who did care for children (for a good deal more than 12 minutes a day)—feeding them, changing and bathing them, playing with them, putting them to bed, and getting up in the night with them—is especially relevant and instructive in the 1980s. In this decade, men are increasingly being pressured or permitted to join or relieve their wives in doing the parenting (Barnett & Baruch, Chapter 5, this volume; C. Cowan, Chapter 16, this volume; Levine, 1976; Radin, Chapter 9, this volume).

A few men reported that when they turned their generative, caregiving energies to their children, fathering seemed to come naturally. It was as if they had always known how to care for babies, play with toddlers, patiently build models with nine year olds, or handle moody adolescents. However, for most men, as for most women, skill and sensitivity in dealing with their children had to evolve, competence in child care had to be learned, confidence in the "goodness" of one's parenting had to be earned. Indeed, some men's concept of fatherhood as a new set of tasks to master and an arena for the expression of competence enabled them to risk a playful intimacy with their children that might otherwise have remained dormant.

David Dessolde is one of the fathers in our study who shared equally with his wife, Dale, in the care of his children from the time they were born. Even as he and Dale were deciding when to have a child, his fathering propensity was unmistakable. It was not sufficient for him to acquiesce to his wife's readiness; he knew he had to feel independently ready. "We weren't going to go ahead and conceive a baby and then Dale would raise it," he said. "Parenthood was something we would both be involved with, which meant that we both had to be ready for it." This insistence that he, too, had to be ready primed him many months in advance to view himself as central to the parenting process. Even so, in response to our question, "What was the biggest surprise about parenthood?" he replied, laughing, "I guess I thought it could be a little more of a sideline."

David described the moment of his daughter's birth as another step in the process of his unfolding receptivity to the experience of parenthood, to his child, and to the father within himself.

Something changed in me the moment she was born. I had gone by the nursery window before Rebecca was born, and I hadn't found newborns very attractive; I didn't have the urge to pick up my camera and photograph them. But I was with Dale during the delivery and the minute Rebecca came out, I thought she was beautiful. I was amazed. I had not expected her to be so beautiful and substantial, and really very much like a person. My whole perspective changed. When I went past the nursery afterward, with all the babies one or two days old lined up behind the window in their little bins, I looked again. They were still all red and puckery, but appealing too, and I said to my-self, "That's really nice."

David was describing not only an aesthetic transformation but an emotional one. The change in his definition of "attractive" and "appealing" signified a shift in self-definition. When his boundaries shifted to make room for his infant daughter, they loosened enough to include all babies.

David's description of his evolving relationship with his daughter and son, who are both now in school, suggests a continuing "boundary-loosened" responsive-ness to them—a minute, immediate, and resilient awareness of their changing lives—which we are used to associating only with mothers (Dinnerstein, 1976; Chodorow, 1978).

> Time has changed for me; my whole sense of a day has changed. Days go by, and I re-alize how small the day is. A month is like what a day used to be. You find yourself having to adjust to *their* pace, *their* readiness to do this or that. Much of the time I find them not quite old enough. For instance, you're making a tree house, but you find they can't quite bang the nails in yet. You're working away and you find that "Gee, I can't really do this *with* them, I can only do it *for* them." And you modify your expectations. You get continuous feedback from them, and you *go* with that.

David Dessolde's way of fathering includes the possibility of controlled merging, "going with" his child. But his was not the only version of "natural" fa-therhood we encountered. For Nate Engel, a product manager for a shoe company, emotional involvement in his forthcoming child was evident during his wife's preg-nancy. "She didn't have morning sickness. I did. For months. I didn't throw up, I just didn't feel like eating breakfast."

Nate reported that the "best thing" in his life, throughout his life, has been his family. In a later era, he might have taken his nurturing propensity to its occupa-tional limit and become the primary parent. As it was, Nate became a father in the late 1940s, 20 years earlier than David Dessolde; the times were traditional, and so was what he did with his children. He did not feed or change his children when they were infants, nor does he remember wanting to. His way of participating in their care was to develop a "specialty" in telling stories and giving baths.

> We used to get up early in the morning. From 6:30 till breakfast, they'd be sitting on top of the potty or playing in the tub, and I'd be shaving and telling them a story. Even when they didn't understand English, I'd tell them stories. I'd put lather all over their faces, scoop it off. We'd make faces to go with the stories. That was the morning rou-tine. In the evening, I got home around 5:30 and we always had dinner together, then more stories and horsing around in the bath until bedtime.

Nate's way of loving and caring for his children when they were young—moments of pleasure bracketing a tedious work day—is a characteristically "masculine" solu-tion. While maintaining his traditional breadwinner role, this deeply nurturant man (by his own and his eldest daughter's account) managed to express that nurturant desire and capacity with his children.

Most men (like most women) do not seem to be "born parents." Feelings of parental love may be reflexive; the capacity for parental care is not. Men learn parenting ways by watching their wives and others playing with children, orchestrating meals, settling sibling squabbles, arranging schedules, comforting, and disciplining. Learning parenting also means learning to pay attention to children's feedback. Fathering (like mothering) depends on practice and opportunity. Ken Brodie is a man who learned how to care for his daughter, Laura, while she was an infant. But it took time. His "politics" and his intellectual grasp of the situation were ahead of his feelings. He wanted to do it and knew that for him and his wife, Barbara, it was the right thing to do, but he didn't know how. He felt no natural affinity for the caregiving rituals of infancy.

> Some men are transformed into fathers instantly. Not me. I had no idea what to do with Laura at first. My feeling was, "My God, I can't relate to this little bundle at all." I was afraid to hold her, to change her diapers. She was such a delicate little thing, I was afraid I would hurt her.

Moreover, Barbara Brodie was always one step ahead of Ken in knowing what to do for Laura, or at least in giving the impression of knowing what to do. "I'm a compulsive person," Barbara admitted. "I like to do the little things my own way. No one can do it as well as I can, no one can touch the child because I can do it best—that was my attitude. Very rigid, very scared." It took the Brodies a while to realize that if Ken was going to share in their daughter's daily care (which Barbara very much needed), *she* was going to have to step back and let him in. Moreover, in order for Ken to do the active fathering that they both envisioned and that he was ready to learn how to do, he needed some tutoring and some "laissez-faire." Barbara gave him both.

Neither parent *assumed* that Ken would take care of his daughter. Indeed, active participation in the daily care of their children has been optional for men, whereas women by and large have had no choice in the matter. Responsibility for nurturance is thrust on them the moment their children are born, and they learn how to take care in a bootstrap operation. Whenever (for whatever reason) men turn actively toward their children, when they experience the fatherhood "click," they, too, must learn what to do.

INDIVIDUAL DIFFERENCES IN THE TIMING
OF THE FATHERHOOD CLICK

In a movie released at the end of 1979, *Kramer vs. Kramer*, Dustin Hoffman plays a successful advertising executive in his mid-thirties whose wife suddenly takes off, leaving him with their six-year-old son. The movie shows us Kramer's transformation from a man who has to ask his son what grade he is in the first morning he takes him to school, to a man whose son is as much a part of his life as his morning

wake-up rituals. Kramer comes to know his son and learns about the nurturant, generative aspects of himself only when his wife leaves home. What does it take for
men to recognize and express the parental side of themselves when the family is intact and children are there in all their immediacy, calling for the devotion, discipline, and imagination of both parents? (Cf., Levine, 1980.) What are the circumstances that encourage active, hands-on fathering to coexist with active, hands-on
mothering?

The fatherhood histories of the men in our study suggest that fatherhood "clicks"
in a way that leads to hands-on fathering when any of a number of individual, interpersonal, and circumstantial factors are favorable to it. A man's memory of when in
his own life *his* father actively turned his attention to him is part of the imagery that
influences the timing of his turning to fathering. A man's perception of what the
culture asks of its fathers—whether they are expected to be participants or observers at home—is another factor. A father's preference for one developmental stage
or another, or his temperamental fit with one child or another, informs the timing of
the fatherhood click. The structure and promotion pattern of his occupation set limits on the timing of a turn toward fathering. Finally, the ways in which wives and
husbands negotiate the balance of parenting between them may affect the sub-
stance, the extent, and the timing of a father's becoming an active parent (Cowan &
Cowan, 1987; Weingarten, 1978). The interplay of these factors determines the moment of the fatherhood click in an individual man's life.

Because there is a split in men's experience between being a father and doing fathering, because the timing of the turn toward active fathering is not automatically
linked with the birth of the first child, there is a wide range of individual variation in
the timing of the fatherhood click. Only when the click occurs does a man know for
sure whether fathering comes naturally to him, or whether he has a great deal to
learn, or both. Time and time again in our interviews, men singled out a precise moment that generated, as it symbolized, the click of fatherhood.

The Early Click

Most of the men for whom fatherhood clicked *early* in their children's lives were
late first-time fathers; their first children arrived when they were 30 or older. These
men reported that they began to experience emotional changes, which in turn had
behavioral consequences, at the moment of their first child's birth, or even during
their wives' pregnancies (cf. Fein, 1976; Phillips, 1978).

Mike Breen was in his early thirties when he became a father in 1975. He re-
members Susan's pregnancy as "a wonderful happy time that we shared. We'd sit
for hours and watch her belly roll, with the baby moving from one side to the other.
And we'd talk to it." Mike was present at his daughter's birth, and spent time with
her in the first few hours afterward. "Nothing was going to stop me from being
there. And it was fantastic. Nobody I knew had even been with their wives in childbirth. The guys at the station thought I was crazy. When Katie was born, I looked at
her and said, 'Man, that's what I wanted.' Fifteen seconds after Katie was out of my
wife I was holding her."

Among his friends and peers, it was unusual for a man to participate in the birth of his child, and yet Mike assumed he would do so. Afterward, supported by a range of facilitating attitudes and circumstances, although he was regarded skeptically by peers at work, Mike stepped into the postpartum role of his daughter's primary daytime parent.

> There was no transition for me at all. I said to myself, "Man, I'm going to have a good time at it." And I have. For the last 21 months I've taken care of my daughter, not more than Susan has, but I'm the one who's here in the daytime.

Like Mike Breen, Bob Berger was present at the birth of his first child, and the experience affected him profoundly:

> I was with Betsy when Jonathan was born, but then she went off to the recovery room, Jonathan was taken to the nursery, and I was left alone. When I called my parents they wanted to know how much he weighed, and I didn't know. So I went down to the nursery to find out. And they said, "Would you like to hold your son?" I said, "Oh yeah, sure. Can I *hold* him? You mean *I* can hold him?" They said "Yes, just put this gown on." So I sat and held him for 20 or 30 minutes. I talked to him, and told him what life was going to be like, if he was a lucky person. I swear I was crying. It was a very emotional, a very special time.

Bob Berger's bonding experience (cf., Fein, 1978) in the nursery with his newborn son was so important to him that he attributes his attachment to his son partly to that first hour they shared together. Though he and Betsy do not divide childcare 50/50, both are hands-on parents.

The Click in Middle Childhood

Unlike Mike Breen or Bob Berger, Tom Adler was and is, in his phrase, "not the baby type." He became a hands-on father later in the family life cycle, when his children were four and six years old. Several interdependent factors triggered the click. Newly launched at the head of his own small consulting firm, Tom was a few years older than Alison when their first child was born in 1959. Shortly before our interview, in addition to her 30-hour-a-week paid job, Alison went back to school part time to earn a business degree, and Tom began to take care of the children weekends while she was at the library. Although he had once imagined having 10 children, he had come to feel that two is enough.

> All anyone has to do to keep me from wanting a third child is to say, "You have to help," and I say, "No, no, no." It takes an unbelievable amount of time. You stretch yourself beyond anything you thought were your normal limits.

Tom described a "theory of child evolution" that dovetailed with and rationalized his evolving interest in his children:

The younger one is four and a half now, and she can keep up. The three of us used to wear each other out. They were too slow, and I couldn't stand being with them after five or ten minutes. But now we're getting to be real friends. Kids are great after five. The problem is getting them to five.

Tom felt that there were many elements in his readiness to agree to take responsibility for the children two days a week. Changes in Alison's schedule seemed to converge with changes in Tom's feelings about his school-aged children, and fatherhood clicked. Did Alison choose that particular year to go back to school because Tom felt differently about the children? Was Tom feeling more at home with the children because he knew he had to spend time with them? Did the children's adaptation to Tom make it easier for him to be with them? Or did all of these events mutually influence each other?

Adam Abernethy's fatherhood click, when his children were well into the middle years of childhood, had a more pervasive impact than Tom's. It both reflected and resulted in fundamental change in the structure of his life. Like Mike Breen and other men of their generation, Adam spent his early twenties in the army, in Vietnam. Unlike Mike, who did not become a father until after his time in the service, Adam's first child was born while he was away. He missed the daytime hours and the nighttimes, too, of the first year of his first child's life. However, at 34 at the time of our interview, Adam was the primary daytime parent of his 11- and 8-year-old children; his academic schedule permitted him to work partly at home while his wife, Jenny, held down a 40-hour-a-week administrative job.

During the early parenthood years, Adam was rarely home. But he became increasingly dissatisfied with this pressured, professional focus of his life:

There's not much advantage to the family in being a college professor unless you can benefit from your flexible hours. I decided I wanted to teach somewhere in the country, so that we could take advantage of a small college community and lead a civilized life. So we moved. Then, when this very good job came along for Jenny, I knew I could arrange my classes so that I could be at the house when the kids came home from school, and that's what we've done. In terms of our family life now, we're very fortunate. Speaking for myself, I've reaped advantages in spades.

Adam took up fatherhood as his second occupation. Without any lead time, with no practice, and with only a few weeks' notice, Adam took over "literally all of the household duties," as Jenny put it. By their joint account, he made the transformation successfully and happily. It is as if the capacity had always been there; he had only to flick the switch to activate his ability to sustain attention to the daily details of family life.

The Click in Slow Motion

Ten years older than Adam Abernethy, Pete Connolly was also at first a remote observer rather than a participant in family life. He followed his first child's development through the lens of his camera, cranking out reel after reel of home movies.

The click that changed his perception did not occur until his first child was almost a year old. And neither he nor his wife knew how, then, to give him "permission" to act on his changed perception. Pete remembered back almost 20 years:

> Chris was home with the baby in a not very nice apartment. She was actually busier than I was, taking care of Jim and studying to finish her senior year and graduate. I had an undemanding nine-to-five job, and spent a lot of time playing golf, going out with the boys, having a couple of drinks.
>
> One day it occurred to me that I too was responsible for that little thing in the crib. I remember that afternoon clearly. "You were barefooted," he said to Chris. "You were wearing turquoise pants and a white top and you were sitting on the long couch against the wall. I knew you were lonely, and suddenly it clicked in my mind—I can't tell you why. This is no damn home movie, this is real." In that lady-of-leisure outfit, Chris was dressed for a part she was definitely not getting to play. From that point on, I put some energy into starting to try to be a father.

It took Pete Connolly 15 years, however, between wanting to "start to try to be a father" and actually becoming a regular, reliable participant in family life. By his own account, it was not until his first child was 16 and his third and last child were well in school that he really became an involved father:

> My relationship with Carey at age 8 was worlds apart from my relationship with Jim at age 8. I'm much closer to Carey now, and I have been for a long time. Only with Carey did I begin to spend time (tentatively, at that) of the quality I wish to God I'd put in with Jim and Lisa.

Pete changed his mind first about the importance of his presence in his children's lives, and then about the importance of their presence in his. And his fathering behavior caught up with his feelings. Several factors seem to have motivated him, after many years, to translate that early click of awareness into action. By the 1970s, the times had changed, permitting and pressuring fathers to become nurturers as well as providers for their children. His first son's adolescence forecast the empty nest and brought him up short with a sense of missing out on his children's lives. His wife was preoccupied with the special medical needs of their middle child, making room in the family system for Pete to step in. And finally, a sense of stagnation and restlessness in a management career he had never enjoyed may have played a part in the redirection of his generative energy.

Fatherhood Clicks as the First Child Grows Up

Mark Fuller said he did not become an active father until his first son, Grant, was a teenager, in the late 1960s. A late first-time father, Mark nevertheless felt that he was not ready to have a child when he and Pat became parents in the 1950s. He knew that those next few years were critical for his career development. His field work and consulting to the Department of the Interior took him away from Pat "at the time when she was facing all the demands little children make."

With hindsight, we understand that my being away made her angry at me. With hindsight we also understand that her deciding she couldn't wait any longer to conceive a child made me damned angry at her.

I was working constantly until Grant was seven or so, and I was away a lot. Of course we'd had Joe and Hal by then. Now I had always thought that being a father was a very reasonable proposition, and that I would be very good at it, that it could be done with grace and success, and so on. In fact, that didn't happen for me, and that was painful to admit.

When Grant was about 13 and I had more time, he proved a very hard child to be a father to. He was having trouble in school and we consulted a psychiatrist. We went as a family; all five of us had therapy for two and a half years. And it was very successful.

Mark became an active father when his son Grant became an adolescent, a timing that fit Pat's sense of her development as a mother.

I feel that I was a terrific mother to the kids when they were infants, and that's what has given them strength. But I would have been the worst mother in the world during adolescence, except that I had Mark to go through it with.

Pat was very clear that their respective temperaments played a large part in Mark's fatherhood click as well as "getting the anger out" in therapy. She sees her husband as having "an enormous calm trust," which she feels was exactly what her children and she needed during the stormy adolescent years. Changes within the Fuller family converged to create psychological space for Mark to join the family. Family therapy enabled Mark and Pat to move beyond their anger at each other, allowing mutual trust to surface and grow. Presumably, Grant felt the shift between his parents, and let his father father him.

It is clear from the parenthood histories of the couples we interviewed that the timing of a man's readiness to do the fathering as well as be a father is an individual matter. A man who never changed a diaper may watch every one of his daughter's basketball games or coach his son's Little League team. A man who never helped a fourth grader with spelling words may sit for hours with a teenager who is ready to talk at 1 A.M. And finally, a man who neither diapered, coached, nor conversed, may go shopping for clothes for his grandchildren, picking sizes and styles perfectly. The full fathering story is not in until it is over.

However, the fatherhood click does not always go "on." Sometimes a hands-on father can turn "off" too. Because fatherhood as an occupation is optional for men in our society, men do not have to sustain hands-on fathering unless circumstances require and encourage it. Mike Breen described a gradual turning off as his daughter Katie neared two years old. Mike found his patience waning, as it does from time to time for most hands-on parents.

I think Katie is going through her terrible twos at 19 months. As much as I love my daughter I'm getting tired of taking care of her. I don't think it's inborn. I don't think it's in a man to be able to care for an infant child for more than two years. If it's hard on a woman, and I think it is, it's doubly hard on a man.

When Katie turned two, Mike and Susan were planning to buy their house, exchange parenting shifts, and have a second child. Was it coincidence that Mike's feelings exactly fit their plan? Very few of the men we met believed that the first two years of fatherhood were the years in which a man would feel most comfortable caring for his child. But Mike, going against the conventions of his peers but with the grain of his times, enthusiastically accepted an arrangement that suited his and Susan's long-range plan, claimed it as an area of competence as well as nurturance, and nurtured in himself feelings of rightness that enabled him to father his baby daughter.

Early- and Late-Timing Fathers: Patterns from Three Decades

When we look at the fatherhood histories of the men in our study one by one, we see that the timing of the fatherhood click makes psychological sense within the particular context of each man's life. Each man was a certain age (and so were his children) when he turned to them directly in a generative way, and each man had his own unique understanding of the click.

Yet if we step back and look at the 72 fathers as a group, it appears that whether couples had their first child early or late, and whether they had young children in the 1950s, 1960s, or 1970s, had some bearing on the timing of the fatherhood click. Almost two-thirds of the late first-time fathers in our study (nearly three times as many as early first-time fathers) had regular responsibility for some part of the daily care of a preschool child (not necessarily the first). And twice as many children born to men in the study in the 1970s were cared for by their father in this way than offspring born in the 1950s and 1960s.

Several reasons may account for late-timing fathers' greater participation in the daily care of their young children. Late first-time parents had developed preparental patterns of collaboration at home that endured throughout the early childhood years. Late first-time mothers often continued with the jobs and careers that had occupied them before their babies were born; though husbands did not usually take over the daytime care of children while mothers were away from home, the model of both parents having a double generativity—two spheres of responsibility and care—had nonetheless been set. Finally, late fathers were usually in more stable work situations than early fathers; whatever the level of their education or the nature of their work, they were more experienced workers, making more money, with jobs and careers more firmly established. They had served their "occupational novitiate" (Levinson, 1978). This allowed them, in principle, a margin of freedom and flexibility to turn to the activities and concerns of family life if they chose to do so.

Nearly two-thirds of the fathers of children born in the 1970s took some regular active part in the care of those children. All 12 late-timing couples who were in their early thirties at the time of the interview (like the Brodies, the Breens and the Bergers) became parents after 1970, and all but one of these fathers is a hands-on parent. It seems clear that fathers as well as mothers were influenced by the changing sex-role prescriptions of the 1970s. Just as women found the support and permission to move out of traditional roles into independent careers and income-generating jobs, men who looked for it found support and permission to become active family men. Had the fathers in their forties and fifties at the time of the interview had children who were preschoolers during the 1970s, we suspect that many of them might have become hands-on parents sooner in their children's lives.

The striking feature of men's parenthood experience is the variation in the timing of the fatherhood click and the turn to hands-on fathering. Biologically, men become fathers and women become mothers at the moment of their first child's birth. But only through daily care, and in sustained emotional engagement in their children's lives, do fathers and mothers become parents in the generative sense. Mothers are expected to become parents instantly, but fathers are not.

It seems clear from our interviews with early and late first-time parents that both men's and their family's well-being are enhanced by fathers' active participation in family life. However, only as we continue to revise our sex-role imagery and ideology, so that there is legitimacy for male nurturance; only when we have institutionalized social policies such as parenthood leaves, flexible working hours, and job-sharing options for parents during the early years of their children's lives; and only when we work out an equitable distribution of child care and householding responsibilities at home will we have created the necessary conditions in which both fathering and mothering can flourish.

REFERENCES

Blum, J. (1980, November). Baby boom. *Atlantic*, pp. 75–85.

Chodorow, N. (1978). *The reproduction of mothering: Psychoanalysis and the sociology of gender*. Berkeley: University of California Press.

Cowan, C.P., & Cowan, P.A. (1987). Men's involvement in parenthood: Identifying the antecedents and understanding the barriers. In P. Berman & F.A. Pedersen (Eds.), *Men: transitions to parenthood*. Hillsdale, NJ: Erlbaum.

Daniels, P., & Weingarten, K. (1982). *Sooner or later: The timing of parenthood in adult lives*. New York: Norton.

Dinnerstein, D. (1976). *The mermaid and the minotaur: Sexual arrangements and human malaise*. New York: Harper & Row.

Epstein, C. (1970). *Women's place: Options and limits in professional careers*. Berkeley: University of California Press.

Erikson, E. (1968). *Identity: Youth and crisis*. New York: Norton.

Fein, R. (1976). Men's entrance into fatherhood. *Family Coordinator, 25*, 341–350.

Fein, R. (1978). Consideration of men's experiences and the birth of a first child. In W.B. Miller & L. Newman (Eds.), *The first child and family formation*. Chapel Hill, NC: Carolina Population Center.

Lerner, M. (1965, May). The vanishing American father. *McCall's*, 95 ff.

Levine, J. (1976). *Who will raise the children? New options for fathers (and mothers)*. New York: Lippincott.

Levine, J. (1978). Fathers are parents too. In B. Sprung (Ed.), *Perspectives on non-sexist early childhood education*. New York: Columbia University Teachers College Press.

Levine, J. (1980, March). *The Kramerization of the American father*. Paper presented at Wheelock College Symposium, Boston.

Levinson, D.J. (1978). *The seasons of a man's life*. New York: Knopf.

Oppenheimer, V. (1974). The life-cycle squeeze: The interaction of men's occupational and family life cycles. *Demography, 11*, 227–245.

Phillips, C.R.N. (1978). "Fathering" involvement in labor and birth. In P. Simkin & C. Reinke (Eds.), *Kaleideoscope of childbearing: Preparation, birth, and nurturing*. Seattle, WA: Pennypress.

Pleck, J.H. (1981a). Husbands' paid work and family role: Current research issues. In H. Lopata (Ed.), *The interweave of social roles: Women and Men:* Vol. 3. Greenwich, CT: JAI Press.

Pleck, J.H. (1981b). *The male myth*. Cambridge, MA: MIT Press.

Ruddick, S. (1980). Maternal thinking. *Feminist Studies, 6*, 342–367.

Vaillant, G., & McArthur, C. (1972). Natural history of male psychologic health. I. The adult life cycle from 18–50. *The Human Life Cycle: A Review of Major Prospective Studies of Human Development, 4*, 415–427.

Weingarten, K. (1978). The employment pattern of professional couples and their distribution of involvement in the family. *Psychology of Women Quarterly, 3*, 43–52.

CHAPTER 4

Fathers, Infants, and Toddlers

A Developing Relationship

MICHAEL W. YOGMAN, JAMES COOLEY, and DANIEL KINDLON

Older theories of child development suggest that parenting is predominantly instinctual, biologically determined, and exclusively maternal. However, a careful look at cross-species, anthropological, and contemporary data in Western cultures does not support the notion of paternal noninvolvement or incompetence with children in the early years of life. There is in fact a growing body of research evidence that indicates that fathers can and do form a unique relationship with young infants and toddlers.

Sociocultural changes in Western societies (notably, the massive entry of women into the labor force) help explain why fathers are becoming more involved with their infants. The fact that families move more often and have fewer long-standing neighborhood friends makes the need for fathers to share in infant care even clearer. However, apart from any response to the women's movement, men are also seeking increased emotional closeness with their infants as part of a men's movement toward fuller personhood, and as a reaction against the alienation and burnout of the purely instrumental role of family provider. While some of the publicity about greater paternal involvement with infants may simply reflect current social acceptability, national surveys in the United States of father participation in family work do suggest a real increase.

In this chapter, we will briefly review the research examining the capacities of fathers and infants to interact with one another, as well as the similarities in behavior and psychological experience between fathers and mothers. We will then address the less well-studied questions of fathers' actual performance with their infants—specifically, what do fathers and infants actually do together, what influences paternal involvement,[1] and how does the father's involvement influence the infant's development? In considering these questions, we will focus on father–infant play during the first few months of life, and on the father's role as limit setter in the family triad during the second year.

---

[1]For further discussion of this topic, see Barnett and Baruch, Chapter 5, this volume.

FATHERS' COMPETENCE AND SENSITIVITY WITH INFANTS

Cross-species and anthropological evidence demonstrate the diversity of the father–infant relationship across species and cultures. While primary maternal caregiving is the predominant mode in most animal species, examples of primary paternal caregiving can be found in animals such as the wolf and the stickleback (Mitchell, 1969; Redican, 1976; Rypma, 1976; Tinbergen, 1952), and even in primates such as the marmoset (a new world monkey) and the gibbon (Chivers, 1972; Hampton, Hampton, & Landwehr, 1966; Ingram, 1978). Male chimps, baboons, and macaques have been found to adopt orphans in the wild (Hrdy, 1976), and even as aggressive a primate as the rhesus male, when reared in a nuclear family environment in a laboratory, interacts playfully with his infant (Suomi, 1977). The evidence suggests that biological constraints are much less significant determinants of male care of infants than ecological influences, such as the modal social structure for each species.

Anthropological data provide further insights into the way social and cultural variables influence paternal involvement with infants. In cultures such as the Arapesh, fathers play an active and joint role with mothers during pregnancy, as well as in caring for infants after birth (Howells, 1969). !Kung San (Bushmen) fathers, representative of the earliest hunter–gatherer societies, have been found to be affectionate and indulgent, often holding and fondling their infants, although they provide little routine care as compared with mothers (West & Konner, 1976). Fathers from the Lesu village in Melanesia, who are gardeners living in monogamous nuclear families, are reported to play with infants for hours. Analysis of social organization in different cultures suggests that males have a closer relationship with their infants when families are monogamous, when both parents live together in isolated nuclear families, when women contribute to subsistence by working, and when men are not required to be warriors (West & Konner, 1976; Whiting & Whiting, 1975).

Within contemporary Western society, the evidence that fathers and infants can develop direct relationships right from birth is impressive. Furthermore, the similarities between the psychological experiences of pregnancy and infant care for mothers and for fathers are striking. Studies of these similarities can be grouped into four developmental periods: prenatal, perinatal, early infancy (1–6 months), and later infancy (6–24 months). The brief discussion of each that follows will illustrate the similarity of maternal and paternal responses and competencies relating to birth and infancy.

Prenatal Period

Bibring (1959) suggests that pregnancy represents a normative psychological crisis for women. Studies by Gurwitt (1976) and Ross (1975) indicate that it is an important psychological event for men as well, in that they are likely to rework significant relationships and events from their early life. The occurrence of physical complaints in men whose wives are pregnant is one manifestation of this turmoil. Taboos and rituals in many cultures, which restrict or enhance the father's role during this process, speak to the intensity of his involvement in it. In the traditional form of the couvade ritual, the father takes to bed during the woman's pregnancy, labor, and delivery, as a means of sharing in the experience (Tylor, 1865). The remnant of this ritual in modern cultures is evidenced by what is called the "couvade syndrome," in which men experience psychosomatic symptoms during their wives' pregnancies (Trethowan, 1972; Trethowan & Conlon, 1965). In a recent survey of patients seen by specialists in internal medicine, almost one-fourth of all men whose wives were pregnant sought medical care for physical symptoms such as nausea, vomiting, anorexia, abdominal pain, or bloating (Lipkin & Lamb, 1982). In other studies, as many as 65% of men complained of similar physical symptoms, also including backache and weight gain, and reported dietary changes and giving up smoking during this period (Liebenberg, 1973).

Perinatal Period

This similarity of emotional responses persists during the perinatal period. Fathers are now almost routinely present during labor and delivery. In an interview study of English first-time fathers, the men emphasized their desire to touch and play with their newborn, and were impressed by the baby's movements (Greenberg & Morris, 1974). In other studies, fathers' descriptions of their feelings after having witnessed their child's birth were almost identical to those of mothers: extreme elation, relief that the baby was healthy, feelings of pride and increased self-esteem, and feelings of closeness when the baby opened its eyes (Lind, 1974; Robson & Moss, 1970). However, not only do fathers and mothers share the exhilaration of the perinatal period, but they also share the lows or the postpartum blues. In an interview study of men in the first few weeks postpartum, 62% reported feelings of sadness and disappointment (Zaslow, Pedersen, Kramer, Cain, Suwalsky, & Fivel, 1981).

Early contact with newborns, which has been found to influence maternal bonding, has been shown to affect the father–infant relationship as well (Keller, Hildebrandt, & Richardson, 1981; Rodholm, 1981). Furthermore, fathers and mothers display similar behaviors when interacting with their newborns. Studies by Parke and Sawin (1975) of father–newborn interaction in the postpartum period suggest that fathers and mothers are equally active and sensitive to newborn cues during that time.

Early Infancy

During the first six months of life, infants become increasingly social as they begin to smile and vocalize. Together with colleagues at Children's Hospital in Boston, we have studied the social interaction of fathers with their infants of two weeks to six months of age. Instead of looking at functional tasks such as feeding and diapering, we studied unstructured face-to-face play, because it placed maximal demands on the social capabilities of the participants. While such play may occupy only a small proportion of an infant's day at home, videotaped interactions in the laboratory allowed us to elicit and study in a detailed way brief exchanges of expressive communication that may reflect the developing father–infant relationship.

We began by demonstrating that infants, by 11½ weeks of age—and as young as six weeks—would interact differently with their parents than they would with strangers, as evidenced by differences in facial expression and limb movements (Dixon, Yogman, Tronick, Als, Adamson, & Brazelton, 1981; Yogman, 1982). We then compared mother–infant and father–infant interaction, and found that by three months of age, infants successfully interacted with both mothers and fathers with a similar, mutually regulated, reciprocal pattern, in which both partners rhythmically cycled to a peak of affective involvement and then withdrew (Yogman, 1977; 1982). Mothers and fathers were equally able to involve the infant in games (i.e., episodes of repeated adult behavior that engaged the infant's attention). For example, father–infant games included such activities as exercising the baby in a "pull-to-sit" game, repeatedly tapping the baby around the mouth, "buttoning" the baby's lips, and "bicycling" the baby's legs. We also found that fathers' and mothers' familiarity with their infant enabled them to synchronize their behavioral rhythms with the infant, whereas the strangers did not do this. Thus our studies of fathers and infants in the first six months of life provide support for the hypothesis that fathers are capable of skilled and sensitive social interaction with young infants.

Later Infancy

Studies of the father–infant relationship with infants aged 6 to 24 months (reviewed in Lamb, 1981) have focused primarily on the development of attachment, as Bowlby (1969) and Ainsworth (1973) have defined it. These studies have asked questions such as: Do infants greet, seek proximity with, and protest on separation from fathers as well as mothers? Such studies provide conclusive evidence that infants are in fact attached to fathers as well as to mothers.

In sum, studies of the father–infant relationship in each of these developmental periods demonstrate both the similarity of the father–infant and mother–infant relationship, and the capacities of fathers and infants to interact successfully with one another.

THE NATURE OF FATHER–INFANT INTERACTION

As definitions of the male role shift, what fathers and infants actually do together is becoming increasingly variable and diverse. In general, however, fathers spend much less time with their infants than mothers do. In research using natural observations in the home, the mother has been found to be the predominant partner with the infant in terms of time spent (Clarke-Stewart, 1980). Reports of father involvement vary from 26 hours per week available at home with awake nine-month-old babies, with eight of those hours spent in play (Pedersen & Robson, 1969), to 3.2 hours per day (one-third that of mother) spent with the infant (Kotelchuck, 1976), to 15–20 minutes per day spent in actual interaction with the infant (Lewis & Weinraub, 1974).

However, while mothers are the predominant social partners for their infants, fathers, in the time they spend with them, are more likely to be their infants' play partners, and fathers' play tends to be more proximal, vigorous, arousing, and state-disruptive for infants than mothers' play. In our studies of infant games during the first six months of life, fathers frequently initiated tactile and limb movement games, which seemed intended to arouse the infant; mothers, on the other hand, more commonly played visual games, in which they displayed distal motor movements that appeared to be attempts to maintain the infant's visual attention (Yogman, 1981).

These findings are surprisingly robust; similar patterns have been observed with infants of different ages, in different situations. Fathers of newborns, while similar to mothers in most behaviors, have been found to hold and rock their infants more (Parke, O'Leary, & West, 1972). In interviews conducted after fathers held their newborns, they emphasized the physical contact, and the feeling of the baby "moving up against them" (Greenberg & Morris, 1974, p. 525). In another study, with six-month-old infants, fathers were found to engage in more play than caregiving activities (Rendina & Dickersheid, 1976). Similarly, they more often picked up their eight-month-old infants to play physical, idiosyncratic, rough-and-tumble games, whereas by comparison, mothers were more likely to hold infants, engage in caregiving tasks, and either play with toys, play distal games, or use conventional games such as peek-a-boo (Lamb, 1977a; Power & Parke, 1979).

These differences in play and quality of vigorous stimulation persist even in studies of primary caregiver fathers in the United States (Field, 1978; Yogman, 1982), and in studies of nontraditional fathers taking advantage of paternity leave in Sweden (Frodi, Lamb, Hwang, & Frodi, 1982; Lamb, Frodi, Hwang, Frodi, & Steinberg, 1982). It is interesting to speculate about whether the play differences will become less tied to gender as a new generation of children, who have been socialized according to different gender-role models, grows up to become parents (for a discussion of fathers' behavior in relation to gender role socialization, see Bronstein, Chapter 1, this volume). In contrast to these persistent play differences, the performance of caregiving tasks seems more modifiable and more linked to role than to gender.

THE FATHERS' ROLE WITH TODDLERS: AN EXPERIMENTAL STUDY

Although father–infant attachment in the second year of life has been well studied, the father's role with his toddler has been characterized primarily as that of play partner (Clarke-Stewart, 1980; Lamb, 1977b). However, we have recently begun to consider that a father may have an important role in fostering his toddler's autonomy during the second year. We propose that a toddler's sense of independence develops through a process of negotiation with father and mother about family and social rules and conventions: "What can I explore, what can I attempt, what is off-limits?" This stage of self-assertion, which has been called the "terrible twos," may pose a challenge for parents. The child, utilizing new skills and testing limits, may have temper tantrums; the parents, on the other hand, have the difficult task of encouraging the child's independence, curiosity, and positive sense of self, while also eliciting the child's compliance in selected situations. Conflicts at this time are especially evident in the areas of safety, eating, sleeping, toilet training, and transitions from one activity to another.

Thus, the infant–mother–father triad is the milieu in which the toddler negotiates a sense of autonomy. In order to understand this process better, we devised an experimental paradigm for the purpose of examining those autonomy negotiations. We were especially interested in whether the father would play a prominent role in limit-setting. Would the stereotype of father-as-disciplinarian manifest itself?

Method

The paradigm consisted of two sequential tasks, with both parents present with the child. The tasks were purposefully ambiguous and slightly frustrating for the child, so that the parents would have to structure them somewhat, and hopefully elicit a show of autonomy/resistance. The family then had to negotiate as a triad to produce the child's compliance in the task. The first episode, after a 5-minute period of free play which gave the child time to adjust to the room, was a 2-minute toy clean-up task. Following this, the family negotiated a 2-minute prohibition episode, in which two attractive objects were introduced, one of which was "off-limits." We chose structured tasks in a laboratory setting rather than naturalistic home observation because we believed that negotiations about limit-setting occur too infrequently to measure easily in a natural setting, even though they peak at this age (Dowdney, Mrazek, Quinton, & Rutter, 1984; Mrazek, Dowdney, Rutter, & Quinton, 1982). In addition, the laboratory playroom, though a new environment for the child, offered constant conditions of lighting, distance, toys, and unobtrusive observation behind one-way mirrors for videotaping and coding.

The parents of 44 healthy, first-born, Caucasian middle-class toddlers, aged 22–26 months, were recruited from local pediatric offices and parent groups. All were traditional two-parent families, in which mother was primary caregiver. Half the toddlers were male and half were female.

Each parent was given detailed instructions, which specified that either parent could initiate each episode on a given cue. The family was then escorted into the laboratory playroom, which is a pleasant, climate-controlled, carpeted, well-lit room, with one-way mirrors on opposite walls allowing unobtrusive observing and videotaping of both toddler and parents. A nonfunctioning electric heater was present on the floor, and a glass of water and a box of tissues were left on a table, to elicit spontaneous limit-setting interactions with parents. The experimenter removed 14 toys from a wooden toy box and invited the child to play. After instructing the parents only "to have a good time," the experimenter exited. After 5 minutes of free-play with the toys, the experimenter began the 2-minute toy clean-up task by tapping on the playroom mirror. At this cue, one parent said, "It's time to put these toys away. We're going to play with another toy now." The parents themselves were left to decide who would state this directive. The parent then put away two toys into the toy box to pattern the task for the child. Parents were asked to elicit compliance from the child however they wished: their behavior or language was not specified or limited in any way after the initial two sentences.

When all 14 toys had been put away in the toy box, or after 2 minutes (whichever came first), the experimenter reentered the room with a child's chair. He invited the triad to sit at the table, and he finished cleaning up the room. Each parent was given three questionnaires and a pencil, and asked to fill out each independently. The questionnaires were the Toddler Temperament Scale (Fullard, McDevitt, & Carey, 1979), the Parental Style Questionnaire (Cohen, Dibble, & Grawe, 1977), and the Dyadic Adjustment Scale (Spanier, 1976). Finally, the experimenter placed a toy jumping frog and an attractive tape recorder (with a bright red foam wind screen on the microphone) across the room, at points equidistant from the child's chair. At the experimenter's exit, one parent said, pointing, "This is the toy frog for you to play with, but don't touch that tape recorder. It might break. There is your frog to play with, but don't touch that tape recorder." Both parents were then to start completing their questionnaires. This segment was regarded as the prohibition task.

Trained observers coded the behaviors both during the episodes and later by reviewing the videotapes. Live coding was necessary for events which could not be adequately recorded on the videotape—specifically, infant looks and glances. In the toy clean-up task, coders recorded each time the toddler looked or glanced at the toys or toy box, the mother, or the father. Observations were divided into 24 5-second segments over the 2-minute period, the segments defined by tape-recorded beeps heard through earphones worn by each coder. In the prohibition task, the coders recorded the toddler's looks/glances at the frog, the tape recorder, the mother, or the father, again at 5-second intervals.

Reviewing the videotaped toy clean-up segments, the coders recorded these details:

1. The number of toys put away by the toddler (5-second intervals)
2. The number of toddler negative vocalizations (10-second intervals), with crying or protest sounds, "no" statements, and negative phrases coded as separate categories
3. The number and type of parental verbal cues (10-second intervals), with directives, questions, prohibitions, compliments, encouragements, explanations, and other behaviors coded as separate categories
4. Which parent gave the first directive to clean up
5. Who the child looked at after the first directive

This coding allowed us to calculate several measures of compliance in each episode: the number of toys put away, the latency until first toy clean-up, and the rate of toy clean-up. In addition, the coding of toddler vocalizations and parental verbal cues enabled us to examine the quality of parent–toddler interaction. Mothers' and fathers' verbal cues were coded separately.

Coding of the videotaped prohibition segments included these variables:

1. The number of toddler touches of the tape recorder (5-second intervals)
2. Toddler negative vocalizations (10-second intervals)
3. Parental verbal cues (10-second intervals)
4. Which parent gave the first prohibition about the tape recorder
5. Who the child looked at after the first prohibition

Inter-coder agreement on 10 pilot tapes was 90%; reliability checks on every fifth subject for the two coders who observed all the experimental videotapes confirmed that agreement remained at greater than 90%. Because of technical difficulties with videotaping, only 40 of the tapes were fully codable and are discussed in these preliminary analyses. Half of these were from sessions with male toddlers and half with female toddlers. Analyses were done using t-tests, or chi-square when appropriate.

Results

Before looking at the entire sample of toddlers, we first looked to see if there were sex differences in toddler compliance. No significant differences were found on any of the coded variables. During the clean-up task, males and females put a similar proportion of their toys away (about two-thirds), and did not differ in the number of negative vocalizations made during this episode. During the prohibition task, there were no differences in the number of times the tape recorder was touched, the mean latency until it was touched (about 10 seconds), or the number of negative vocalizations. Similar findings have been reported recently by Easterbrooks and Emde (1985).

When we compared fathers' and mothers' interactions with toddlers of both sexes, the similarities were much more striking than the differences, at least in these preliminary analyses. Fathers and mothers were evenly divided as to who gave the first directive during the prohibition episode, and although mothers more often gave the first directive during the clean-up episode, the differences were not significant. There were no differences between mothers and fathers in the total number of directive statements made during either episode, although both parents gave more directives during the clean-up task.

Parents differed on only one measure: total number of verbal statements. Mothers verbalized significantly more than fathers during both the clean-up task and the prohibition task. Toddlers looked significantly more at their mothers than their fathers during the prohibition episode; presumably, they would have been more likely to look at the parent who was talking. No relationships were found between who gave the first directive or gave more directives, and eventual toddler compliance.

These preliminary analyses suggest that the father's role with toddlers is neither simple nor unidimensional, in terms of his being the disciplinarian. Certainly in this selected population of families, the stereotype of the father as disciplinarian does not appear to be accurate. A previous study of parental prohibitions and toddler compliance has similarly found few differences related to parent gender

(Easterbrooks & Emde, 1985). The degree of consistency between parents in directing the child, the parental style (authoritarian vs. accommodative, as measured by the Parental Style Questionnaire), and the presence or absence of marital conflict (as measured by the Dyadic Adjustment Scale), may be more highly related to toddler compliance than gender alone. Further analyses of the observational data, combined with the measures of parental style, marital relationship, and infant temperament, may help clarify the relationship between those variables and toddler compliance. We anticipate that the father's role in fostering his toddler's autonomy is embedded in the context of a triadic family system, and that the father–infant relationship may be influenced by both the mother–father relationship and the mother–infant relationship.

INFLUENCES ON PATERNAL INVOLVEMENT

A father's actual ongoing involvement with his child is influenced by forces both within and external to the family. Probably the single most important influence on father involvement is the mother's feelings, which are likely to have been influenced by her relationship with her own father (Radin, 1981). The mother seems to function much as a gatekeeper, regulating the father's involvement with the infant (Yogman, 1984), and she continues to influence his relationship with the infant even when he is not at home, in the way she refers to him in his absence (Atkins, 1981). In addition, if a mother returns to full-time employment, a transitional period occurs during which she spends more time with the infant in the evening, and this is associated with lower levels of father–infant interaction (Pedersen, Zaslow, Suwalsky, & Cain, 1982).

The quality of the marital relationship may also affect fathers' involvement with their infants. However, while mothers' perceptions of their spouse's support in the marriage have been found to be related to mothers' enhanced sensitivity to infant signals (Fiering & Taylor, in press), a similar association between marital cooperation and the father–infant relationship has not yet been empirically studied. Conversely, in marriages filled with conflict, spouses may attempt to undermine the partner's parenting role. Fathers have been found to experience feelings of competition with their wives after the birth of an infant, particularly if the father has a close relationship with the baby and the mother is nursing. Husbands of nursing mothers have described feelings of inadequacy, envy, and exclusion, and the competition may actually undermine the mother's attempts at breast-feeding, unless these feelings are addressed (Lerner, 1979; Waletzky, 1979). The effects of these feelings on *fathers'* involvement with their infants, however, have not yet been addressed.

Forces outside the family or beyond the couple's control may also have a major impact on father involvement. Stressful events such as maternal illness, a Caesarean section birth, or premature birth of an infant may act to increase paternal involvement, as a family coping mechanism to support the mother. In the case of prematurity, our data suggest that increased paternal involvement may actually be beneficial to the infant's developmental outcome (Yogman, 1985). Conversely, paternal job loss with accompanying depression, or even job insecurity, is likely to diminish the psychological (if not physical) availability of the father to the child; in fact, paternal job insecurity has been found to be associated with increased illness in children (Margolies, 1982). Cultural practices, economic constraints, and employment policies such as paternity leave and flexible work schedules can all have major influences on paternal involvement.

CONCLUSION

Studies of fathers and infants are beginning to provide a basis for theorizing about the influences of paternal involvement on infant personality development. First, it appears that fathers can have a meaningful and direct relationship with their infants right from birth, and that the pregnancy experience is a time of developmental transition for fathers as well as for mothers. Second, in spite of different research strategies and samples, studies have found considerable consistency in the ways that fathers interact with infants. They have been found to be sensitive to infant cues (Parke & Sawin, 1975) and to be skilled in their interactions (Yogman, 1977). In addition, consistent differences have been found in fathers' and mothers' behaviors with their infants. Fathers have proved more likely to develop a heightened, arousing, and playful relationship with their infants (Clarke-Stewart, 1980; Parke, 1979; Yogman, 1982), and to provide a more novel and complex environment (Pedersen, Yarrow, Anderson, & Cain, 1979). During the second year, differences in play style apparently persist, but in limit-setting tasks, there are more similarities between fathers and mothers than differences. The father's role in fostering his toddler's autonomy seems to be embedded in the context of a triadic family system. Future research will need to understand the influence of the marital relationship, parenting styles, and consistency between the parents during limit-setting encounters.

It is tempting to speculate that the father–child patterns of play we have described will facilitate the child's exploration of novelty in later life, and will encourage curiosity and independence. We can also speculate that infants will develop into more resilient children if their parents have a harmonious marriage, and if fathers and mothers can support and buffer each other in their role as parents.

REFERENCES

Ainsworth, M. (1973). The development of infant-mother attachment. In B. Caldwell & H. Ricciuti (Eds.), *Review of child development research*, vol. 3. Chicago: University of Chicago Press.

Atkins, R. (1981). *Discovering daddy: The mother's contributions to father-representations*. Paper presented to the American Psychiatric Association, New Orleans.

Bibring, G. (1959). Some considerations of the psychological processes in pregnancy. *Psychoanalytic Study of the Child, 14,* 113.

Bowlby, J. (1969). *Attachment and loss*, (vol. 1). New York: Basic Books.

Chivers, D.J. (1972). The siamang and the gibbon in the Malay Peninsula. *Gibbon and Siamang, 1*, 103–135.

Clarke-Stewart, K.A. (1980). The father's contribution to children's cognitive and social development in early childhood. In F.A. Pedersen (Ed.), *The father-infant relationship: Observational studies in a family setting*. New York: Holt, Rinehart & Winston.

Cohen, D.J., Dibble, E., & Grawe, J.M. (1977). Fathers and mothers perceptions of children's personality. *Archives of General Psychiatry, 34*, 480–487.

Dixon, S., Yogman, M.W., Tronick, E., Als, H., Adamson, L., & Brazelton, T.B. (1981). Early social interaction of infants with parents and strangers. *Journal of the American Academy of Child Psychiatry, 20*, 32–52.

Dowdney, L., Mrazek, D., Quinton, D., & Rutter, M. (1984). Observation of parent-child interaction with two- to three-year-olds. *Journal of Child Psychology and Psychiatry, 25*, 379–407.

Easterbrooks, M.A., & Emde, R.A. (1985). *When Mommy and Daddy say no: A longitudinal study of toddler compliance*. Paper presented at the biennial meeting of the Society for Research in Child Development, Toronto.

Field, T.M. (1978). Interaction behaviors of primary versus secondary caretaker fathers. *Developmental Psychology, 14*, 183–184.

Fiering, C., & Taylor, J. (in press). The influence of the infant and secondary parent on maternal behavior: Toward a social systems view of infant attachment. *Merrill-Palmer Quarterly*.

Frodi, A., Lamb, M.E., Hwang, C., & Frodi, M. (1982). *Increased paternal involvement and family relationships*. Paper presented to the International Conference on Infant Studies, Austin, Texas.

Fullard, W., McDevitt, S., & Carey, W. (1979). The Toddler Temperament Scale. Unpublished test form, Temple University, Philadelphia.

Greenberg, M., & Morris, N. (1974). Engrossment: The newborn's impact upon the father. *American Journal of Orthopsychiatry, 44*, 520–531.

Gurwitt, A.R. (1976). Aspects of prospective fatherhood. *Psychoanalytic Study of the Child, 31*, 237–271.

Hampton, J.K., Hampton, S.H., & Landwehr, B.R. (1966). Observations on a successful breeding colony of the marmoset: Oedipomidas Oedipus. *Folia Primatologica, 4*, 265–287.

Howells, J.G. (1969). Fathering. In J.G. Howells (Ed.), *Modern perspectives in international child psychiatry*. Edinburgh, Scotland: Oliver and Boyd.

Hrdy, S.B. (1976). Care and exploitation of nonhuman primate infants by conspecifics other than mothers. In J.R. Rosenblatt, R.A. Hinde, E. Shaw, & C. Beer (Eds.), *Advances in the study of behavior* (vol. 6). New York: Academic.

Ingram, J.C. (1978). Social interactions within marmoset family groups. In D. Chivers & J. Herbert (Eds.), *Recent advances in primatology* (vol. 1). New York: Academic.

Keller, W.D., Hildebrandt K.A., & Richardson, M.E. (1981). *Effects of extended father-infant contact during the newborn period*. Paper presented at the biennial meeting of the Society For Research in Child Development, Boston.

Kotelchuck, M. (1976). The infant's relationship to the father: Experimental evidence. In M.E. Lamb, (Ed.), *The role of the father in child development*. New York: Wiley.

Lamb, M.E. (1977a). Father-infant and mother-infant interaction in the first year of life. *Child Development, 48*, 167–181.

Lamb, M.E. (1977b). The development of mother-infant and father-infant attachments in the second year of life. *Developmental Psychology, 13*, 637–648.

Lamb, M.E. (1981). The development of father-infant relationships. In M. E. Lamb (Ed.), *The role of the father in child development* (2nd ed.). New York: Wiley.

Lamb, M., Frodi, A., Hwang, C., Frodi, M., & Steinberg, J. (1982). Mother and father-infant interaction involving play and holding in traditional and nontraditional Swedish families. *Developmental Psychology, 18*, 215–221.

Lerner, H. (1979). Effects of the nursing mother-infant dyad on the family. *American Journal of Orthopsychiatry, 49*, 339–348.

Liebenberg, B. (1973). Expectant fathers. In P. Shereshefsky & L. Yarrow (Eds.), *Psychological aspects of a first pregnancy and early postnatal adaptation*. New York: Raven.

Lind, J. (1974). *Observations after delivery of communication between mother-infant-father*. Paper presented at the International Congress of Pediatrics, Buenos Aires, Argentina.

Lipkin, M., & Lamb, G.S. (1982). The couvade syndrome: An epidemologic study. *Annals of Internal Medicine, 96*, 509–511.

Lewis, M., & Weinraub, M. (1974). Sex of parent × sex of child: Socioemotional development. In R.C. Friedmand, R.M. Richart, & R.L. Vande Wiele (Eds.), *Sex differences in behavior*. New York: Wiley.

Margolies, L. (1982). Work in progress at University of North Carolina School of Public Health. Personal communication.

Mitchell, G.D. (1969). Paternalistic behavior in primates. *Psychological Bulletin, 71*(6), 399–419.

Mrazek, D.A., Dowdney, L., Rutter, M.L., & Quinton, D.L. (1982). Mother and preschool child interaction: A sequential approach. *Journal of American Academy of Child Psychiatry, 21*, 453–464.

Parke, R. (1979). Perspectives on father-infant interaction. In J.D. Osofsky (Ed.), *Handbook of infancy*. New York: Wiley.

Parke, R.D., O'Leary, S.E., & West, S. (1972). Mother-infant-newborn interaction: Effects of maternal medication, labor and sex of infant. *Proceedings of the American Psychological Association*, 85–86.

Parke, R., & Sawin, D. (1975). *Infant characteristics and behavior as elicitors of maternal and paternal responsibility in the newborn period*. Paper presented at the Society for Research in Child Development, Denver.

Pedersen, F.A., & Robson, K.S. (1969). Father participation in infancy. *American Journal of Orthopsychiatry, 39*. 466–472.

Pedersen, F., Yarrow, L.J., Anderson, B.J., & Cain, R.L. (1979). Conceptualization of father influences in the infancy period. In M. Lewis & L. Rosenblum (Eds.), *The child and its family*. New York: Plenum.

Pedersen, F., Zaslow, M., Suwalsky, J., & Cain, R. (1982). *Infant experience in traditional and dual wage-earner families*. Paper presented at the International Conference on Infant Studies, Austin.

Power, T.G., & Parke, R.D. (1979). *Toward a taxonomy of father-infant and mother-infant play patterns*. Paper presented at the Society for Research in Child Development, San Francisco.

Radin, N. (1981). Child rearing in intact families. *Merrill-Palmer Quarterly, 27*, 489–514.

Redican, W.K. (1976). Adult male-infant interactions in nonhuman primates. In M.E. Lamb (Ed.), *The role of the father in child development*. New York: Wiley.

Rendina, I., & Dickerscheid, J.D. (1976). Father involvement with first-born infants. *Family Coordinator, 25*, 373–379.

Robson, I., & Moss, H. (1970). Patterns and determinants of maternal attachment. *Journal of Pediatrics, 7*, 976–985.

Rodholm, M. (1981). Effects of father-infant interaction at the first contact after delivery. *Early Human Development, 5*, 79–85.

Ross, J.M. (1975). The development of paternal identity: A critical review of the literature on nurturance and generativity in boys and men. *Journal of American Psychoanalytic Association, 23*, 783–817.

Rypma, C.B. (1976). The biological basis of the paternal responses. *Family Coordinator, 25*, 335–341.

Spanier, G.B. (1976). Measuring dyadic adjustment: New scales for assessing the quality of marital and similar dyads. *Journal of Marriage and the Family, 38*, 15–28.

Suomi, S. (1977). Adult male-infant interactions among monkeys living in nuclear families. *Child Development, 48*, 1215–1270.

Tinbergen, N. (1952). The behavior of the stickleback. *Scientific American, 187*, 28–38.

Trethowan, W.H. (1972). The couvade syndrome. In J. Howells (Ed.), *Modern perspectives in psycho-obstetrics*. Edinburgh, Scotland: Oliver and Boyd.

Trethowan, W., & Conlon, M.F. (1965). The couvade syndrome. *British Journal of Psychiatry, 111*, 57.

Tylor, E.B. (1865). *Researches into the early history of mankind in the development of civilization* (2nd ed.). London: Murray.

Waletzky, L. (1979). Husbands' problems with breast-feeding. *American Journal of Orthopsychiatry, 49*, 349–352.

West, M.M., & Konner, M.J. (1976). The role of the father: An anthropological perspective. In M.E. Lamb (Ed.), *The role of the father in child development*. New York: Wiley.

Whiting, B.B., & Whiting, J.W.M. (1975). *Children of six cultures*. Cambridge, MA: Harvard University Press.

Yogman, M.W. (1977). *The goals and structure of face-to-face interaction between fathers and infants*. Paper presented at the biennial meeting of the Society for Research in Child Development, New Orleans.

Yogman, M.W. (1981). Games fathers and mothers play with their infants. *Infant Mental Health Journal, 2*, 241–248.

Yogman, M.W. (1982). Development of the father-infant relationship. In H. Fitzgerald, B. Lester, & M.W. Yogman (Eds.), *Theory and research in behavioral pediatrics* (vol. 1). New York: Plenum.

Yogman, M.W. (1984). Competence and performance of fathers and infants. In A. Macfarlane (Ed.), *Progress in child health*. London: Churchill Livingston.

Yogman, M.W. (1985). The father's role with preterm and fullterm infants. In J. Call, E. Galinson, & R. Tyson (Eds.), *Frontiers in infant psychiatry* (vol. 2). New York: Basic Books.

Zaslow, M., Pedersen, R., Kramer, E., Cain, R., Suwalsky, J., & Fivel, M. (1981). *Depressed mood in new fathers*. Paper presented at the Society For Research in Child Development, Boston.

CHAPTER 5

Correlates of Fathers' Participation in Family Work

ROSALIND C. BARNETT and GRACE K. BARUCH

The 1980s have seen a dramatic change in attitudes toward the role of fatherhood. Now the joys of fatherhood and shared parenting are touted in commercials, television programs, books, and magazine articles. This view of fathering is especially striking when we realize that as recently as the 1960s children and the care of children were seen as the exclusive domain of the mother (Nash, 1955; Parsons, 1955). Until recently it was assumed that the father's role in child care was essentially indirect, and defined through his primary function of providing financial support for the family and emotional support for the mother. There was little concern with changing this pattern, nor was change viewed as desirable. The current popularly held view of fatherhood, on the other hand, makes different assumptions; specifically, that enlightened fathers would participate in childrearing, were it not for the constraints of their work, and that shared parenting is the solution to the problems faced by mothers who are simultaneously employed and responsible for their children. In other words, if one could remove the obstacles to participation, fathers would participate, and if they did, the consequences would be positive, both for fathers and for mothers.

The reality is that there are a variety of forms of fathers' participation, that these forms may not be highly correlated (Carlson, 1984), and that they may have different determinants as well as different consequences (Barnett & Baruch, 1987; Baruch & Barnett, 1986a, 1986b). For example, Russell (1982) reports that among highly participant Australian fathers, the amount of time that fathers alone were in charge of their children was related to maternal employment status, but the total amount of time fathers spent jointly with their children and wife was not. Current research suggests that the factors that determine the extent of fathers' participation in family work—child care and household chores—and the consequences of their participation are much more complex than has popularly been assumed.

Since most of the research in this area is cross-sectional, it is not really possible to determine cause-and-effect relationships. Thus the distinction between determinants and consequences must be somewhat arbitrary. For example, maternal employment status might be a consequence as well as a determinant of fathers' participation. This chapter will focus mainly on correlates of father participation that can be viewed as potential determinants; a short section at the end will consider briefly those correlates that can be considered consequences.

PREVIOUS RESEARCH ON DETERMINANTS OF FATHERS' PARTICIPATION

Understanding the determinants of fathers' participation became a concern of researchers initially because of the massive entry of women, especially married women with children, into the paid labor force. The early research focused on fathers' own work constraints and sex-role attitudes. More recent studies, however, have considered other potential determinants, reflecting an awareness that fathers' participation, especially in families with employed wives, may be less voluntary, less reflective of individual preference, and more controlled by wives' needs (Feldman, Nash, & Aschenbrenner, 1983; Radin, 1981; Rossi, 1984), or by the demands of child care. Further, recognition that fathers' participation is an outgrowth of an interactive process determined in part by mothers' needs, has fostered research in which data are collected from both members of the marital dyad.

Five categories of determinants have been identified as important in previous research: mothers' and fathers' employment status and pattern, socioeconomic indicators, family structure, parental sex-role attitudes, and parental socialization.

Initially, researchers assumed that whether or not the mother worked outside the home determined whether the father got involved in family work. However, findings on the relationship between mothers' employment status and fathers' participation are inconsistent (Hoffman, 1983; Perrucci, Potter, & Rhoads, 1978; Pleck, 1981; Russell & Radin, 1983). One reason for this inconsistency may be that aspects of the paid work pattern of each parent (such as number and/or flexibility of hours worked) have been found to be more influential on fathers' participation than mothers' employment status alone (Russell & Radin, 1983; Staines & Pleck, 1983). It may also be that maternal employment status indirectly affects other determinants, which then emerge as significant predictors of fathers' participation. For example, the needs and attitudes of the employed mother may to a large extent determine her husband's level of participation in family work, whereas in families in which the mother is not employed, fathers' own attitudes may be the more significant determining factor.

Socioeconomic indicators, such as parental age and occupational attainment, have been hypothesized to affect men's family participation patterns; more specifically, the greater a father's involvement in his traditional role as economic provider, the less obligation he may feel to share in family work inside the home (Mortimer, Hall, & Hall, 1976). Here the research findings are contradictory. For example, fathers' income has been found to be negatively related to participation (Blood & Wolfe, 1960; Eriksen, Yancy, & Eriksen, 1979), but Coverman (1985) found no relationship between fathers' education, income, or occupational prestige, and participation in family work. Findings about parents' age and participation are also inconsistent (Pleck, 1983).

Among family structure variables thought to be important determinants are the sex, age, and number of children in the family. Most of the research on family structure determinants of fathers' participation has involved families in which the children are infants or toddlers, with relatively few studies focusing on paternal involvement with older children (Montemayor, 1982; Tasch, 1952; Zeigler, 1980). Available findings suggest that fathers spend fewer hours interacting with their children as the children get older, while the number of hours they spend relative to mothers increases with the age of the child. Again, these conclusions are drawn primarily from studies of younger children (Lamb, Pleck, Charnov, & Levine, 1985). With older children, who are more independent and have their own activities, fathers' absolute and proportional involvement may decrease. With regard to differential involvement by sex of child, the literature on young children indicates "surprisingly few differences in parents' treatment of boys and girls" (Huston, 1983; see also Block, 1976; Maccoby & Jacklin, 1974 for reviews and critiques of this literature). However, as children get older, fathers may find it easier to relate to a male child because they share a larger repertoire of commonly enjoyed and familiar activities (Tasch, 1952). Thus fathers may participate more with sons than with daughters in particular kinds of activities.[1]

With respect to parental sex-role attitudes, most research in this area has focused on the sex-role attitudes of fathers as determinants of involvement in child care (Coverman, 1985). However, the sex-role ideology of both fathers *and* mothers has been found to influence fathers' participation patterns (Baruch & Barnett, 1981; Pleck, 1983). Indeed, recent reviews suggest that high paternal participation is unlikely to occur unless there is approval and support for this behavior from significant others, such as spouses and peers (Cowan & Cowan, 1987; Lamb, et al., 1985; Lamb, Pleck, Charnov, & Levine, in press; Lein, 1979). Thus, mothers' sex-role attitudes may play a crucial gate-keeping role, either fostering or impeding fathers' participation in family work.

Finally, with respect to parents' own socialization experiences, two views have been advanced: (1) that fathers tend to *imitate* their own fathers' patterns, and (2) that they tend to *compensate* for them: that is, the lower the level of their fathers' involvement in their family of origin, the more involved men are likely to become in their own families (Lamb, et al., in press; Radin, 1981, 1985).

FATHERS' PARTICIPATION IN FAMILY WORK: AN INTERVIEW STUDY

In this chapter we present findings from an interview study concerning both determinants and consequences of fathers' participation in family work.[2] In an ef-

---

[1]For further discussion of father–son participation and interaction, see Bronstein, Chapter 8, this volume.

[2]The data come from a study of both determinants and consequences of fathers' participation in family work. The study was funded by the National Institute of Mental Health (MH #34225), and received additional funding from the Henry A. Murray Research Center of Radcliffe College. The determinants of fathers' participation on fathers and mothers are examined in Baruch and Barnett (1987); the effects of fathers' participation on children's sex-role development can be found in Baruch & Barnett (1986b); and the effects of mothers' participation are reported in Barnett & Baruch (1987).

fort to shed light on inconsistencies in the literature and to answer several as yet unanswered questions we addressed the following questions: (1) do the determinants of fathers' participation vary depending on the form of participation? and (2) do the determinants vary depending on whether or not the mothers are employed? To obtain this information, we collected parallel data from mothers and fathers on the five categories of potential determinants previously discussed, asked about different forms of fathers' participation, and compared families of employed and nonemployed mothers (see Barnett & Baruch, 1987, for a complete description).

Method

We conducted the study in 1980–1981 on a sample of 160 fathers and mothers of kindergarten or fourth-grade children, in a mainly white, middle-class suburb in the greater Boston area. The sample was stratified so that at each grade level half of the children were boys and half were girls. Within each of the four groups, half the mothers were employed, which was defined as working at least 17.5 hours per week for at least three months prior to being interviewed for this study. Nonemployed mothers were defined as employed less than eight hours per week; families with mothers who worked more than 8 but less than 17.5 hours per week were not included in this study. All families were Caucasian, with both biological parents of the target child living in the home, and middle-class, which was defined as the father's occupation being Class III or above on the Hollingshead Scale (Hollingshead, 1957).

The mean age of fathers was 41 years; of mothers, 39. All of the fathers were employed full time. Of the 80 employed mothers, roughly half worked between 17.5 and 29 hours per week and half worked 30 or more hours per week. For employed mothers, the mean occupational prestige level (Siegel, 1971) corresponded to that of a bookkeeper and the owner of a real estate agency; for fathers, it was the level assigned to an accountant and a social worker. On average, both mothers and fathers had completed a college degree. For the total sample, mean family income was in the mid-$30,000s; fathers' mean income was approximately $28,000; that of employed wives, $7,600, reflecting the high proportion of part-time workers among women, and lower pay scales for women's jobs. Moreover, some wives were employed by their husbands and reported especially low salaries. The average family had 2.6 children (Mode = 2.0; range 1–11). Eighteen percent of the families had a child under three, and 21 percent had no children younger than nine.

Average income for fathers with employed wives was $16,000, and for fathers with nonemployed wives, $29,000, a significant difference. However, there were no significant differences between the two groups in total family income, number of children, father's or mother's age, educational attainment, occupational prestige of husbands, or number of hours per week the husband worked.

Fathers and mothers were interviewed in their homes for approximately two hours by a team consisting of a male and a female staff member. Parents were interviewed together about the extent of their separate and joint participation in child care and home chores, in paid employment, and in other activities. Demographic data about the family, such as income and educational attainment, were also obtained at that time. Each parent was then interviewed in a separate room by a same-sex interviewer to obtain data on parental role strain and well-being. Finally, a questionnaire packet, which included a self-esteem measure, was left with each parent to be filled out independently and returned by mail. Each parent received $5 for participating.

Assessing Potential Determinants.

Mothers and fathers provided us with the following data on the five categories of determinants:

1. The measures of *employment status and pattern* were the number of hours worked, the flexibility of their work schedules, and their satisfaction with that flexibility
2. The indexes of *socioeconomic status* were the parents' age, educational attainment, income (both total family income and the amount earned separately by each parent), and occupational prestige (Siegel, 1971)
3. *Family structure* indicators were the number, sex, and ages of all children
4. *Parental sex-role attitudes* were assessed by both the Brannon and Juni *Attitude toward Masculinity Scale,* short form (Brannon & Juni, 1984) and the question, Who should provide the economic support for the family: the father, the mother, or both?
5. Our index of *parental socialization* was a rating by each father and mother, on a 7-point scale, of the quality of fathering he or she received between the ages of 5 and 10, the same age range as that of the children in the study. The Brannon and Juni Scale asks subjects the extent to which they agree with such statements as, "It bothers me when a man does something that I consider feminine."

Measures of Fathers' Participation.

We selected particular dimensions of fathers' participation based on distinctions made in recent research (Baruch & Barnett, 1981; Goldberg, 1981; Lamb, et al., in press; Pleck, 1983), including:

1. The quality of father–child interactions
2. The amount of interaction time he spends alone (i.e., without his wife) in interaction with his child
3. The total amount of interaction time the father spends with the child proportional to his wife's total interaction time with the child
4. The amount of time he spends performing specific child care and household tasks alone compared to the amount of time he spends on those tasks jointly with his wife
5. His *responsibility* for child care and household tasks versus his simply performing those tasks.

Specifically, we looked at these five dimensions of father participation, as follows:

1. *Quality of Father–Child Interactions.*   To measure the quality and intensity of a father's interactions with his child, we devised a chart that allowed parents to indicate jointly for five typical weekdays and two typical weekend days, the hours during which the target child and each parent were home and awake. They then indicated the nature of the parent–child interaction that typically occurred during each of those hours. Three levels of interaction were described to parents:

Level 1, *No Interaction.*   Parent and child are not involved together. Each is engaged in independent activity with no interaction.

Level 2, *Intermittent Interaction.*   Parent and child are each doing their own thing, aware of each other's activities, and interacting periodically.

Level 3, *Intensive Interaction.*   Parent and child are actively involved together, as in doing homework, playing a game, or being engaged in a project.

Since parents reported only a very small number of hours in which they were at home but unavailable to the child, Level 1 scores were omitted from the analyses. To our surprise, many parents in fact found this category difficult to understand. As one father of five explained, "There's no time when I'm not there for the kids. When I'm home, I'm home. There's no way to be home and be off limits." Level 2 and 3 scores were combined into a *Total Interaction Time* score because, although conceptually clear to both parents and researchers, the distinction between the levels was difficult to apply. For example, conversations held while a parent was chauffeuring a child were experienced as intensive interaction, yet, according to our definition, were intermittent. This score reflects the total number of hours per week the father spends in quality interaction with his child.

2. *Father's Solo Interaction Time.*   On the basis of the data from the chart, we calculated the number of hours per week the father spent in intermittent and intensive interaction with the child when the mother was out of the house or not available.

3. *Father's Proportional Interaction Time.*   In addition, we calculated the number of hours the father spent per week in intermittent and intensive interaction both with and without the wife present, divided by the total number of hours both parents spent in such interactions.

4. *Father's Participation in Child Care and Household Tasks.*   Fathers' participation in child care was measured by a checklist of 11 tasks, modified from Baruch and Barnett (1981). For each task, parents were asked to estimate jointly what percent of the time it was done by the father alone, by the parents together, and by the mother alone. The 11 tasks included such things as: go to teacher conference, supervise morning routine, buy clothes, take on outing (e.g., museum, park) stay home, or make arrangements for care when child is sick. To provide a measure of fathers' performance of home chores, parents jointly reported the hours each spent for a typical week on nine household tasks. Five were chores commonly viewed as "feminine": meal preparation, cleaning house, laundry, grocery shopping, and meal

clean-up. Four were "masculine" tasks: general repairs, yard work, car repairs, and paying bills. Because a major focus of the larger study was on the children's sex-role attitudes, the variable used in these analyses concerned the father's involvement in feminine tasks only—that is, nontraditional behavior by the father.

For both child care tasks and home chores, we focused on the proportion of the total time for both parents that was spent by the father. One objective of the study was to examine the effects of fathers' involvement on children's sex-role attitudes. It seemed likely that, from a child's perspective, the relative involvement of fathers and mothers would matter more than the absolute involvement of each.

5. *Responsibility for child care and household tasks.*   Responsibility was defined as "remembering, planning, and scheduling," and was assessed both for the 11 child-caretasks and the nine home chores.

Results

Fathers' Level of Involvement.

First, we found that the five forms of fathers' participation were only moderately correlated with one another. With the exception of proportional interaction time, which correlated .54 with total interaction time and .65 with the proportion of feminine chores, the remaining correlations ranged from .15 to .37.

Second, our findings revealed a definite overall pattern: fathers' participation in the areas of family work we examined was substantially lower than that of mothers. Looking first at the total time fathers spent interacting with their children—both alone and when mothers were present—we found that fathers spent significantly less time with children than did mothers, regardless of whether the mothers were employed or at home. Fathers spent about two-thirds the number of hours that mothers did with the child, with mothers averaging 44 hours per week and fathers averaging 29 hours. The disparity was even greater when we looked at time spent alone with the child. In both groups of families, mothers spent nearly four times as many hours interacting alone with the child than did fathers. In contrast to these measures of absolute time, the proportional measures showed that fathers' involvement relative to mothers' was affected by whether or not their wives were employed outside the home. On each proportional measure, fathers with employed wives interacted more with their children relative to their wives than did fathers with nonemployed wives. This reflects, in part, the fact that their wives were interacting with the children less than mothers who were not working outside the home.

Finally, perhaps the most striking of our findings was that overall, fathers reported extremely low levels of responsibility for child-care tasks and home chores. That is, they might *perform* various tasks, but they were not responsible for "remembering, planning, and scheduling" them. Of 160 fathers, 113 reported that they were responsible for *no* child-care tasks, 35 were responsible for one, and 12 for 2 or 3. For "feminine" home chores, 150 fathers were not responsible for any, 8 were responsible for 1, and 2 for 2 or 3. Because of the very limited range of these two "responsibility" variables, we omitted them from further analyses. However, it should be noted that fathers did not generally perceive themselves as lacking in responsibility for their home and children; rather they saw their responsibilities in a more global and traditional way. For example, in one family with a nonemployed mother, the interviewer arrived just after the mother came home from doing the grocery shopping, yet during the interview, when the couple was asked who is responsible for the food shopping, the husband immediately answered, "I am." When he was asked in what way he was responsible, he responded, "It's obvious. I have to earn all the money."

Determinants of Fathers' Involvement.

Although there were substantial differences between fathers and mothers in their level of participation in family work, there were also differences among the fathers themselves. In order to answer our questions about what determines the degree to which a father actively participates in child-care and household tasks, we computed regression equations both for the total sample and for the two groups of fathers (with employed and nonemployed wives), with each of the five forms of fathers' participation treated as a separate outcome. Thus we were looking at which of the specific measures (such as father's income, child's age, mother's attitude toward masculinity) from the five categories of determinants (employment status and pattern, socioeconomic status, family structure, parental sex-role attitudes, and parental socialization) might be significantly related to fathers' level of participation. Only determinants correlating $>.20$ with at least one father-participation variable were included in the regression analyses.

For the total sample, the most consistent predictors of fathers' absolute interaction time, both total and solo, were some of the family structure variables. Fathers of younger children spent more time with their children, both alone and when their wives were present, than fathers of older children, and fathers with larger families had higher levels of interaction with their children alone and relative to their wives than fathers with smaller families. Mothers' employment status was also significant, predicting all proportional measures of fathers' participation, child-care tasks, and feminine home chores. In addition, mothers' sex-role attitudes and fathers' feelings about the parenting they had received were important to fathers' involvement in their own families. Specifically, fathers who spent more time alone with their kindergarteners or fourth graders were more likely to wish that their own fathers had been more involved in fathering, and to have wives who believed that men should share the care of children.

Different patterns of predictors emerged, depending on whether or not the wife was employed. For fathers with employed wives, the number of hours the wife worked was a significant predictor of the husband's total interaction time, proportional interaction time, and "feminine" home chores. The more hours she worked outside the home, the more time he spent on chores like cooking, laundry, and caring for the children. In addition, her attitude toward the male role was a significant predictor both of her husband's involvement in "feminine" home chores and the time he spent interacting with the child relative to her. The demands of her employment and her nontraditional attitudes about men's roles appear to have created more demand for her husband's participation in the family, and may have created an atmosphere that encouraged him to be more participatory. It is especially noteworthy that none of the variables reflecting fathers' own employment pattern correlated highly enough with any of the participation variables to be included in the regression analyses.

For fathers with nonemployed wives, on the other hand, their attitudes toward the quality of fathering they received were significant predictors of involvement; fathers with less favorable attitudes toward the fathering they received spent more time with their child in total interaction, proportional interaction, and solo interaction. For example, one of the more highly involved fathers reported that while he was still in high school, he had resolved never to become like the distant figure that his own father had been—a very successful lawyer who had had no time for his children, and had sent them to boarding school. As a result of that decision, this man broke with his family's educational and occupational traditions, and became a carpenter. "I'm very involved with my children, on a daily basis," he told the interviewer. "I wouldn't have it any other way." Note, however, that although these men's feelings about the fathering they received tended to predict their level of involvement with their children, there was no relationship between those feelings and their participation in either child-care tasks or feminine home chores. Additional consistent findings that emerged for husbands of nonemployed wives were that they spent more time interacting with the child both on their own and with their wives when the target child was younger, and that fathers with more children had a higher level of proportional interaction time with their child.

Discussion and Conclusions

A major finding of this study is that in families with five- and nine-year-olds, the significant predictors of fathers' participation differed, depending on whether the mothers were employed or nonemployed. In dual-earner families, the number of hours the mothers worked and their sex-role attitudes were important predictors of fathers' involvement with the children. In contrast, in single-earner families, fathers' feelings about the quality of the fathering they received as youngsters were the most consistent predictor of their involvement with their own children. These findings suggest that mothers' employment status may create conditions that help determine which aspects of fathers' lives affect their involvement with their children, and how involved they will be.

The findings that in dual-earner families the more hours the mother worked, the greater was the fathers' involvement with the child, is consistent with Russell's report (unpublished manuscript). He found that in families where fathers were highly participatory, the decision about roles had been mainly influenced by the wife. However, as Pleck (1983) has pointed out, a wife's employment status and pattern is confounded with other variables affecting families, such as the husband's earning power. Further, the greater influence of wives' versus husbands' work hours may be a statistical artifact of the greater range in wives' hours found in most studies (Pleck, 1983).

Also in dual-earner families, the mother's attitude toward the male role, but not the father's, was a major predictor of the father's involvement with the child. When her attitude was more liberal, he did more; when it was more traditional, he did less. Many prior studies have failed to inquire about mothers' sex-role attitudes, perhaps explaining why the findings in this area have been so inconsistent.

For both groups of families, of the five classes of determinants, only socioeconomic indicators were consistently unrelated to fathers' participation. This finding may be due to the relative affluence and homogeneity of the sample; in a less advantaged sample, family income and education might have had a greater influence. In dual-earner families, the lack of a significant relationship between fathers' participation and family structure is especially noteworthy. Apparently fathers' participation is not primarily a function either of resources or of demands placed on him by the children; rather, it is related more to the wife's attitudes and needs. In single-earner families, however, family structure had a significant influence: the younger the target child, the more time the father spent in interaction, both totally and proportional to his wife. Further, the more children he had, the greater was his solo and proportional interaction time.

This study casts doubt on the validity of the recent belief that fathers with liberal sex-role attitudes and few work constraints will participate more with their children. In fact, fathers' sex-role attitudes and work-related variables were not systematically related to their participation. In addition, as will be shown, further analyses of the same data set have raised questions about the validity of the second part of this belief—namely, that the effects of fathers' participation will be uniformly positive for fathers and mothers.

SOME CONSEQUENCES OF FATHERS' INVOLVEMENT IN FAMILY WORK

In contrast to popular notions of basically positive effects of fathers' involvement in the family, recent research suggests that the effects may be quite complex; they differ for fathers and mothers (Pleck, 1983), and for families with employed and nonemployed wives (Hoffman, 1983; Lamb, et al., in press; Pleck, 1983; Russell & Radin, 1983). They also differ according to the domain considered (e.g., effects on the parenting role or effects on the marital relationship) and the particular form of family work being considered (e.g., child care or home chores). Finally, father involvement effects also differ according to whether the focus is on immediate and specific problems such as time pressures and conflicts in commitments, or more long-term generalized outcomes such as role satisfaction and self-esteem.

We studied two types of "consequence" correlates of fathers' participation: parents' role strain and well-being. For each parent, we assessed four groups of role-strain variables related to work/family conflicts, and three domains of well-being, including the parental role, the marital role, and overall life satisfaction and self-esteem. Contrary to our expectations, the effects of fathers' participation on these two categories of consequences did not differ by maternal employment status per se.

While previous research had suggested that such a difference would be found, those studies had not controlled for level of participation.

What we did find was that there were mixed consequences of fathers' participation. Overall, as fathers' involvement with children and child-care tasks increased, so did their worry about having enough time for their work. In addition, while fathers who participated more in total interaction and child-care tasks enjoyed benefits in the parental role, they experienced tensions in the marital role. They described themselves as more involved with their child and more competent as fathers, but they were also more critical of their wives as mothers, expressing more dissatisfaction with both the amount of time their wives spent with the children and with the way their wives allocated their time.

In contrast, the wives of the more participant fathers were quite self-blaming. The more their husbands did, the more likely they were to say that they experienced conflict between work and family—specifically, that their work interfered with their family responsibilities. The more time a husband spent interacting with the child, the more positive his wife's evaluation of him as a father, but the less her satisfaction with *her* overall life. This pattern suggests that one of the risks of fathers' greater involvement in family work is that wives may feel less satisfied with their own family role.

Finally, different forms of fathers' participation were associated with different consequences. For example, fathers who spent more time alone with their child described more tension in the marriage. On the other hand, fathers who spent more time with their child when their wives were present described themselves as more involved with the child and more competent as fathers, and they did not report the marital tensions that men spending more time alone with their child described. Thus whether fathers were responding to their wives' work-related demands or sex-role attitudes, or their own socialization experiences, participation itself had mixed effects.

The research perspective on the role of father seems to have arrived at a third stage. In the first stage, fathers were barely represented in psychological thinking and writing about parenting. In the second, fatherhood was glorified, and men's increased participation in family work was assumed to be both the panacea for the beleaguered employed mother and the solution to the tensions faced by dual-earner couples as they confronted the problems of rearing children. The third stage represents a recognition that fathers' increased participation will have stressful as well as positive consequences on some aspects of family life, and that as it generates solutions to some problems, it may also be creating new problems for which the solutions are yet to be found.

REFERENCES

Barnett, R.C., & Baruch, G.K. (1987). Determinants of fathers' participation in family work. *Journal of Marriage and the Family, 49*, 29–40.

Barnett, R.C., & Baruch, G.K. (1987). Mothers' participation in child care: Patterns and consequences. In F. Crosby (Ed.), *Spouse, parent, worker: On gender and multiple roles*. New Haven, CT: Yale University Press.

Baruch, G.K., & Barnett, R.C. (1981). Fathers' participation in the care of their preschool children. *Sex Roles, 7*, 1043–1054.

Baruch, G.K., & Barnett, R.C. (1986a). Consequences of fathers' participation in family work: Parents' role-strain and well-being. *Journal of Personality and Social Psychology, 51*, 578–585.

Baruch, G.K., & Barnett, R.C. (1986b). Fathers' participation in family work and children's sex-role attitudes. *Child Development, 57*, 1210–1223.

Block, J.H. (1976). Issues, problems, and pitfalls in assessing sex differences: A critical review of "The psychology of sex differences." *Merrill Palmer Quarterly, 22*, 283–308.

Blood, R.O., Jr., & Wolfe, D.M. (1960). *Husbands and wives.* Glencoe, IL: Free Press.

Brannon, R., & Juni, S. (1984). A scale for measuring attitudes about masculinity. *Psychological Documents, 14*, 6–7.

Carlson, B.E. (1984). The fathers' contribution to child-care: Effects on children's perceptions of parental roles. *American Journal of Orthopsychiatry, 54*, 123–136.

Coverman, C. (1985). Explaining husband's participation in domestic labor. *Sociological Quarterly, 26*, 81–97.

Cowan, C.P., & Cowan, P.A. (1987). Men's involvement in parenthood: Identifying the antecedents and understanding the barriers. In P. Berman & F.A. Pedersen (Eds.), *Men's transitions to parenthood.* Hillsdale, NJ: Erlbaum.

Eriksen, J.A., Yancey, W.L., & Eriksen, E.P. (1979). The division of family roles. *Journal of Marriage and the Family, 41*, 301–303.

Feldman, S.S., Nash, S.C., & Aschenbrenner, B.G. (1983). Antecedents of fathering. *Child Development, 54*, 1628–1636.

Goldberg, R.J. (1981). *Adapting time budget methodology for child development research: Effects of family variables on allocation of time to child rearing activities and developmental outcomes.* Paper presented at the biennial meeting of the Society for Research in Child Development, Boston.

Hoffman, L.W. (1983). Increased fathering: Effects on the mother. In M. Lamb & A. Sagi (Eds.), *Fatherhood and social policy.* Hillsdale, NJ: Erlbaum.

Hollingshead, A. (1957). *Two factor index of social position.* New Haven, CT: Yale University Press.

Huston, A.C. (1983). Sex-typing. In P.H. Mussen (Ed.), *Handbook of child psychology* (Vol. 4). New York: Wiley.

Lamb, M.E., Pleck, J.H., Charnov, E., & Levine, J.A. (1985). Paternal behavior in humans. *American Zoologist, 25*, 883–894.

Lamb, M.E., Pleck, J.H., Charnov, E., & Levine, J.A. (in press). A biosocial perspective on paternal behavior and involvement. In J.B. Lancaster, J. Altman, A. Rossi, & L. Sherrod (Eds.), *Parenting across the lifespan: Biosocial perspectives.* Chicago: Aldine.

Lein, L. (1979). Male participation in the home: Impact of social supports and breadwinners' responsibility on the allocation of tasks. *Family Coordinator, 28*, 489–496.

Maccoby, E.E., & Jacklin, C.N. (1974). *The psychology of sex differences.* Stanford, CA: Stanford University Press.

Montemayor, R. (1982). The relationship between parent-adolescent conflict and the amount of time adolescents spend alone and with parents and peers. *Child Development, 53*, 1512–1519.

Mortimer, S., Hall, R., & Hall, R. (1976). *Husbands' occupational attributes as constraints on wives' employment.* Paper presented at meeting of American Sociological Association, New York.

Nash, J. (1955). The father in contemporary culture and current psychological literature. *Child Development, 56*, 261–297.

Parsons, T. (1955). Family structure and the socialization of the child. In T. Parsons & R.F. Bales (Eds.), *Family, socialization and interaction processes*. Glencoe, IL: Free Press.

Perrucci, C., Potter, H.R., & Rhoads, D.L. (1978). Determinants of male family-role performance. *Psychology of Women Quarterly, 3*, 53–66.

Pleck, J.H. (1981). *Changing patterns of work and family roles*. Paper presented at meeting of American Psychological Association, Los Angeles.

Pleck, J.H. (1983). Husbands' paid work and family roles: Current research issues. In L. Lopata & J.H. Pleck (Eds.), *Research in the interweave of social roles: Vol. 3, Families and jobs*. Greenwich, CT: JAI Press.

Radin, N. (1981). Child rearing fathers in intact families. *Merrill Palmer Quarterly, 27*, 489–514.

Radin, N. (1985). *Antecedents of stability in high father involvement*. Paper presented at Conference on Equal Parenting: Families of the Future, University of California, Chico, CA.

Robinson, J.P., Yerby, J., Fieweger, M., & Somerick, N. (1977). Sex Role difference in time use. *Sex Roles, 3*, 443–459.

Rossi, A. (1984). Gender and parenthood. *American Sociological Review, 49*, 1–10.

Russell, G. (1982). Shared-caregiving families: an Australian study. In M.E. Lamb (Ed.), *Non-traditional families: Parenting and child development*. Hillsdale, NJ: Erlbaum.

Russell, G. (1981). *A multivariate analysis of fathers' participation in child care and play*. Unpublished manuscript, Department of Psychology, Macquarie University, Sydney, NSW.

Russell, G., & Radin, N. (1983). Increased paternal participation: The fathers' perspective. In M. Lamb & A. Sagi (Eds.), *Fatherhood and social policy*. pp. 139–165. Hillsdale, NJ: Erlbaum.

Siegel, P.M. (1971). *Prestige in the American occupational structure*. Unpublished doctoral dissertation, University of Chicago, Chicago.

Staines, G.L., & Pleck, J.H. (1983). *The impact of work schedules on the family*. Ann Arbor, MI: University of Michigan Press.

Tasch, R.J. (1952). The role of the father in the family. *Journal of Experimental Education, 20*, 319–361.

Zeigler, M. (1980). *The father's influence on his school age child's academic performance and cognitive development*. Unpublished doctoral dissertation, University of Michigan.

CHAPTER 6

Changing Perspectives on the Role of the Black Father

JOHN LEWIS MCADOO

The role of the father in the socialization of his children has become an issue of great interest in social science literature. Until fairly recently, however, very little research had been done in this area. What studies there were that considered the father's role have been described as "matricentric" (Lamb, 1981) in that they most often focused on the mother's *perception* of the role of the father in the family, rather than focusing on the father directly. Or, they considered the impact of father absence on children's development, with the effects of father presence considered only as a control.

In keeping with this general tradition, there has also been very little research on Black fathers. Cazenave (1979) extensively reviewed a number of family studies, as well as texts and readers in the social sciences, and found no articles, sections, or index references about the Black father in the home. Several studies focused on the negative impact of the absent Black father, but the researchers did not evaluate the role, if any, that such fathers might continue to play in the rearing of their children.

Thus the role of the Black father has generally been portrayed in terms of deficiencies. Developmental and family research on absent fathers has not statistically controlled for or reported the influences of the economic, political, racial, and social barriers that help maintain the marginal status of many Black men within society, and serve to restrict their ability to assume the traditional, socially prescribed role of father within the family (McAdoo, 1979). Furthermore, there is very little research that examines the family roles and relationships of the many Black fathers in two-parent families who are deeply involved in the parenting of their children.

In this chapter I will discuss some of the historical, social, and economic factors affecting Black family structure, and review the emerging research on Black fatherhood. In addition, I will present and discuss some of my own findings on the role of the Black father in two-parent families.

HISTORICAL BACKGROUND

It is particularly useful to explore the Black family from a historical perspective. Some social scientists feel that the Black father has been hampered in his ability to nurture his family by the long-enduring effects of enslavement. Several historians have documented the cruel, inhumane effects of enslavement on Blacks in this country (Blassingame, 1979; Elkins, 1959; Fogel & Engerman, 1974; Franklin, 1967). Myrdal (1944) has suggested that these effects did not disappear when enslavement ended and Blacks moved into a caste system.

While historians have often been vague about the Black father's role in the family, two views have emerged. The first is that since enslavement law did not sanction marriages (Green, 1975; Nichols, 1972), Black fathers were not expected to play any role in the socialization of their children. The other view is that the family system was recognized and encouraged by many enslavers (Blassingame, 1979; Franklin, 1967; Genovese, 1976), and that many Black fathers were able to provide nurturance for their children.

Nichols (1972) found some support for the first view in his extensive analysis of narratives by men who escaped bondage. He notes that enslavement diminished the Black man's ability to provide the same protection for his family as other men. Both Nichols (1972) and Green (1975) suggest that the Black man was systematically denied his role as a father. The law did not recognize his authority over his household, and in many instances he was forbidden to discipline his children; the provider's role and the control of rewards and punishments were in the hands of the plantation owner. Under these conditions, Nichols and Green maintain that some of the enslaved fathers abandoned their parental obligations.

On the other hand, Blassingame (1979) notes that many plantation owners allowed the enslaved family to exist as a unit, and that the family provided mechanisms for survival. Both plantation records and the narratives of those men who escaped bondage provide us with some clues regarding the enslaved father's role in his family. He hunted and trapped small animals to supplement the family diet. He was the authority in the cabin who disciplined his children. He also entertained his children with stories and songs, and won their affection with little gifts.

Some enslaved fathers were perceived by their children to be stern disciplinarians, and some of these fathers, in fact, were abusive toward their children (Genovese, 1976). The relationship within the family was not always idyllic. In some instances, the enslaved father imposed his authority over his family by force; although punishing his wife was usually forbidden by the master and led to his own punishment, he did it anyway. The evidence on these matters is fragmentary, but it suggests that in some cases, the enslaved father asserted his authority as much as he could. His wife was expected to defer to her husband, and both tried hard to keep their master out of their lives (Blassingame, 1979; Genovese, 1976; Gutman, 1976).

Genovese (1976), summarizing much of the historical evidence on the quality of Black family life during slavery, suggests that the average enslaved Black male lived in a family setting, developed strong family ties, and held the nuclear family as the proper norm. Enslaved fathers, though living under highly adverse conditions, were apparently able to enact a variety of fathering roles.

Emancipation of enslaved families left them under extreme economic, political, and social pressures, as they traded bondage for a caste system. However, Frazier

(1966) notes that the family life of the emancipated Negro was to a large extent influenced by his social development under slavery. If under slavery the family had been allowed to remain intact and acquire stability, the transition to freedom did not result in disorganization. Fathers had generally developed a deep and permanent attachment to their wives and an interest in their children. In some cases, as they assumed responsibility for their families, they remained on the plantation as tenants. The more ambitious fathers acquired land, and with this property ownership laid the foundation for patriarchal authority in the family. Frazier's conclusions are based on his examinations of slave narratives. Gutman (1976) and Furstenberg, Hershberg, and Model (1975) cite census data that support these findings. Gutman, analyzing postenslavement census data and data from the Freedman's Bureau, found that 70–90% of Black fathers were present in the home. Furstenberg and colleagues, looking at the 1850 and 1880 census for Philadelphia, found no significant differences between Black and White family structural patterns.

The Black family structure experienced extreme pressures during the twentieth century, when many migrated north. The men found themselves shut out of employment, not so much by their lack of skills, as by fierce discrimination (Genovese, 1976). Families were also forced apart by public welfare laws that provided more economic support for the family when the father was not in the home. However, in spite of the extreme economic and social pressures on the family, more than two-thirds of Black fathers were living with their families in 1970 (Neckerman & Wilson, 1986).

CURRENT SOCIOECONOMIC FACTORS AFFECTING BLACK FATHERHOOD

Many social scientists evaluating Black families have failed to take into consideration some important demographic characteristics that affect the Black father's ability to carry out prescribed traditional roles within the family. The rate of unemployment in 1984 for all Black males was 16%, which, in the peak child rearing ages of 16 to 44, was double that of White males (U.S. Bureau of the Census, 1986b). The greatest disparity in unemployment between Black and Whites occurred in the 16- to 19-year age range, in which 43% of Black males versus 17% of White males were unemployed—and here we need to keep in mind that the census figures do not reflect those who have given up and are no longer looking for work. In 1984, the median income for Black families was $15,432, which was 56% of White family income (U.S. Bureau of the Census, 1986c). According to the U.S. Census (1986d), 33% of Black families as opposed to 10% of White families were below the poverty level in 1984.

These constantly high unemployment and underemployment levels mean that many Black fathers cannot adequately fulfill a provider's role in the family, which in turn may seriously influence their ability to fulfill other roles related to the rearing of their children. Marital and family stress have been found to be related to conditions of unemployment, job insecurity, and poverty (Albee, 1982). In addition, a negative perception of their ability to provide adequately for their children may lead some Black fathers to withdraw from the family. These factors, combined with public welfare policies that inadvertently provide economic incentive for fathers to leave the family, may contribute to the rising number of single-parent female-headed Black families, which were reported to be 23% of all nonwhite families in 1962 (Moynihan, 1965) and 59% of all Black families in 1984 (U.S. Bureau of the Census, 1986a).

RESEARCH ON BLACK FATHERS

Father Absence

The findings from empirical research into father absence seem to be mixed, because the studies focused on its outcome for children, and not on the absent fathers themselves. Boys in father-absent Black families have been found to be more likely to have lower IQs (Deutsch & Brown, 1964) and to score lower than their classmates on achievement tests (Deutsch, 1960). However, Elder (1968), in a review of the empirical studies of adolescent achievement, points out that findings on the effects of father absence have frequently been confounded with economic and cultural factors: when economic factors have been satisfactorily controlled, household structure has turned out to have little if any effect on the academic performance of children and adolescents. Coleman, Campbell, Hobson, McParland, Mood, Weinfeld, and York (1966), examined the 6th, 9th, and 12th grade achievement test scores of Black and White students, controlling for socioeconomic factors, and found no significant differences between those from father-absent and those from father-present homes. These findings have been supported in other studies (Cortes & Fleming, 1968; Hess, Shipman, Brophy, & Bear, 1968; Wasserman, 1969).

Many studies (Bacon, Child & Barry, 1963; Bandura & Walters, 1959; Miller, 1958; Pettigrew, 1964; Scarpitti, Murray, Dinitz, & Reckless, 1960) have found a relationship between father absence and problems in developing a secure masculine identity, with juvenile delinquency sometimes viewed as a resulting overcompensation. Biller (1976) reviewed a series of studies, including his own, that found father absence to be related to problems in sex role, personality, and independence development in boys. While his research indicated consistent sex differences and some social class differences in the influence of father absence on children's development, no racial differences were found. Similarly, Pettigrew noted that both Black and White boys from fatherless homes tended to be markedly more immature, submissive, dependent, and "effeminate" than other boys. However, Herzog and Sudia (1973), extensively reviewing the literature on the effects of family structure on sex-role development, found insufficient data to indicate that father absence affects masculine identity in the direction of either underdevelopment or overcompensation. In addition, they provided evidence that the most significant factors associated with juvenile delinquency are lack of general family cohesiveness and lack of supervision. Overall, Herzog and Sudia conclude that the empirical evidence does not support the popular notion of a father having to be present in the home in order for his son to develop a positive masculine identity.

From this large body of literature on father absence, some of which focuses on Black families, we learn almost nothing at all about the men whose children have been left "fatherless." However, there are some sociological studies of Black families and communities which suggest that many lower-income Black fathers who do not live with their children continue to play a role in their children's lives. Stack (1986), in her early 1970s study of domestic life in a poor, Black Midwestern community, found that 70% of the fathers of 1000 children on welfare recognized their children, and provided them with kinship affiliation, though only 12% of those who acknowledged paternity also provided some financial support. Stack also discusses the importance of kin networks to economic survival, pointing out that a man in such a community was expected to contribute to his own kin network, rather than dissipating his services and finances in a marital relationship. Liebow (1967), in his study of Black "streetcorner men" in an urban ghetto, found a broad spectrum of father–child relationships among those men who did not live with their children. Some did not acknowledge paternity, while others had frequent brief and affectionate contact with their child, though the mother was entirely responsible for the child's care and upbringing. Sometimes, a man's child lived with *his* relatives, in which case there tended to be a closer father–child relationship. The closest father–child relationships that Liebow observed involved men who lived with and cared for children who were not biologically their own. Thus as Liebow points out about these nonresident fathers, "Some fathers are not always 'absent' and some are less 'absent' than others" (p. 73). In a recent interview study of 100 Black teenage fathers, Rivara, Sweeney, and Henderson (1986) found that, 18 months after the birth of their child, in addition to the 12% who were living with the child, 25% reported that they saw the child daily, and 28% reported that they saw the child 3–6 times per week; only 2% reported that they maintained no contact at all. In addition, these fathers reported that they not only played with their child during visits (which, for 75% of the fathers, generally lasted anywhere from four hours to a whole day), but commonly fed and diapered the child, and stayed home alone with the child or took the child out. Clearly, the roles 'absent' Black fathers play in the lives of their children may vary widely, and are at least in part determined by social and economic factors that are beyond the control of the men themselves.

The Co-Parenting Relationship in Two-Parent Families

Though limited in scope, there has been some research on Black fathers' role in family decision making. A number of researchers (Cromwell & Cromwell, 1978; Jackson, 1974; Middleton & Putney, 1960; TenHouten, 1970; Willie, 1976) have found that Black fathers in their studies tended to report that they shared equally with their wives in decisions relating to family matters. While Cromwell and Cromwell (1978) found some disagreements between the spouses about who made the decisions, other researchers (Middleton & Putney, 1960; TenHouten, 1970) reported

substantial agreement between parents on the role the father played in family decision making.

Mack (1974) has suggested that socioeconomic status may make a difference in
the role Black men perceive themselves to be playing in these family decisions, and
that egalitarian decision-making patterns might be a middle-class phenomenon.
However, other researchers (Jackson, 1974; TenHouten, 1970; Willie, 1976) found
few if any social class differences, and Jackson (1974), looking at a working-class
sample of Black fathers, reported that the majority of them shared equally with their
wives in household and family decisions.

In sum, the studies on family decision making in Black families found Black fathers to be as involved as mothers, and this was true of a majority of the families
within the studies reviewed, regardless of social class. Further, in most of the studies, the perceptions of the Black men of their equal role were supported by their
wives. This egalitarian pattern in family decision making in Black families is similar to the pattern generally found in White families (Mack, 1974; Middleton &
Putney, 1960).

The Father–Child Relationship in Two-Parent Families

A number of studies have examined the Black father's perception of himself in the
parenting role. Some have compared Blacks with Whites, or with other ethnic
groups. Some have focused on the father's role definition, others on child rearing
attitudes and behaviors, and still others on the father's degree of involvement in
child care.

Role Definition

Daniel's (1975) study of Black fathers and their preschool sons found that these fathers perceived themselves as mediators between their sons' inner selves and the
outside world. However, Cazenave (1979), in a study of 54 Black middle-income
fathers who were postal carriers, found that they rated their role as provider higher
than their other parental roles.

Child Rearing Attitudes and Behavior

A number of studies have found that Black fathers tended to have strict behavioral
expectations of their children emphasized parental control in their child rearing attitudes. Allen (1985), in a survey of 120 Black and while lower-income families of
adolescent boys, found that fathers (regardless of race) tended to expect less independent behavior from their children as compared with mothers, and reported punishing their sons more frequently. Bartz and Levine (1979), in a survey of 455 lower
income Black, Chicano, and White families, found that Black fathers, more than fathers in other ethnic groups, believed in the value of strictness, expected children to
assume early control of their own bodily functions and emotions, and expected the
children to use their time wisely. However, while along with other fathers, the
Black fathers in this sample encouraged their children's involvement in decision

making, and expressed loving concern and care for their children, at the same time they expressed a desire to regulate closely their children's behavior, in order to assure the attainment of goals, such as obedience and achievement. Similarly, in my own study of middle-income Black fathers and their preschool children (McAdoo, 1979), I found that the fathers considered themselves to be moderately strict in their child rearing attitudes, tended to expect their children to respond immediately to their commands, and almost never allowed temper tantrums from their children. However, although the fathers in this study tended to expect obedience and good behavior from their children (as opposed to assertive and independent behavior), they reported that they were not as strict with their children as their fathers had been with them.

Other studies, on the other hand, have not found Black fathers to be more restrictive than White fathers in controlling their children. Baumrind (1972), in a laboratory study of parenting styles in Black and White families, found the fathers in both groups to be similar in their expectations that their sons behave in a mature, independent fashion, although Black fathers more than White fathers were observed to encourage independence or individuality in their daughters. Price-Bonham and Skeen (1979), in a study of Black and White fathers' child rearing attitudes, found more similarities than differences in disciplinary methods, particularly in the use of physical punishment, withdrawal of privileges, isolation of children and explanation of the reasons for discipline to them, with 60% of both groups stating that they seldom if ever explain the reasons for discipline to their children. In addition, the Black fathers saw themselves as less strict than did White fathers, and compared with White fathers, reported being less likely to ignore their children as a disciplinary technique.

In addition, warm and supportive paternal behaviors have been reported in some studies. Bartz and Levine (1979) found that fathers in all three ethnic groups studied reported that they encouraged their children's involvement in decision making, and expressed loving concern and care for their children. Daniel (1975) found that Black fathers tended to favor discipline that both controlled and changed their child's behavior through positive, supportive means. Hornig and Mayne (1981), in an observational study of 60 middle- and lower-income Black fathers interacting with their preschool children in the home, found that middle-income fathers were significantly more responsive to their children's developmental needs than were lower-income fathers, and that the middle-income fathers' level of responsiveness was identical to that of middle-income White mothers found in one of her previous studies. Allen (1985) found that Black fathers reported rewarding their sons by hugging and kissing them, whereas White fathers reported rewarding their sons with gifts as the children grew older. In contrast to Allen's findings, the fathers of preschoolers in my study (McAdoo, 1979) were more likely to report rewarding their children's good behavior with praise than with hugs and kisses. Thus Black fathers appear to favor child rearing strategies that involve some combination of warmth and support, as well as firm control, which is consistent with Baumrind's (1971) model of authoritative parenting, and which may help foster positive social and emotional development in children.

Fathers' Involvement in Child Rearing

A number of studies of Black fathers in two-parent families have found them to be involved in child care actively. Cazenave's (1979) study of 54 Black postal carriers found that they reported being involved in the disciplining of their children, helping them with homework, and transporting them for medical appointments. These men felt that they were more involved in routine child-care activities than their own fathers had been, and that they had close relationships with their children. Similarly, the Black fathers in Daniel's study (1975) felt that it was essential for the optimum growth and development of their children that they spend time with them. And while Allen (1985) found that Black fathers were the least likely of all groups to read child-care magazines, and most likely to feel that parents know as much as experts about child rearing, they were rated by Black mothers as being slightly more actively involved with their teenage sons than White mothers rated White fathers. On the other hand, Price-Bonham and Skeen (1979) found that Black fathers talked less often with their children than did White fathers, yet were more likely to feel that their children should be like them.

BLACK FATHERS WITH THEIR CHILDREN: AN OBSERVATIONAL STUDY

Naturalistic observation of parent–child interaction has become a preferred methodological approach in child rearing and socialization research (see, for example, the chapters by Bronstein, Tinsley & Parke, and Yogman, Cooley & Kindlon, Chapters 8, 17, and 4 respectively, this volume). However, studies of Black fathers' parenting behavior have generally depended solely on parents' self-reports, with very few looking at actual parent–child behaviors in either a home or laboratory setting (e.g., Hornig & Mayne, 1981; Baumrind, 1972). The study I will be describing here, of parenting behavior in Black and White middle-income families, was an attempt to apply this emerging methodology in an area where there are many stereotypes and misperceptions, and very little empirical evidence.

Method and Instruments

The subjects were 40 Black and 44 White intact families of preschoolers living in a suburban town in the Baltimore–Washington metropolitan area. The children, 39 girls (20 Black and 19 White) and 45 boys (20 Black and 25 White), were between the ages of three and six. The families, rated on the fathers' educational and occupational level, were all at least at a middle-income socioeconomic level, with 46% of the Black fathers and 65% of the White fathers judged to be at an upper-middle income level. While the study included both parents, for the purposes of this chapter only the findings relevant to fathers will be discussed.

Several data collection instruments were used:

1. The Radin (1972) Cognitive Home Environment Scale (CHES) to obtain background data on the fathers

2. The Radin Verbal Interaction Scale (1972) to gather data on the verbal interaction that took place between each father and his child
3. A modified version of the Thomas Self-Concept Values Test (1967), which
   used Polaroid pictures of the children as a basis for asking them how they
   felt about themselves, and how they felt significant others in their lives perceived them, specifically, their father, mother, preschool teachers, and
   peers.

In addition, four interviews were conducted, two with each father–child pair and
two with the child alone, the latter to gain further understanding of the child's self-
concept. The interviewers were trained Black and White male college graduates,
who were matched with the father by race to preclude cross-race interviewer effects.

During the first meeting the interviewer introduced the project to the father in the
presence of the child, explained the interviewing procedures, and stressed the need
to have the child present throughout the interviewing process. The interviewer's
goals for the first interview were to gather background data on the family, become
acquainted with the child, and have the family become comfortable with his
presence.

Data on verbal interactions were gathered in the second interview, which was
tape recorded. Each father was interviewed for an hour and a half with the child
present; the child's presence was requested ostensibly because he or she would play
a game later in the session with the father. However, the real interaction data was
recorded during the interview. The assumption of this study was that the child
would become restless during the interview and make demands to which the father
would respond. Later, the tapes were analyzed to determine the 2 consecutive
15-minute segments that contained the most verbal interaction. These segments
were then coded by two assistants working independently, using Radin's (1972) 26
categories for coding parents' verbal interactions. The coders, who were trained by
Radin's staff, achieved an intercoder reliability of .92.

A factor analysis done by Radin on the 26 categories had identified 2 major
categories—nurturance and restrictiveness. Nurturant behavior referred to the
father's warmth, his meeting the implicit and explicit needs of his child, his reinforcing and motivating positive behavior in his child, and his setting limits, with explanation, on the child's behavior. An example of this limit setting would be a father saying to his child, "No, you cannot turn on the television now, because I am
talking to this interviewer and it would disturb us." Restrictive behavior was defined
as exercising sharp verbal control of the child, usually in the form of reprimands,
demands, or threats, without explanation, when the child violated family expectations or standards. An example of this type of behavior would be the father's raising
his voice and demanding that the child stop jumping on the sofa. Or he might repri-
mand the child by saying, "You're being a real pest today." The father might even
physically restrain the child in his lap if the negative behavior persisted. Separate
nurturance and restrictiveness frequency totals were obtained, and proportional
scores were then calculated by dividing the nurturance and restrictiveness frequency
totals by the combined frequency of both categories. Verbal interactions initiated by

the child were also coded, because we were interested in examining the relationship between the child-initiated interactions and types of father responses.

Results and Discussion

Among both Black and White fathers, 75% were predominantly warm, loving, and nurturant in their interactions with their children, with no differences found between fathers of boys and fathers of girls. In addition, no socioeconomic differences in paternal nurturance patterns were found. White fathers interacted significantly more with their children in the interview situation than Black fathers, White mothers, or Black mothers, whereas Black fathers (though the finding was not statistically significant) had the lowest amount of interaction of all four groups. However, the amount of interaction between father and children was not significantly related to the way the children evaluated themselves (McAdoo & McAdoo, 1986).

Children whose fathers were predominantly nurturant sat and played contentedly during the 90-minute session, and made very few demands on their fathers' time. Their fathers seemed to be aware of them throughout the interview, and cognizant of their needs. For example, if a predominantly nurturant father thought his child might need to go to the bathroom, he would interrupt the interview to check that out, and he would also interrupt the interview to respond to any questions from the child. Or he might simply cuddle the child on his lap for a time, while he was talking. On the other hand, the children of the 25% of the fathers who were identified as predominantly restrictive were more restless, and made repeated demands for their fathers' attention. They more frequently wanted to go to the bathroom or turn on the television, and in many instances, did not accept their father's first negative response. The restrictive fathers seemed to be forced to respond in more controlling ways, as their children did not appear to understand or accept their attempts to control their behavior.

The interactions between the restrictive fathers and their children seems to have been a reciprocal process, with the children playing an active role. The children's misbehavior and demands for attention tended to evoke restrictive parental responses. This perspective has been discussed in a review by Bell (1968), and supported in a study by Osofsky and O'Connell (1972), who reported significant changes in parents' behavior in response to their children. Similar reciprocal patterns have been reported in studies of mother–child interaction, particularly with behaviorally aggressive children (e.g., Patterson, 1980).

The findings suggest that children of more restrictive fathers may not have been as able to pick up cues from their fathers to control their own behavior. It is also possible that these fathers may not have been as involved in the child-rearing process as the more nurturant fathers, and thus were less sensitive to their children's needs. It is important to note, however, that while children with restrictive fathers apparently suffered no seriously distressing consequences from their misbehavior, a study of fathers and children in more stressful economic or social environment might reveal a different outcome.

No differences were found on the Thomas Self-Concept Values Test between the

Black and White children on how they felt about themselves, or how they felt their fathers perceived them. The self-esteem scores of the children were all in the positive range. In addition, there was no relationship between the child's self-esteem and the father's pattern of interaction, which suggests that the relationship, if any, between father–child interaction and self-esteem may be indirect, mediated by factors not measured in the present study. For example, an important direction for future research on families would be to consider the connection between patterns of interaction between husband and wife, and the development of their children's self-esteem and psychological and social competence (McAdoo & McAdoo, 1986).

These findings add to the growing body of evidence, from recent research on Black fathers' parenting behaviors, that middle income and well-to-do Black fathers look very much like their White counterparts in their relationships with their children. This supports the hypothesis stated earlier, that the existing stereotype of the absent or otherwise deficient Black father is very much a product of research that focused in a very limited way on economically disadvantaged Black families, with the results often generalized to all Black fathers and their families.

CONCLUSION

This chapter briefly considered the research on Black fathers from their enslavement to the present. I reviewed some of the literature on Black father absence, which appears to be related to unique economic, social, and historical factors affecting many Black families in this country, such as persistent poverty and long-term unemployment. However, though the causes for father absence may generally differ for Black and White families, no differences have been found for the two groups in the effects on children.

I then examined the role of Black fathers within the family unit, comparing them across socioeconomic levels and with fathers from other racial/ethnic groups. Overall, Black fathers in maritally intact families seemed to show child-rearing attitudes and perceived levels of involvement with their children that are very similar to those of fathers from other groups. Black and White fathers and their wives generally reported sharing equally in household and family decision making. Fathers of both races tended to be firm in their expectations of their children's behavior, and were similar in expecting their sons to behave in a mature, independent fashion—though Black fathers in some studies tended to be more restrictive in their expectations and reported behaviors. Further, both Black and White fathers were found to be predominantly nurturant, warm, and loving towards their children.

Variations in these findings from different studies on fathering attitudes and behavior may have been influenced by attitudes and values in the region of the country where a family lives, and by socioeconomic differences. Future research should address regional differences in child rearing attitudes, as well as differences related to socioeconomic status. One important question is the degree to which economic stress influences a father's ability to remain within his family and provide consistent nurturance and guidance for his children. Finally, future research on the Black father's role within the family should ideally include both cross-sectional and longitudinal observations, and take into account the perceptions of all family members on the father's role in the child-rearing process.

REFERENCES

Albee, G.W. (1982). Preventing psychopathology and promoting human potential. *American Psychologist, 37*(9), 1043–1050.

Allen, W.R. (1985). Race, income and family dynamics: A study of adolescent male socialization processes and outcomes. In M.B. Spencer, G.K. Brookins, & W.R. Allen (Eds.), *Beginnings: The social and affective development of black children*. Hillsdale, NJ: Erlbaum.

Bacon, M.K., Child, I.L., & Barry, H., III. (1963). A cross-cultural study of correlates of crime. *Journal of Abnormal and Social Psychology, 66*(4), 291–300.

Bandura, A., & Walters, R.H. (1959). *Adolescent aggression*. New York: Ronald.

Bartz, K.W., & Levine, E.S. (1979). Childrearing by Black parents: A description and comparison to Anglo and Chicano parents. *Journal of Marriage and the Family, 40*(4), 709–720.

Baumrind, D. (1971). Current patterns of parental authority. *Developmental Psychology Monographs, 4*, 1–103.

Baumrind, D. (1972). An exploratory study of socialization effects on black children: Some black-white comparisons. *Child Development, 43*(1), 261–267.

Bell, R.Q. (1968). A reinterpretation of the direction of effects in studies of socialization. *Psychological Review, 75*(2), 81–95.

Biller, H.B. (1976). The father and personality development: Paternal deprivation and sex-role development. In M.E. Lamb (Ed.), *The role of the father in child development*. New York: Wiley.

Blassingame, J.W. (1979). *The slave community: Plantation life in the antebellum south*. New York: Oxford University Press.

Cazenave, N.A. (1979). Middle income black fathers: An analysis of the provider role. *Family Coordinator, 28*(4), 583–593.

Coleman, J.S., Campbell, E.Q., Hobson, C.J., McParland, J., Mood, A.M., Weinfeld, F.D., & York, R.L. (1966). *Equality of educational opportunity*. Washington, DC: U.S. Government Printing Office.

Cortés, C.F., & Fleming, E. (1968). The effects of father absence on the adjustment of culturally disadvantaged boys. *Journal of Special Education, 2*, 413–420.

Cromwell, V.L., & Cromwell, R.E. (1978). Perceived dominance in decision making and conflict resolution among Anglo, Black, and Chicano couples. *Journal of Marriage and the Family, 40*(4), 749–769.

Daniel, T.E. (1975). *A definition of fatherhood as expressed by black fathers*. Unpublished doctoral dissertation, University of Pittsburgh.

Deutsch, M. (1960). Minority group and class status as related to social and personality factors in scholastic achievement. *Monograph of the Society for Applied Anthropology, 2*. Ithaca, NY: Society for Applied Anthropology.

Deutsch, M., & Brown, B. (1964). Social influences in negro-white intelligence differences. *Journal of Social Issues 20*(2), 24–35.

Elder, G.H., Jr. (1968). Adolescent socialization and development. In E.F. Borgatta & W.W. Lambert (Eds.), *Handbook of personality theory and research*. Chicago: Rand McNally.

Elkins, S.M. (1959). *Slavery: A problem in American institutional life*. Chicago: University of Chicago Press.

Fogel, R.W., & Engerman, S.L. (1974). *Time on the cross: Evidence and methods*. Boston: Little, Brown.

Franklin, J.H. (1967). *From slavery to freedom: A history of Negro Americans*. New York: Knopf.

Frazier, E.F. (1966). *The Negro family in the United States*. Chicago: University of Chicago Press.

Furstenberg, F.F., Jr., Hershberg, T., & Model, J. (1975). The origins of the female-headed black family: The impact of the urban experience. *Journal of Interdisciplinary History*, 6(2), 211–233.

Genovese, E. (1976). *Roll, Jordan, roll: The world the slaves made*. New York: Vintage.

Green, M.A. (1975). Impact of slavery on the black family: Social political, economic. *Journal of Afro-American Issues*, 3, 347–356.

Gutman, H.G. (1976). *The black family in slavery and freedom, 1750–1925*. New York: Pantheon.

Herzog, E., & Sudia, C. (1973). Children in fatherless families. In B.M. Caldwell & H.N. Ricciuti (Eds.), *Review of child development research (vol. 3)*. Chicago: University of Chicago Press.

Hess, R.D., Shipman, V.C., Brophy, J.E., & Bear, R.M. (1968). *The cognitive environments of urban preschool children*. Chicago: University of Chicago Press.

Hornig, A.S., & Mayne, G. (1981). Black fathering in three social class groups. Unpublished manuscript, College of Human Development, Syracuse University.

Jackson, J.J. (1974). Ordinary black husband-fathers: The truly hidden men. *Journal of Social and Behavioral Sciences*, 20(2), 19–27.

Lamb, M.E. (1981). Fathers and child development: An integration view. In M.E. Lamb (Ed.), *The role of the father in child development*. New York: Wiley.

Liebow, E. (1967). *Tally's corner*. Boston: Little, Brown.

Mack, D.E. (1974). The power relationship in black families and white families. *Journal of Personality and Social Psychology*, 30, 409–413.

McAdoo, J. (1979). Father-child interaction patterns and self-esteem in black preschool children. *Young Children*, 34(2), 46–53.

McAdoo, J., & McAdoo, H. (1986 Nov.). *The impact of paternal interaction patterns on the self-esteem of black and white preschool children*. Paper presented at the annual meeting of the National Council on Family Relations, Dallas.

Middleton, R., & Putney, S. (1960). Dominance in decisions in the family: Race and class differences. *American Journal of Sociology*, 65, 605–609.

Miller, W.B. (1958). Lower class culture as a generating milieu of gang delinquency. *Journal of Social Issues*, 14(3), 5–19.

Moynihan, D.P. (1965). *The Negro family: The case for national action*. Washington, DC: U.S. Government Printing Office.

Myrdal, G. (1944). *An American dilemma: the Negro problem and modern democracy*. New York: Harper.

Neckerman, K.M., & Wilson, W.J. (1986). Poverty and family structure: The widening gap between evidence and policy issues. In S.H. Danziger & D.H. Weinberg (Eds.), *Fighting poverty: What works and what doesn't*. Cambridge, MA: Harvard University Press.

Nichols, C.H. (1972). *Black men in chains: Narratives by escaped slaves*. New York: Hill.

Osofsky, J.D., & O'Connell, E.J. (1972). Parent-child interaction: Daughters' effects upon mothers' and fathers' behaviors. *Developmental Psychology*, 7(2), 157–168.

Patterson, G.R. (1980). Mothers: The unacknowledged victims. *Monograph of the Society for Research in Child Development*, 45(5).

Pettigrew, T.F. (1964). *A profile of the Negro American*. Princeton, NJ: Van Nostrand.

Price-Bonham, S., & Skeen, P. (1979). A comparison of black and white fathers with implications for parents' education. *Family Coordinator*, 28(1), 53–59.

Radin, N. (1972). Father-child interaction and the intellectual functioning of four-year old boys. *Developmental Psychology*, 6(2), 353–361.

Rivara, F., Sweeney, P., & Henderson, B. (1986). Black teenage fathers: What happens when the child is born? *Pediatrics*, 78(1), 151–158.

Scarpitti, F.R., Murray, E., Dinitz, S., & Reckless, W.C. (1960). The "good" boy in a high delinquency area: Four years later. *American Sociological Review*, 25(4), 555–558.

Stack, C.B. (1986). *Sex roles and survival strategies in an urban black community*. In R. Staples (Ed.), *The black family: Essays and studies* (3rd ed.). New York: Harper & Row.

TenHouten, W.D. (1970). The black family: Myth and reality. *Psychiatry*, 33, 145–173.

Thomas, W. (1967). The Thomas Self-Concept Values Test. Grand Rapids, Michigan: Educational Service Co.

U.S. Bureau of the Census statistical abstracts of the United States. (1986a). Family groups with children under age 18 by race and type, 1970 to 1984. Washington, DC: U.S. Government Printing Office.

U.S. Bureau of the Census statistical abstracts of the United States. (1986b). Civilian labor force employment by status, sex, race and age: 1984. Washington, DC: U.S. Government Printing Office.

U.S. Bureau of the Census statistical abstracts of the United States. (1986c). Median family income by number of earners and race of household: 1983. Washington, DC: U.S. Government Printing Office.

U.S. Bureau of the Census statistical abstracts of the United States. (1986d). Median family income in current and constant (1984) dollars by race and Spanish origin of householder: 1950–1984. Washington, DC: U.S. Government Printing Office.

Wasserman, H.L. (1969). Father-absent and father-present lower-class Negro families: A comparative study of family functioning. *Dissertation Abstracts*, 29(12-A), 4569–4570.

Willie, C.V. (1976). *A new look at black families*. Bayside, NY: General Hall.

CHAPTER 7

Chicano Fathers

Traditional Perceptions and Current Realities

ALFREDO MIRANDÉ

One of the most significant consequences of the Women's Movement of the 1970s and 1980s was an increased awareness of and sensitivity to changing and emergent gender roles. While there has been considerable interest on the part of social scientists in the way women respond and adapt to change, only recently has attention turned to the response and adaptation of men to alterations in traditional gender roles (Lewis & Pleck, 1979; Pleck, 1981; Pleck & Brannon, 1978). Ethnic and sociocultural factors have in some cases been taken into account; the topic of Black male roles and masculinity, for example, has received considerable scholarly attention (Coles, 1977; McAdoo, this volume; Taylor, 1977; Turner, 1977; Wilkinson & Taylor, 1977). On the other hand, systematic study of the role of the male within the Chicano family has been virtually nonexistent.

That Chicano male roles have not been studied empirically is surprising, given that social scientists have had a long-standing interest in and concern with Chicano masculinity or machismo (Baca Zinn, 1982; Mirandé, 1985). Generalizations concerning the male role in the Chicano family abound, but tend, unfortunately, to be based on meager or nonexistent evidence. Much of this literature depicts an authoritarian, patriarchal unit where the macho (i.e., male) is lord and master of the household and the woman is a quiet, submissive, servile figure. Although the traditional view has begun to be called into question by recent findings (which suggest that Chicano males may be less dominant and Chicano females less submissive than was previously believed), such studies have typically been concerned with the female role or with conjugal decision making rather than with the male role per se. Especially neglected has been the role of the father within the Chicano family. A systematic analysis of changing male roles and masculinity, and specifically of the Chicano father role is therefore long overdue.

Partial support for this project was provided by a grant from the Academic Senate Committee on Research, University of California, Riverside, and by a Rockefeller Foundation Research Fellowship for Minority-Group Scholars. During the 1985–86 academic year I was in residence as a postdoctoral fellow at The Stanford Center for Chicano Research (SCCR) and SCCR greatly facilitated completion of this chapter.

This chapter includes an analysis of the male role within the Chicano family, and a comprehensive assessment of the literature on Chicano fathers. Specifically, two conflicting theoretical models of the Chicano family are examined and critically evaluated: The traditional authoritarian, male-dominated model described above, and a more recent, emerging perspective on *la familia*, which depicts it as less rigid and authoritarian, and more child-centered than was previously believed. In the former, the father is the provider and the instrumental leader of the family, and the wife–mother is the socioemotional leader and the source of warmth, affection, and succor, especially to her children. In the latter, the Chicano family is seen as warm, nurturing, and supportive, with the father assuming a significant role within that unit.

CHICANO FAMILY ROLES: CONFLICTING MODELS

The Traditional Model

While there has been little research on the role of the father in the Chicano family, there is an extensive literature characterizing both the Mexican and Chicano family in terms of the traditional model. Such studies have had a heavy psychoanalytic focus, and have attempted to isolate a model Mexican personality. The traditional model has infused the works of many scholars such as Bermúdez (1955), Díaz-Guerrero (1975), and Gilbert (1959), with perhaps its most noteworthy proponents being Ramos and Paz. The renowned Chicano folklorist Américo Paredes (1967) has identified Ramos as the originator of this viewpoint and Paz as its most eloquent defender.

The Mexican male, according to this view, is driven by a pervasive feeling of inferiority and by the rejection of authority. According to Ramos (1962):

> One must presuppose the existence of an inferiority complex in all those people who show an excessive concern with affirming their personality, who take vital interest in all things and situations that signify power, and who demonstrate an immoderate eagerness to excel, to be first in everything. (p. 81)

Thus the male's overly masculine (or macho) response is but a futile attempt to mask pervasive feelings of inferiority and ineptitude (Baca Zinn, 1975; Montiel, 1970). This pathological force or cult of machismo is said to permeate and color all aspects of life, especially relations between the sexes.

In his treatise on Mexican national character, *The Labyrinth of Solitude*, Paz (1961) similarly depicts the macho as the *gran chingón*. *The verb chingar* has numerous and diverse meanings but it always connotes some form of violence, or "an emergence from oneself to penetrate another by force" (p. 76). The *gran chingón* is aggressive, insensitive, unpredictable, and invulnerable, but what most clearly identifies him is power, in that "He opens the world; in doing so, he rips and tears it, and this violence provokes a great, sinister laugh" (p. 81). By contrast, women are believed to be passive and inert. Both the "bad woman" as represented by the violated mother (*La Chingada*), and the "good woman" as represented by the Virgin Mary (Guadalupe-Tonantzin[1]), are passive symbols, according to Paz:

> Guadalupe is pure receptivity, and the benefits she bestows are of the same order; she consoles, quiets, dries tears, calms passions. The *Chingada* is even more passive. Her passivity is abject: she does not resist violence, but is an inert heap of bones, blood and dust. Her taint is constitutional and resides, as we said earlier, in her sex. (p. 85)

While *La Chingada* was clearly a victim of the Conquest, symbolizing the thousands of Indian women who were raped or otherwise sexually assaulted by the Spanish, she is chastised in Mexican folklore for somehow "opening herself up" to the conqueror. According to this view, all women, even those who willingly enter a sexual liaison, are believed to be "torn open" by the man.

Other social scientists have similarly described the Mexican family as a patriarchal unit, in which the married man is permitted to pursue the same life style he maintained as a bachelor. Women, on the other hand, are described as protected and isolated before marriage, and severely restricted after marriage. A very strong element of machismo, according to this view, is that a woman be respectful of her husband.

One of the foremost proponents of this model of the Mexican family is cultural anthropologist Oscar Lewis, who has carried out ethnographic field work in both urban (1961) and rural (1960) settings. After three years of field work in Tepoztlán, a village located south of Mexico City, Lewis (1960) concluded that the ideal Mexican cultural pattern, which may not always be observed, is for the husband to be master of the household and to make all major decisions. The father supposedly avoids intimacy with other family members in order to maintain their respect, and his sense of security is said to be often gauged by the extent to which he is able to control and instill fear in his wife and children.

> Wife beating, more common in the past than now but still widespread, is resorted to for offenses that range from not having a good meal ready on time to suspicion of adultery. A jealous wife or a wife who objects to her husband's activities or judgment may also receive a beating. (p. 56)

Despite the power vested in the father role, family life, according to Lewis, revolves primarily around the mother, who is seen as having more ways of demonstrating affection toward children. The father, on the other hand, is depicted as being severely limited in this area. Rather than being directly affectionate, he may demonstrate his affection by buying them small gifts, giving them pennies, or taking them to a *fiesta*. Severe punishment is common and, although mothers punish more often, fathers are said to administer more extreme punishment. The father

---

[1]Tonantzin was the Pre-Columbian Goddess of fertility. The apparition of *La Virgen de Guadalupe* to a young converted Indian named Juan Diego took place on the site of an ancient religious sanctuary to this Indian Goddess (Mirandé, 1985, p. 126). For many followers, Guadalupe and Tonantzin are one and the same.

is described as assuming an important role in the lives of male children after they are old enough to work in the fields. But "regardless of age or marital status, a son is subject to his father's authority as long as he lives with his father" (p. 61).

Social scientists have often assumed that this rigid, authoritarian model of the Mexican family and the father role is also applicable to Mexicans living in the United States. Despite the absence of empirical evidence to support this view, until very recently the Chicano family and the Mexican family were considered to be isomorphic.

Madsen's (1973) ethnographic study of Mexican Americans in South Texas, with its description of the Mexican-American family, for example, is very similar to Lewis' depiction of the Mexican family and Mexican cultural values. Fieldwork was carried out in four communities in Hidalgo County ranging from a rural-folk society to an urban center. According to Madsen, among Mexican cultural values, machismo ranks second in importance only to devotion to family. Thus men are driven by the cult of machismo and an incessant preoccupation with sex. The macho is likened to a rooster, so that the better man is the one who can have the most girlfriends or, if married, the most extramarital affairs. A real man is "proud, self-reliant, and virile" (p. 22). Women, on the other hand, are expected to honor and respect their husbands, despite infidelity or abuse. The cult of machismo, as seen by Madsen, also dictates that Mexican-American men prove themselves stronger, smarter, and superior to women in every respect. "Where he is strong, she is weak. Where he is aggressive, she is submissive. While he is condescending toward her, she is respectful toward him" (p. 22). Not only are wives who are not compliant subjected to physical punishment and abuse, but they are expected to accept this punishment as being somehow deserved. Some wives are even "grateful for punishment at the hands of their husbands for such concern with shortcomings indicates profound love" (p. 22).

As a father, according to Madsen, the Mexican-American man may be affectionate with very small children, but his authoritarian role is clearly established by the time children enter puberty. Whereas the mother is loved and adored, the father is feared and obeyed. His role is one of policing family members to assure that they stay in line and do not dishonor the family. The position of the father is such that "Ideally the Latin male acknowledges only the authority of his father and God. In case of conflict between these two sources of authority, he should side with his father" (p. 20).

Robert G. Hayden's (1966) description of the Hispanic family in the Southwest closely parallels Madsen's. The family, according to Hayden, is under the firm control of the father. Whereas the woman is quiet and subservient, defining her role primarily in terms of bearing and rearing children and being a homemaker, the man sees his role as dictated by the values of machismo or *hombría* (manliness). The male stresses attributes such as male dominance, assertiveness, pride, and sexual prowess. Hayden contends, moreover, that large families are taken as a sign of virility and machismo, and that physical punishment of a wife by her husband is culturally accepted and justified (p. 20).

Carroll (1980), in a comparison of violence in Mexican-American and Jewish families, takes the argument a step further by suggesting that the authoritarian Chicano family structure produces a very high level of family violence. After reviewing literature that supports the traditional view of the Mexican/Chicano family, Carroll concludes that values and norms that are an accepted part of Chicano culture engender family violence, and hypothesizes that

> the higher level of violence in Mexican-American families [is] associated with the values of severe male dominance, strict discipline, and submission to the father. . . . Perpetuation of this subculture is accomplished through the desire of boys to be like their fathers even though they fear them, and because a child turned adult treats his wife and children the same way his father treated his family. (p. 80)

In short, the authoritarian role of the older male within the Mexican-American family is proposed to lead to distant and severe relations between fathers and children, especially male children, and to the acceptance of violence as a legitimate mechanism for resolving family conflicts.

In another ethnographic study in a Texas community, *Across the Tracks*, Rubel (1966) argues that respect for elders and male dominance are the two most basic organizing principles of the Mexican-American family, so that ideally "the older order the younger, and the men the women" (p. 59). The belief that a man's home is his castle is widely accepted and the husband/father is expected to dominate the nuclear family. Respect for the father is such that children, even as adults, according to Rubel, often do not drink or smoke in his presence. They may even be reluctant to laugh or tell jokes in front of him, as illustrated by the following account given by one of Rubel's respondents.

> My mother is quiet and seldom laughs or tells jokes. I never tell jokes to my mother because I have respect for her; but my younger sister is the clown of the family. . . . Sometimes I, too, will tell jokes to my mother, when we're with my younger sister. I *never* tell jokes to my father! We [the children] don't even talk with him! If we are laughing in his presence, he right away wants to know what we are laughing about. He thinks that maybe we are laughing about something that he did. (p. 61)

Furthermore, as *jefe de la casa* (head of the household), the father represents the family to the outside world and, according to Rubel, the conduct of each member of the family is seen as ultimately reflecting on him. Thus because of the strong imperative for paternal respect, one of the worst things that a person can do is to bring shame or dishonor to *la familia*.

An Emergent Model

The traditional view of the Mexican/Chicano family has been called into question by a more recent perspective, which proposes that the Chicano family is more egalitarian and the power of the male less absolute than was previously believed. This new model is buttressed by empirical studies of conjugal decision making and ac-

tion taking which, while not focusing on the father roles per se, suggest that decisions are typically shared by Chicano husbands and wives.

Hawkes and Taylor (1975), for example, hypothesized that male dominance
would prevail among their sample of migrant farm families in California, but found
instead that the dominant pattern of decision making and action taking was essentially egalitarian. Similarly, findings from the Mexican-American Study Project
(Grebler, Moore, & Guzman, 1970), a major study carried out in Los Angeles and
San Antonio, did not support the patriarchal pattern. In fact, the authors found not
only that income, age, and gender had insubstantial effects on family decision making, but that a basically egalitarian division of household tasks prevailed.

While male dominance may have been considered the ideal pattern of decision
making among Mexican Americans, Grebler and colleagues (1970) argue that it has
probably never been the actual behavioral norm, either in Mexico or the United
States. Although most respondents said that the father "ran things," the mother was
the one seen as making the day-to-day decisions. Decisions relative to large pur-
chases and the like, moreover, were made jointly by husband and wife. In addition,
respondents were more likely to identify the mother, rather than the father, as having had "greater influence on them" (pp. 360–361). Thus according to the authors,
patriarchy and machismo are rooted in the rural past, and while the value of male
dominance persists as a cultural ideal, it is a value often breached among urban
Chicano families.

A study of 100 married couples in Fresno, California carried out by Ybarra
(1977, 1982) also did not find patriarchy to be the prevailing pattern, but instead
found conjugal roles that ranged from patriarchal to egalitarian. The factor that appeared to have the greatest impact on the type of conjugal role structure exhibited
was whether the wife worked outside the home. If the wife was employed, couples
were more likely to share household chores and child care, and have an egalitarian
role structure. Yet, according to Ybarra, "whether or not a wife was employed outside the home, the majority of husbands and wives in both groups shared decision
making" (1982, p. 173).

Others have suggested that while the prevailing cultural ideology is one of male
dominance, the Chicano family is, in actuality, mother-centered. Baca Zinn (1975)
has done much to resolve what appear to be contradictory tendencies in the literature
by suggesting that *la familia* is both patriarchal and mother-centered. Men traditionally represent the family in matters outside the home, while women are responsible
for the day-to-day functioning of the family. Thus, "Chicana's control of household
and family matters is the source from which their power is derived" (p. 27). However, she disagrees with Grebler and colleagues' contention that patriarchal values
are somehow more ideal than real, arguing that

> what appears more likely is that patriarchal values continue to provide the basic organ-
> izing principle for Chicano interaction, and that while women do have power in the do-
> mestic sphere, generalized male authority legitimates males to exercise power when
> and if Chicano males choose to exert their will. (p. 27)

Tuck's (1946) ethnographic study of *Descanso* in San Bernardino, California also challenges the traditional model of the Mexican/Chicano family. She observes that despite the alleged lowly status of women in Latin American society, women are honored and revered within the family. Legally, women have very little power or status.

> But the "good" woman, entrenched with her children in the circle of the great family, has some peculiar and wide-reaching powers. As the *madrecita* [beloved mother], entitled to respect and homage, she may actually dominate in all matters that affect her children. Hers may be the deciding voice in every important decision. (p. 123)

Most children acknowledge that it is the mother who generally makes critical decisions such as whether children will get new clothing or continue in school, and even if the father will move from one job to another. "My father did the talking," said a young Mexican American, "but it was my mother who really decided things" (p. 115).

MACHISMO, MASCULINITY, AND THE FATHER ROLE

While the traditional view of the Mexican/Chicano family as patriarchal and authoritarian has been challenged in recent years, available research, unfortunately, has tended to focus either on the female role or on the process of conjugal decision making, rather than on the male role as such. As a result, there is very little actual data on important topics such as the role of the father in the family, the relationship between fathers and children, changing conceptions of masculinity, or the way Chicano men have responded to alterations in traditional gender roles and conceptions of masculinity.

It is only recently that researchers have considered the father role as a worthy area of study. The research, although limited and sometimes based on impressionistic findings, has brought into question the image of the Mexican/Chicano father as a cold and distant figure. Luzod and Arce (1979), in a study based on 88 interviews from a sample of Mexican ancestry households in southwest Detroit, found that fathers play a much more important role in the family than is commonly thought. They concluded that

> it therefore appears erroneous to focus only on maternal influence in the Chicano family since Chicano fathers are seen as being important to their children, and moreover, may provide significant positive influences on the development of their children."
> (p. 19)

The results showed that husbands and wives each defined their role as parent as being very similar to that of their spouse, and that there were no significant sex differences on any of the three parenting scales they administered. These findings are inconsistent with the traditional model of the Chicano family, and instead support a more egalitarian view of Mexican/Chicano family roles.

A study of 78 parent–child dyads in 19 Mexican families carried out by Bronstein (1984) found that fathers were much more playful and companionable with their children than one would expect from the traditional image of Mexican parental roles. Further, she found that compared with mothers, fathers spent a significantly greater proportion of their time with their children engaged in playful, companionable interaction. Bronstein concluded that fathers

> played a distinct and salient role of their own, different from mothers, and very different from the traditional view of the aloof Mexican patriarch. Although there is no measure of the hours per day each father in the present sample spent at home, most did seem to spend most of their non-working hours and their days off there or in recreational pursuits with their families. Furthermore, when they were with their children, many of the fathers seemed genuinely involved with them, in friendly, nonauthoritarian interaction. (p. 1000)[2]

Similar findings have been reported among Mexican Americans. Rubel (1966), in his ethnographic study of a Texas city, noted that despite the fact that fathers were generally viewed as distant and aloof, especially by young men, they were observed to be very warm and affectionate in relating to very young children.

> Without exception, direct observations note the warmth and affection exhibited by fathers with their young sons and daughters, children under 10 years of age. In several instances the field notes comment that the father was, in fact, far more gentle with his children than was their mother. (p. 66)

In applying an Adlerian perspective to the Mexican-American family, Zapata and Jaramillo (1981) also raise a number of significant questions about the prevailing literature, which depicts *la familia* as rigidly structured along sex and gender lines. Their findings, based on a sample of 32 sets of Chicano parents and 123 children in a large Southwestern city, are inconclusive, but they fail to support the view that Chicano fathers are dominant and distant, and the mothers passive and dependent, or that children are socialized into rigid gender roles. The results indicate that children perceive females as being somehow "socially more cooperative," and alliances within the family as tending to be sex-based. Parents, on the other hand, appear to allocate family responsibilities irrespective of the sex of the family member. Significantly, whereas children clearly differentiate sibling roles and alliances, "neither parents nor children clearly nominate either parent as responsible for 'managing' the household" (p. 286).

Machismo or Male Chauvinism?

While these more recent findings indicate that Mexican/Chicano family roles are more egalitarian and fathers less dominant than was suggested by the traditional view, there is reason to believe that male dominance prevails, nonetheless, not only

[2]For further description of this study, see Bronstein, Chapter 8, this volume.

among Chicanos but in society at large. After presenting an extensive review of male roles and masculinity, Baca Zinn (1982) concludes that "although male dominance may not typify marital decision making in Chicano families, it should not be assumed that it is nonexistent either in families or in other realms of interaction and organization" (pp. 33–34). She contends, moreover, that the ideology of patriarchy can exert an influence despite the presence of egalitarian decision making. It is thus essential to distinguish between male dominance as a cultural ideal and male dominance as a behavioral reality.

Perhaps the most significant contribution of Baca Zinn's analysis is that it seriously questions the assumption that male dominance is necessarily a cultural phenomenon. She proposes that masculine roles and masculine identity are shaped by a wide range of structural factors. That is, rather than viewing machismo in exclusively cultural terms, it is possible to see it as a response to the position of Chicanos in the stratification system, and their exclusion from public roles within society. White males, on the other hand, have generally had more roles open to them.

> However, this has not been the case for Chicanos or other men of color. Perhaps manhood takes on greater importance for those who do not have access to socially valued roles. Being male is one sure way to acquire status when other roles are systematically denied by the workings of society. . . . To be "hombre" may be a reflection of both ethnic and gender components and may take on greater significance when other roles and sources of masculine identity are structurally blocked. (p. 39)

However, although Baca Zinn presents an intriguing perspective on Chicano masculinity, her emphasis on structural variables is such that it virtually negates the possibility of any cultural impact. Thus it does not explain the apparent pervasiveness of the ideology of machismo across social classes in Mexico and the United States, or account for the prevalence of male dominance among white males. An additional problem in her conceptual analysis is the use of the terms male dominance, masculinity, gender segregation and stratification, masculine roles, and machismo interchangeably without defining them. Her perspective appears to regard machismo solely as male dominance effecting the subordination and exploitation of women.

On the other hand, other scholars have suggested that machismo may entail much more than male dominance, and that it is, in fact, a cultural value that transcends both gender and national boundaries. It is said to persist not only among men on both sides of the border but among women as well, with *la hemra* being the female counterpart of *el macho*. While this viewpoint acknowledges the presence of male dominance within Mexican/Chicano culture, it holds that male dominance is not peculiar to this group, and has little, if anything, to do with machismo or *hombría*. One can dominate and oppress women without being macho and one can certainly be *muy hombre* (very manly) without abusing or controlling them. Delgado (1974–75) maintains that

> a man who beats up his wife is not a macho, but a coward and an abuzon. A man who steps out on his old lady and has extramarital affairs is not macho but a sinverguenza,

two-timing bato. A man who gets plastered, stoned or pulls a knife on his compas for no reason at all is not a macho but a drunk and troublemaker. These and other such attributes have been erroneously labeled as displays of Machismo.[3] (p. 6)

Mendoza (1962) has identified such behavior as "false" machismo. Genuine machismo is characterized by true bravery or valor, courage, generosity, and ferocity, while false machismo uses the appearance or semblance of these traits to mask cowardliness and fear.

Utilizing Adler's theory of "masculine protest," Ramos (1962) similarly argues that excessive demonstrations of masculinity, as found in the Mexican *pelado* (nobody), are in fact attempts to mask deeply ingrained feelings of inferiority and ineptitude. The *pelado* is said to be fixated on phallic symbolism, frequently consoling himself by holding his genitals and exclaiming *tengo muchos huevos!* ("I've got a lot of balls"). Another favorite expression, "I am your father," is also used to symbolize power and control. The success of any man is thus ultimately attributed to his "balls." Despite these external trappings, the *pelado*, like the false macho, is neither strong nor brave, but weak and cowardly, for ultimately his aggressiveness and assertiveness are designed to conceal inferiority and impotence. Insecurity and anxiety, moreover, are said to engender a pervasive feeling of distrust, a quality which Ramos believes is the most distinguishing aspect of Mexican national character.

While Baca Zinn (1982) categorically rejects the view that male dominance among Chicanos is essentially a cultural phenomenon, she does suggest that the patriarchal ideology, which she found manifested among both male dominant and egalitarian families, may be associated with family solidarity. She argues that perhaps

the father's authority is strongly upheld because family solidarity is important in a society that excludes and subordinates Chicanos. The tenacity of patriarchy may be more than a holdover from past tradition. It may also represent a contemporary cultural adaptation to the minority condition of structural discrimination. (p. 40)

If male dominance, aggressiveness, and a propensity toward violence are characteristic of false machismo, what then distinguishes true or genuine machismo? Delgado (1974–1975) contends that a true macho does not pick fights or abuse drugs and alcohol. Rather than being irresponsible, he is extremely reliable and responsible. A man's sense of accomplishment and self-worth is, in fact, determined largely by his ability to provide for and protect his wife and children. One who is a drunkard, a troublemaker, or does not take care of his family, would hardly qualify as a macho. Sanchez (1979) also notes that the literature has emphasized the negative aspects of machismo and neglected its more positive implications, such as "responsibility, being a good husband and father, providing for one's family, strength in adversity" (p. 55). Although maintaining honor and integrity within the family and in the community are very important elements of machismo, perhaps its most

[3]Translations from Spanish of terms quoted are—*abuzón*, bully; *sinverguenza*, shameless; *bato*, dude; and *compas*, buddies.

pervasive characteristic, according to Delgado, is a noncompromising or intransigent nature. "This does not mean that a macho does not change his mind or that he doesn't bargain on a trade or issue, but he does this before arriving at a noncompromising level from which he is immovable even if it costs his life" (p. 6).

Ramirez (1979) similarly observed that the negative aspects of machismo have been stressed to the point where it has become synonymous not only with Mexican-American males, but with male chauvinism. The problem with such a conceptualization is that it transforms male chauvinism, which is cross-cultural, into a culture-specific trait. Ramirez argues that in order to gain a better understanding of Chicano culture and the role of the male within the family, it is necessary to redefine machismo, and to recognize its positive elements.

> *Machismo's* new definition translates into such positive cultural characteristics as respect, honesty, loyalty, fairness, responsibility and trustworthiness. A *macho* is affectionate, hard working, amiable and family oriented. He can admit his mistakes and knows when to ask for help. (p. 62)

Chicano Fathers Today: Emerging Roles

A study of the father role in Anglo-American and Mexican-American families carried out by Mejia (1975) concluded that despite the prevalence of the theoretical paradigm that depicts the Mexican-American family as rigid and authoritarian, cross-ethnic comparisons suggested that parental roles are more similar than dissimilar (p. 179). Mejia found that "Mexican Americans did not adhere to published conceptions of authoritarianism-traditionalism, extended family or the submissive wife concept as noted in the literature" (p. 179). In terms of self-ratings, Anglo-American mothers were most permissive in their treatment of children and Mexican-American mothers were most restrictive, but Anglo- and Mexican-American fathers did not differ in their level of permissiveness (p. 96). In addition, both Anglo-American and Mexican-American fathers mentioned responsibility as an important component of the father role. Mexican-Americans stressed fulfilling paternal responsibility "in the context of providing needs such as finances and basic necessities like food and shelter" (p. 115). One Mexican-American described his childhood view of his father as "a person that is responsible. One who supplies the money to survive. I saw my father as the guy who was gone in the daytime and home at night" (pp. 115–116). Although the Chicano respondents were middle-class and on a par economically with their Anglo counterparts, their experience with poverty in childhood appeared to have shaped their conception of the father role as adults.

Findings from a qualitative study of 22 Chicano house husbands in Southern California carried out by Chavez (1984) suggest that Hispanic males are able to adjust to drastic alterations in traditional gender roles. Although some of the men in the study were employed part time outside the home, in all instances the female was defined as the principle breadwinner and the man as the house husband. Some men were teased by friends, called *chavalas* (girls), or said to be "pussy whipped," but most were able to reconcile their new role and retain their masculine identity. One reason for this may have been that, despite the fact that men's primary role centered around the maintenance of the home, and that they assumed more household and child-care responsibilities than they had in the past, women continued to perform most of the traditional female chores such as doing the laundry, cooking, paying the bills, and feeding and caring for children. Another reason for the acceptance of the house husband role was that it was defined as a temporary status necessitated by economic contingencies over which the men had little or no control.

One of the few studies to focus on Mexican/Chicano fathers, and specifically on single custodial fathers, was carried out by Nieto (1983), who notes that while the phenomenon of single fatherhood has received national attention, virtually no information is available on Hispanic single fathers. Based on findings from a sample of 200 questionnaire responses and 50 personal interviews in four metropolitan areas in Texas, as well as on clinical experience as a psychotherapist and interviews with five custodial fathers in a large Mexican city, Nieto concludes that while the single Hispanic father deviates from the cultural norm, "it can be reasonably expected that once 'permission' for the family style is granted, the full resources of the Hispanic family will be mobilized in its support" (p. 19). Nieto believes that Chicano fathers face a paradoxical situation, in the sense that the strong family orientation of a single-parent household provides a great deal of impetus for the male to be family-oriented, and thus to assume custody of his children, yet at the same time he has been socialized to play an instrumental, rather than an expressive parental role. Interestingly, a factor that appears to be especially significant for single Hispanic men on deciding to become custodial parents is the relationship that they had with their own fathers.

> *Almost* without exception, this relationship has been characterized by the fathers in question as reliable *but* distant, aloof and lacking in warmth. It is as if the potential single father, contemplating the disruption of his relationship with his children considers that "while I could not control my own father's attitudes and behaviors toward me, I—and only I—can and will control the quality of the relationship between my children and their father!" (pp. 17–18)

Thus the traditional view of the Mexican/Chicano family is being challenged not only by the presence of a growing number of Chicano house husbands and single fathers, but by recent research which indicates that *la familia* may be more egalitarian, and fathers less cold and aloof, than was once thought. In retrospect, the traditional model appears to have been based on a view of Mexican/Chicano culture that was deeply rooted in a romanticized, rural past. The bulk of the support for this model was derived from field research carried out by outsiders, who all too often lacked genuine knowledge and understanding of the cultural patterns they observed. Hence many of their conclusions simply served to reinforce or verify prevailing stereotypes and misconceptions about Chicano culture and family life. Paredes (1977) maintains that the problem with Anglo ethnographers like Madsen and Rubel was not that they were overtly racist, but that they were essentially ignorant of Chicano language and culture and had unconscious biases, which led them to force their data to fit "preconceived notions and stereotypes" (p. 2). Clearly, there is a need for research that is not only free of such preconceived notions and stereotypes, but which captures the subtlety and complexity of the father role within *la familia*, and enhances our understanding of machismo and masculinity.

REFERENCES

Baca Zinn, M. (1975). Chicanas: Power and control in the domestic sphere. *De Colores, 2*, 19–31.

Baca Zinn, M. (1982). Chicano men and masculinity. *Journal of Ethnic Studies, 10*, 29–44.

Bermúdez, M.E. (1955). *La vida familiar del mexicano*. Mexico City: Robredo.

Bronstein, P. (1984). Differences in mothers' and fathers' behaviors toward children: A cross-cultural comparison. *Developmental Psychology, 20*, 995–1003.

Carroll, J.C. (1980). A cultural consistency theory of family violence in Mexican-American and Jewish-ethnic groups. In M.A. Straus & G.T. Hotaling (Eds.), *The social causes of husband-wife violence*. Minneapolis: University of Minnesota Press.

Chavez, Virginia. (1984). Hispanic househusbands. Unpublished manuscript.

Coles, R. (1977). Black fathers. In D.Y. Wilkinson & R.L. Taylor (Eds.), *The Black male in America*. Chicago: Nelson-Hall.

Delgado, A. (1974–75). Machismo. *La Luz, 3*, no. 9, 6, and nos. 10–11, 7.

Díaz-Guerrero, R. (1975). *Psychology of the Mexican: Culture and personality*. Austin: University of Texas Press.

Gilbert, G.M. (1959). Sex differences in mental health in a Mexican village. *International Journal of Social Psychiatry, 3*, 208–213.

Grebler, L., Moore, J.W., & Guzman, R.C. (1970). *The Mexican-American people*. New York: Free Press.

Hawkes, G.R., & Taylor, M. (1975). Power structure in Mexican and Mexican-American farm labor families. *Journal of Marriage and the Family, 37*, 807–811.

Hayden, R.G. (1966). Spanish-Americans of the Southwest: Life style patterns and their implications. *Welfare in Review, 4*, 14–25.

Lewis, O. (1960). *Tepoztlan*. New York: Holt, Rinehart & Winston.

Lewis, O. (1961). *The children of Sanchez*. New York: Random House.

Lewis, R.A., & Pleck, J.H. (1979). Men's roles in the family. Special Issue. *Family Coordinator, 28*, 429–432.

Luzod, J.A., & Arce, C.H. (1979 December). *An exploration of the father role in the Chicano family*. Paper presented at the National Symposium on the Mexican American child, Santa Barbara, CA.

Madsen, W. (1973). *The Mexican-American of South Texas*. New York: Holt, Rinehart & Winston.

Mejia, D.P. (1975). Cross-ethnic father roles: Perceptions of middle class Anglo-American and Mexican-American parents. Doctoral dissertation, University of California, Irvine.

Mendoza, V.T. (1962). El machismo en Mexico al traves de las canciones, corridos y cantares. In *Cuadernos del instituto nacional de antropologia III*, 75–86. Buenos Aires: Ministerio de Educacion y Justica.

Mirandé, A. (1985). *The Chicano experience: An alternative perspective*. Notre Dame, IN: University of Notre Dame Press.

Montiel, M. (1970). The social science myth of the Mexican American family. *El Grito: A Journal of Contemporary Mexican American Thought*, *3*, 56–63.

Nieto, D.S. (1983). Hispanic fathers: The growing phenomenon of single fathers keeping their children. *National Hispanic Journal*, *1*, 15–19.

Paredes, A. (1967). Estados Unidos, Mexico, y el machismo. *Journal of Inter-American Studies*, *9*, 65–84.

Paredes, A. (1977). On ethnographic work among minority groups: A folklorist's perspective. *New Scholar*, *6*, 1–33.

Paz, O. (1961). *The labyrinth of solitude*. (Translated by L. Kemp.) New York: Grove. First published 1950.

Pleck, J.H. (1981). *The myth of masculinity*. Cambridge, MA: MIT Press.

Pleck, J.H., & Brannon, R. (1978). Male roles and the male experience: Introduction. *Journal of Social Issues*, *34*, 1–4.

Ramirez, R. (1979). Machismo: A bridge rather than a barrier to family and marital counseling. In P. Preciado Martin (Ed.), *La frontera perspective*. Tucson, AZ: La Frontera Center.

Ramos, S. (1962). *Profile of man and culture in Mexico*. (Translated by P.G. Earle.) Austin: University of Texas Press. First published 1938.

Rubel, A.J. (1966). *Across the tracks: Mexican-Americans in a Texas city*. Austin: University of Texas Press.

Sanchez, A.F. (1979). History and culture of the tecato (Chicano "junkie"): Implications for prevention and treatment. In P. Preciado Martin (Ed.), *La frontera perspective*. Tucson, AZ: La Frontera Center.

Taylor, R.L. (1977). Socialization of the Black male role. In D.Y. Wilkinson & R.L. Taylor (Eds.), *The Black male in America*. Chicago: Nelson-Hall.

Tuck, R.D. (1946). *Not with the fist: Mexican-Americans in a Southwest city*. New York: Harcourt, Brace.

Turner, W.H. (1977). Myths and stereotypes: The African man in America. In D.Y. Wilkinson & R.L. Taylor (Eds.), *The Black male in America* (pp. 122–144). Chicago: Nelson-Hall.

Wilkinson, D.Y., & Taylor, R.L. (1977). *The Black male in America*. Chicago: Nelson-Hall.

Ybarra, L. (1977). Conjugal role relationships in the Chicano family. Unpublished Ph.D. dissertation, University of California, Berkeley.

Ybarra, L. (1982). When wives work: The impact on the Chicano family. *Journal of Marriage and the Family*, *44*, 169–178.

Zapata, J.T., & Jaramillo, P.T. (1981). The Mexican American family: An Adlerian perspective. *Hispanic Journal of Behavioral Sciences*, *3*, 275–290.

CHAPTER 8

Father–Child Interaction

Implications for Gender-Role Socialization

PHYLLIS BRONSTEIN

In the past 10 years, widespread changes in family roles and structures, accompanied by a growing interest in gender-role development, have led developmental researchers to become more aware of the father's role in the family. Earlier research, based on the notion that mothers were the main agents of socialization in the child-rearing process, tended to disregard fathers, or else investigated father *absence* for its effects on gender-role development. Currently, however, in recognition of the likelihood that father *presence* has important effects on gender-role socialization, researchers have begun to look more closely at the kinds of direct involvement and interaction fathers have with children.

Parents can affect gender-role socialization both directly and indirectly. Direct ways involve the intended communication of cultural norms and values; for example, parents may directly teach children the activities that are considered gender-appropriate within a particular culture, such as fathers teaching sons to hunt or fish, cut firewood, or drive a tractor. Or parents may verbally communicate and reinforce what are considered to be appropriate gender-role behaviors, such as telling sons that big boys don't cry, or telling daughters that it is unladylike to sit with their legs apart. A slightly less direct approach is to structure the child's environment so as to foster different behaviors and self-perceptions in girls and boys; for example, without overtly assigning gender labels, parents may provide sex-typed toys or assign sex-typed chores, or may allow later curfews for sons than for daughters. Indirect messages, on the other hand, are generally conveyed through the frequency and quality of parent–child interaction—by how much time parents spend with sons versus with daughters, what kinds of activities they engage in with girls as compared to with boys, and how attentive, affectionate, or restrictive they may be with each sex in different situations. Finally, indirect messages are conveyed by modeling; parents, in everything they do in the family, are providing prototypes of male and female behavior for their children.

This chapter will consider the father's role in that transmission process. Since it would be too extensive a task to examine all aspects, and since the direct aspects have been well covered by anthropologists and sociologists, my focus will be on some of the more indirect ways that gender-role socialization messages are communicated. In particular, I will examine research on father–child interaction that may shed light on the process at different stages of children's development, comparing findings from the different age groups studied, and from other cultures, when available. Finally, I will describe some of my own research on parent–child interaction in Mexican and U.S. families, and consider father–child interaction and gender-role socialization from a broader cross-cultural perspective.

FATHERING BEHAVIOR: A REVIEW

Earlier research involving the father-child relationship was generally based on mothers' reports of parenting behaviors (Newson & Newson, 1963, 1968; Pedersen & Robson, 1969; Schaffer & Emerson, 1964), or on children's reports of their parents' child-rearing behaviors. In the latter studies, fathers tended to be perceived as being less accepting or affectionate than mothers (Armentrout & Burger, 1972; Bronfenbrenner, 1961; Droppelman & Schaeffer, 1963; Kagan & Lemkin, 1960), and more dominant, strict, and punitive, especially with sons (Bronfenbrenner, 1961; Droppelman & Schaeffer, 1963; Kagan, 1956). In addition, in one study, tenth grade boys perceived fathers as spending more time in instrumental companionship with them than mothers did (Bronfenbrenner, 1961), while in another, seventh grade girls perceived fathers as neglecting and ignoring them more than mothers did. (Droppelman & Schaeffer, 1963). Though these studies did not focus specifically on gender-role socialization, they suggested differences between fathers' and mothers' relationships with children, which could conceivably impact on that aspect of development.

Recent research on fathering has dealt more directly with fathers, interviewing them about their involvement with their children, and observing them in interaction with them—though some data on fathering behavior are still being obtained through mother interviews and child questionnaires. Since it is difficult to know in an absolute way what effects fathers may be having, most of the studies compare them with mothers, so that in effect, mother–father differences are being measured, rather than fathering behavior per se. In these studies, as in the previously mentioned research, gender-role socialization has generally not been the specific focus, nor are there child outcome measures assessing the effects of particular patterns of fathering behavior on gender-role development. Still, from the many studies that have been done, an overall picture begins to emerge that suggests some of the ways that the process occurs.

Early Behavior Patterns: Fathers with Infants and Toddlers

Some of the more recent studies of fathers and infants have shown ways that fathers' parenting behaviors are similar to mothers'. Parke and colleagues (Parke & O'Leary, 1976; Parke, O'Leary, & West, 1972; Parke & Sawin, 1975) found that U.S. fathers showed the same kinds of nurturant behaviors (e.g., touching, kissing, vocalizing) to newborns that mothers did, with similar results found in a study of

German fathers (Parke, Grossman, & Tinsley, 1981). On the other hand, much of the recent research has found sex differences in parenting behaviors. In addition to the consistent finding that fathers spend much less time interacting with infants than mothers do (Ban & Lewis, 1974; Kotelchuck, 1976; Lewis & Weinraub, 1974; Pederson & Robson, 1969; Rebelsky & Hanks, 1971; Weinraub, 1980), there appear to be some persistent differences in the kinds of interactions they have. Numerous studies in the United States have found that whereas mothers spend a greater proportion of their interaction time with infants in caregiving activities, fathers spend a greater proportion in playful and sociable activities (Clarke-Stewart, 1978; Field, 1978; Katsh, 1981; Kotelchuck, 1976; Lamb, 1977a, 1977b; Parke & Sawin, 1980; Pedersen & Robson, 1969; Rendina & Dickerscheid, 1976). Similar findings have emerged in a mother-interview study involving English fathers (Richards, Dunn, & Antonis, 1977), and in a study of Australian fathers (Russell, 1982); in the latter instance, fathers who were the primary caregivers for their infants still spent less time on child-care tasks than their spouses did.

Another persistent finding that has emerged is a difference in U.S. parents' behavioral styles, with fathers tending to engage in more active and stimulating interaction than mothers throughout the infancy period.[1] In their studies of newborns, Parke and colleagues found that fathers were more likely than mothers to hold, rock, and provide auditory and physical stimulation for their infants (Parke & O'Leary, 1976; Parke, et al., 1972; Parke & Sawin, 1975). Yogman (1982), reporting studies of parents' interactions with infants from two weeks to six months of age, found that fathers more than mothers engaged their infants in tactile, arousing, unpredictable games, often involving limb movement. Mothers, on the other hand, were more likely to engage their infants in soothing, nontactile games (especially verbal ones), and when they played limb movement games, they were usually predictable and contained ones, such as peek-a-boo and pat-a-cake. Similar patterns of father–infant interaction in the first year of life have been found by Field (1978), Pedersen, Anderson, and Cain (1980), Power and Parke (1981), and Lamb (1977a). The same patterns have also been found with older infants. Smith and Daglish (1977) found in a home study of parents with 12- to 24-month old infants that fathers joined in physical play more than mothers did, and Clarke-Stewart (1978, 1980), studying parent interaction with infants from 15 to 30 months of age, found that fathers' play was more likely than mothers' to be physical and arousing, and less likely to be didactic or mediated by objects. Other studies have found fathers to be less sociable, verbal, and affectionate than mothers with their infants (Belsky, Gilstrapp, & Rovine, 1984; Landerholm & Scriven, 1981), and to be less responsive to infant cues of interest and attention (Power, 1985; Power & Parke, 1983), though Clarke-Stewart (1978, 1980), studying parents with older infants, did not find sex differences in parental responsiveness.

Another consistent finding throughout the infancy period is that fathers much more than mothers tend to differ in their behaviors toward boys and girls. On the most basic level, fathers tend to show more interest in sons than in daughters. Parke

[1]For further discussion of father–infant interaction patterns, see Chapter 4, Yogman, Cooley, and Kindlon, this volume.

and colleagues found that with very young infants, fathers looked at, touched, and vocalized and responded to sons more than daughters (Parke and O'Leary, 1976; Parke & Sawin, 1975), and fed and diapered sons more than daughters (Parke & Sawin, 1980). With older infants, Rendina and Dickerscheid (1976) found that fathers watched and played with sons more than daughters, Lamb (1977a, 1977b) and Belsky (1979) found that fathers vocalized more to sons than to daughters, and Kotelchuck (1976) found that fathers spent more time playing with sons than with daughters. This evidence of fathers' greater interest in infant sons is consistent with the finding that fathers, to a much greater degree than mothers, acknowledge a preference for having male children (Hoffman, 1977; Parke, 1979; Rendina & Dickerscheid, 1976). There is also cross-cultural evidence of fathers' tendency to be more interested in sons during the infancy period: !Kung San fathers of Botswana were found to spend more time with sons than daughters (West & Konner, 1976), and Israeli kibbutzim fathers were found to spend more time visiting infant sons than infant daughters (Gewirtz & Gewirtz, 1968).

In addition to fathers' tendency to show a higher level of interest in infant sons, they also have been found to interact with them differently from the way in which they interact with daughters. Most notable is that their higher level of physical and arousing play (compared with that of mothers) tended to occur much more with sons than with daughters (Lamb, 1977b; Power & Parke, 1981), with fathers playing more interactive games (Field, 1978; 1979) and encouraging more visual, fine-motor, and locomotor exploration (Power & Parke, 1981) with sons, and encouraging more vocal behavior with daughters (Field, 1978; Power & Parke, 1981). Other findings of interest are that fathers of toddler daughters in one study were found to encourage proximity more than fathers of toddler sons (Fagot, 1978), and that fathers more often than mothers showed negative responses to sons' play with dolls and soft toys (Fagot, 1978; Snow, Jacklin, & Maccoby, 1983), though a study by Eisenberg, Wolchik, Hernandez, and Pasternack (1985) did not find parental differences in response to children's toy preferences.

Piecing together some of these behavioral findings from the first two years of life, can we then come to any conclusions about fathers' early effects on gender-role socialization? First, it appears that most children, starting at birth, come to see that mothers are more frequently there, that they take care of bodily needs, that they are attentive and responsive, and that they tend to offer a soothing kind of play. Fathers, on the other hand, are less often there, and when they are, they are less predictable and more exciting. They tend to initiate activity more, and be less responsive to the infant's cues. Thus right from the beginning it would seem that children are being shown very different models of male and female behavior.

Second, if the babies are male, something additional appears to be happening. Not only are they likely to be getting extra attention from their fathers, which may enhance their sense of importance in a way that does not generally occur for female babies, but they are also getting a message from the manner of that attention. Fathers, in their more physical and arousing play with infant and toddler sons, frequently do things like lift them high in the air, toss them up and catch them, and swing them around upside down. There are data suggesting that infants at certain stages especially enjoy the arousing kinds of play that fathers offer (Clarke-Stewart, 1978; Lamb, 1977b). However, there are no data on infants' *initial* responses to these kinds of gross motor stimuli, such as those provided by Yogman's (1982) video microanalyses of parent play with infants who are confined to seats. If such microanalytic data were available, it is conceivable that they might show that a baby's initial reactions to being tossed in the air, or swung around upside down, are startle and fear—until he catches sight of his father's excited face, and hears the enthusiastic "Whee!" which defines the situation as fun rather than danger. What we may be seeing in this very early pattern of father–son interaction is a process that teaches boys to equate fun with gross physical involvement, sudden movement, a sense of risk or danger, and the translation of fear into excitement. Carrying this speculation further, we can relate this early socialization process to the findings that, throughout childhood, boys consistently show more gross motor play activity and more impulsive behavior than girls (Block, 1983; Maccoby & Jacklin, 1974). We can also consider it in relation to the fact that from toddlerhood on, many more males than females are treated in hospital emergency rooms for accidental injury (Block, 1983), and that the accidental death rate at all ages is much higher for males than for females.

Fathers with Preschoolers and Older Children

Much less research has been done on fathers' interaction with preschool-age children than has been done on fathers with infants. With this older group, the research context has generally been a structured play, task, or teaching situation, rather than naturalistic observation of caregiving or spontaneous play. Even so, particular patterns of behaviors that have been found in father–infant studies have emerged here as well. Several studies have found fathers to engage in more active and physical play than mothers (DiPietro, Jacklin, & Maccoby, 1981; Osofsky & O'Connell, 1972; Stuckey, McGhee, & Bell, 1982). Others found fathers to show a kind of verbal rather than physical dominance, interrupting and talking simultaneously with children more than mothers did (Greif, 1979), giving more directives and imperatives than mothers (Bellinger, 1982; Bright & Stockdale, 1984), and giving more functional information and encouraging children's task performance more than mothers (Mazur, 1980). In addition, fathers were again found to differ more than mothers in behaviors to girls as compared with boys. They interacted more positively and socially with daughters than with sons (Block, Block, & Harrington, 1974; Tauber, 1979), were more controlling and directive with sons than with daughters (Bright & Stockdale, 1984), showed more concern for cognitive achievement for sons than for daughters in one set of studies (Block, et al., 1974), and showed more concern with cognitive achievement for daughters than for sons in another study (Mazur, 1980). And, as in several father–infant studies, fathers of preschoolers were found to encourage play with same-sex toys and discourage play with cross-sex toys with both sexes, but particularly with sons (Langlois & Downs, 1980).

Because there has been relatively little research on father–preschooler interaction, it is difficult to offer more than tentative conclusions. It does appear, however, that with preschoolers (as with infants), fathers tend to maintain a more active, initiating, and dominant role than do mothers, and that this behavioral style carries over from the physical into the verbal realm as children get older. It also seems that fathers assume a more instrumental, or task-oriented, role in their interactions (Parsons & Bales, 1955), and that this behavior may be more often directed toward sons than toward daughters. Thus it appears that fathers are providing a distinct model of male behavior for their children, different from that provided by mothers.

Furthermore, their differing behaviors to preschool boys versus girls would also seem to be contributing to gender-role socialization. They appear to give more cognitive input and direction to sons than to daughters, and to engage in more purely social interaction with daughters than with sons, similar to the findings that fathers more often encouraged visual, fine-motor, and locomotor exploration in infant boys (Power & Parke, 1981), and vocal behavior in infant girls (Field, 1978; Power & Parke, 1981). In addition, fathers of preschoolers (and toddlers) seem to be concerned that their children—in particular their sons—play with toys traditionally considered appropriate for their gender. Thus fathers, more than mothers, may be transmitting traditional gender-role messages to their children, and reinforcing any such messages that the children may have heard elsewhere.

Research on fathers' interactions with older children has generally involved either clinical studies of problem behaviors, or studies of parent–adolescent communication around a structured task. Since they are less relevant to the topic at hand, they will not be considered here. I have found only two published studies (other than my own) that examine father–child interaction with older children in naturalistic settings. Mackey and Day (1979), observing naturally occurring groups in public places in five different cultures, found that mothers were in more frequent and closer contact with children than fathers were. Margolin and Patterson (1975), in a study of parents' interactions with children between 5 and 12 years of age, found that fathers showed almost twice as many positive responses to their sons as to their daughters. Tasch (1952), interviewing fathers of older children, found that fathers reported more concern for daughters' safety than for sons' safety, more rough-and-tumble play with sons than with daughters, harsher control of sons than of daughters, and more participation in the development of sons' motor skills than daughters'. Thus the data suggest that some of the patterns of fathering behavior observed in parent–infant and parent–preschooler studies may be present cross-culturally, and with older as well as younger children.

FATHERS WITH OLDER CHILDREN: A STUDY OF MEXICAN FAMILIES

The research I will be describing here investigated that possibility. It considered fathering behavior from several perspectives: (1) whether the parental roles traditionally ascribed to Mexican culture were realistic; (2) whether or not there were substantial differences between fathers' and mothers' behavior to older children; and

(3) whether the differences, if found, corresponded to those found in other cultures, with younger children.

Mexican parental roles have traditionally been described in ways that are not very different from the perceptions children have provided of their parents in the U.S. studies mentioned previously. The mother has been portrayed as the more nurturant and affectionate parent, self-sacrificing for her children, who in turn place her on a pedestal. The father has been portrayed as more aloof, more likely to provide discipline, and overall, more likely to maintain an authoritarian relationship with his children and with his wife, who respect and obey him (Diaz-Guerrero, 1955; Fromm & Maccoby, 1970; Staton, 1972). Although these portrayals have recently been called into question, in particular for Mexican–American fathers (see Chapter 7, Mirandé, this volume), empirical data are needed to substantiate or alter the traditional perspective. The present study represents a start in that direction.

Method

My sample consisted of 78 parent–child dyads, in 19 two-parent families of lower and middle socioeconomic levels, living in a small city high in the mountains of central Mexico. The families at the lower end of the economic spectrum lived in two-room houses with no inside plumbing. The families at the upper end lived in six- to eight-room houses, and had cars, a servant, and numerous electrical appliances. Lower-income fathers were miners (mining was the city's main industry) or construction workers; middle-income fathers were professionals or middle-level managers. Mothers were primarily housewives, though five women did part-time work to supplement the family income, and one was a law student. Target children included all those between 7 and 12 years of age, with an average age of 9 for both boys and girls. Number of target children per family ranged from one to four, with a median and mode of two.

To obtain observational data on parent–child interaction, I trained five Mexican fieldworkers in two concurrent systems for the act-by-act coding of behavior. The first, developed at the research locale with the help of local advisors, consisted initially of 81 culturally relevant behaviors (both verbal and nonverbal), such as Agree, Instruct, Scold, and Ignore. The second was a more global measure of interpersonal style (from Bales, 1970; Bales, Cohen, & Williamson, 1979) rating each act on three dimensions: Dominant/Submissive, Positive/Negative (or friendly/unfriendly), and Expressive/Controlled (perceivably expressing vs. controlling emotion). About 18,000 acts were coded using these two systems.[2]

There were six 15-minute observational sessions per family. During each visit, the fieldworker set up a tape recorder, retired to an unobtrusive corner, and took notes on the interaction between parents and target children—twice when only mother was present, twice when only father was present, and twice when both parents were present. Other people were allowed to be there as well, though acts in-

---

[2] A more extensive discussion of the methodology, and some of the additional findings from this study, can be found in Bronstein (1984; 1986) and Bronstein-Burrows (1981).

volving them were not coded. Actual coding of behaviors took place afterward, away from the family, when the fieldworker transcribed the tape recording of the session, and then coded the behaviors using the tape, the transcript, and notes made during the session. There were 109 sessions of parent–child interaction observed, with two dropped from the final analysis because of inadequate data.

During the data analysis, low-frequency categories were eliminated or subsumed. The remaining 25 parent behavior categories and the Bales measures of interpersonal style were then totaled across sessions for each parent–child dyad, and the totals were converted to percentage scores to adjust for differences in family environment (such as number of people present at the sessions). These percentage scores indicated what percentage of a parent's acts to a given target child were in a particular category (e.g., that 12% of a mother's acts to her oldest son were coded as Disagree). Behavior clusters were then formed, based on an exploratory factor analysis of the categories. In addition, for families with several same-sex children in the study, the interactions with these children were averaged, to create a new set of dyad scores that represented interaction with a composite "son" or "daughter." This assured that families with several children between 7 and 12 years of age would not be unduly weighting the data by having, for example, three father–son dyads in the sample. I then did t-tests on the individual behaviors, the behavior clusters, and the dimensions of interpersonal style, to see what differences there might be between mothers' and fathers' behavior to children. Since with 78 dyads from 19 families, the cases could not be regarded as independent, the number of families rather than the number of dyads was used to determine the degrees of freedom for those tests.

Results

Mothers were, in fact, significantly more nurturant than fathers in a physical sense; that is, offering food, helping the child with grooming, and showing concern for safety and health. However, contrary to the traditional perception of Mexican family roles, fathers were more *emotionally* nurturant and more playfully involved with their children than mothers were. They were significantly higher than mothers on the behavior category Act Playful, and on a behavior cluster called Supportive Involvement, which consisted of agreeing, complying, showing affection, encouraging, participating with, acting playful, explaining, giving opinion, and suggesting. In addition, they were somewhat higher than mothers on showing a Positive (or friendly) interpersonal style with their children. In terms of cognitive input, fathers more frequently explained things to their children than mothers did, though they did not offer instruction or direction any more frequently. During the observation sessions, while mothers spent a greater proportion of time than fathers in caregiving and chore activities, fathers were more likely than mothers to be involved in an educational or entertaining activity with their children. For example, one father, a civil engineer, spent an observation session looking at a butterfly collection with his children, and explaining to them about insect life cycles:[3]

[3]The transcript segments are translated from the original Spanish. Names have been changed to protect the identity of the families.

Father: No, they only live a few hours, those little bugs.

Roberto: Really?

Father: Yes, generally when they hatch, it's in the evening, and by the morning, they've already died.

Leticia: And why, Papa?

Father: Because it is the cycle of life, Leticia. All the insects don't live a long time like we do.

Leticia: It's lucky we're not insects.

Another, a chemist, played shoe store with his children:

Laura: Well, do they fit? Are they slipping off?

Father: Well, a little, but it's because I'm wearing socks that are a little thin.

Laura: Well yes, because of the heat. Then what are you saying—are you taking them or not?

Father: Well, let me walk a little more in them, because . . .

Laura: Okay, walk here on the rug.

Given the preceding findings, it is not surprising that, despite the traditional image of the Mexican father as authoritarian and intimidating, there was no difference between fathers and mothers on a behavior cluster called Authoritarian Control, which consisted of scolding, criticizing, ordering, threatening, interrogating, and acting angry. Nor was there any difference on a more affectively neutral parental control cluster (Instrumental Directive), which consisted of ordering, prohibiting, and setting limits. Likewise, there were no differences between fathers and mothers on showing a Dominant or Negative (unfriendly) interpersonal style.

However, as has been found in studies of parent–child interaction in other cultures, there were differences between mothers' and fathers' interactions with boys and girls, in that mothers tended to treat them similarly, and fathers tended to interact with them in a distinctly different manner. Fathers used direct control strategies significantly more often with sons than with daughters; they were higher to sons on the behavior clusters Authoritarian Control and Instrumental Directive, and on showing a Dominant interpersonal style. However, these findings reflected fathers' especially gentle treatment of daughters, compared with all other dyad combinations, rather than harsh treatment of sons; in fact, fathers were no higher than mothers on Authoritarian Control and Instrumental Directive to sons, and were substantially lower than mothers on these behavior clusters to daughters. In a similar vein, there was a nonsignificant trend for fathers to be higher to daughters than to sons on a behavior cluster called Psychological Control, an indirect approach which consisted of moralizing, correcting, pressuring, manipulating, interrogating, asking opinion, and belittling.

Fathers also differed toward girls and boys on measures of attention and cognitive/intellectual involvement. They more frequently provided instruction for sons than for daughters, often within a play context; for example, during the previously described shoe store game, the father interacted sociably with his nine-year-old daughter—and taught his seven-year-old son how to polish shoes. Another father (an architect), playing marbles with his three sons, provided guidance to the youngest, an impulsive, easily frustrated seven year old, helping him master the technique:

Father: You have to do it gently, Armando, gently, gently.

Armando: I'm going now.

Father: Where are you going to shoot from? Ah!

Armando: It's behind the sofa.

Father: Well, it's a little difficult, right? Let's see how you do it. Ah!

Armando: (complaining) It always goes over there.

Father: Well, yes, since your finger was crooked . . . . Now that shot was better.

In addition, fathers tended to ask sons more frequently than daughters to explain or give information, though this trend did not reach statistical significance. On the other hand, fathers were more likely to show a behavioral pattern called Inattentive Imposing (which consisted of interrupting, ignoring, answering in monosyllables, precautioning, giving opinion, proposing, and disagreeing), in their interactions with daughters than in their interactions with sons. In the following segment, the father (an electrician) was talking with his three children—his 10- and 7-year-old daughters and his 9-year-old son—about what they would like to be when they grow up:

Father: (to Maria, aged 10) What do you want to study, when you finish elementary school?[4]

Maria: I'd like to study . . . that is . . .

Father: How about you, Manuel? Now that you're graduating elementary school, what do you want to study?

Manuel: To be a lawyer.

Father: A lawyer?

Maria: I want to be a doctor.

Father: (to Manuel) And you think you'll be able to do that, do you? You think your brain is going to help you do it?

Manuel: Yes.

Father: (to Manuel) You do? Well, listen, you get distracted all the time around here. You don't pay attention to me, to what I tell you to do, or to what your mother tells you to do. You're very disobedient. And for that profession, you have to be very conscientious and obedient, right?

Maria: I'd like to study to be a doctor.

[4]In the Mexican educational system, vocational training and tracking for higher education begin after sixth grade.

Father: A doctor, hmm? And you, Josefina?

Josefina: Also a doctor.

Father: You'd like to study to be a ballerina, because you really like to dance.

Josefina: Yes, a doctor and a ballerina.

In this segment, the father seemed concerned with his son's achievement—and was direct and not very gentle about letting him know it. Most of his conversation was directed to Manuel; he questioned him, asked him to explain himself, and listened and responded to his answers. With his daughters, on the other hand, he was quite gentle—but he also interrupted them, ignored their responses, and imposed his own opinions.

Cross-Cultural Comparisons

It appears, from the findings of the present study, that Mexican fathers of 7- to 12-year-old children have a lot in common with U.S. fathers of infants and preschoolers. First, in comparison with mothers, the fathers in this sample, during the times they were observed interacting with their children, spent a smaller proportion of time in caregiving activity and a larger proportion of time in play and sociable activity. This is very similar to patterns that have been found in the U.S. parent–infant studies discussed earlier. Second, the fathers in the present sample explained things and gave information to their children more often than mothers did, which is similar to Mazur's (1980) finding that fathers of preschoolers gave more functional information and encouraged children's task performance more than mothers did. Third, Mexican fathers differed more than mothers in their interactions with girls and boys, in ways that were similar to fathers in U.S. studies of parent–child interaction. The fathers in the present sample were more directive and restrictive with sons and more gentle with daughters, which is similar to the findings from U.S. studies of father–preschooler interaction that fathers were more controlling and directive with sons than with daughters (Bright & Stockdale, 1984), and that they interacted more positively and socially with daughters than with sons (Block, et al., 1974; Tauber, 1979). In addition, the Mexican fathers more often showed their sons how to do things, and more often asked their sons to explain things, which is similar to the finding by Block and colleagues (1974) that fathers of preschoolers showed more concern for the cognitive achievement of sons than of daughters. Finally, the finding that fathers paid less direct attention to daughters than to sons, in that they more often interrupted and ignored them, and answered them in monosyllables, suggests that the Mexican fathers in this sample, like the fathers in the parent–infant interaction studies described earlier, were more interested in sons than in daughters. It is interesting to note that the last two findings are similar to the patterns reported by older children in U.S. studies of parenting behavior described at the beginning of the chapter (Bronfenbrenner, 1961; Droppelman & Schaeffer, 1963).

FATHERS AND PREADOLESCENTS IN U.S. FAMILIES:
SOME PRELIMINARY FINDINGS

As part of a longitudinal study I am presently conducting, of 43 fifth graders and their families in Vermont, I have obtained 240 segments of parent–child interaction in the home. The conditions under which the data were gathered were very similar to those of the Mexican study, except that in the Vermont study, there was only one target child per family, and the number of people present at observation sessions was usually smaller than in the Mexican study. Though the actual behavioral observations are not yet fully analyzed, the activities fathers and mothers chose to participate in with their children during the observation sessions are revealing. It appears that the roles and patterns observed in parent–infant and parent–preschooler studies are also apparent in parents' interactions with preadolescent children. Specifically, given free choice of what to do during observation sessions, fathers were twice as likely as mothers to play a game with their child, but were only half as likely to bake or cook or do a project together. Thus, as in the parent–infant studies, fathers opted for play, while mothers tended more to get involved in caregiving activities with their children—though the children were now old enough to be coparticipants in caregiving activities, rather than the recipients. In addition, whereas mothers of daughters and mothers of sons spent an equal percentage of their sessions doing projects, only fathers of sons did projects with their children, and fathers were 4 times more likely to work on a computer with sons than with daughters. On the other hand, fathers of daughters were 3½ times more likely to spend their sessions in simple social conversation than were fathers of sons. These findings are similar to those from the research with younger children discussed earlier, that fathers engaged in more purely social interaction with daughters than with sons, but were more invested in the cognitive achievement of sons than of daughters.

CONCLUSIONS

Across a wide age range of children, and across several different cultures, certain consistencies in fathering behavior have emerged. Many studies have found fathers to participate much less than mothers in caregiving, to spend a larger proportion of their time with children in play, to engage more than mothers in physical and arousing play, and to be more verbally dominant and information-providing than mothers. Thus in terms of gender-role socialization, fathers seem to be providing a particular model or prototype of male behavior, for boys to emulate and girls to eschew. Children may be learning from this model (and from mothers' model as well) that the physical nurturance of others is a female responsibility, whereas for males, it is unnecessary—or off-limits. Children may be learning from their fathers' model that physical play, involving gross motor activity and risk-taking, is appropriate male (but not female) behavior. They may be learning that verbal dominance is an appropriate male (but not female) trait, socializing them for a world where men have been found to exert more control in male–female conversation—by speaking more than women (Argyle, Lalljee, & Cook, 1968; Bernard, 1972), interrupting more, and more often answering in monosyllables (Fishman, 1973; Zimmerman & West, 1975), while women more carefully phrase their assertions as questions (Lakoff, 1973). Children may be learning from their fathers' model that it is more appropriate for males than for females to know things—or at least to sound knowledgeable.

A substantial number of studies have found fathers to differ more than mothers in their behaviors toward male and female children; in particular, to show more interest in sons than in daughters. In addition, fathers have been found to be more restrictive and demanding with sons, and more sociable and gentle with daughters, more physically active in their play with sons, more concerned with their sons' cognitive development and achievement, and more concerned with their sons' playing with "masculine" and not "feminine" toys. In terms of gender-role socialization, fathers' greater interest in and attention to sons may communicate to children the belief that what boys have to say is more worth listening to, whereas girls can more readily be interrupted or ignored, and may need to be told what to think. Fathers' greater demandingness with sons and their greater concern with sons' cognitive development and achievement may communicate to children that higher levels of competence and performance are expected of boys than of girls—a message that could conceivably affect children's developing sense of efficacy, and eventual levels of academic and occupational achievement. Fathers' higher level of physical activity in their play with sons may communicate to children that boys are better equipped to handle and enjoy the challenges of the physical world, and that girls, for their own safety, had best be more cautious. And of course, as they are communicating different attitudes to and about girls and boys, fathers are differentially imparting skills in these areas, so that they may in fact be creating self-fulfilling prophecies. In support of this hypothesis is a finding that has emerged in numerous studies (reviewed in Radin, 1981), across a wide age range of children, that the more fathers are involved with sons, the higher the sons' cognitive performance— whereas this relationship has not consistently been found for fathers and daughters.

However, we also need to consider whether certain aspects of fathers' behavior may have limiting effects on boys' social and emotional development. In their greater restrictiveness with sons and greater gentleness with daughters, fathers may be communicating the expectation that boys, if not handled firmly, are more likely to be out of control, whereas girls can be trusted to behave more reasonably and responsibly. These are messages that may shape children's self-concepts along traditional gender-based lines, thereby reinforcing aggressive behaviors in male children, while providing them with less opportunity to learn cooperation and empathy. In treating sons more instrumentally and less sociably than daughters, fathers may be providing their sons with less opportunity to learn the interpersonal skills necessary for establishing and maintaining intimate relationships, while also providing an early model of a traditional male–male relationship—of *doing* things together, rather than verbally connecting in a more intimate way. In their concerns that their sons play mainly with "masculine" toys, fathers may, on the one hand, be furthering their sons' cognitive and motor development, in that construction sets and model airplanes may enhance spatial ability, fine-motor coordination, and problem-solving skills. On the other hand, in communicating that it is not appropriate for boys to play with dolls and tea sets, fathers may be discouraging their sons from owning and developing their nurturant selves, thereby suggesting that those characteristics are not relevant to boys' and men's lives.

Of course, all of this presents a somewhat one-sided picture, which may seem to imply that fathers are doing things "wrong." We need to keep in mind that research findings generally represent matters of degree and comparison (e.g., fathers vs. mothers or boys vs. girls) rather than the total presence or absence of a behavior, and they also tend to blur the wide range of individual differences among fathers. Also, since this chapter deliberately focused on the effects of father–child interaction, it has not examined *mothers'* effects. For example, Malatesta (1980) found that whereas mothers responded less to negative facial expressions of emotion than to positive ones in infants of both sexes, they responded almost *not at all* to infant boys' expressions of pain; and Moss (1972) found that mothers tended to offer contact to crying three-month-old female infants, but for male infants, the more they cried, the *less* the mothers offered contact. Obviously mothers, too, contribute to the gender-role socialization of their children, in ways that may limit children's options.

One clear fact that emerges from the data reviewed and presented here is that fathers have very special and important contributions to make to children's development. The research clearly shows that in their interactions with their children, fathers have taught, demonstrated, or encouraged physical competence, adventurousness, confidence in asserting opinions, learning of new information, and mastery of new skills—and the effects of paternal involvement on boys' cognitive development and achievement have been well documented (Radin, 1981). In addition, with children of all ages, fathers have been found to show warmth, sociability, and playfulness. Studies of single-parent custodial fathers and fathers who are the primary caregivers in two-parent families (see Hanson, Chapter 11, and Radin, Chapter 9, this volume) clearly demonstrate that fathers are capable of providing both physical and emotional nurturance for their children, modeling both instrumental and expressive roles, and finding that kind of parenting experience deeply gratifying. As men become more aware of their own capacities for nurturance as well as achievement, connectedness as well as mastery, and as more and more fathers come to own these qualities as part of their identity as men, they will more fully and equally be able to transmit those qualities to their sons and daughters.

REFERENCES

Argyle, M., Lalljee, M., & Cook, M. (1968). The effects of visibility on interaction in a dyad. *Human Relations, 21*, 3–17.

Armentrout, J.A., & Burger, G.K. (1972). Children's reports of parental child-rearing behavior at five grade levels. *Developmental Psychology, 7*(1), 44–48.

Bales, R.F. (1970). *Personality and interpersonal behavior*. New York: Holt, Rinehart & Winston.

Bales, R.F., Cohen, S.P., & Williamson, S.A. (1979). *SYMLOG: A system for the multiple level observation of groups*. New York: Free Press.

Ban, P., & Lewis, M. (1974). Mothers and fathers, girls and boys: Attachment behavior in the one-year-old. *Merill-Palmer Quarterly, 20*, 195–204.

Bellinger, D. (1982). Sex differences in parental directives to young children. *Sex Roles, 8*, 1123–1139.

Belsky, J. (1979). Mother-father-infant interaction: A naturalistic observational study. *Developmental Psychology, 15*(6), 601–607.

Belsky, J., Gilstrapp, B., & Rovine, M. (1984). The Pennsylvania Infant and Family Development Project, I: Stability and change in mother-infant and father-infant interaction in a family setting at one, three, and nine months. *Child Development, 55*, 692–705.

Bernard, J. (1972). *The sex game*. New York: Atheneum.

Block, J.H. (1983). Differential premises arising from differential socialization of the sexes: Some conjectures. *Child Development, 54*, 1335–1354.

Block, J.H., Block, J., & Harrington, D. (1974, April). *The relationship of parental teaching strategies to ego-resiliency in pre-school children*. Presented at the annual meeting of the Western Psychological Association, San Francisco.

Bright, M.C., & Stockdale, D.F. (1984). Mothers', fathers', and preschool children's interactive behaviors in a play setting. *Journal of Genetic Psychology, 144*, 219–232.

Bronfenbrenner, U. (1961). Some familial antecedents of responsibility and leadership in adolescents. In L. Petrullo & B.M. Bass (Eds.), *Leadership and interpersonal behavior*. New York: Holt.

Bronstein, P. (1984). Differences in mothers' and fathers' behaviors toward children: A cross-cultural comparison. *Developmental Psychology, 20*(6), 995–1003.

Bronstein, P. (1986). Children's social behavior: A cross-cultural comparison. *International Journal of Behavioral Development, 9*, 153–173.

Bronstein-Burrows, P. (1981). Patterns of parent behavior: A cross-cultural study. *Merrill-Palmer Quarterly, 27*, 129–143.

Clarke-Stewart, K.A. (1978). And daddy makes three: The father's impact on mother and child. *Child Development, 49*, 466–468.

Clarke-Stewart, K.A. (1980). The father's contribution to children's cognitive and social development in early childhood. In F.A. Pedersen (Ed.), *The father-infant relationship: Observational studies in the family setting*. New York: Praeger.

Diaz-Guerrero, R. (1955). Neurosis and the Mexican family structure. *American Journal of Psychiatry, 112*, 411–417.

DiPietro, J., Jacklin, C.N., & Maccoby, E.E. (1981, April). *Sex-typing in parent and child interaction*. Paper presented at the biennial meeting of the Society for Research in Child Development, Boston.

Droppelman, L.F., & Schaeffer, E.S. (1963). Boys' and girls' reports of maternal and paternal behavior. *Journal of Abnormal and Social Psychology, 67*(6), 648–654.

Eisenberg, N., Wolchik, S.A., Hernandez, R., & Pasternack, J.F. (1985). Parental socialization of young children's play: A short term longitudinal study. *Child Development, 56*, 1506–1513.

Fagot, B. (1978). The influence of sex of child on parental reactions to toddler children. *Child Development, 49*, 459–465.

Field, T. (1978). Interaction patterns of primary versus secondary caretaker fathers. *Developmental Psychology*, *14*, 183–185.

Field, T. (1979). Games parents play with normal and high-risk infants. *Child Psychiatry and Human Development*, *10*, 41–48.

Fishman, P. (1973). *Interaction: The work women do*. Unpublished Master's thesis, Department of Sociology, University of California, Santa Barbara.

Fromm, E., & Maccoby, M. (1970). *Social character in a Mexican village: A sociopsychoanalytic study*. Englewood Cliffs, NJ: Prentice-Hall.

Gewirtz, H.B., Gewirtz, J.L. (1968). Visiting and caretaking patterns for Kibbutz infants: Age and sex trends. *American Journal of Orthopsychiatry*, *38*, 427–443.

Grief, E.B. (1979, April). *Sex differences in parent-child conversations: Who interrupts whom*. Presented at the biennial meeting of the Society for Research in Child Development, San Francisco.

Hoffman, L.W. (1977). Changes in family roles, socialization, and sex differences. *American Psychologist*, *32*, 644–658.

Kagan, J. (1956). The child's perception of the parent. *Journal of Abnormal and Social Psychology*, *53*, 257–258.

Kagan, J., & Lemkin, J. (1960). The child's differential perceptions of parental attributes. *Journal of Abnormal and Social Psychology*, *61*(3), 440–447.

Katsch, B.S. (1981). Fathers and infants: Reported caregiving and interaction. *Journal of Family Issues*, *2*, 295–296.

Kotelchuck, M. (1976). The infant's relationship to the father: Experimental evidence. In M.E. Lamb (Ed.), *The role of the father in child development*. New York: Wiley.

Lakoff, R. (1973). Language and women's place. *Language in Society*, *2*, 45–79.

Lamb, M.E. (1977a). Father-infant and mother-infant interaction in the first year of life. *Child Development*, *48*, 167–181.

Lamb, M.E. (1977b). The development of mother–infant and father–infant attachment in the second year of life. *Developmental Psychology*, *13*(6), 637–648.

Landerholm, E.J., & Scriven, G. (1981). A comparison of mother and father interaction with their six-month-old male and female infants. *Early Childhood Development and Care*, *7*, 317–328.

Langlois, J.H., & Downs, A.C. (1980). Mothers, fathers, and peers as socialization agents of sex-typed play behaviors in young children. *Child Development*, *51*, 1217–1247.

Lewis, M., & Weinraub, M. (1974). Sex of parent × sex of child: Socioemotional development. In R.C. Friedman, R.M. Richart, & R.L. VandeWiele (Eds.), *Sex differences in behavior*. New York: Wiley.

Maccoby, E.E., & Jacklin, C.N. (1974). *The psychology of sex differences*. Stanford, CA: Stanford University Press.

Mackey, W.C., & Day, R.D. (1979). Some indicators of fathering behaviors in the United States: A cross-cultural examination of adult male-child interaction. *Journal of Marriage and the Family*, *41*(2), 287–298.

Malatesta, C.Z. (1980). *Determinants of infant affect socialization: Age, sex of infant, and maternal emotional traits*. Unpublished doctoral dissertation, Rutgers University, New Brunswick, NJ.

Margolin, G., & Patterson, G.R. (1975). Differential consequences provided by mothers and fathers for their sons and daughters. *Developmental Psychology*, *11*(4), 537–538.

Mazur, E. (1980). Parent-child interaction and the acquisition of lexical information during play. *Developmental Psychology, 16,* 404–409.

Moss, H.A. (1972). Sex, age, and state as determinants of mother–infant interaction. In J.M. Bardwick (Ed.), *Readings on the psychology of women.* New York: Harper & Row.

Newson, J., & Newson, E. (1963). *Infant care in an urban community.* London: Allen & Unwin.

Newson, J., & Newson, E. (1968). *Four years old in an urban community.* London: Allen & Unwin.

Osofsky, J.D., & O'Connell, E.J. (1972). Parent-child interaction: Daughters' effects upon mothers' and fathers' behaviors. *Developmental Psychology, 7*(2), 159–168.

Parke, R.D. (1979). Perspectives on father-infant interaction. In J.D. Osofsky (Ed.), *The handbook of infant development.* New York: Wiley.

Parke, R.D., Grossman, K., & Tinsley, B.R. (1981). Father-mother-infant interaction in the newborn period: A German-American comparison. In T. Field (Ed.), *Culture and early interactions.* Hillsdale, NJ: Erlbaum.

Parke, R.D., & O'Leary, S.E. (1976). Father-mother-infant interaction in the newborn period: Some findings, some observations, and some unresolved issues. In K. Riegel & J. Meacham (Eds.), *The developing individual in a changing world, Vol. 2: Social and environmental issues.* The Hague, Netherlands: Mouton.

Parke, R.D., O'Leary, S.E., & West, S. (1972). Mother-father-newborn interaction: Effects of maternal medication, labor, and sex of infant. *Proceedings of the 80th Annual Convention of the American Psychological Association, 7,* 85–86.

Parke, R.D., & Sawin, D.B. (1975, April). *Infant characteristics and behavior as elicitors of maternal and paternal responsivity in the newborn period.* Paper presented at the Society for Research in Child Development, Denver.

Parke, R.D., & Sawin, D.B. (1980). The family in early infancy: Social interactional and attitudinal analyses. In F.A. Pedersen (Ed.), *The father-infant relationship: Observational studies in the family setting.* New York: Praeger.

Parsons, T., & Bales, R.F. (1955). *Family, socialization, and interaction process.* Glencoe, IL: Free Press.

Pedersen, F.A., Anderson, B., & Cain, R. (1980). Parent-infant and husband-wife interactions observed at age five months. In F.A. Pedersen (Ed.), *The father–infant relationship: Observational studies in a family setting.* New York: Praeger.

Pederson, F.A., & Robson, K.S. (1969). Father participation in infancy. *American Journal of Orthopsychiatry, 39,* 466–472.

Power, T.G. (1985). Mother- and father-infant play: A developmental analysis. *Child Development, 56,* 1514–1524.

Power, T.G., & Parke, R.D. (1981). Play as a context for early learning: Lab and home analyses. In L.M. Laosa & I.E. Sigel (Eds.), *The family as a learning environment.* New York: Plenum.

Power, T.G., & Parke, R.D. (1983). Patterns of mother and father play with their 8-month-old infant: A multiple analyses approach. *Infant Behavior and Development, 6,* 453–459.

Radin, N. (1981). The role of the father in cognitive, academic, and intellectual development. In M.E. Lamb (Ed.), *The role of the father in child development.* New York: Wiley.

Rebelsky, F., & Hanks, C. (1971). Fathers' verbal interaction with infants in the first three months of life. *Child Development, 42,* 63–68.

Rendina, I., & Dickersheid, J.D. (1976). Father involvement with first-born infants. *Family Coordinator*, *25*, 373–379.

Richards, M., Dunn, J.F., & Antonis, B. (1977). Caretaking in the first year of life: The role of fathers' and mothers' social isolation. *Child: Care, Health, and Development*, *3*, 23–26.

Russell, G. (1982). Highly participant Australian fathers: Some preliminary findings. *Merrill-Palmer Quarterly*, *28*, 137–156.

Schaffer, H.R., & Emerson, P.E. (1964). The development of social attachments in infancy. *Monographs of the Society for Research in Child Development*, *29*, Serial No. 94.

Smith, P.K., & Daglish, L. (1977). Sex differences in parent and infant behavior in the home. *Child Development*, *48*, 1250–1254.

Snow, M.E., Jacklin, C.N., & Maccoby, E.E. (1983). Sex of child differences in father-child interaction at one year of age. *Child Development*, *54*, 227–232.

Staton, R.D. (1972, July). A comparison of Mexican and Mexican-American families. *Family Coordinator*, 325–330.

Stuckey, M.F., McGhee, P.E., & Bell, N.J. (1982). Parent-child interaction: The influence of maternal employment. *Developmental Psychology*, *18*, 635–644.

Tasch, R.J. (1952). The role of the father in the family. *Journal of Experimental Education*, *20*, 319–361.

Tauber, M.R. (1979). Sex differences in parent–child interaction styles during a free-play session. *Child Development*, *50*, 981–988.

Weinraub, M. (1980, August). *The changing role of the father: Implications for sex role development in children*. Paper presented at the annual meeting of the American Psychological Association, Montreal, Canada.

West, M.M., & Konner, M.J. (1976). The role of the father: An anthropological perspective. In M.E. Lamb (Ed.), *The role of the father in child development*. New York: Wiley.

Yogman, M.W. (1982). Observations on the father-infant relationship. In S.H. Cath, A.R. Gurwitt, & J.M. Ross (Eds.), *Father and Child: Developmental and clinical perspectives*. Boston: Little, Brown.

Zimmerman, D.H., & West, C. (1975). Sex roles, interruptions, and silences in conversations. In B. Thorne & N. Henley (Eds.), *Language and sex: Differences and dominance*. Rowley, MA: Newbury House.

PART 3

Fathers and Family Relationships:

Variations and Change

CHAPTER 9

Primary Caregiving Fathers of Long Duration

NORMA RADIN

A new phenomenon has been attracting considerable interest in recent years in both the professional literature and the mass media—that of the father who stays home much of the day to care for his young children while his wife goes to work. Although this arrangement has many advantages, it appears from the growing research data in the field that there tends to be little stability to the pattern. A study of Swedish fathers who had taken paternity leave to become actively involved in rearing their infant found the average length of time men played the role of primary caregiver was 2.8 months (Radin & Russell, 1983). A study of 23 families in Australia, in which the fathers were described as highly participant in their children's care, discovered that only 22% of the 18 families who could be located two years later had maintained that arrangement (Russell, 1982). In my own Michigan study of families of preschoolers with varying degrees of paternal participation, only 25% of the 20 fathers who were primary caregivers of a child in 1977 were still playing that role four years later (Radin & Goldsmith, 1985). And a two-year follow-up of 17 intact Connecticut families, in which fathers were the major caregivers of children aged 2 to 24 months, revealed that only 47% of the men were still functioning in that role (Pruett, 1983).

The number of long-term primary caregiving men is so minuscule that it might seem that nothing can be learned from these families of persisters. However, if we think in terms of case studies rather than quantitative analyses of large samples, a good deal of valuable information can be obtained, particularly when the persisters are compared to families who were nontraditional when initially interviewed, but who subsequently reverted to a traditional pattern. At the very minimum, a close examination of the persisters should generate hypotheses to be tested in more extensive studies. From another perspective, any gleam of light that can be shed on factors that contribute to stability in high levels of fathering may help clinicians who are counseling couples considering that arrangement, or who already have a reversed-role child-care pattern.

PREDICTORS OF FATHER INVOLVEMENT: THE SHORT-TERM VIEW

While data on antecedents of long-term paternal care are scarce, some information is available on factors predictive of active fathering when duration of the arrangement is not known or not considered. These findings will be summarized so that they may be compared to data concerning determinants of longer-term active fathering. One recent investigation conducted in Massachusetts (Barnett & Baruch, 1984), on a group of middle-class families with five- or nine-year-old children, found that mothers' employment status predicted how involved fathers were with children. In families where the mother was employed, the number of hours she worked and her attitude toward the male role were the strongest predictors of the father's participation. If the mother was not employed, the major determinant of paternal participation in child care was the father's perception of the quality of fathering he received as a youngster, with the lowest quality being predictive of the most participation.[1]

Similarly, in a California study of parents of infants, Feldman, Nash, and Aschenbrenner (1983) found that the wives' characteristics were more predictive of their husbands' styles of involvement with the babies than were the husbands' own characteristics. For example, they found the wives of husbands involved in caregiving were often women who had had positive relations with their own fathers. Our study of parents of preschoolers in Michigan gives additional support to the hypothesis that mothers' characteristics are important determinants of their husbands' child-care activities (Radin, 1981, 1982). We found that one of the most powerful determinants of father involvement was the mother's feeling that her own father had been nurturant but not sufficiently available when she was growing up. The fathers' views of their own fathers were not systematically related to their involvement with their children, nor did parents' sex-role orientation predict how involved men were in child rearing. However, when mothers and fathers had both been reared in a home with a working mother, it was more common for the father to be the primary caregiver than when the family roles had been traditional. In contrast to both the Massachusetts and Michigan studies, an Israeli investigation found that highly participant men had had fathers who were both involved and nurturant (Radin & Sagi, 1982; Sagi, 1982).

A major limitation of all four studies was their confinement to middle-class families. In Russell's (1982) Australian study of families spanning a wide socioeconomic range, however, it was found that the financial situation, particularly the employment potential of the mother, was a major contributor to a couple's deciding to share the child-care role. If it was likely that she could obtain a good job and the father could not, it was often agreed that he would become actively involved in child rearing. Other predictive factors emerging in that study were the father's prior knowledge of child care, nonstereotyped beliefs about appropriate parental roles, and flexible hours or part-time employment for at least one parent. Sex-role orientations of the parents as measured by the Bem Sex Role Inventory (1974) were also

---

[1]For a more complete description of this research, see Chapter 5, Barnett and Baruch, this volume.

relevant; a combination of a high femininity score for fathers and a high masculinity score for mothers was associated with a pattern of shared child rearing. Contrary findings emerged in another culture, however. Lamb and colleagues (Lamb, Frodi, Hwang, Frodi, & Steinberg, 1982) interviewed two groups of Swedish fathers from a wide range of social classes: those who took paid paternity leave, and a matched control group of fathers who did not. These researchers found sex-role orientation was unrelated to father involvement in child care. There was also no clear cut evidence that the income of the parent was an important contributor to the couple's decision to take advantage of the fairly lucrative paternity leave program (Lamb & Levine, 1983). Similarly, in the Pruett (1985) investigation of families where fathers were major caregivers of very young children, only one-third of the parents were pressed into the choice for economic reasons, although the families ranged across a wide socioeconomic spectrum, from welfare status through professional occupations.

In sum, there appears to be persistent support across cultures for only one antecedent of paternal participation in rearing children: parents' perceptions of the fathering they had received as children. Only mixed support was obtained for the other potential determinants (e.g., beliefs about parental roles, sex-role orientation, and financial factors).

PREDICTORS OF PATERNAL INVOLVEMENT: THE LONG-TERM VIEW

Are the same variables predictive of stability in high father involvement over a period of years? There are early suggestions that they are not. In Russell's (1982) two-year follow-up of couples sharing child care, he found no difference between the sex-role orientation of parents who maintained their original nontraditional arrangement and that of those who reverted to a traditional pattern. Nor did beliefs about parental roles differentiate the two groups. However, all nine families reverting to a traditional pattern had experienced problems in the role reversal arrangement. The only other longitudinal investigation in the literature that can shed light on the question of predictors is the one I conducted with my colleagues. Our findings will be the focus of the rest of this chapter, along with some speculations about the children raised in father-primary-caregiver families over a period of years.

The Michigan Study of Primary Caregiving Fathers

Our sample in 1977 consisted of 59 middle-class, intact, primarily white families with a preschool child, who lived within a radius of 50 miles of Ann Arbor, Michigan, a university community. Included in this group was a subsample of highly involved fathers, obtained through local newspaper and radio announcements, and notices on bulletin boards of student housing units, asking families with fathers participating in the rearing of a preschooler to contact us. The control subsample of traditional families, who were matched in age of child, social class, and race, was found through word of mouth. Because families were not always sure who was the primary caregiver, we developed a scale to measure the amount of father involvement in child care. The instrument contained five components: the father's role in the socialization of the child, his participation in the physical care of the child, his availability to the child, his power in decision making about the child, and a global estimate of the amount of paternal involvement in child rearing. The scale was administered to each parent separately, and a total score computed for each respondent's view of father involvement; father's and mother's scores were then added in each family, to arrive at a grand total score. The 59 grand totals were rank ordered, and the 20 families with the highest scores were classified as father primary caregiver, the 20 with the lowest scores as mother primary caregiver, and 19 with scores in the middle as intermediate. There was strong evidence that the titles selected were valid. For example, parents were asked to estimate the amount of time during which the father was the primary caregiver. In the father-primary-caregiver group, the average of the figures cited by fathers was 58%, and by mothers, 56%. In the mother-primary-caregiver group, however, the averages of the figures given by fathers and mothers were 22% and 23%, respectively. When we interviewed the families we learned that all of the mothers in the father-primary-caregiver group worked or went to school on a full-time basis.

For the follow-up investigation four years later (Radin & Goldsmith, 1983; 1985), we sent letters to the last known address of each family, and asked families living in or near Ann Arbor for an interview, to be conducted separately with each parent, as before. Financial constraints precluded our observing father–child interactions as we had done in the initial study. For families living beyond 50 miles, we mailed them copies of the interview questionnaire, and asked each parent to complete one separately and return it to us. As a result of diligent efforts, 57 of the 59 families were contacted, and of those, only one family (who had been in the mother-primary-caregiver group) refused to participate. One of the lost families was also in that group, and the second lost family was in the intermediate group. Thus the 1981 sample consisted of the 20 families originally in the high-father-involvement group and 18 in each of the other two groups. Although, there were five separations or divorces in the first group and two each in the other two groups, the difference was not significant. It was evident, however, from the follow-up interviews, that custody disputes when a divorce occurred were much more heated and bitter in the father-primary-caregiver group than in the other two groups.

The follow-up questionnaire contained questions identical to those initially used in 1977 to assess the amount of father involvement in child care, except for minor changes in a few items to make them more appropriate for children aged seven to nine; for example, a question about who feeds the child was replaced with one inquiring as to who prepares meals for the child. Some new questions were also incorporated into the second questionnaire, such as what changes in child-care arrangements were made since the first interview, and what were the reasons for those changes. A score was again computed for the 47 still-intact families, representing the parents' perceptions of the father's level of involvement in child care, and the same cutoff points from four years earlier were used to determine whether the fam-

TABLE 9.1   Differences between 1977 and 1981 Indexes of Paternal Involvement in Child Care

Group	n	1977 Mean Score	S.D.	1981 Mean Score	S.D.	t Value
Mother as primary caregiver	16	67.2	6.0	68.1	10.4	.71
Boys	8	66.4	6.4	72.1	10.3	1.42
Girls	8	67.9	5.8	64.0	9.4	−2.13
Intermediate	16	80.9	1.9	78.5	7.4	−1.29
Boys	9	80.4	1.4	77.3	7.6	−1.15
Girls	7	81.6	2.4	80.1	7.4	−1.49
Father as primary caregiver	15	93.0	5.3	81.0	15.6	−3.81[a]
Boys	7	92.8	7.1	75.9	21.1	−2.66[b]
Girls	8	93.2	3.6	85.4	5.0	−5.86[c]

[a]$p<.01$.
[b]$p<.05$.
[c]$p<.001$.

ily was father-primary-caregiver, mother-primary-caregiver, or intermediate. In this way we were able to determine how many families remained in the same group and how many had shifted.

In Table 9.1 we present data pertaining to the changes we found in child-care arrangements, organized by original father involvement group and sex of child. It can be seen from the table that it was in the father-primary-caregiver group that all of the significant changes occurred, and the pattern was one of decreased paternal involvement.

Of the 15 still-intact families in the original father-primary-caregiver group, five remained in the same category in 1981, eight were now in the intermediate group, and two were classified as mother-primary-caregiver. This chapter will discuss only the first and last groups, comparing a clearly stable nontraditional arrangement with a clearly unstable pattern, in order to highlight the differences between the two types of families. No clear-cut pattern of relevant variables emerged among the families that started out with high father involvement and then changed to intermediate participation.

Father-Primary-Caregiver Families Who Persisted Over Time

To start with demographic characteristics of the stable group, all of the families had remained in the Ann Arbor area. As this was true of only roughly two-thirds of the total sample in the follow-up, maintaining residence in or near a town known to be tolerant of nontraditional behavior may be a factor facilitating stability in an unusual parenting pattern. In four of the five families, or 80%, the target child (the child who was a preschooler in the initial study) was a girl. This sexual imbalance is notable because in the original group of 20 father-primary-caregiver families, 50% of the target children were daughters, and in the 15 still-intact families from this original group in 1981, the figure was 53%. The preponderance of daughters among the persisters is surprising, but is concordant with the literature emerging about the differential impact of maternal employment on sons and daughters. As Bronfenbrenner, Alvarez, and Hendersen (1984) have noted, an appreciable body of evidence has accumulated indicating that the mother's working outside the home tends to have a salutary effect on girls, but may exert a negative influence on boys. Further, according to Bronfenbrenner and colleagues, the results indicate that whereas daughters from families in which the mother works tend to be more independent, this trend is not apparent for boys. The authors add that the strongest effects have been obtained for samples in which the mothers have worked since the children were of preschool age. Thus it is possible that girls of primary-caregiving fathers were generally easier to rear than boys, and that this sex-of-child factor contributed to the stability of the arrangement.

The small size of the family also appears to be a possible predictor of stability in parental role reversal. In 1977, two of the persisting father-primary-caregiver families had one child and three had two children; at the time of the follow-up, none of those families had any additional children. Since the average age of the five mothers at the time of the follow-up was 35, it seemed unlikely that many more children would be added.

The education of both mothers and fathers ranged from some college to a graduate degree—a well-educated group, even for a middle-class sample. However, while the mothers in general appeared to be making rapid progress in their careers, their husbands, for the most part, were either at the same stage in their careers as they had been in 1977, or had gone down. For example, in one family the mother was a part-time lecturer at a university in 1977, and an assistant professor and the director of a writing program at a university in 1981, working full-time. Her husband remained a faculty member of a university throughout this period. In another family, the mother was a medical technician in 1977, and the supervisor of a clinical pathology lab at a large university hospital in 1981. Her husband was unemployed in 1977 and working 10 hours a week as a baker in his own home in 1981. It should be noted that all five men had flexible working hours at both times, but this was true for only three of the mothers, all of whom were working full-time by 1981.

Perception of parents in the family of origin, which has been found to be a significant predictor of high father involvement in child care in nonlongitudinal studies, turned out to be a salient variable for the persisting families in the present study. Overall, the women in the persisting group had positive views of their own fathers, while the men had negative views of theirs. In 1977, the parents had been asked to rate aspects of their fathers' behavior relevant to nurturance. With possible scores ranging from 5 to 18, the mean in the total sample of 59 was 12 for both mothers and fathers. However, for the five mothers in the persisting group, the mean was 14, while for the five fathers, it was 10.

Another predictor of stability of paternal involvement in child care was the work status of the mother in the family of origin—that is, the grandmother of the target child. Whereas a little over 50% of the parents in the total sample had had mothers who worked while they were growing up, among the persisters, all five of the mothers and two of the fathers had had employed mothers. When asked in 1977 how they felt about their own mothers' employment, all seven parents indicated that they felt positive or neutral about it, at the present time or when they were young.

Russell's (1982) findings suggest that financial need is an important determinant both of women working outside the home, and of fathers' participation in child care. Our findings are similar; two of the women in the persisting group said they were working because they had to, and two said they both had to and wanted to (in the fifth interview, the question was inadvertently omitted). However, all parents responded positively when asked how they felt about the wife's employment, and all the parents indicated that they were satisfied with their current child-care arrangement.

We also asked parents in 1977 how long the family had had the current child-care arrangement; all of the families in the persisting group had maintained that pattern for a number of years prior to 1977. All five of the fathers and four of the mothers indicated that the arrangement had been the same for the child's entire life except for a short period of time (at most, eight months). The fifth mother said the arrangement had been the same for the last three years but the child had been with a sitter since 18 months of age while the mother worked. Noteworthy about these replies was the very short time any of the mothers in the persisting group had been the primary caregiver of the target child. This suggests that a predictor of stability in a father-primary-caregiver arrangement may be the mother's weak identification with the role of principal caregiver of the child.

In 1981, we asked the parents why they had selected their initial child-care arrangement. The reasons were diverse; if there was a belief involved, it was that a child should not be left with a sitter, not that a father should be involved in child rearing, as Russell (1982) found. Some parents indicated that the wife's job was important, either for personal satisfaction or for financial reasons; some saw the arrangement as allowing the husband to do a job he enjoyed. Others commented on the feasibility or efficiency of the arrangement. The husbands' views concurred with those of their wives to a remarkable extent. In addition, three of the men explicitly referred to the fact that they felt a child should be with one parent or another, and not with a sitter.

When asked about changes in the arrangement, three of the couples said that there had been none. One of these fathers said it had worked well and there were no difficulties to overcome. His wife commented, "It's a comfortable arrangement that we fall into naturally, and my husband won't quit child care even if there is a change in his job status." One father, who was uninterested in his career, said he was enjoying his life, felt well-suited to staying home, and felt the arrangement was good for the child. The major problem he had to overcome was missing some contact with other adults. His wife said there were no problems, and mentioned that Ann Arbor is supportive of this arrangement. Two families reported change in the direction of greater father involvement, either because of the father's own life choice or because of the mother's increased involvement in her career. Concurrent with this, however, was the observation in one family that the child was getting older and more independent, and thus able to care for herself to a great extent. Thus overall it can be said that the persisters were satisfied with their lives, and seemed likely to maintain the same arrangement for the next four years.

Father-Primary-Caregiver Families Who Reverted to the Traditional Pattern

We will present a fairly brief portrayal of the two families who reverted to a traditional child care pattern, to highlight the differences between the reverters and the persisters. These differences are summarized in Table 9.2. Acknowledging that an *n* of 2 is exceedingly small, we nevertheless, feel that some pertinent information can emerge from a case study approach.

TABLE 9.2   Summary of Differences between Persisters and Reverters

Persisters	Reverters
Mother raised in home with working mother and experience is not aversive	Mother raised in home where mother didn't work or if she did, experience was aversive
Mother views her own father as nurturant	Mother does not view her father as nurturant
Father views his own father as not very nurturant	Father views his own father as nurturant
Mother was not a primary caregiver for a long period, usually under 6 months	Mother was a primary caregiver for a prolonged period of time
Both parents are satisfied with the child care arrangement and with mother's employment	At least one parent is ambivalent or dissatisfied with child-care arrangement or with mother's employment
Family continues to reside in a community supportive of nontraditional child-care arrangements	Family moves to a community with very traditional values regarding parenting
Parents are in their thirties and/ or well-established in their careers	Parents are in their twenties or just starting in their careers
Mother does not feel guilty about leaving her child to go to work	Mother experiences guilt in leaving child to go to work
Mother's investment in her career grows	Mother becomes dissatisfied with her career
Family members do not pressure couple to revert to traditional child-rearing pattern	Family members pressure couple to resume traditional child-care arrangement
Family remains small and no catastrophic illness occurs	Number of children increases or a catastrophic illness occurs to one of the children

Looking first at age, we found that the reverting parents were considerably younger that the persisters. The average age for the mothers in families resuming a mother-primary-caregiver pattern in 1981 was 31; for persisters it was 35. For the reverting fathers the average age at time 2 was 32, while for the persisters it was 39. The education of the reverters was also somewhat more limited than that of the persisters. Both mothers and fathers in the reverting group had either some college or an undergraduate degree, but none had a graduate degree. In both reverting families, the target child was a boy, whereas among the persisters, 80% were girls.

Concerning the work status of the mothers of the reverting parents, one of the husbands and one of the wives had had an employed mother when growing up. However, the latter expressed very negative feelings about the situation. She stated that "I WANTED MOM," although she now feels that that was a selfish view. Even more significant, she disliked her mother's going to work because she was "scared to be left with Dad because he would get violent."

Concerning the reverting parents' views of their own father's nurturance, the pattern was the reverse of that found for persisting families. Here it was the men who perceived their fathers as very nurturant, not the women. For example, the mother who described her father as violent commented about his nurturance as follows: "He would tell the children to come to him with their problems and then yell at them when they did." When the mean scores for parental perceptions of the grandfathers' nurturance were compared in the persisting and reverting groups, it was evident that the wives of men who persisted as primary caregivers perceived their fathers to be more nurturant than did reverting mothers, and persisting fathers perceived their own fathers to be less nurturant than did the reverting men.

Both mothers who had resumed a primary caregiver role four years later were employed when initially interviewed, one full time as a nurse (RN) and one part time as a licensed practical nurse (LPN), but their feelings about their jobs in 1977 were much more conflicted than were those of the women whose husbands persisted as primary caregivers. The RN described her feelings about her job as ambivalent; she liked it but also disliked it, because she both enjoyed working and enjoyed being home. The LPN said she liked her job, but her husband felt ambivalent about it. He liked her working because it gave her fulfillment, but disliked it because it was very difficult to arrange their schedules. Lending some support to the hypothesis that perceived financial necessity is a precursor of long-term parental role reversal, is the 1977 statement of the LPN that she worked because she wanted to, and not because she had to.

In contrast to the families maintaining the nontraditional arrangement, all the mothers and fathers who were reverters had expressed some dissatisfaction in 1977 with their child-care arrangement. The RN said she was resentful when she had to work and be away from home. The LPN saw the problem as her husband and herself not having enough time together, adding that "When we do, we regret it. We can't go out much and we go our separate ways." The change desired by the RN in 1977 was to work part time, because she felt guilty about being out of the house so much. The LPN said at that time that she would like to change her hours so that the family could have weekends together.

There was also a major difference between the persisters and reverters in the length of time the families had had the current child-care arrangement as of 1977. For the LPN it was only six months; for the RN, though she had been working full time for two years, for the first two years of the child's life, she had worked only part time. Thus both women had had ample time to experience the primary caregiver role.

Finally, when the families were asked in 1981 why they had selected the original child-care plan, the RN said that her husband was in school to develop a new career and she had to work. The LPN indicated that she had just graduated and wanted to use her practical nursing skills. Neither she nor her husband wanted to use a sitter, and he wanted to have something to do with the children. The husbands' views generally agreed with those of their wives, with the LPN's spouse commenting that his wife wanted to pursue her career, and to support her, he had to help with the child care. Thus it appears that the families reverting to traditional parenting roles, like the persisting couples, had had diverse reasons for selecting the father-primary-caregiver arrangement in 1977.

When the follow-up interview took place, it was learned that both reverting families had increased the size of their family; one had added one child and the other, two children, the youngest of whom had Down's Syndrome. Both families now had three children, which was more than any of the persister families had.

Both sets of reverting parents also said that large changes had taken place since the time of the last interview. The RN was no longer working outside the home, and her husband was now employed in a well-paying job in a city about 100 miles from Ann Arbor. She said she had "burned out" on the job, and had felt guilty about not being home and around her child more. In addition, there had been pressure from her family, especially her mother, who had not worked while rearing children, and she was frequently told that a mother's place is in the home. She saw the advantage of the current arrangement as one of not being stressed by having to leave for work outside the home.

The LPN and her spouse also told of big changes in their lives. The mother said that she had given up her career as an LPN because she could not make much money, and "it wasn't worth my working outside the home." She is now occupied with caring for the three children, especially the handicapped infant, who is receiving intensive physical therapy at home. The family is living on a farm on the West Coast, caring for some farm animals and homesteading. The ex-LPN said that she would like to have her husband spend more time with the children, but he works an afternoon shift and this makes it difficult. He voiced the same views. In contrast, the RN's spouse indicated that he was now satisfied with the child-care arrangement, and would not want any changes.

PREDICTORS OF LONG-TERM HIGH FATHER INVOLVEMENT: GENERAL CONCLUSIONS

From this myriad of details, we can generate some hypotheses about antecedents of stable high father involvement in child care, in white middle-class families with young children. The predictors can be put into four categories: (1) background factors: the early childhood experiences of the parents; (2) precipitators of the decision to try the arrangement; (3) conditions fostering the stability of the arrangement in the short range; and (4) conditions fostering the perpetuation of the arrangement in the long range. The subcategories falling within these broader classifications will be discussed, along with comparable findings from other investigations.

Background Factors: Early Childhood Experiences

Three predictors emerge here: (1) the mother was raised in a home in which her mother worked, and she did not find the experience very aversive or traumatic; (2) the mother views her own father as having been relatively nurturant and nonthreatening; (3) the father views his own father as having been relatively nonnurturant.

Thus the wife of a man who maintained the role of primary caregiver for at least four years tended to have had two positive role models: a working mother and a nonthreatening, fairly nurturant father. In contrast, the child-rearing husband appeared to have had a more negative role model—a father who was not very warm and loving. It may be that the father was attempting to compensate with his own children for the deficits in his family of origin, and that the wife's background dovetailed with those efforts. These conclusions tend to be concordant with data collected on antecedents of paternal involvement in child rearing assessed at a single time. The presence of a negative role model for the involved father was found by Barnett and Baruch (1984), and by De Frain (1979), who studied androgynous parents. The presence of a nurturant paternal model for the wife of the stable caregiving father is congruent with the data obtained by Feldman and colleagues (1983), and with our own data (Radin, 1981, 1982), collected in 1977 on the entire sample of 59 families, in which perceived nurturance of the mother's father correlated with the amount of participation in child rearing by her husband. The conclusions drawn about the family of origin of the persisting parents differ most from the findings of the Israeli study, in which caregiving men were found to have nurturant fathers (Sagi, 1982). Cultural differences between Israel and the United States, as described in the paper by Radin and Sagi (1982), may well explain the discrepancy. Further support of the hypotheses that having a working mother may predispose a woman to a father-caregiving arrangement is provided by Pruett's (1983) finding that 13 of the 17 wives of the primary caregiver fathers in his sample had had mothers who were employed.

Precipitators of the Decision to Try the Arrangement

Four antecedents are relevant here:

1. The mother was not the primary caregiver of the child for more than 18 months, and in most cases, for not more than 6 months after the child's birth.
2. The family holds the belief that young children should not be left with a sitter for a prolonged period of time.

3. The father's hours are flexible or he is not working at all.
4. One of four alternative conditions prevail relevant to the parents' occupational status: the mother has a strong career interest and the father is supportive; the father has a weak or negative view of his career and the mother is supportive; both parents have strong career interest and also flexible hours; or the father is obtaining additional training or education and the wife is able to work and help support the family.

The first antecedent may be powerful because it prevents mothers from developing a central role that is difficult to relinquish—that of primary caregiver of the child. The hypothesis that a central role is related to one's self-definition and tends to be maintained, is in keeping with social role theory and related topics pertaining to role-leaving (Feld & Radin, 1982). The second antecedent, attitudes pertaining to the use of babysitters, had not been considered critical in this study or in other published reports on involved fathering. The focus, as in Russell's (1982) work, has almost always been on attitudes about parental roles. Attitudes about substitute caregiver roles warrant further investigation, given that the percentage of working mothers with children is now over 56% (Hoffman, 1984).

Having flexible hours was also found by Russell (1982) to be an important predictor in his study of shared child rearing in Australia. The most significant aspect of parents' employment as a predictor is that both the mother's and father's perspectives must be considered together. We cannot look only at the mother's career or the father's career—it is the combination that is critical. This systemic orientation is congruent with the current theoretical focus on the total family in explaining behavior, rather than on single-person variables.

Conditions Fostering the Stability of the Arrangement in the Short Range

A number of conditions are predictive of persisting high father involvement:

1. The parents are generally satisfied with the child-care arrangement.
2. Both parents have positive feelings about the mother's working, with no ambivalence involved.
3. The family resides in a community supportive of such arrangements.
4. The parents are in their thirties rather than their twenties, and have started in their careers or are fairly well established in them.
5. The mother does not feel great guilt about leaving her child.
6. The mother feels she has to work.

Russell (1982) also found that the more satisfied parents felt with the role-reversed pattern, the more fathers tended to stay highly involved in the care of their children. In regard to positive attitudes about the mother's working, Pruett (1983), in his two year follow-up, reported that regardless of socioeconomic status, the wives of caregiving fathers continued to report high satisfaction with their work.

Lamb (1982) found that it was not the fact of maternal employment that influenced the outcomes for the family, but the mother's feeling about her life. He concluded after reviewing the literature, that mothers who are satisfied with their lives—whether or not they are employed—have well-adjusted children.

Conditions Fostering the Perpetuation of the Arrangement in the Long Range

The following conditions appear to predict long-term high father involvement:

1. The mother's investment in her career grows.
2. The father finds caring for the child gratifying.
3. The mother's salary is sufficiently large to warrant her working outside the home.
4. Family members do not pressure the mother to stay home.
5. The father's hours continue to be flexible, or he works on a part-time basis.
6. The family remains small and no catastrophic illness occurs.
7. The child the father is caring for over a prolonged period of time is a daughter, or more likely, an independent child.

It appears that for long-term stability, once again, the parents' positions must be considered conjointly. One factor not appearing previously, and which merits further inquiry, is the presence or absence of pressure to conform to traditional roles. This type of social influence has been found in numerous studies to bring about conformity, particularly in small groups and families (Feld & Radin, 1982). There is some support in Pruett's (1985) work for the finding that the sex of the child may be a factor contributing to the stability of involved fathering. In his four-year follow-up of primary caregiving fathers of very young children, he mentions "some hints that some of the boys are doing a bit worse affectively during the fourth and fifth years." Taking a psychoanalytic perspective, Pruett speculates that this finding may be attributable to the fact that whereas girls may still have their mothers as rivals, boys must be rivalrous with the primary nurturing figures in their lives.

Pruett's (1985) data also lend support to the hypothesis that a small family size may foster stability in father caregiving. All of his 17 families with caregiving fathers had only one child when initially interviewed. Pruett reported that in the seven families in which the father continued as the primary caregiving parent for two years, 50% had had no additional child, whereas in the three families that reverted to a mother-primary-caregiver pattern, 100% had had second children.

Along with the list of antecedents, variables that are *not* predictive of a stable high father involved pattern should be noted. Russell's (1982) follow-up data, our own findings (Radin, 1982), and the results of Lamb and colleagues' short-term investigations (Lamb, et al., 1982) show that the sex-role orientation of the parents does not systematically predict how involved fathers stay in the day-to-day care of their young children. When average scores on the Bem Sex Role Inventory (Bem & Watson, 1976) were computed in the Michigan study for all mothers and fathers, there were virtually no differences between persisters and reverters for either men or women. Similarly, whether the father had child-care skills before the target child was born, and whether the parents had positive role models currently available (such as friends who were highly involved fathers) do not appear to differentiate the persisters from the reverters. Neither does expressed paternal nurturance, as rated in an observation of father–child interaction in 1977 in the Michigan study.

In sum, it is clear from even this very small sample that the reasons for establishing an arrangement of high father involvement are not the same as the reasons for maintaining it over a period of years. It is also evident that there are alternate paths to selecting and persevering in that role-reversed plan, and many factors contribute to its stability. Perhaps the reason there are so few families in which fathers are primary caregivers over prolonged periods of time is not merely because of prior socialization in the traditional role, as has often been suggested, but because it is difficult to find the combination of conditions which may be necessary for a family to withstand the powerful societal pressures on those who try to create new parental patterns of behavior (cf. Cowan & Cowan, 1987).

CONSEQUENCES OF HIGH FATHER INVOLVEMENT

Thus far, few data are available about the consequences for children raised in homes with high father involvement over a prolonged period of time. However, from the data thus far collected, some extrapolations can be drawn about short-term effects (Radin, 1981, 1982; Radin & Sagi, 1982). There were indications that children's intellectual functioning was stimulated more in families with high father involvement. We attribute this effect to the fact that fathers appear to have a different way of interacting with children; they tend to be more physical, more provocative, and less stereotyped in their play behavior than mothers (Radin, 1986). There are also strong indications that father presence is linked to children's mathematics ability (Radin, 1976). For example, Landy, Rosenberg, and Sutton-Smith (1969), studying the American College Entrance Examination Scores of college sophomores, found that the quantitative scores of women whose fathers were absent during childhood were significantly lower than the quantitative scores of women whose fathers were present, but started working on a night shift after the girls were 10 years of age. (There were no significant differences in the language scores of the two groups.) Since there were no significant differences between the quantitative scores of the father-absent group and those of a group whose fathers started working on the night shift when the girls were *under* 10, the authors concluded that the ages of one through nine composed a critical period for the development of quantitative skills in girls, and that fathers who were available influenced this development. In addition, it was found by several investigators (Carlsmith, 1964; Nelsen & Maccoby, 1966) that high school and college males whose fathers were absent were more likely than boys whose fathers were present to have a feminine patterning on standard aptitude tests—that is, a higher verbal than mathematics score. Thus it is reasonable to conjecture that greater father involvement in child care will have beneficial effects on children's cognitive growth, particularly on the mathematical competence of both sons and daughters.

Further support for this view is the finding that primary caregiving fathers spend more time than do traditional fathers in cognitively stimulating activities with children, particularly with daughters (Radin, 1981, 1982). These data suggest that the effect of more involved fathering on girls' cognitive functioning may be especially powerful. In addition, Pruett's (1985) initial findings indicate that children raised primarily by men can be vigorous, competent, and thriving infants. Many of the infants functioned well above the expected norms on a standardized test of development. On both problem-solving tasks and social skills, the infants were 2 to 10 months ahead of schedule.

It can also be anticipated that such children will make more nontraditional career choices. The preschool-aged children in families where there were primary caregiving fathers were found to have a more internal locus of control (Radin, 1981, 1982; Radin & Sagi, 1982; Sagi, 1982), suggesting that they were not greatly influenced by the views of others in making their decisions. Further, social learning theory (Bandura, 1967) would suggest that when relatively nurturant parents play nontraditional parental and occupational roles over a period of time, this modeling should have a major impact on children's later performance in similar roles.

Whether these predictions prove to be accurate can best be determined by longitudinal research; my own work in the coming year will include a follow-up of these families eight years after the initial caregiving patterns were assessed. It is important that clinicians, sociologists, and child development researchers learn more about families who are on the forefront of change; these mothers and fathers may prove to be the harbinger of patterns that will become commonplace in the years to come.

REFERENCES

Bandura, A. (1967). The role of modeling processes in personality development. In W.W. Hartup & N.L. Smothergell (Eds.), *The young child: Review of research*. Washington, DC: National Association for the Education of Young Children.

Barnett, R.C., & Baruch, G.K. (1984). *Determinants of fathers' participation in family work*. Wellesley, MA: Center for Research on Women, Wellesley College. (Duplicated)

Bem, S.L. (1974). The measurement of psychological androgyny. *Journal of Consulting and Clinical Psychology, 42*, 155–162.

Bem, S.L., & Watson, C. (1976). *Scoring packet: Bem sex-role inventory*. Stanford, CA: Stanford University.

Bronfenbrenner, U., Alvarez, W.F., & Hendersen, C.R., Jr. (1984). Working and watching: Maternal employment status and parents' perception of their three year old children. *Child Development, 55*, 1362–1378.

Carlsmith, L. (1964). Effect of early father absence on scholastic aptitude. *Harvard Educational Review, 34*, 3–21.

Cowan, C.P., & Cowan, P.A. (1987). Men's involvement in parenthood: Identifying the antecedents and understanding the barriers. In P. Berman & F. Pedersen (Eds.), *Men's transition to parenthood*. Hillsdale, NJ: Erlbaum.

De Frain, J. (1979). Androgynous parents tell who they are and what they need. *Family Coordinator*, *28*, 237–243.

Feld, S., & Radin, N. (1982). *Social psychology for social work and the mental health professions*. New York: Columbia University Press.

Feldman, S.S., Nash, S.C., & Aschenbrenner, B.G. (1983). Antecedents of fathering. *Child Development*, *54*, 1628–1636.

Hoffman, L.W. (1984). Work, family, and the socialization of the child. In R.D. Paarke (Ed.), *The family*. Chicago, IL: University of Chicago Press.

Lamb, M.E. (1982). Maternal employment and child development: A review. In M.E. Lamb (Ed.), *Nontraditional families: Parenting and child development*. Hillsdale, NJ: Erlbaum.

Lamb, M.E., Frodi, A.M., Hwang, C-P., Frodi, M., & Steinberg, J. (1982). Mother- and father-infant interaction involving play and holding in traditional and nontraditional Swedish families. *Developmental Psychology*, *18*, 215–221.

Lamb, M., & Levine, J.A. (1983). The Swedish parental insurance policy: An experiment in social engineering. In M.E. Lamb & A. Sagi (Eds.), *Fatherhood and family policy*. Hillsdale, NJ: Erlbaum.

Landy, F., Rosenberg, B.G., & Sutton-Smith, B. (1969). The effect of limited father absence on cognitive development. *Child Development*, *40*, 941–944.

Nelsen, E.A., & Maccoby, E.E. (1966). The relationship between social development and differential abilities on the scholastic aptitude test. *Merrill-Palmer Quarterly*, *12*, 269–289.

Pruett, K.D. (1983, April). *Two year follow-up of infants of primary-nurturing fathers in intact families*. Paper presented to the Second World Congress in Infant Psychiatry, Cannes, France.

Pruett, K.D. (1985). Oedipal configurations in young father-raised children. In A.J. Solnit, R.S. Eissler, & P.B. Neubauer (Eds.), *The psychoanalytic study of the child* (Vol. 40). New Haven, CT: Yale University Press.

Radin, N. (1976). The role of the father in cognitive/academic and intellectual development. In M.E. Lamb (Ed.), *The role of the father in child development* (Second ed). New York: Wiley.

Radin, N. (1981). Childrearing fathers in intact families I: Some antecedents and consequences. *Merrill-Palmer Quarterly*, *27*, 489–514.

Radin, N. (1982). Primary caregiving and role-sharing fathers. In M.E. Lamb (Ed.), *Nontraditional families: Parenting and child development*. Hillsdale, NJ: Erlbaum.

Radin, N. (1986). The influence of fathers upon sons and daughters and implications for school social work. *Social Work in Education*, *8*, 77–91.

Radin, N., & Goldsmith, R. (1983, April). Predictors of father involvement in childcare. Paper presented at the biennial meeting of the Society for Research in Child Development, Detroit, MI. (ERIC Document Reproduction Service No. ED 248 031.)

Radin, N., & Goldsmith, R. (1985). Caregiving father of preschoolers. Four years later. *Merrill-Palmer Quarterly*, *31*, 375–383.

Radin, N., & Russell, G. (1983). Increased father participation and childcare development outcomes. In M.E. Lamb & A. Sagi (Eds.), *Fatherhood and family policy*. Hillsdale, NJ: Erlbaum.

Radin, N., & Sagi, A. (1982). Childrearing fathers in intact families in Israel and the U.S.A. *Merrill-Palmer Quarterly, 28*, 111–136.

Russell, G. (1982). Shared-caregiving families: An Australian study. In M.E. Lamb (Ed.), *Nontraditional families: Parenting and child development*. Hillsdale, NJ: Erlbaum.

Sagi, A. (1982). Antecedents and consequences of various degrees of paternal involvement in child-rearing: The Israeli project. In M.E. Lamb (Ed.), *Nontraditional families: Parenting and child development*. Hillsdale, NJ: Erlbaum.

CHAPTER 10

Parent–Child Relationships in Stepfather Families

JOHN W. SANTROCK, KAREN A. SITTERLE, and RICHARD A. WARSHAK

In the last 10 to 15 years, family and child development researchers have become increasingly aware that fathers play an important and unique role in their child's life from infancy onward (Lamb, 1981). From the time of conception until adulthood, children form a very special relationship with their fathers—a relationship that is as significant as the relationship they have with their mothers, and yet very different. Along with this recognition of the importance of the father's role has emerged an interest in studying special groups of fathers such as single-parent fathers, teenage fathers, Black fathers, and gay fathers. One group that has remained relatively neglected, however, is stepfathers. Yet, if current statistics are accurate, more and more men will find themselves joining the ranks of stepfatherhood, trying to fill an ambiguous and ill-defined role for which they will have had little or no preparation (Visher & Visher, 1979).

Remarried families (i.e., families in which one or both of the spouses bring children from a prior marriage to live in the newly formed stepfamily) are among the fastest growing social phenomena in the United States. Divorces in this country are being granted at a rate of over 1.2 million a year, and most involve minor children. Four out of five of these divorced adults remarry within three years (Glick, 1980). Thus many of the children of divorce become children of remarriage. It is estimated that if present rates of childbearing, divorce, and remarriage continue, by 1990 as many as 25–33% of *all* children will, by the age of 18, have lived at least part of their lives as a member of a stepfamily (Glick, 1984). And of all remarriages that will occur, almost half will include a stepfather (Robinson, 1984).

It is important to keep in mind that remarried families are families in *transition*. Remarriage represents just one event in a long sequence of events that follow in the

A number of people contributed in substantial ways to the research project described in this chapter. Cathy Dozier performed the duties of project coordinator with organization and cheer. Majorie Stephens provided invaluable help with data coordination and statistical analysis. Pamela Blumenthal provided helpful comments on an earlier version of the chapter. This research was made possible through a grant from the National Institute of Mental Health #5-RO1-MH-34954. Also, a grant from the Hogg Foundation of Mental Health provided continued support of this research.

wake of family disruption. It is one of many steps, beginning with the difficult process of making the shift from life in a two-parent family to life in a single-parent household to yet another step—life in a remarried family. The first transition period following separation and divorce is characterized by disequilibrium and disorganization, in which family members are experimenting with a variety of coping mechanisms, some more effective than others (Hetherington, 1981). Ideally, this period is then followed by reorganization and eventual attainment of a new pattern of equilibrium in the single-parent household. However, when a single parent remarries and a new family is formed, another period of disequilibrium may occur. Family members may be confronted with a number of major changes, including assumption of new roles and responsibilities, reorganization of household routines, new attachments, a new financial status, and perhaps relocation of residence and school—and the eventual formation of a new family system.

The most common permutation of the various remarried family arrangements is one in which a man marries a woman with children. In these instances, while the mother and her children share common background, history, and cultural values, the new stepfather has a different background and history, and his values may differ considerably from those of his new stepfamily. Thus the new stepfather is often in the position of trying to break into a unit of mother and children, whose bonds predate the association between the spouses. The longer this unit has existed, the more difficult it may be for the stepfather to be assimilated into the new family system (Visher & Visher, 1979). While a nuclear family can gradually develop a set of commonly agreed-upon values, a stepfamily plunges in and starts to struggle almost immediately. Many stepfathers have reported feeling poorly prepared for the many problems they face in trying to integrate into a new household and establish new roles of husband and father simultaneously (Messinger, 1976; Messinger, Walker, & Freeman, 1978).

As the number of stepfamilies seeking professional help continues to increase, it becomes imperative that rigorous empirical studies be carried out to inform clinical work. Stepfamily research, however, is at a formative stage. Investigators must contend not only with the complexities of research measurement and design involved in doing family research in general, but also with the problems specific to working with stepfamily populations (Esses & Campbell, 1984). One of the major problems is the reliance on data collected from surveys and questionnaires, which have been completed by only one family member, usually the stepparent or stepchild (Bowerman & Irish, 1962; Wilson, Zurcher, McAdams, & Curtis, 1975). Other studies have used clinical reports of unknown reliability (Fast & Cain, 1966; Visher & Visher, 1979). Most stepfamily studies also fail to include a control group of intact families or behavioral observations of the family members, while others combine stepmother and stepfather families into a single group when conducting statistical analyses. Not surprisingly, the stepfamily research provides a mixed and confusing picture of children's development and adjustment in stepfamily homes. Some studies indicate that children from stepfamilies are less well-adjusted (Bowerman & Irish, 1962; Fast & Cain, 1966; Langner & Michael, 1963), while others claim that children in stepparent homes are functioning just as well as their counterparts living with biological parents in nondivorced families (Bernard, 1956; Burchinal, 1964; Duberman, 1973; Wilson, et al., 1975).

This situation, however, has improved considerably in the past few years, as several major studies and numerous small-scale investigations are underway. A recent special issue of *Family Relations* (Pasley & Ihinger-Tallman, 1984) on stepfamily research and clinical work with remarried families, for example, signals a scholarly commitment to empirical research on remarriage and stepfamily life. In this chapter, we will be presenting the results and findings from our own investigation of stepfamilies. We will focus particularly on stepfather families, by which we mean families consisting of a mother who obtains custody of her children following divorce, her children, and a stepfather, all living together in the same home. In the first section, we will briefly review and critique the prior research on family relations in stepfather families, with particular emphasis on findings regarding the stepfather–child relationship. We will then turn to our own research investigation of stepfather families.

STEPFATHER FAMILY RESEARCH

The findings in the stepfather family research are somewhat inconclusive and at times mixed. Positive or negative outcomes seem all too often to be a function of the methods used to obtain data (Robinson, 1984). Typically, stepfather family studies have been conducted from three different research traditions: (1) clinical, (2) family sociological, and (3) quasi-experimental/developmental. There are inherent strengths and weaknesses in each of these three traditions that affect the nature of the findings and conclusions (Santrock & Sitterle, 1985).

Clinical studies of stepfather families who are being seen for counseling or therapy indicate an array of adjustment problems, particularly in the stepfather–child relationship. The clinical evidence suggests that how stepchildren view their relationships with stepfathers depends in part on how old they are at the time their mothers remarry (Visher & Visher, 1979). It seems that children below the age of nine are more likely to accept the stepfather and form a warm, intense attachment (Hetherington, Cox, & Cox, 1982) than children who are between nine and 15 years of age when their mothers remarry.

In addition, clinical reports suggest that stepfathers have a set of common problems unique to their role. Some of the most frequently mentioned problems are feeling poorly prepared for the task of integrating themselves into a new household and role, uncertainty about the degree of authority they have in the role of father, loyalty conflicts, tension over leaving children from a previous marriage, and confusion about the amount and manner of showing affection to their stepchildren, particularly their stepdaughters (Messinger, 1976; Messinger, Walker, & Freeman, 1978; Mowatt, 1972; Stern, 1982; Visher & Visher, 1979).

However, the extent to which these difficulties occur in stepfather families not seeking help is unknown, since the clinical tradition in stepfamily research is characterized by the study of small, heterogeneous samples that usually do not include a control group. Stepfather families seeking counseling may be a select group undergoing considerably more stress than those who are not involved in therapy (Robinson, 1984). Providing evidence for this is the fact that clinical studies report more pathology and adjustment problems in stepfather families than do studies of larger, more representative samples of stepfather family populations, which tend to find more positive outcomes in family functioning. This is especially true when stepfather families are systematically compared with other family structures, such as single parent or father-absent families. (Robinson, 1984).

In the family sociology tradition, surveys and questionnaires typically are given to large random samples of stepfather families. In two of the earliest and most widely cited studies (Bowerman & Irish, 1962; Duberman, 1973), contradictory results were found on practically every dimension. For example, in the Bowerman and Irish study, the relationships in stepfamilies were characterized by more stress and ambivalence and less cohesiveness than those in nonstepfamily homes. In contrast, in the Duberman study, 64% of the stepfamilies rated themselves as having excellent relationships, while only 18% rated themselves as having poor relationships. Of course, the fact that adolescent stepchildren were surveyed in the former study and stepparents in the latter makes it difficult to compare outcomes.

As these studies illustrate, a major shortcoming of most questionnaire research is that conclusions are based on the perceptions of only one family member, usually a parent or child, but not both. It makes sense that the perceptions of children and parents are different, and that both groups evaluate their relationships differently. Not only have these factors generally not been considered, but both survey/questionnaire and clinical investigations have generally not included two-parent families or stepmother families as comparison groups. For example, adjustment may be better for children in stepfather families than for those in conflict-ridden intact families. Age at onset of the dissolution of the original family, reason for parental absence (death or divorce), and the length of time the child has lived in the stepfamily are important demographic variables that can be controlled for in studies of different family structures (Santrock, Warshak, Lindbergh, & Meadows, 1982).

Two large surveys that did include comparison groups (Burchinal, 1964; Wilson, et al., 1975) confirmed the positive findings reported by Duberman. Wilson and his colleagues, who collected data from two national surveys on a large array of variables, including several related to mental health, found no differences between respondents living in stepfather families and those living in nonstepfamily homes. However, neither Burchinal nor Wilson and his colleagues assessed the quality of interpersonal relations within the stepfamily (as did Duberman and also Bowerman and Irish), but rather focused primarily on global personality traits and psychological and demographic characteristics. Also, both of these studies examined only children's responses, failing to include responses from stepparents or biological parents (Robinson, 1984).

Moving beyond earlier survey research on stepparent families, Bohannan and Erickson (1978) included comparison groups and responses from both stepchildren and stepparents. In this investigation, positive outcomes in stepparent families were reported from the perspective of both parents and children. The stepchildren viewed themselves as being just as happy as biological children, and were found to be just as successful and achieving as their biological counterparts. Children in stepfather families got along as well with their stepfathers as children in nondivorced families got along with their fathers. Mothers' survey responses were similar to those of the children. In contrast, however, biological fathers rated their children as significantly happier than stepfathers rated their stepchildren, and biological fathers rated themselves as significantly better fathers than stepfathers rated themselves. In other words, stepfathers viewed themselves and their children as less successful and happy, even though the children and their mothers did not feel that way.

The experimental/developmental approach to the study of stepfather families emphasizes a careful matching of demographic variables, inclusion of a control group (usually of intact nuclear families), and a multimethod assessment that often includes behavioral observations and extensive use of statistical analyses. However, research on stepparent families that controls for or investigates such important variables as the age at onset of the divorce, the reason for the natural parent's absence, and the length of time the child has lived in the stepparent family, is very limited. Chapman (1977) investigated the cognitive development of 96 college students who came from father-absent, stepfather, or intact family backgrounds. Age at onset of father absence was controlled, but the reason for the father absence and length of time in the stepfather family were not. He found that the presence of a stepfather attenuated the negative effects of father absence on cognitive development. In another investigation of the effects of a stepfather family structure on cognitive development, Santrock (1972) found that the entrance of a stepfather, when the child's natural father and mother had become divorced before the age of five, had a positive effect on 6- to 11-year old boys, but not girls. In a third investigation, focused on the effects of stepfather family structure on children's development, Oshman and Manosevitz (1976) gave a questionnaire based on Erikson's eight stages of development to late adolescent males from father-absent, stepfather, and intact family backgrounds. The questions required the subjects to evaluate themselves on such personality characteristics as trust versus mistrust and identity versus identity diffusion. The personality characteristics of the boys from stepfather families were more positive than those of boys from father-absent families.

These studies of stepfather families suggest that the entrance of a stepfather into a previously father-absent home has a positive effect on boys' cognitive and personality development; the effects on girls' cognitive and personality development are virtually uncharted. However, the nature of the data collected provides an incomplete picture of boys growing up in stepfather families as well. The dependent variables in studies of children in stepparent families characteristically have been one or two paper and pencil measures, usually achievement, intelligence, or personality tests. None of the stepfamily studies reviewed so far has included actual observations of children, their parents, and their stepparents.

Recently, several behavioral studies have been conducted in the quasi-experimental/developmental tradition. Santrock and colleagues (1982) examined the social behavior of boys and girls, ages 6 to 12, from nondivorced, divorced, and remarried families. The study included videotaped observations of the interactions between the parent–child and the stepparent–child dyads. The most consistent findings were that boys in stepfather families showed more competent social behavior than boys in intact families, which corresponded with more competent parenting behavior in stepfather families. In contrast, girls in stepfather families were observed to be more anxious than girls in intact families. Further, boys showed more warmth toward their stepfathers than did girls, while there was a trend for girls in these families to show more anger toward their mothers than did boys. Children from divorced and stepfather families differed only in a trend for boys from stepfather families to show more mature behavior than boys from divorced homes; correspondingly, mothers of boys in stepfather families made more meaningful statements to their sons than divorced mothers of boys made to theirs. Few differences were found between divorced and intact families. It was concluded that the social behavior of children is not necessarily less competent in stepfather families than in intact or divorced families, and that in any type of family structure, such factors as parenting behavior, sex of child, and marital conflict may be predictors of children's social behavior.

Hetherington and colleagues (1982) followed 60 custodial mothers, their ex-spouses, and their children in the two years immediately following marital dissolution, and then did a follow-up at six years following the divorce. In the follow-up study, the investigators found that 70% of the custodial mothers had remarried, thus making the transition from a single-parent family to a stepfather family. Examining this subset of stepfather families, the investigators found that stepfathers tended to show more variability than natural fathers in their family relationships—either being disengaged, inattentive, and nonsupportive of the mother, or being active and involved in raising their stepchildren, particularly their stepsons. Stepfathers often reported dissatisfaction with their wives' lack of control over sons, and expressed a wish to help them regain control. If the natural mother welcomed the involvement of the stepfather, and the stepfather was an authoritative parent (warm, willing to set limits, and to participate in verbal give-and-take), children in stepparent families, particularly boys, functioned better than those in divorced, unremarried families or in conflict-ridden intact families. In such cases the stepfather proved to be an effective support to both the natural mother and stepson, and his presence was associated with a reduced frequency of coercive interactions between mother and son. Young boys often formed intense, warm attachments with their stepfather, and a positive relationship with the stepfather was associated with more mature, independent, and controlled behavior in boys at home and at school. However, if the remarriage occurred when the boy was older (9 or 10), the child's relationship with the stepfather was more likely to be negative and problematic than in the case of younger children. Hetherington and colleagues noted that even if a supportive stepfather was present for sons, a continued positive relationship with the natural father played an important role in the development of social and cognitive competence. On the other hand, few significant differences were observed in the mother–daughter relationship, or in the behavior of girls in remarried, divorced, or intact families. This last finding contrasts with the previously mentioned results reported by Santrock and colleagues (1982), who found the presence of a stepfather to be associated with more adverse outcomes for girls. These differences may be attributable to the fact the preadolescent daughters in the study by Santrock and colleagues, who were slightly older than those in the study by Hetherington and colleagues, may have been experiencing different dynamics with their stepfathers.

A study of parents and children in stepfamilies by Clingempeel, Brand, and Ievoli (1984) also found that nine-year-old girls had more problematic relationships with their stepfathers *and* stepmothers than did their brothers. These investigators examined the quality of stepparent–child relationships in 16 stepfather and 16 step-mother families, using both self-report questionnaires and behavioral observations. Biological parents, stepparents, and children all rated the stepparent–stepdaughter relationship as more detached and less intimate than the other pairs. The observa-tional data also were consistent with family members' self-reports. Girls displayed a lower proportion of positive and a higher proportion of negative verbal problem-solving behavior toward their stepparents than did boys. Interestingly, stepparents did not differ in their observed interactions with either boys or girls. Unfortunately, Clingempeel and colleagues did not look at either the remarried biological par-ent–child interactions or parent–child relationships in intact families, so we do not know how the stepparent–child relationships compared with those in other family constellations.

A multimethod approach to the study of stepfamilies is necessary before a comprehensive picture of stepfamily members can be obtained (Robinson, 1984; Santrock, Warshak, & Elliott, 1982). Perceptions of all stepfamily members, as-sessed by questionnaires, should be used in conjunction with behavioral observa-tions assessed by outside observers. Standardized personality and cognitive mea-sures given to stepparents and stepchildren can further contribute to creating a comprehensive portrait of the psychological makeup of the stepfamily (Robinson, 1984). A multimethod, multisource (natural parent, stepparent, and child), multi-family structure approach may help to reduce some of the inconsistent conclusions in stepfather research. In our own investigation of interpersonal relationships in stepmother and stepfather families, which is presented in the remainder of the chap-ter, we have taken that approach.

A COMPARISON STUDY OF STEPFATHER FAMILIES

Subjects

Participating in the study were 69 children and their parents and stepparents, from three types of family structures: (1) families where the father retained custody fol-lowing a divorce and remarried (18 families; 10 girls, 8 boys); (2) families where the mother retained custody following a divorce and remarried (26 families; 13 girls, 13 boys); and (3) two-parent or intact families where both biological parents were living in the home, with no history of divorce (25 families; 12 girls, 13 boys).

Participating children and their families were recruited from the Dallas-Fort Worth metropolitan area using referrals from university students, churches, the

Dallas Stepfamily Association, and responses to newspaper articles and radio and television advertisements. As might be expected, the stepmother families were the most difficult to obtain. An elaborate and prolonged search for these families was pursued over an 18-month period, and finally terminated after obtaining 18 families meeting the criteria.

The children were all from White, middle-class families, with one child in the family who was between the ages of 7 and 11 serving as the target child. The mean age of target children was nine years, six months, and the average grade level was fourth grade. In all the stepparent families, the reason for dissolution of the child's biological parents' marriage was divorce, and the biological parent in the stepfamily was always the parent who had received custody of the child following the divorce. The stepparent families had lived together for at least one year, and none of the children had been identified as having emotional problems.

An attempt was made to match parents and stepparents on age, education, and socioeconomic status.[1] The mean total family income was $47,000, indicating that the participating families were clearly from the middle to upper middle class. The men in the sample tended to be high school graduates in their mid-to-late thirties who had completed some college or advanced training. The women were somewhat younger and less well-educated than their spouses; most were in their early- to mid-thirties and had completed high school. Noncustodial parents, on average, had completed some college or advanced training beyond high school. Another difference between the male and female parents in the sample is worth noting. The male parents were all working 40 hours or more a week, while most of the female parents worked on a part-time basis, with the women in the stepparent groups more likely to be holding down full- or part-time jobs than their counterparts in intact families. As anticipated, the parents in intact families had been married significantly longer than the couples in the stepparent groups, on average nearly 15 years as compared to three years. The two stepparent groups were closely matched on the length of marriage.

Characteristics of Stepfather and Stepmother Families

Stepfather and stepmother family groups were well-matched on most variables. In general, the children in stepparent families were about three and a half years old when their parents separated and about six years old when their custodial parent later remarried. The average length of the custodial parents' first marriage had been about seven and a half years, and they had tended to wait about two years before marrying again. Not surprisingly, during the time they were single parents, the income of later remarried fathers was nearly twice as much as that of later remarried mothers. Also, as would be expected, noncustodial fathers were making greater annual child support payments compared to the almost negligible payments made by noncustodial mothers.

---

[1] An additional intent of this investigation was to obtain children who could be closely matched to a group of children from single-parent father custody and single-parent mother custody families who had been previously studied (Santrock & Warshak, 1979; Santrock, Warshak, & Elliott, 1982).

Procedure

In our investigation, we obtained information on family interactions from a variety of data sources. We interviewed biological parents and stepparents and gave them a battery of questionnaires to complete. We included children as informants via paper-and-pencil tests and interviews, and obtained observations of their interactions with peers in a laboratory play group. We observed parent–child and stepparent–child dyads interacting with each other in our laboratory. Finally, we asked teachers to rate the children's adjustment and behavior in the school setting. However, although a number of measures were used, we will describe only those relevant to the findings we will be reporting here.

Parent Involvement with Children: Adult Form

We asked biological parents and stepparents to indicate on a five-point scale how involved they were with their children in 11 different areas of parenting, such as discipline, celebrating holidays, discussing problems, and recreation (adapted from Ahrons, 1987). The parental involvement inventory was designed to provide a global rating of the degree to which the parent or stepparent was emotionally and physically available to the child both in day-to-day activities, and in the low-frequency, but salient events in the child's life (e.g., major holidays and birthdays). Thus the measure assessed the emotional responsiveness and sensitivity of the adult to the child's needs, as well as the degree to which the parent or stepparent was a stable and dependable figure in the child's life. We also asked parents and stepparents to complete the same questionnaire regarding the noncustodial parent's current involvement with the target child.

Parent Involvement with Children: Child Form

We also measured the child's perception of parental involvement, on the same 11 dimensions. The child's version was a nonverbal rather than a pencil-and-paper task, intended to minimize differences in cognitive and reading ability, and to increase children's interest in the task. We constructed a felt-covered board with five different colored pockets, ranging in size, with the largest pocket corresponding to the most involvement and the smallest pocket corresponding to the least involvement. Each area of parental involvement was phrased as a question, and printed on a card with a picture depicting the activity being inquired about. We then asked the child to place the card in the pocket that best described the amount of involvement by the parent. At separate times during the interview process, the child was asked to complete the involvement task to show the remarried parent's, the stepparent's, and the noncustodial parent's current involvement with him or her.

Parent Interview

We interviewed parents and stepparents individually, using a schedule designed to assess child-rearing practices, the parent–child relationship, the quality of the relationship with the spouse, and perceptions of the child's adjustment and self-esteem. We also asked remarried parents and stepparents about issues related to being in a stepfamily, such as the development of the stepparent's relationship with the child, previous parenting experience, loyalty conflicts, and perceptions of the stepparent role.

Observed Peer Interactions

Each child participated in a play group with two other participants in the study of the same sex and approximately the same age. Specifically, the play groups consisted of one child from an intact family and two children from stepparent families. It has been found that there is a high correspondence between children's behavior in contrived play groups of unacquainted peers and their behavior and social status with familiar peers at school (Coie & Kupersmidt, 1981).

The children met for one hour in a room equipped with toys suitable for both sexes, which were likely to elicit both active interaction as well as solitary play. The play group procedure consisted of a series of controlled tasks designed to elicit a range of situations that confront most children during their everyday encounters with their fellow peers such as cooperation, competition, play, and negotiation of conflicts with other children. The children were also given an opportunity for unstructured free play.

The play group sessions were videotaped and the taped interactions were later coded, using a system derived from previous coding schemes for studying laboratory play groups (Coie & Kupersmidt, 1981; Dodge, 1983). Categories focused on task-directed behavior, prosocial behavior, aversive behavior, and the degree of social interaction.

The Perceived Competence Scale for Children

Each child was asked to complete the Perceived Competence Scale for Children (Harter, 1982), a 28-item questionnaire designed to assess a child's sense of competence in different skill domains: cognitive (e.g., doing well at schoolwork, being smart, feeling good about one's classroom performance); social (e.g., having a lot of friends, being easy to like, and being an important member of one's class); and physical (e.g., doing well at sports, learning new outdoor games readily, and preferring to play sports rather than merely watch others play). In addition to these subscales, there is a fourth subscale which assesses the child's general feelings of worth or self-esteem, independent of any particular skill domain.

Teacher Ratings

The child's teacher at school rated the child using the Teacher's Rating Scale of Child's Competence (Harter, 1982), which is designed to parallel the Perceived Competence Scale for Children. Its subscales provide an independent assessment of the child's actual cognitive, social, and physical competence, plus an appraisal of the child's general sense of self-worth or self-esteem.

Parental Ratings of the Child's Behavior

Intact-family parents and remarried parents and stepparents were asked to complete the Child Behavior Checklist (Achenbach & Edelbrock, 1979, 1981), a widely used assessment device for evaluating a variety of problem behaviors that are of clinical concern. In addition, they were asked to complete The Parent Rating Form of Actual Competence (Harter, 1982), which is a modified version of the rating scale completed by teachers.

Data Analysis

We used a multivariate analysis of variance involving sex of child and family composition (stepfather, stepmother, and intact families). In some of the analyses, the intact families were used as the comparison group for the stepfather families, while in others the comparison group was the stepmother families. Rather than present the results separately for each measure, we have summarized the combined findings from the self-report measures of parental involvement completed by the child, stepparent, and biological parents. Using the results from these different data sources, it is possible to construct a profile of the interaction patterns between the different members in stepfather families. In our discussion, we will also be comparing the relationship patterns of stepfather families with those of intact and stepmother families.

Findings: The Experience of Stepfathers

We spent considerable time interviewing stepfathers about their views of stepfamily life and their role as a stepparent. In our group of stepfathers, we found that for over half, their current marriage was their second attempt at matrimony. Many of them also had children from their first marriage (54%), most of whom lived with their ex-wives and only occasionally visited the stepfather's remarried household. Thus while about half of our stepfathers had previous experience at parenting, for the other half, this was their first attempt at being a parent.

For many of the stepfathers, their current wife's children seemed to play a central role in their relationship with their spouse early on. Although half of the men said their stepchildren's feelings did not play a part in their decision to marry, the other 50% said that if their stepchildren had disapproved of the marriage, they would have seriously thought more about it, or postponed the decision. Thus for those stepfathers, children's acceptance played a key role in their entrance into the stepfamily arrangement, almost from the beginning.

In addition, many of the stepfathers acknowledged one or more areas of difficulties in assuming the stepparent role. One-fourth of the stepfathers reported some reservations around issues of discipline. For example, one stepfather said, "It's hard to discipline because her father tells her she doesn't have to do a certain thing after I tell her she does." Some felt they had initially been too strict or harsh in their relationship with their stepchildren, or that they were often impatient, and frequently became too easily annoyed by their stepchildren's normal behavior.

One-third of our stepfathers reported that there had been a critical incident, event, or confrontation that facilitated their stepchildren's acceptance of them as a parental figure, and nearly every one of those incidents had revolved around issues of discipline and limit-setting. Usually, it involved the stepfather asserting his authority for the first time, and enforcing a limit or rule that he had set, which the step-child was unwilling to obey. For example, one stepfather said, "It happened after a visit with his father. Joey said he didn't have to mind me because I wasn't his Dad. Since I put my foot down, we haven't had any more problems." There was a great deal of variability when this incident occurred; for some, it was early on, often only months after the stepfather had met the child, whereas for others, it did not occur until two to three years following the marriage. These preliminary findings support Visher and Visher's (1979) observation that such instances can do a great deal to build a bond between a child and a stepfather, helping to integrate the stepfather into the family system.

We were also interested in seeing how this group of men viewed their role as a stepparent. Interestingly, the most frequent responses to the question of what the proper role of a stepparent is, was "father figure" and "parent." Only two of our stepfathers said being a "friend" was the best way to negotiate the stepparent–child relationship. Some stepfathers, particularly those with stepsons, also mentioned the importance of serving as a male role model, and said that they felt their presence had at times, bolstered their stepson's self-confidence.

However, it is also interesting to note that one-fourth of the stepfathers in our study reported that a major problem had been that they had expected to assume the parental role too quickly. These men said that this often resulted in ill feelings and conflict between them and their stepchild; such conflict usually revolved around the stepfather trying to discipline the child too early in the history of the stepfather-child relationship. In fact, when asked about advice they would give to new step-fathers, they frequently referred to the need to move slowly and be patient, empha-sizing that developing a relationship with the stepchild takes time. It seems that gradual participation in the parenting process by the stepfather may often be the best answer (Visher & Visher, 1979).

Findings: Parental Involvement

According to the stepfamily literature, one of the most common tasks facing stepfa-thers is the question of how much to be a parent (Visher & Visher, 1979). In fact, some authors have questioned whether any stepfather can successfully assume a parent role, no matter how skillful his efforts (Fast & Cain, 1966). We were inter-ested in finding out how much of the parenting stepfathers assumed, and how their parental involvement compared with that of the other types of fathers who were con-sidered in our study. To answer this question, we examined the results from the pa-rental involvement scale, which was completed by biological parents, stepparents, and children.

Overall, there was no difference between never-divorced and remarried families in the quality of relations between children and their biological parents. The levels of closeness, affection, shared activity, and involvement were about the same. However, when it came to the relationship between children and their stepfathers, the story was quite different. There were huge disparities in how children felt about natural biological parents and how they felt about stepfathers. In addition, feelings toward stepfathers appear to have been reciprocated. This pattern of differences will become clearer as we compare stepfathers with their spouses (the remarried mothers in these families), and also with natural fathers in nondivorced families.

Stepfathers and Remarried Mothers

First, we were interested in how much of the responsibility for parenting and child-rearing stepfathers were assuming, as compared to their spouses—who up until the remarriage had been carrying the burden of child-rearing pretty much single-handedly. When we compared children's relationship with their stepfather to their relationship with their biological mother, we found highly consistent results across measures from different family members. The reports of parental involvement from the stepfathers, their wives, and their stepchildren clearly indicated that the step-father–child relationship was more detached and uninvolved, while the remarried mother–child relationship was closer, warmer, and characterized by more shared activity. Specifically, stepfathers were less likely to take the child along with them when running errands, were less likely to go to watch the child, whether a son or daughter, in outdoor activities such as soccer practice, and were less involved in disciplining the child or attending school-related functions. In addition, stepfathers were less likely to provide comfort and support to their stepchildren when they were upset, or to discuss problems that their stepchild might be having. One stepfather described the distance he felt in his relationship with his stepson: "It's close but sep-arate. There's a gap to reach across. It doesn't come with ease for either of us. He's afraid to ask me some things."

Stepfathers and Never-Divorced Family Fathers

We were further interested in comparing our group of stepfathers with fathers from never-divorced families. It is possible, for example, that fathers are generally less involved in the day-to-day activities of their children's lives, and that the pattern of less parental involvement that we saw in stepfather families was no different from the degree of involvement of fathers in never-divorced families.

However, when we compared these two groups of fathers, we found a somewhat mixed picture. On the one hand, the two groups of fathers and their wives reported few differences, suggesting that stepfathers were about as involved in the care and supervision of their stepchildren as never-divorced fathers were with their children. On the other hand, there were strong disparities between adults' and children's per-ceptions of children's relationships with their fathers and stepfathers. In all areas, children of stepfathers reported less paternal involvement than did children of intact family fathers.

Stepfathers and Stepmothers

When we compared our group of resident stepfathers with our group of resident stepmothers, we found a very interesting pattern of differences. Stepfathers were much less likely to be active participants in the lives of their stepchildren than were their stepmother counterparts, according to both their own and their children's per-ceptions. The analyses comparing stepfather–child relationships with stepmother–

child relationships, in fact, produced one of the clearest findings obtained in our research. Comparing their self-reports, we found that stepfathers were much less likely to take their stepchildren to and from recreational activities, were less available for providing emotional support and comfort to their stepchildren, and were less likely to discuss problems with their stepchildren than were stepmothers. The children, too, tended to perceive stepmothers as much more actively involved, particularly in discipline and school activities, as compared to stepfathers.

Remarried and Intact Family Mothers

Up until now, we have been discussing to what degree the stepfather is involved in the parenting of his stepchildren. In our study, we were also interested in looking more closely at the child's relationship with his/her biological remarried mother. In general, there were few differences in the way that remarried mothers perceived their relationship with their children compared to the mother–child relationship in intact families. Remarried mothers and mothers in intact families reported that they were actively involved in child-rearing, disciplining their children, taking them to sports activities, and meeting with teachers at school. Further, remarried mothers were as emotionally responsive and available as mothers in intact families. They talked to their children about their problems and comforted them when necessary. Children's reports generally concurred: remarried mothers were rated as being as actively involved with their children as intact family mothers were rated.

We also asked remarried mothers to rate the change in their relationship with their children by comparing the six months prior to their remarriage with the present. Mothers from intact families were asked to rate the amount of change in their relationship with their child in the last four years (four years was the average length of time remarried mothers included in their assessment of change). Intact-family mothers did not report any significant change in their relationship with their children over that time period. However, remarried mothers felt that they had become closer, more affectionate, and generally able to spend more quality time with their children than they had been able to as single parents before the remarriage. As one remarried mother stated, "Now I can be a full-time mom."

Children's Adjustment Following Remarriage

A critical question is how relations within stepfamilies affect the child's performance and adjustment outside the family. In our ongoing analysis, we compared intact families and stepfamilies along a number of indicators measuring the adjustment of children. Provisional results reveal that on a variety of outcomes including behavior problems, self-esteem, competence, and peer relations, children in stepfather families fared about as well as did children living with both biological parents. For example, on mothers' ratings of children's competence, children in stepfather families were equally as competent in physical, social, and cognitive skills as children from never-divorced families. Mothers' reports of children's behavior problems also suggest that children in stepfather families were as emotionally well-adjusted as their counterparts living in never-divorced families. Further, children's self-perceptions across the three competence domains were congruent with their mothers' reports.

Teachers also perceived children in stepfather families as being as competent in their academic performance (cognitive competence), and as well-accepted by peers (social competence) as children from never-divorced families. Many of the teachers said that they did not feel sufficiently confident about rating the child's degree of competence in physical sports and outdoor games. However, of the teachers who were able to complete those ratings on the children, there were no differences between the two groups of children (stepfather and intact-family) in the physical competence domain. The teachers also felt that children living in remarried families with a stepfather felt positively about themselves, and did not rate them differently from children from intact homes on general feelings of worth. Overall, these findings reveal that teachers did not perceive children differently as a function of the family's marital status.

From the preceding discussion, it seems that whether hearing from parents, teachers, or the children themselves, all tended to perceive children in stepfather families as socially competent and well-liked by peers. This description was further confirmed by our research team's assessment of the children's social behavior, when we observed them interacting with each other in play groups in our laboratory (Sitterle & Santrock, 1985). We noted that the children in stepfather families tended to have confident and positive encounters with their age-mates, much like the children living in two-parent families. Specifically, during the laboratory play groups, the children in stepfather families were talkative, supportive of others, and worked well with the rest of the group during structured activities; they refrained from inappropriate and antisocial behavior, such as verbal or physical aggression. In addition, according to the global ratings, the emotional quality of their interaction was judged as happy, enthusiastic, and even-tempered.

One important domain in children's development and adjustment, however, did yield some interesting differences between the children living in these two family structures. Two different measures indicated that children from stepfather families may have had a more negative view of themselves than children from never-divorced families. Mothers in stepfather families rated their childrens' feelings of self-worth significantly lower than did mothers in intact families. On another rating of self-esteem obtained from the interview with the parents, we again found that mothers from stepfather families viewed their children as having a more negative self-concept than their intact-family counterparts viewed their children as having. And when the children rated their own general self-worth, they confirmed their parent's reports: children from stepfather families felt more negatively about themselves than children from never-divorced families. Thus children in stepfather families may have, in fact, been experiencing some difficulties, but these difficulties appear to have been more global in nature, and not restricted to any single realm of the child's functioning.

It is important to put the magnitude of the risk associated with family structural differences into perspective. The majority of children in stepfather families were not experiencing significant or widespread problems, if we rely on reports of their parents, their own self-reports, evaluations from their teachers, and independent ratings of their interactions with their age-mates. In other words, if we were trying to predict whether a child were prone to have emotional, behavioral, or academic problems, it would be of little help to know only the marital history of his or her parents. Marital disruptions and rearrangements do appear to be associated with some kind of developmental risk, but this risk may be neither ameliorated nor worsened by remarriage (Furstenberg, 1987).

Discussion

In summary, these results revealed a fairly consistent profile of the role of the stepfather, the family interaction patterns in stepfather families, and the adjustment of children living in these families. What emerged was a pattern in which the stepfather functioned as a more distant and detached observer, and the biological, remarried mother was more responsive to and actively involved with her children. We suspect that there are a number of reasons why the stepfathers in our study were less involved and more distant with their stepchildren. The stepfamilies in the study had been together an average of three years, so that a level of involvement equal to that of the biological mothers could hardly be expected. Furthermore, stepfathers had not shared early experiences with the children such as birth and infancy, or the relationship history that existed between the children and their biological parents. One of our stepfathers commented, "Communication isn't as good because bonding in the early years wasn't there." The stepfathers were obviously not attached to their stepchildren in the same way as the natural mothers were. Thus it would have been unrealistic to expect the same degree of closeness found between the child and the remarried mother.

Interestingly, one of the themes that we heard repeatedly in talking with our group of stepfathers was the need to move slowly in establishing the stepfather–child relationship. Frequent advice to other stepfathers included comments such as "Move slowly," "Be patient," and "It takes time." In describing the gradual process of developing a relationship with the stepchild, one of our stepfathers commented, "Our relationship gradually evolved from friendship to one in which I am the father figure," while another stepfather said, "Brian is different now. At first he was reclusive and jealous and he saw me as infringing. It was a slow progression." As mentioned earlier, nearly one-fourth of our stepfathers said that they had expected to assume a parental role too quickly, and that this had in turn created difficulties in their relationships with their stepchildren.

Of course, it can often be very frustrating to wait out the child's period of adjustment. As Visher and Visher (1979) point out, the dilemma is that if the new stepfather attempts to become a co-parent and disciplinarian immediately, he may be undermined by the mother, the child, or both; on the other hand, if he remains out of the management picture he may become isolated and treated as an intruder. Stern (1978) has found that is important for the stepfather to first become a friend to the stepchild before he can be effectively integrated into the family. A child who has a stepfather–friend is usually more willing to cooperate with the rules of the household and to accept the stepfather's disciplinary actions. The willingness to be disciplined is essential, and this willingness can only be based on mutual respect and friendship. In addition, acceptance of the stepfather is likely to be even more difficult if the child continues to be involved with his noncustodial father. In simple logistical terms, if the child visits the biological father on a frequent basis, then he or she may not be at home on weekends or holidays, which means less time available for consolidating the child's relationship with the stepfather.

This finding of the distant stepfather also emerged in a series of studies conducted by Furstenberg and colleagues, on the transition from divorce to remarriage (Furstenberg, 1987). Specifically, they found that "children are less likely to report doing things with stepparents, much less likely to feel close to them, and most do not want to be like them when they grow up." He also found that a higher proportion of biological parents in stepfamilies complain that their spouse assumes too little responsibility for child rearing, and does not have a great deal of influence over the child.

An interesting question to consider is whether children grow closer to their stepfathers with more time. Earlier work on this issue by Stern (1978) found that one and a half to two years are usually necessary to integrate a stepfather into a remarried family system. However, Furstenberg and his colleagues, comparing stepfamilies of differing duration, found no consistent pattern in the quality of relations between children and their stepparents, leading them to conclude that the "ties between children and their stepparents do not become progressively stronger over time" (Furstenberg, 1987). Thus it may be reasonable to expect that most children in stepfamilies will experience some problems or limitations in establishing close ties with their stepfathers.

It is important to note, despite this pattern of less involvement and greater distance, that the majority of the stepfathers in our study reported that they were "somewhat" involved in the care and supervision of their stepchildren, and most stepchildren expressed positive feelings about their stepfathers. In addition, the majority of the children in stepfather families appeared to function well. We could find little to differentiate the overall descriptions of family life offered by both parents and children in stepfamilies and never-divorced families. This seems to suggest that an absence of closeness between stepparents and children typically does *not* disturb the adjustment of children in these families, or the overall family functioning—or else there may be compensations that offset the relative distance between stepfathers and their stepchildren (Furstenberg, 1987).

We also found that remarried mothers were as involved with their children as were mothers in intact marriages. There appeared to be extensive communication between these mothers and their children. The children described their mothers as people who are available for talking about feelings and problems, and as the adults who are responsible for their caregiving. Overall, then, remarried mothers came across as highly involved, available, and nurturant parents, even though many of them were managing full-time careers or working part time as well. Very few of our intact-family mothers, on the other hand, had jobs. It would seem that these remarried mothers had found a way to successfully balance the demands of work and child rearing.

Our group of remarried mothers reported that their current degree of involvement with their children was a major change that had occurred since their remarriage. This is a noteworthy finding in light of accumulated evidence indicating that common complaints of many single parents are task overload, disorganization, and problematic relationships with children during the divorce period (Hetherington, et al., 1982). It seems that remarriage may have a positive and stabilizing effect on custodial mothers, which is then reflected in their relationships with their children. More money is available for child support and other aspects of running a household than was likely the case as a single parent. Also, stepfathers are available to help with family work, and perhaps more important, to offer nurturance and support to their wives—which in turn gives wives more time and emotional energy to direct toward their children. Hetherington and colleagues (1982) found that women's economic concerns and household disorganization, which had been pervasive problems during the divorce, diminished when they remarried. We found this to be the case as well.

Regardless of whether we were observing or interviewing stepfather or stepmother families, we sensed the significance of the child's enduring attachment to the biological custodial parent (Santrock & Sitterle, 1987). Children in stepparent families had undergone considerable disruption in their lives. Generally, the most longstanding and unchanging relationship that they had was with their custodial parent, whether it was a remarried mother in a stepfather family or a remarried father in a stepmother family. We sensed that the positive nature of the relationship between the remarried parent and the child was a key ingredient in helping the child through the disruption and disequilibrium, as the family moved from the status of intact to divorced to becoming a stepfamily.

Limitations of the Present Study and Suggestions for Future Research

Our research focused on a fairly small sample of elementary school children, from middle-class White families. Clearly, future research should include a wider socioeconomic and age range, and, where possible, larger samples of stepfather families. In particular, it is likely that child development and family processes will differ in stepfather families, depending on the age of the child; for example, Furstenberg and colleagues (1987) has found that a sizable number of children in stepfamilies report troubled relations with their stepparents when they enter adolescence.

The theme of equilibrium–disequilibrium in stepfamilies over time is of utmost importance. At the beginning of this chapter, we described the stepparent family as undergoing a series of major transitions across a number of years, rather than as experiencing a single outcome. Longitudinal studies would provide us with valuable information about the unfolding of lives through intact, divorced, and stepfamily configurations. Even when longitudinal studies are not possible, it is important for researchers to discover the manner in which the members of the stepfamily reconstruct the past and carry forward previous relationships (Sroufe & Fleeson, 1985), as these reconstructions can influence the nature of present parent–child interactions in the family. It also is important to learn more about how the nature of relationships in stepfamilies may influence relationships in other interpersonal contexts, such as interaction with peers. While Hetherington, Cox, and Cox (1979) revealed how mother-custody divorce influences children's play and peer interactions, there is virtually no information available about the ways that entrance into a stepfamily and continued life there might influence children's peer relationships. No significant differences were found in our study between the peer relations of children in stepfather and intact families. However, we did find that children living with their remarried custodial fathers and a stepmother exhibited difficulties in interactions with age-mates (Sitterle & Santrock, 1985). Thus the influence of significant relationships within the family on the development of relationships outside the family may be an important area for future inquiry in stepfamily research.

Finally, the nature of the attachment process in stepfamilies may be an important variable in the quality of functioning of the various family members. While extensive information has been collected on the attachment of infants in intact families, we know little about the nature of attachment in divorced or stepparent families. We believe the concept of secure attachment, as developed by Ainsworth (1979), Bowlby (1969), and Sroufe and Fleeson (1985) is important throughout development, and needs to be carefully looked at in stepfather and stepmother families.

Along similar lines, we need to begin investigating a broader range of relationships in stepfamilies, including intergenerational attachments. Entrance into a stepfamily increases not only the number of "parents" children must relate to, but also the number of grandparents as well, particularly in a complex stepparent family. There have been virtually no investigations of intergenerational relationships in stepparent families, although there are some studies of children in intact families that examine the attachment process and the nature of parent–child relationships that are carried through generations, and their influence on children's development (e.g., Main, Kaplan, & Cassidy, 1985). In one investigation of the effects of remarriage and divorce on the kinship network (Furstenberg & Spanier, 1984), it was found that grandparents were included in the kinship network of stepparent families. However, this investigation did not touch on the developmental outcome of such experiences for children, or examine how intergenerational experiences are carried forward in time.

Research into the nature of life in stepparent families is complex and time consuming. We need to build an empirical base of information on stepfather families that will challenge existing stereotypes and provide resources both for the stepfamilies and for those involved in working with the children and adults in such families. Stepfather families function differently than never-divorced families in a number of ways, but these differences may not be harmful to the children involved. We need to be aware of these differences, but also not to manufacture or exaggerate the difficulties. An important task is to become able to identify the stepfather families that may truly be at risk, and that may require assistance from helping professionals. On the other hand, research can help to identify the positive coping mechanisms and factors that mitigate against the stresses associated with remarriage. Such information can, in turn, serve as the building blocks for enlightened parenting and clinical intervention.

REFERENCES

Achenbach, T.M., & Edelbrock, C.S. (1979). The child behavior profile, II. Boys aged 12–16 and girls aged 6–11 and 12–16. *Journal of Consulting and Clinical Psychology*, *47*, 223–233.

Achenbach, T.M., & Edelbrock, C.S. (1981). Behavioral problems and competencies reported by parents of normal and disturbed children aged 4 through 16. *Monographs of the Society for Research in Child Development*, *46* (1, Whole No. 188).

Ahrons, C.R. (1987). Parenting in the binuclear family: Relationships between biological and stepparents. In K. Pasley & M. Ihinger-Tallman (Eds.), *Remarriage and stepparenting: Current research and theory*. New York: Guilford.

Ainsworth, M.D.S. (1979). Infant-mother attachment. *American Psychologist*, *34*, 932–937.

Bernard, J. (1956). *Remarriage: A study of marriage*. New York: Holt, Rinehart & Winston.

Bohannan, P., & Erickson, R. (1978, January). Stepping in. *Psychology Today*, pp. 53–59.

Bowerman, C., & Irish, D. (1962). Some relationships of stepchildren to their parents. *Marriage and Family Living*, *24*, 113–121.

Bowlby, J. (1969). *Attachment* (Vol. 1). London: Hogarth.

Burchinal, L.G. (1964). Characteristics of adolescents from unbroken, broken, and reconstituted families. *Journal of Marriage and the Family*, *26*, 44–50.

Chapman, M. (1977). Father absence, stepfathers, and the cognitive performance of college students. *Child Development*, *48*, 1155–1158.

Clingempeel, W.G., Brand, F., & Ievoli, R. (1984). Stepparent–stepchild relationships in stepmother and stepfather families: A multimethod study. *Family Relations*, *33*(3), 465–473.

Coie, J.D., & Kupersmidt, J.B. (1981, April). *A behavioral analysis of emerging social status in boys' groups*. Paper presented at the Biennial Meeting of the Society for Research in Child Development, Boston.

Dodge, K.A. (1983). Behavioral antecedents of peer social status. *Child Development, 54* (6), 1386–1399.

Duberman, L. (1973). Step-kin relationships. *Journal of Marriage and the Family*, *35*, 283–292.

Esses, L., & Campbell, R. (1984). Challenges in researching the remarried. *Family Relations*, *33*(3), 415–424.

Fast, I., & Cain, A. (1966). The stepparent role: Potential for disturbance in family functioning. *American Journal of Orthopsychiatry*, *36*, 485–491.

Furstenberg, F.F., & Spanier, G.B. (1984). *Recycling the family: Remarriage after divorce*. Beverly Hills, CA: Sage.

Furstenberg, F.F. (1987). The new extended family: The experience of parents and children after remarriage. In K. Pasley & M. Ihinger-Tallman (Eds.), *Remarriage and stepparenting: Current research and theory*. New York: Guilford.

Glick, P.C. (1980). Remarried: Some recent changes and variations. *Journal of Family Issues, 1*, 455–478.

Glick, P.C. (1984). Prospective changes in marriage, divorce, and living arrangements. *Journal of Family Issues, 5*, 7–26.

Harter, S. (1982). The perceived competence scale for children. *Child Development, 53*, 87–97.

Hetherington, E.M. (1981). Children and divorce. In R. Henderson (Ed.), *Parent-Child Interaction: Theory Research and Prospects*. New York: Academic.

Hetherington, E.M., Cox, M., & Cox, R. (1979). Play and social interaction in children following divorce. *Journal of Social Issues, 35*, 26–49.

Hetherington, E.M., Cox, M., & Cox, R. (1982). Effects of divorce on parents and children. In M.E. Lamb (Ed.), *Nontraditional families: Parenting and child development*. Hillsdale, NJ: Erlbaum.

Lamb, M.E. (1981). Fathers and child development: An integrative overview. In M.E. Lamb (Ed.), *The Father's Role in Child Development*. New York: Wiley.

Langner, L., & Michael, S. (1963). *Life stress and mental health*. New York: MacMillan.

Main, M., Kaplan, N., & Cassidy, J. (1985). Security in infancy, childhood, and adulthood: A move to the level of representation. In I. Bretherton & E. Waters (Eds.), Growing points of attachment theory and research. *Monographs of the Society for Research in Child Development*, Vol. 50, Nos. 1–2 (Serial No. 209).

Messinger, L. (1976). Remarriage between divorced people with children from previous marriages: A proposal for preparation for remarriage. *Journal of Marriage and Family Counseling, 2*, 193–200.

Messinger, L., Walker, K.N., & Freeman, S.J. (1978). Preparation for remarriage following divorce: The use of group techniques. *American Journal of Orthopsychiatry, 48*(2), 263–272.

Mowatt, M.H. (1972). Group psychotherapy for stepfathers and their wives. *Psychotherapy: Theory, Research and Practice, 9*(4), 328–331.

Oshman, H., & Manosevitz, M. (1976). Father-absence: Effects of stepfathers upon psychological development in males. *Developmental Psychology, 12*, 479–480.

Pasley, K., & Ihinger-Tallman, M. (Eds.). (1984). *Family Relations: Remarriage and Stepparenting* [Special issue], *33*, 3.

Robinson, B.E. (1984). The contemporary American stepfather. *Family Relations, 33*(3), 381–388.

Santrock, J.W. (1972). The relations of type and onset of father absence to cognitive development. *Child Development, 43*, 455–469.

Santrock, J.W., & Sitterle, K.A. (1985). The developmental world of children in divorced families: Research findings and clinical implications. In D.E. Goldberg (Ed.), *Contemporary marriage: Special issues in couples therapy*. Homewood, IL: Dorsey.

Santrock, J.W., & Sitterle, K.A. (1987). Parent-child relationships in stepmother families. In K. Pasley & M. Ihinger-Tallman (Eds.), *Remarriage and stepparenting: Current research and theory*. New York: Guilford.

Santrock, J.W., Warshak, R.A., & Elliott, G.W. (1982). Social development and parent–child interaction in father custody and stepmother families. In M.E. Lamb (Ed.), *Nontraditional families: Parenting and child development*. Hillsdale, NJ: Erlbaum.

Santrock, J.W., Warshak, R.A., Lindbergh, C., & Meadows, L. (1982). Children's and parent's observed social behavior in stepfather families. *Child Development, 53*, 472–480.

Sitterle, K.A. & Santrock, J.W. (1985, April). *Remarriage: The family and peer system*. Paper presented at the annual meeting of the Southwestern Society for Research in Human Development, Denver.

Sroufe, L.A., & Fleeson, J. (1985). Attachment and the construction of relationships. In W.W. Hartup & Z. Rubin (Eds.), *Relationships and Development*. Hillsdale, NJ: Erlbaum.

Stern, P.N. (1978). Stepfather families: Integration around child discipline. *Issues in Mental Health Nursing*, 1(2), 50–56.

Stern, P.N. (1982). Affiliating in stepfather families: Teachable strategies leading to step-father-child friendship. *Western Journal of Nursing Research, 4*, 76–89.

Visher, E.G., & Visher, J.W. (1979). *Stepfamilies: A guide to working with stepparents and stepchildren*. New York: Bruner/Mazel.

Wilson, K., Zurcher, L., McAdams, D., & Curtis, R. (1975). Stepfathers and stepchildren: an exploratory analysis from two national surveys. *Journal of Marriage and Family, 37*, 526–536.

CHAPTER 11

Divorced Fathers with Custody

SHIRLEY M.H. HANSON

Family structures in the United States are undergoing a metamorphosis, with a marked increase in marriage dissolutions, remarriages, single-parent families, and two-earner families. There is also a movement on the part of men toward greater participation in family, household, and child-care activities. Nowhere have the changes in men's roles been more evident than with the growing group of parents called single-custodial fathers—men who have physical (though not necessarily legal) custody of their children. These men, who have assumed primary parental responsibility without a co-parent living in the home, include fathers who are separated, divorced, or widowed, or who are adoptive parents; most generally, however, they are divorced fathers.

The purpose of this chapter is to describe divorced, single, custodial fathers, and their lives with their children. First, it will review the research literature on this special group of parents, integrating common themes and findings. Then it will consider implications for social policy and future research.

FATHER CUSTODY: A BRIEF HISTORY

Fathers with custody are not a new phenomenon. Throughout history until the middle of the nineteenth century, custody of children under most circumstances almost always went to fathers. Not only did the law regard men as owning their children as well as their wives (Orthner & Lewis, 1979), but their economic status assured power. Thus men were more able than women to provide financially for their offspring.

At the beginning of the Industrial Revolution, at about the turn of the century, when families moved to cities and fathers left homes to work for companies, courts began to award children to their mothers. Fathers then received custody only when mothers were proven unfit or died—most commonly from childbirth—though the children were not generally reared by their fathers, but by women in the fathers' ex-

The author of this chapter would like to acknowledge the hard-working secretarial staff at the Oregon Health Sciences University for their assistance in preparing this manuscript: D. Ceresero, B. Edwards, V. Nufer, and C. Peart-Peterson.

tended families. However, with the advent of modern medicine, the number of widower families greatly declined, and this decline has continued into the present, down from 124,000 in 1970 to 97,000 in 1984 (Hanson & Sporakowski, 1986; U.S. Bureau of the Census, 1985b). Concurrently, in recent years, many changes have occurred in the means by which fathers receive custody of minor children, the main ones now being separation/divorce, death of spouse, and adoption.

Adoption is the most recent way by which men receive custody of children. Single parent adoption first became legally possible in 1950, with the first reported case in 1965; the first formal single father adoption took place about 1980 (Curto, 1983). The U.S. Bureau of the Census (1985b) estimates that there are 166,000 single fathers in the category of never married father-headed families, which includes legal and informal adoption.

The largest number of men receive custody of children following separation and divorce, with these father-custodial families growing from 241,000 in 1970 to 683,000 in 1984, almost a 300% increase (U.S. Bureau of the Census, 1985b). These fathers obtain custody by both legal and nonlegal means. There are three types of legal or court ordered custody: (1) sole custody is when one parent is given sole responsibility and the other parent may be granted visitation rights; (2) split custody is when each parent receives sole custody of one or more children; and (3) joint custody is when both parents have equal responsibility for the health, education, and welfare of all children. Most single fathers have sole custody, but the occurrence of joint custody is increasing. Nonlegal custody means that the children live with one parent while the other retains legal custody. This is a common occurrence for custodial fathers, and usually involves the mother's consent. However, child snatching is another way that men have obtained nonlegal custody (Palmer & Noble, 1984).

One-parent families account for 25.7% (nearly 8 million) of all family groups, an increase from 12.9% or 3.8 million since 1970 (U.S. Bureau of the Census, 1985a, 1985b). What this means is that approximately one out of every four children lives with a single parent. Of single parent families, 89% are headed by mothers, with 11% headed by fathers. The number of father-headed families has increased 127% between 1970 and 1984.

REVIEW OF RESEARCH

There has been a paucity of research about fathers in general and single custodial fathers in particular. However, since 1976 an increasing number of studies have been published. The purpose of the following narrative is to synthesize the findings of the past 12 years. Table 11.1 summarizes some of the major studies in the United States, Canada, Great Britain, and Australia on single-custodial fathers according to common themes or variables of interest across studies.[1]

[1]Due to space limitations, only selected studies were included in the tables. Other works of interest included in this analysis are: DeFrain & Eirick, 1981; Orthner & Lewis, 1979; Santrock & Warshak, 1979; and Schlesinger, 1974, 1977, 1978a, 1978b, 1985.

TABLE 11.1 Landmark Studies on Single Parent Fathers, 1976–Present

Author(s), Year	Gasser & Taylor, 1976	Mendes, 1976	Orthner, Brown, & Ferguson, 1976	Bartz & Witcher, 1978
Subjects/Locations	40 divorced, widowed, Ohio	32 separated, divorced, and widowed, California	20 divorced, never married, North Carolina	34 divorced, Iowa
Methodology	Questionnaire	Interview	Interview	Interview
Variables/Purpose	Role conflict, role adjustment, household activities, society's attitude toward single fathers	Psychological-social adjustment; child supervision, home-making, child's emotional needs, rearing girls	Father's lifestyle, problems, successes	Learn about single families' adjustment, problems, pleasures
Socioeconomic status		43% Middle Class 46% Working Class	60% Professional 25% Blue collar 80% Post h.s.ed. Mean income $18,000	82% Upper SES
Race		43% Black 46% White		
Religion				
Age		30–44	Mean: 37	40 and under
Employment	50%: problems pursuing job possibilities, business trips	Synchronization between job and family	33% public assistance	Greater occupational adjustment Greater job flexibility
Family of origin/ Procreation	Involved in child care before divorce			60% more involved in child care than pre-divorce

Homemaking skills	Involved prior to divorce	87% manage home by self		No problem, share cooking, cleaning, shopping, dishes with children
Motivation for custody			Wives did not want or could not care for children	Custody < 3 yrs. Majority via spousal allocation
Visitation/Child support			Rare child support	5% receive child support from mother
Support networks	Divorced men: New friends, singles groups. Widowed men: Old friends.	Lack of help from kin for children	50% singles groups 66% family support	Friends & neighbors helpful; sought single friends; not cohabitating
Age, sex, and number of children		Majority 6–9 years; range 3–17 years. 62% rearing girls	50% preschool 50% school age Mean: < 2.0 children	Mean: 2 children: 50% male, 50% female; Range: 1–17 years. 44% under 6 years
Child care	Father himself	School age unsupervised; Preschool: daycare	Day care, nursery schools	Preschool daycare; private; neighbors; cost a problem
Father–child relationships	Share household activities	Increased affect with preadolescent children	Good parent–child relationship; demand more child independence	Increased father/child affection; changed parental style
Child rearing problems		Some conflict with teens; female sexuality; lack of female role model	Sex education for adolescent girls; time and patience; gone from home too much	Decreased time and patience; emotional adjustment; school stigma

TABLE 11.1 Landmark Studies on Single Parent Fathers, 1976–Present (*continued*)

Author(s), Year	Gasser & Taylor, 1976	Mendes, 1976	Orthner, Brown, & Ferguson, 1976	Bartz & Witcher, 1978
Problems	50%: dating	Coordinate house tasks, job and child care; emotional needs of children	Making decisions alone; expect children to be too independent; two parents better than one	Insufficient time; children's initial adjustment; financial adjustment
Strengths	70%: more active in organizations, homemaking skills		Active social life; happy with being single; more child-oriented; pride in coping	80%: active sex life; children more responsible; single father a hero; children—good adjustment
Future study				Adjustment of children; fathers who do not succeed; objective evaluation of father
Social policy needs	More programs for widowed	Family life curriculum on single-parent family: teach homemaking, budgeting, marketing, child development; support group for fathers only	Day care hours; baby-sitting co-ops; classes on parenting; Big Sisters	Better child care
Future	Father's role adjustment better in future; more models to emulate	More single-parent fathers; more custodial & noncustodial men in child care	Need family policy	If role-sharing pre-divorce, less adjustment required later

Author(s), Year	Gersick, 1979	Katz, 1979	Hanson, 1979, 1981, 1985, 1986	Rosenthal & Keshet, 1981
Subjects	40 divorced, 20 with custody and 20 without custody, Massachusetts	409 divorced and widowed, Australia	80 divorced, Washington	128 separated, divorced custodial and noncustodial, Massachusetts
Methodology	Interview	Questionnaire, interview subset	Interview, questionnaire, standardized instruments	Interview, questionnaire
Variables/Purpose	Factors related to custody: demographic, family of origin, child rearing, sex-role orientation;	Define problems of single families and suggest social policy	Characteristics of single parent; parent–child relationships: SES, history, custody, nurturance/support	Relationship between father and child; effect of relationship on life style; growth of men and children
Socioeconomic status	Above average family	24% tradesmen; 15% laborers; 53% professional; mean income $6,356; mean education 10 years	Educational mean 15 years; 75% professional or business. Mean income: $23,500	College educated, professional, or semi-professional; increased income
Race	Caucasian		92% Caucasian	Caucasian
Religion	48% Catholic		38% Protestant; 16% Catholic; 43% Other	
Age	Median age: 38 years. Custodial fathers older & better established than noncustodial	62% between 30-49 years	Mean: 42 years Range: 31-54 years	
Employment		89% employed; 51% work fewer hours since divorce	95% employed, restraints on job prospects	

171

TABLE 11.1 Landmark Studies on Single Parent Fathers, 1976–Present (*continued*)

Author(s), Year	Gersick, 1979	Katz, 1979	Hanson, 1979, 1981, 1985, 1986	Rosenthal & Keshet, 1981
Family of origin/ Procreation	Single fathers middle or last-born child; 22% parents divorced, closer relationships with mother. No difference between custodial/noncustodial fathers in child rearing participation during marriage		Relationships with own parents not significant; 22% parents divorced	
Homemaking skills		75%: no problem	No problem	90%: no problems
Motivation for custody	Wife unfaithful; provisional marriage; incapacitated wife; incompatibility	Multiple causes for divorce and custody	53% seeking fathers 46% assenter fathers 65% sole custody 11% joint custody	
Visitation/Child support			10% receive child support; problems with visitation	
Support networks		New male & female friends; decreased old friends; 70% help from multiple sources	Single mothers, friends, family	Single mothers
Age, sex, and number of children		Mean: 2.8 children. 71% children 7–18 yrs., 54% male	Mean: 15 years. Mean: 2 children. 66% male	
Child care		36% not in school 22% need help	After school care	Day care, babysitter

Father–child relationships	Participation in child care pre-divorce varied	80%: more time with children since divorce	Fathers and children rated nurturing and support better than pre-divorce	Enjoy recreation with children
Child rearing problems	37%: difficulty with children		Time/energy demands	Guidance, nurturance of children; meet emotional needs
Problems	Money; child care; visitation; social life	26%: financial; 46%: household; 26%: role overload, lonely; 37%: not coping well; 47%: school doesn't understand	Custody and visitation issues; lack of support from other single fathers	Time constraints; role strain; social opportunity
Strengths	No regrets about new role; male sex-role identification in single-father homes	70% sought help	Feel good about self	Positive self-esteem; grow emotionally; 75% closer to children now
Future study		Larger samples; study problems and successes	Study younger children; compare male/female children; compare single females to single males; Compare divorced to widowed; study healthy single-parent families	
Social policy needs	Better legal system	Income support beyond unemployment for single families; intervention with children; policy initiatives and interventions to support single fathers	Group support for fathers; cooperative parenting pursued; teach parenting to males; encourage joint custody	Information regarding counseling
Future		Increase in single fathers	Increased number of single parents; increased number of joint custody	

TABLE 11.1 Landmark Studies on Single Parent Fathers, 1976–Present (*continued*)

	Chang & Deinard, 1982	McKee & O'Brien, 1982	Grief, 1982, 1983, 1984, 1985	Risman, 1986
Author(s), Year				
Subjects	80 divorced, Minnesota	59 separated and divorced, England	1,136 divorced and separated across United States and Canada	141 divorced, Washington and Massachusetts
Methodology	Questionnaire	Interview	Survey questionnaire with subset of 180 interviews	Questionnaire
Variables/Purpose	Reason for divorce; past and present roles; problems, assistance needed	Men's process into lone fatherhood	Who are single fathers; how managing; suggestions to other single fathers	Can they nurture children? individualist vs. structuralist; homemaking; satisfaction with father–child relationship
Socioeconomic status	67% post high school education; 46% +$20,000; 52% professional	44% middle class 56% working class	Mean income $30,000 Range $10,000–$100,000	50% less than high school grad 50% B.S. + Income: less than $15,000 to $50,000; $\overline{X}$ = $20,000–$25,000
Race	90% White 1% Black 9% Other		Most Caucasian	90% White
Religion			Protestant or Catholic	30% No preference 39% Protestant 20% Catholic 4% Jewish
Age	Mean = 35 years	75%: 30-44 years	Mean = 40 years	
Employment	91% employed; decrease in employment flexibility post-divorce		All occupations; middle management; mean salary post-divorce $28,000	51% white collar 25% blue collar 80% work full-time

	Family of origin/ Procreation	More domesticity and parenting before divorce	Involved in child rearing during marriage		
Homemaking skills		"Better than average father"		Little prior experience; no problems now	80%: No outside help; share with children
Motivation for custody		80% uncontested custody. Cause of divorce: change of wife's lifestyle, incompatibility. Sought custody: better parent, love for kids	Majority of wives wanted divorce; routes into single fatherhood: conciliatory negotiations, hostile seekers; passive acceptors	Custody for 4 years; custody decision mutual agreement with wife or children; custody battle 16% of time; 20% fathers win; minority didn't want custody	87 passive acceptances; 26 conciliatory negotiations; 28 hostile; Fathers who fought more satisfied
Visitation/Child support				24% mothers visit once/ week; 22% visit every other week; 14% once a month	
Support networks				Other single parents	Relatives, dates, and friends
Age, sex, and number of children		More boys (p < .005)	35% one child; 40% two children	1,996 children; 39% had one child; 43% had 2 children; 57% boys; mean age 11–12 years	90% pre-teen
Child care				Involved in child rearing during marriage; arranging child care okay	
Father–child relationships			Parental competence	Satisfaction with father–child relationship; fathers rated themselves high	Comfortable and competent; parent–child disclosure
Child rearing problems					

TABLE 11.1 Landmark Studies on Single Parent Fathers, 1976–Present (*continued*)

Author(s), Year	Chang & Deinard, 1982	McKee & O'Brien, 1982	Grief, 1982, 1983, 1984, 1985	Risman, 1986
Problems	Adjustment; time for children and social life; lack of employment flexibility; child care; initial problems with job; day care; daughters; children interfere; depression; anxiety; loneliness	Adjustment to singlehood and parenthood; time; financial problems; emotional difficulties	Adjustment to single life; reestablish social life; care of adolescent girls; balancing work–home demands; lack of role clarity	Income inversely related to satisfaction
Strengths	Better than average father in household; adaptation		Admired by friends and relatives	Satisfaction with life; fathers can "mother"
Further study				
Social policy needs			Counseling before divorce; concrete assistance; support group; child-care costs; income support beyond unemployment	Societal perspective better than individualist; judges consider child's best interest; fathers good parents and homemakers
Future	Fathers win more custody cases			More single parents in future

176

Hypotheses and variables investigated in the studies presented in Table 11.1 have become increasingly more sophisticated since the first reports came out in 1976. The questions asked most by early investigators were:

Who were single fathers? How were they faring as primary caregivers of children?

How did the roles of single fathers conflict with those for which they were socialized?

What were single fathers' problems and successes?

Were they able to handle homemaking and child rearing activities?

What were their reasons for divorce, and did a typology emerge that would explain why they assumed custody?

As knowledge progressed, studies went from descriptive to correlational investigations. For example, was there a relationship between the background characteristics of single custodial fathers and the present parent–child interaction?

Currently, researchers have been trying to discern if and why some families are healthier and cope better than others. Since sole custody favoring one parent over another is being replaced by joint custody, it is important to assess and determine how parents can most effectively meet the "best interests of the child" imperatives that prevail in family law. Examples of questions being asked include:

What are the characteristics of single mothers and fathers that are most predictive of eventual success given the sex, age, and personality of children?

How can courts of law best determine custody or assist parents to arrive at the most beneficial caregiving arrangement for children?

Does divorce mediation help parents focus on meeting the needs of children?

How can investigators use standardized instrumentation in measuring and predicting the various outcomes?

Methodology

Most investigations were descriptive in nature, obtaining information through interviews and questionnaires. The majority focused on what single fathers had to say about their parenting and their children. Some studies collected data directly from the children (Ambert, 1982, 1984; Hanson, 1979, 1981, 1985a, 1985b, 1985c, 1986a, 1986b, 1986d; Santrock & Warshak, 1979). Additionally, some studies went beyond description, utilizing more standardized measurements, and comparing single-father families to more traditional family units (Gersick, 1979; Hanson, 1986b; Santrock & Warshak, 1979). Other studies compared different kinds of single fathers such as custodial versus noncustodial fathers (Gersick, 1979), widowed versus separated/divorced custodial fathers (Grief, 1985; Katz, 1979), and fathers with different kinds of custody (sole, joint, split) (Fricke, 1982; Hanson, 1986b; Hanson & Trilling, 1983).

Studies were conducted on subjects across North America as well as in England and Australia. The number of subjects in most research studies was generally small, with the majority of the samples consisting of 30–40 people. Subjects were self-selected, which resulted in nonrandomized samples.

Larger samples have been obtained, however. Researchers at the University of Nebraska analyzed data from a large study of single parents (n = 738). The initial report of this work compared single mothers to single fathers, compared different custodial arrangements (sole, joint, and split), and studied the adjustment of children to divorce (Fricke, 1982). Grief (1982, 1983, 1984, 1985) obtained a large sample (n = 1,136) of single fathers (both widowers and separated/divorced men) and has published many articles from this work.

Characteristics of Single Custodial Fathers

Demographics

Not all studies reported the demographics of their subjects. In the United States, however, fathers who had custody of their children were generally better educated, occupied more prestigious occupational roles, and received higher income than fathers in the average two-parent households (Chang & Deinard, 1982; Espenshade, 1979; Gersick, 1979; Hanson, 1986b). For the most part, single fatherhood requires men with special resources and motivation to obtain custody through existing legal systems, so this finding is not very surprising. However, higher socioeconomic status was not the rule of thumb in England, Australia, and Canada where single fathers included men from all social and economic strata (Bain, 1973; George & Wilding, 1972; Katz, 1979; Schlesinger, 1985), and there is now some evidence of a shift in the United States as well.

Although racial representation varied widely, the majority of single custodial fathers were Caucasian. This is consistent with higher socioeconomic levels for White males in this country. An exception is the military, where there is a high percentage of single custodial fathers, many of whom are non-White (Orthner & Bowen, 1985).

Very little information was available on the religious affiliations and practices of single fathers. Hanson (1981) and Risman (1986) reported a cross-section of religious preferences, with the percent of Catholic, Protestant, and Jewish fathers approximate to that of the general U.S. population.[2]

Single fathers in the research literature ranged in age from 30 to 54 years, which are traditional child rearing years for most male parents in this country. Researchers comparing separated/divorced versus widowed fathers generally found widowers to be about five years older than their separated/divorced counterparts (Grief, 1983, 1985; Kohn & Kohn, 1978).

[2]According to the U.S. Bureau of the Census (1985a) Protestants made up approximately 54% of the U.S. population, Roman Catholics 37%, and Jews 4%.

Most of the fathers studied remained in the same jobs they had before becoming single parents. Since many of the fathers in the U.S. studies had high occupational status, they possessed a certain degree of flexibility in their jobs, with some fathers reporting changing positions or changing the hours of their employment in order to accommodate child-care needs. On the other hand, one study found that single fathers experienced some curtailment of job-related travel or upward career mobility because of their more restricted home circumstances, but that this did not present a psychological problem for most of them (Gasser & Taylor, 1976). It should be noted that the military has been concerned about the combat readiness of single fathers in the service—that is, their ability to leave children at the spur of the moment for extended periods of time (Orthner & Bowen, 1985).

Most of the single fathers studied worked for a living, and did not avail themselves of the various income enhancement programs that are used by many single mothers in the same position. This was especially true in the United States, where most of the single custodial fathers were not on welfare, aid to dependent children, food stamps, or other assistance programs (Grief, 1985; Hanson, 1985b, 1986a; Risman, 1986). This scenario may change as more and more lower-income men take on single fatherhood and claim equal rights to government assistance programs. It appears that a higher proportion of the Canadian, English, and Australian single fathers utilize these options (Katz, 1979; McKee & O'Brien, 1982; Schlesinger, 1978b, 1985).

Family of Origin

Some researchers asked single fathers questions about their upbringing in their families of origin. Several theories (social learning theory, identification theory, and concepts of intergenerational continuity) have been used in an attempt to explain why these men took on the nontraditional role of primary parenting (Gersick, 1979; Hanson, 1985c). The research suggests that there are links between the parenting these men experienced in their families of origin and their choice to continue as primary parent of their children following divorce. For example, Mendes (1976a, 1976b) found that single fathers who actively sought custody seemed to identify with and emulate their mothers more than their fathers as role models. Gersick (1979) found that custodial fathers, compared with their noncustodial counterparts, reported more intense relationships with their mothers but felt distant from their fathers. In addition, these custodial fathers were more likely to have had mothers who were full-time homemakers, and said they would have chosen to reside with their mothers rather than their fathers if they had had to make such a choice when they were youngsters. Gersick also found that single custodial fathers were not more "feminine" on the Bem Sex Role Scale than fathers in his comparison sample. Hanson (1979, 1981, 1985b) reported that, although single custodial fathers named their male parents as their primary parental model, they felt they were much more emotionally involved with their own young children than their own fathers had been with them. In other words, single fathers were making a conscientious effort to be more expressive and physically affectionate with their children. A major question remains: Since they were not socialized in that way, where did these single fathers acquire the attitudes, knowledge, and skills necessary to assume the primary nurturing roles that their children needed and required?

Motivation for Custody

Single fathers have sought and/or received custody for a number of reasons. Some researchers have made a distinction between two distinct and different motivational origins, utilizing a typology that differentiates fathers who obtain custody by seeking it (adjudication) from fathers who assent to it (allocation) (Gasser & Taylor, 1976; Greene, 1977; Hanson, 1981; Mendes, 1976a, 1976b; Orthner, Brown, & Ferguson, 1976; Risman, 1986). One end of the continuum implies activity and aggressiveness, while the other end implies passivity and/or resistance. In the studies reported, fathers who actively sought custody adjusted faster and better to their roles as single parents, performed more adequately as parents, and viewed themselves as more nurturing parents. However, even though seeking fathers spent more time initially in the parenting role, there was evidence that men who assented to custody also learned or adjusted to their roles.

Reasons for fathers assuming custody have generally been positive. Fathers who had been involved in child care since their children's early infancy were more likely to have actively sought custody and were better equipped both physically and emotionally to assume the primary care of their children (Hanson, 1986d; Mendes, 1976a, 1976b; Risman, 1986). In the research to date there is little indication that men who sought custody did so to spite their former wives, or that men who had custody wished they did not. In fact, some custodial fathers thought that their former spouses were equally fit to be custodial parents, and that they, the fathers, just happened to have custody at this time (Grief, 1985; Risman, 1986). Chang and Deinard (1982) found that newly separated/divorced single fathers sought custody because they considered themselves to be better parents, because of their love for their children, or because their wives did not want to have custody. Very few of their subjects reported their former wives to be unfit for parenthood.

The Fathering Role

Sex and Age of Children

Although single fathers had custody of both boys and girls of all ages, such arrangements were not typical. Characteristically, single mothers had custody of younger children, both male and female. If fathers had custody the children were more likely to be adolescent. In addition, studies showed that on average, 57% of father-only households had custody of boys, whereas 43% had custody of girls (Ambert, 1982; Chang & Deinard, 1982; Hanson, 1981). In contrast, the ratio between male and female children was equal in single-mother households (U.S. Bureau of the Census, 1980). The higher incidence of male children living with single fathers may reflect a greater tendency both for men to seek custody of sons, and for judges to grant it. However, though single custodial fathers were more likely to rear boys, nearly one-half of single custodial fathers were rearing daughters ranging in age from infancy to young adulthood. These fathers did not appear to have anxiety over raising daughters without their mothers, although the issues of sex education, appropriate clothing, and hair styles became concerns for which they tended eventually to seek help (Lynn, 1979).

For years, scholars have been troubled about the effects of parental absence on the sexual and social development of children. Most of the work in this area investigated the effects of father absence on boys (Biller, 1981; Robinson & Barrett, 1986). In one study comparing children from single-mother, single-father, and two-parent homes, Santrock and Warshak (1979) investigated the interaction between the sex of child(ren), the sex of custodial parent(s), the type of custody, and the social development of the children. They reported that children of single parents living with the same sex parent were better socially adjusted than children living with opposite sex parents.[3] That is, boys seemed to fare better with fathers and girls with mothers. If these findings are substantiated through further research, they may affect custody decisions in the future.

The Single Father as Homemaker

Although not all single fathers actively engaged in homemaking activities (house-cleaning, cooking, or laundry) before becoming single parents, there was evidence that most fathers experienced little difficulty in taking on these additional duties (Gasser & Taylor, 1976; Mendes, 1976a, 1976b; Orthner, Brown, & Ferguson, 1976; Risman, 1986; Victor & Winkler, 1977). In fact, contrary to common assumption, single fathers did not hire someone or coerce relatives to take on these responsibilities for them. One study reported that single fathers perceived themselves as having more ability with homemaking and parenting skills than the "average" father in a two-parent family (Chang & Deinard, 1982). In most studies reported, the household chores were shared with children, and when problems arose, it was because of the time and energy needed for meal preparation and housecleaning (Chang & Deinard, 1982; Hanson, 1986b). Weiss (1979) suggested that the responsibility for additional chores placed on children in single-parent homes has resulted in positive outcomes—helping children of divorce to "grow up faster."

Father–Child Relationships

The relationships between fathers and children appear to have been affected by the quality and quantity of earlier interactions. That is, single fathers who reported interacting frequently and effectively with their children from very early infancy, adjusted more readily to single-parent roles (Gasser & Taylor, 1976; Orthner & Lewis, 1979), felt warmer and more comfortable with their custodial children (Lynn, 1979), were more likely to have sought custody, and felt they were doing a good job (Greene, 1977; Hanson, 1979, 1981; Mendes, 1976a, 1976b).

One of the common concerns expressed about men serving as primary custodians

---

[3]It should be noted that the type of parenting style and the amount of contact with additional adult caregivers were also associated with positive social behaviors demonstrated by these children.

of young children is their ability to provide emotional support and understanding as well as physical and psychological nurturance. Hanson (1979, 1981) studied the relationship between single fathers and their children, with a focus on the nurturing quality of their interaction. On four separate measures, she found that fathers viewed themselves as affectionate, nurturing parents, and children perceived their fathers as being loving and concerned. Furthermore, fathers who sought custody viewed themselves as more supportive and nurturing than men who assented to custody. One of the more interesting findings of this particular study was that children of single fathers rated their fathers as more nurturing than children from two-parent families rated either parent.

Smith and Smith (1981), in an investigation pertaining to the ability of single fathers to meet the emotional requirements of children, found that single fathers did fulfill the age- and sex-appropriate emotional needs of their children. These needs varied, however, according to individual families rather than general developmental tasks.

Finally, in relation to parent–child interactions, Ambert (1982) studied children's behavior toward their custodial parents in one-parent families. When comparing children's behavior toward custodial mothers versus to custodial fathers, she found that (1) custodial fathers reported better child behavior in the home than did custodial mothers, and (2) the children of custodial fathers verbalized their appreciation for their fathers, but children of custodial mothers rarely did so. Not surprisingly, single custodial fathers reported more satisfaction with their roles than single mothers, and children appeared to be happier in those households than children in single-mother households.

Child Care

Single fathers relied on available child-care resources in the community. Despite their favorable economic position, these men did not hire housekeepers, nor did they rely on relatives or friends to provide babysitting. Fathers with preschool children utilized nursery and day-care centers, fathers with young school-age children paid neighbors to tend the children after school, and fathers of older children (age 10 and above) usually left the children on their own after school, until they came home from work (Lynn, 1979). Since single custodial fathers were not in frequent communication with each other, they were not likely to exchange babysitting services. The lack of high-quality, low-cost child-care services was a reported concern of fathers in the United States more than in other English speaking countries.

Social Support

There is little doubt that strong social and kinship network systems have provided important emotional sustenance to single-parent families, and promoted their healthy adjustment following divorce (Burden, 1979, 1982; Grief, 1985; Hanson, 1986b; Santrock & Warshak, 1979). Simply because of their uniqueness, single fathers have tended to elicit more community sympathy and support than single mothers, though it has commonly been believed that fathers have not been as active as mothers in community organizations, due to differences in the ways that males and females have been socialized. One study found that single fathers utilized, to a high degree, their professional and community resources as well as their extended families (Santrock & Warshak, 1979). On the other hand, Gasser & Taylor (1976) and Hanson (1986b) found that single fathers became involved with community agencies primarily to assist them through the pre- and post-divorce period, but relinquished these associations over time. Single fathers appeared to know of other men in similar circumstances, but they did not seek their companionship or support. Instead, they turned to single mothers for help and friendships, although many men complained of the lack of suitable social and sexual partners (Chang & Deinard, 1982; Hanson, 1986c).

Single custodial fathers tended to provide consistency in their children's living environment. DeFrain and Eirick (1981) found that single fathers were less likely than single mothers to move from their homes and communities following divorce, which they believe may have enhanced the adjustment of single-father families. No doubt this phenomenon was due to the more stable job situation most men experience following divorce, in comparison to women in similar circumstances.

Visitation and Child Support

There were a variety of visitation arrangements with noncustodial mothers, providing the mothers were around. Some single fathers reported good relationships between themselves and their former spouses regarding visitation issues, but most fathers discussed some of the same problems that single mothers reported about noncustodial fathers: that is, mothers spent too much time with the children, they did not spend enough time, they did not show up when they were supposed to, the children returned upset when they had been with their mothers, the fathers did not like their former spouses' boyfriends (lifestyle, behavior), the children did not want to see their mothers, or mothers did not contribute anything to the children's financial welfare (Folberg, 1984; Hanson, 1985b).

In one comparative study of single mothers and single fathers, DeFrain and Eirick (1981) reported that single fathers were more likely to say negative things to their children about noncustodial mothers than single mothers say about noncustodial fathers. However, children in father-custody homes were in more frequent contact with their noncustodial mothers than were their counterparts in mother-custody homes (Santrock & Warshak, 1979).

There seemed to be fewer demands that "you pay child support or you do not see the kids" in single-father homes than in single-mother homes. This may be primarily due to the fact that few mothers paid child support. While Fox (1985) reported that less than 50% of noncustodial fathers met their court mandated support obligations, corresponding comparisons for mothers were unavailable. Hanson (1979, 1981) reported that only 10% of all noncustodial mothers paid child support. These differences may well be due to the overall discrepancy between men's and women's education and salaries in our society. Child support will be an interesting issue to follow, now that most noncustodial mothers are working, and more and more states endorse child support enforcement laws.

Problems Encountered

Although as reported earlier, single fathers felt successful in their child rearing practices, they also experienced a variety of problems, a few of which will be summarized here (see Table 11.1 for additional information). In one English study, Hipgrave (1982) found that single fathers questioned their competence as parents. Bartz and Witcher (1978), Orthner, Brown, and Ferguson (1976), and Hanson (1981) all reported that some fathers did not feel they had enough time and patience to do everything they would have liked to with their children. Grief (1985) found that, although fathers rarely reported unhappiness about their children or unhappiness at having custody, some reported conflict with adolescent offspring, particularly daughters. Similarly, 37% of the fathers in Katz's study of Australian fathers (1979) reported behavioral problems with children. Smith and Smith (1981), who found that single fathers in their sample encountered a number of problems in child rearing, suggested the following strategies for solving them:

1. Earlier preparation of men for parenthood
2. More participation by men in household activities while still married
3. Increased involvement in the early discipline and limit setting with children
4. Learning to provide more nurturing, supportive interaction with women and children early in the family's history.

On the other hand, there were so few reports of difficulties with child rearing that one wonders if men had any problems as sole parents, or if they just failed to report problems in order to give a positive impression. Data collected directly from children themselves might have yielded different findings.

Katz (1979) found that 69% of his Australian fathers were more willing to discuss their personal problems than their child rearing problems. Fathers' issues varied, but some of the more commonly mentioned challenges were role overload (not enough time to work, socialize, parent, and keep house), financial problems (having to buy services that were free when married), and loneliness (making decisions by themselves and the lack of social life). The fathers studied by Chang and Deinard (1982) reported their difficulties as restricted opportunities to date, inability to pursue employment opportunities when they arose, and a dearth of time and energy. Half of the men from this latter study also reported depression and loneliness, as well as an increase in drinking and smoking since divorce.

Strengths of Single Custodial Fathers

In sum, the research on single fathers demonstrates that they are doing well as primary caregivers. Those who were doing the best had been involved in child-care and household tasks before divorce, had actively sought additional counseling and education prior to or following the divorce, and had purposefully worked toward a more meaningful interaction between themselves and their offspring (Ambert, 1982, 1984; Chang & Deinard, 1982; Grief, 1985; Hanson, 1986d; Keshet &

Rosenthal, 1976). Many were willing and able to use the resources that the community offered them and their children, and were not afraid to become joiners and admit their need for help from others. Even if they did not know how to do housework before divorce, they quickly learned these skills and involved their children in these activities. For the most part, these fathers worked very hard to fulfill the emotional and psychological needs of their children, and from the few reports available from the children themselves, these ends were accomplished. Initially, single fathers hoped to find female companions who would assume the role of surrogate mothers, but as time passed, fathers became more confident as well as capable, and the need for substitute mothers disappeared (Chang & Deinard, 1982; Hanson, 1985a; Robinson & Barrett, 1986). Most fathers were happy with their decision to have sought or consented to custody, and they felt that they were clearly the better choice of parent. Children reported happiness with this arrangement, and there did not appear to be much yearning to live with the noncustodial parent.

IMPLICATIONS FOR SOCIAL POLICY

The number of single fathers who assume primary responsibility for raising their children will almost certainly continue to increase. It is important, therefore, to examine the effects of existing social policy on the lives of these fathers and their families, and to consider the implications of the research findings for future policy decisions. The rest of this chapter will examine some of the areas and ways in which social policy affects single father families.

Child Custody Laws

Of all the issues that have had ramifications for family policy pertaining to single fathers, marriage and custody laws have been the most debated in recent years. No-fault divorce laws were instituted in the early 1970s, with individual states amending their statutes governing the judicial award of child custody (Pearson, Munson, & Theonnes, 1982). In 1973, the American Bar Association drafted the Uniform Marriage and Divorce Act, which began the repeal of mother preference in custody cases. Instead of the proscribed standards of maternal preference, sex neutral standards, commonly called the "best interests of the child doctrine," were instituted. By 1979, only three states were still automatically awarding children to mothers by law (Burden, 1982).

As it has become easier for men to obtain custody of minor children, more fathers have sought custody—despite the discouragement they receive from lawyers (Bartz & Witcher, 1978)—so that presently, 11% of all children are awarded to fathers. Of all custody decisions, 80% are, in fact, decided between parents; of the 20% that are disputed, approximately half are won by fathers (Burden, 1982),[4] and

---

[4]Various percentages have been reported, depending on the sample studied. For a further discussion of custody issues, see Chapter 12, Loewen, this volume.

with more families undergoing divorce, custody disputes are on the increase (Pearson, Munson, & Theonnes, 1982; Schwartz, 1984).

By 1984, the Uniform Child Custody Jurisdiction Act (UCCJA) was enacted in 48 states in an effort to curb child snatching by disgruntled parents. Prior to this, frustrated fathers deprived of contact with their children, kidnapped their own offspring at an estimated rate of 25,000 to 100,000 per year (Palmer & Noble, 1984). However, these newer custody laws, which were designed to curtail parents from abducting their children from one state and gaining legal custody in another, have not provided the entire solution to the problem (Folberg, 1984).

The most recent controversial issue pertaining to custody is that of joint custody. An activist group, the Joint Custody Association, has advocated that joint custody be given first preference following divorce. By 1985, 35 states had adopted joint custody laws (Folberg, 1984); for example, California enacted a law by which joint legal custody was presumptive and seen to be in the "best interest of children." These new laws mandated joint *physical* as well as joint *legal* custody to both parents, except where one parent did not agree to this arrangement, or where this arrangement was not viewed to be in the best interest of the children.

Professionals from a variety of disciplines support the joint custody movement that is taking place right now. Studies have indicated that children least adversely affected by divorce have been those whose fathers have continued to be actively involved with them (Burden, 1982; Cook, 1980), and fathers with joint custody certainly fall into that category (Grief, 1985). Presumably joint custody has helped both to prevent the recourse of excluded parents to "child snatch," and to reduce the incidence of abandonment and loss of financial support, which are thought to be due to the lack of meaningful, frequent contact with children (Cook, 1980). However, these arguments in support of joint custody have not addressed the larger issue of parents' equal access to their children.

When the American Bar Association developed the Uniform Marriage and Divorce Act, they also called for the protection of children's rights. Some of the questions raised have been: Should there be a separate attorney or *guardian ad litem* appointed to represent children's best interests when parents are in turmoil, and/or when both parents are equally qualified to parent? How can children be protected in family conflicts when their parents are antagonists? Should courts invite opinions from children of all ages concerning their parental preference?

There are many unresolved issues and problems pertaining to child custody. Suffice it to say that it appears that mandatory joint custody is likely to become the most common custodial arrangement. This will, in turn, force social and legal agencies into taking action on many other issues that affect single fathers, some of which are discussed below.

Child Support

Child support is a volatile issue for divorcing families. In the research reported earlier, only 34–51% of noncustodial fathers and 10% of noncustodial mothers were found to be paying child support (Burden, 1979; Fox, 1985; Hanson, 1981; Weiss, 1984).

The 1975 amendments to the Social Security Act created the Child Support Enforcement Program in all states and territories (U.S. Department of Health and Human Services, 1975). The major purpose of this federal/state/local program is to collect child support from parents who are legally obligated to pay. Its goals include: to ensure that children are supported by their parents, to foster family responsibility, and to reduce the costs of welfare to the taxpayer. State enforcement programs locate absent parents, establish paternity, establish and enforce support orders, and collect child support payments. Should this program actively seek child support from fugitive noncustodial employed and nonemployed mothers? Should child support be vigorously enforced for parents of both sexes? If the ERA passed, what would be its implications for child support, spousal support (alimony), and adherence to property settlement after divorce?

Income Support

Although single fathers enjoy higher socioeconomic circumstances than single mothers, the fathers in the studies reported here felt little choice as to whether or not they wanted to continue to work outside of the home. In the United States it is more acceptable for women with dependent children to make choices between child care or outside employment. Most men with higher incomes continue with present employment when they become divorced and obtain custody, while some lower-income men quit jobs and stay home with children. But how many men from across the socioeconomic spectrum would choose to be custodial parents if they had the option of drawing welfare and staying home with children? There is a strong stigma attached in our culture to able-bodied men tending house and caring for children.

There are no income support programs for families in the United States beyond aid-to-dependent children, welfare, and unemployment insurance. Moreover, some people believe that our welfare system has turned child rearing into paid employment for women, thus transforming children into sole providers for families. It can be argued that supplemental income programs of all kinds should apply equally to single mothers and single fathers. Recently, some states have started providing welfare support to families when men remain in the home, even when mothers are present. A logical extension of this support would be to provide this option for single custodial fathers.

Child Care

The problems that single fathers reported concerning child care were not much different than problems that single mothers and dual career two-parent families have had in obtaining economical, quality care for their children. The research to date indicates that single fathers did not hire live-in babysitters, but used the same resources that were available to all parents in the community—resources that have been under attack for years for their scarcity, variable quality, and high cost. In contrast to many other governments, the United States has not regarded the provision of child care as being within the jurisdiction of public or family policy. Consistent efforts have been made since 1971 to pass comprehensive child-care legislation, but it has been voted down, or vetoed by successive presidents. According to Kamerman and Kahn (1981), who advocated that funds be allocated to parents with financial need, and that low-cost loans be given to day care centers for construction and renovation, the United States has had a "do nothing approach."

Economical and quality child care is not just a single father issue. Day-care facilities are needed for children of working single custodial mothers and fathers after school, with extended hours to accommodate parents who have job requirements into the evening or weekend hours. In addition, fathers may also need some assistance in the establishment of baby-sitting cooperatives.

Community Resources

If there was one common theme from most of the literature about single fathers, it was their fierce independence—their belief that they could do almost everything by themselves and did not need assistance from anyone. This autonomous stance suggests that single fathers are not generally inclined to seek the help or services that may be available. Yet, the problems that single fathers encounter during separation and divorce suggest that they would benefit from services provided by family courts early in the divorce process, to assist with issues such as child custody, visitation, and child support. Mediation and counseling services can help parents separate their personal struggles from what is in the best interest of the children, as well as help avoid custody battles in the courtroom by facilitating custody/co-parenting compromises. In addition, individual and group counseling can be very effective in helping men move through this difficult transition period toward a satisfying life as a single parent. For a discussion of clinical work with divorced fathers, see Chapter 17, Schwebel, Fine, Moreland and Prindle, this volume.

There are a number of community programs that would be of interest and assistance to single custodial fathers. Single-parent groups have become popular with women, but there are few such groups for custodial or noncustodial fathers. Fathers-only groups as well as combined single-mother/single-father self-help groups could be sponsored and funded by local agencies. Special classes could be offered to men who want to learn more about parenting, children's growth and development, and children's emotional lives (Tedder, Libbee, & Scherman, 1981); in particular, fathers in one study expressed interest in understanding and helping their preadolescent and teenage daughters in their psychological-social-sexual development (Hanson, 1981). Furthermore, although many men reported social isolation, few were actively seeking out each other. Classes for information and support would put single fathers in touch with one another and would provide critical networking. It may require active recruitment on the part of professionals working in these areas to inform single fathers about these programs.

In addition, as a primary prevention measure, parenting class should be a required high school course. Although the majority of people become parents, there is little or no education provided to assist in this endeavor—and this is especially true for men. With 12% of all men becoming primary parents, and with the likelihood of this number increasing, education for parenthood is critical for both sexes (Klinman & Kohl, 1984). For a full discussion of fatherhood education programs for men and boys, see Chapter 15, Levant, this volume.

Business and Industry

What is the responsibility of business, industry, and the professional community to single fathers? What are the rules, regulations, and policies of businesses, and how can they be helpful? Sweden adopted a paternity leave policy for the purpose of encouraging early bonding and participation of men in child care. Should industries in the United States do something similar? Some research (Hanson, 1981, 1985b) has shown that single fathers who were faring particularly well as parents reported early involvement in the lives of their children, so this appears to be an important issue.

Many businesses and organizations could incorporate flextime into their work schedules so that single custodial fathers could adjust their hours according to their families' needs. Dempsey (1981) has suggested a written "family responsibility statement" by organizations which would enable prospective employees to decide if an organization's requirements were compatible with their desired family style. A family sick-leave policy where parents can stay home with sick children while saving their personal sick leave time is also a viable notion. Some companies provide on-site day care, but this is still not widely available. For further discussion of workplace policies relevant to child care, see Chapter 18, Catalyst, this volume.

The banking and housing industry could make some adjustments. There are a number of single fathers who would like to buy homes together and share in the cost benefits and satisfaction that such arrangements provide. Thus far, under our present loan and ownership policies, this kind of arrangement has been very difficult. There is also recent interest in multiple-family dwellings built specifically for single-parent families, where they can share common core facilities but maintain their privacy.

Working parents have difficulty with getting to the bank or taking care of problems with their utilities in the day time. Many businesses are not open on the weekends. Society is still oriented to the traditional nuclear family where the nonemployed mother takes care of family business during the daytime hours. Additionally, health care services may not be readily available for working parents, unless they take time off from work. Inexpensive clinics could be established and kept open in the evening or on the weekend when single parents with children can attend.

CONCLUSIONS

The purpose of this chapter has been to synthesize current empirical knowledge about single custodial fathers and their children. Most of the research on this group of fathers has been carried out in the past 12 years. Even though there are fairly good empirical data about common themes in single-father research, methodologically there is a need to move beyond descriptive studies toward more sophisticated research designs. Longitudinal analyses of fathers and children during the process of divorce adjustment would be of particular value. In addition, collaborative research between a variety of disciplines should be encouraged.

There are many issues to be explored, such as the following:

1. What are the long-term sequelae of joint custody on male and female children and on male and female parents?
2. Does early attachment and bonding of fathers and children result in a higher quality of single fatherhood (custodial or noncustodial) during subsequent years?
3. What are the effects of mother-absence on children living with single fathers?
4. How do different kinds of father-only homes differ from one another? For example, are there differences and similarities among widowed, separated, divorced, and adoptive fathers?
5. Thus far, only successful single-custodial fathers are reported in the literature. Who are the "unsuccessful" single custodial fathers and how can they be helped?

Although admittedly risky, speculations can be made about the future. Demographers prophesy that by 1990 more than 50% of all U.S. children will have lived in a single-parent household before the age of 18 years (Glick, 1975, 1979, 1984; Masnick & Bane, 1980; Norton & Glick, 1986). With increasing divorce rates, increasing employment of women, increasing acceptance of men in nurturing roles, and with the demonstrated viability of single-parent homes, there will be many more single-parent families in the future. There will be an increase in male-only headed families as a result not only of separation/divorce, but also adoption, and the awarding of custody to never-married biological fathers. Additionally, more fathers will continue to receive sole, joint, or split custody, allowing even more men to remain active in child rearing after divorce. In the past, single-custodial fathers were privileged in education, income, and occupation, but increasingly more working-class and middle-class fathers will experience this family structure.

Researchers are beginning to examine the way this society socializes males. Similarly, there appears to be a growing popular awareness about changing men's roles. In the future, it is likely that single fathers will not have to struggle as hard to maintain meaningful relationships with their children after divorce, as more judges, lawyers, and former spouses come to view men as capable, nurturing parents with whom children can live. As women's status in the world changes, they will be more willing to support men in these kinds of roles. Times are changing and so are families. Single-custodial-father families are here to stay, and represent an acceptable and viable option for family life in this country.

REFERENCES

Ambert, A. (1982). Differences in children's behavior toward custodial mothers and custodial fathers. *Journal of Marriage and the Family*, *44*, 73–86.

Ambert, A. (1984). Longitudinal changes in children's behavior toward custodial parents. *Journal of Marriage and the Family*, *46*(2), 463–467.

Bain, C. (1973). Lone fathers: An unnoticed group. *Australian Social Welfare*, *3*, 14–17.

Bartz, K.W., & Witcher, W.C. (1978). When father gets custody. *Children Today*, *7*(5), 2–6.

Biller, H. (1981). Father absence, divorce, and personality development. In M.E. Lamb (Ed.) *The role of the father in child development*. New York: Wiley.

Burden, D. (1979 August). *The single parent family: Social policy issues*. Paper presented at the annual meeting of the American Sociological Association, Boston.

Burden, D. (1982). *Parental custody after divorce*. Unpublished manuscript, Brandeis University, The Florence Heller Graduate School for Advanced Studies in Social Welfare, Waltham, MA.

Chang, P., & Deinard, A. (1982). Single father caretakers: Demographic characteristics and adjustment process. *American Journal of Orthopsychiatry*, *52*(2), 236–243.

Cook, J.A. (1980). Joint custody, sole custody: A new statute reflects a new perspective. *Conciliation Courts Review*, *18*, 1–14.

Curto, J.J. (1983). *How to become a single parent*. Englewood Cliffs, NJ: Prentice-Hall.

DeFrain, J., & Eirick, R. (1981). Coping as divorced parents: A comparative study of fathers and mothers. *Family Relations*, *30*(2), 265–274.

Dempsey, J.J. (1981). *The family and public policy*. Baltimore, MD: Brookes.

Espenshade, T.J. (1979). The economic consequences of divorce. *Journal of Marriage and the Family*, *41*, 615–621.

Folberg, J. (1984). *Joint custody and shared parenting*. Portland, OR: Association of Family and Conciliations Courts.

Fox, G.L. (1985). Noncustodial fathers. In S.M.H. Hanson & F.W. Bozett (Eds.), *Dimensions of fatherhood*. Beverly Hills: Sage.

Fricke, J.M. (1982). *Coping as divorced fathers and mothers: A nationwide study of sole, joint, and split custody*. Unpublished master's thesis, University of Nebraska.

Gasser, R.D., & Taylor, C.M. (1976). Role adjustment of single fathers with dependent children. *Family Coordinator*, *25*(4), 397–401.

George, V., & Wilding, P. (1972). *Motherless families*. London: Routledge and Kegan Paul.

Gersick, K.E. (1979). Fathers by choice: Divorced men who receive custody of their children. In G. Levinger & O. Noles (Eds.), *Separation and divorce*. New York: Basic.

Glick, P.C. (1975). A demographer looks at American families. *Journal of Marriage and the Family*, *37*, 15–26.

Glick, P.C. (1979). Children of divorced parents in demographic perspective. *Journal of Social Issues*, *35*, 170–182.

Glick, P.C. (1984). American household structure in transition. *Family Planning Perspectives*, *16*(5), 205–211.

Greene, R.S. (1977). *Atypical parenting: Custodial single fathers*. Unpublished doctoral dissertation, University of Maryland.

Grief, G.L. (1982). Dads raising kids. *Single Parent*, 25(9), 17–23.

Grief, G.L. (1983). Widowers. *Single Parent*, 26(7), 29–32.

Grief, G.L. (1984). Custodial dads and their ex-wives. *Single Parent*, 27(1), 17–20.

Grief, G.L. (1985). *Single fathers*. Lexington, MA: Heath.

Hanson, S.M.H. (1979). Characteristics of single custodial fathers and the parent-child relationship (Doctoral dissertation, University of Washington, 1979). *Dissertation Abstracts International*, 40, 6438A.

Hanson, S.M.H. (1981). Single custodial fathers and the parent-child relationship. *Nursing Research*, 30, 202–204.

Hanson, S.M.H. (1985a). Fatherhood: Contextual variations. *American Behavioral Scientist*, 29(1), 55–78.

Hanson, S.M.H. (1985b). Single custodial fathers. In S.M.H. Hanson & F.W. Bozett (Eds.), *Dimensions of fatherhood*. Beverly Hills, CA: Sage.

Hanson, S.M.H. (1985c). Single fathers with custody: A synthesis of the literature. In B. Schlesinger (Ed.), *The one-parent family in the 1980's: Perspectives and bibliography 1978–1984*. Toronto: University of Toronto Press.

Hanson, S.M.H. (1986a). Father-child relationships: Beyond Kramer vs. Kramer. *Marriage and Family Review*, 9(3,4), 135–150.

Hanson, S.M.H. (1986b). Father-child relationships: Beyond Kramer vs. Kramer. In R.S. Lewis & M.B. Sussman (Eds.), *Men's changing roles in families*. New York: Haworth Press.

Hanson, S.M.H. (1986c). Healthy single parent families. *Family Relations*, 35(1), 125–132.

Hanson, S.M.H. (1986d). Parent-child relationships in single father families. In R. Lewis & B. Salts (Eds.), *Men in families*. Beverly Hills, CA: Sage.

Hanson, S.M.H., & Sporakowski, M.J. (1986). Single parent families. *Family Relations*, 35(1), 3–8.

Hanson, S.M.H., & Trilling, J. (1983). A proposed study of the characteristics of the healthy single-parent family. *Family Perspectives*, 17(2), 79–88.

Hipgrave, T. (1982). Lone fatherhood: A problematic status. In L. McKee & M. O'Brien (Eds.), *The father figure*. London: Tavistock.

Kamerman, S., & Kahn, A. (Eds.). (1981). *Child care, family benefits, and working parents*. New York: Columbia University Press.

Katz, A.J. (1979). Lone fathers: Perspectives and implications for family policy. *Family Coordinator*, 28(4), 521–527.

Keshet, H.F., & Rosenthal, K.N. (1976). Single-parent families: A new study. *Children Today*, 7(3), 13–17.

Klinman, D.G., & Kohl, R. (1984). *Fatherhood U.S.A.* New York: Garland.

Kohn, J.B., & Kohn, W.K. (1978). *The widower*. Boston: Beacon Press.

Lynn, D.B. (1979). *Daughters and parents: Past, present, and future*. Monterey, CA: Brooks/Cole.

Masnick, G., & Bane, M.J. (1980). *The nation's families: 1960–1990*. Boston: Auburn House.

McKee, L., & O'Brien, M. (1982). *The Father Figure*. London: Tavistock.

Mendes, H.A. (1976a). Single fatherhood. *Social Work, 21*(4), 308–312.

Mendes, H.A. (1976b). Single fathers. *Family Coordinator, 25*(4), 439–444.

Norton, A.J., & Glick, P.G. (1986). One parent families: A social and economic profile. *Family Relations, 35*(1), 9–17.

Orthner, D.K., & Bowen, G.L. (1985). Fathers in the military. In S.M.H. Hanson & F.W. Bozett (Eds.), *Dimensions of fatherhood.* Beverly Hills, CA: Sage.

Orthner, D., Brown, T., & Ferguson, D. (1976). Single-parent fatherhood: An emerging family life style. *Family Coordinator, 25*(4), 429–437.

Orthner, D., & Lewis, K. (1979). Evidence of single father competence in child rearing. *Family Law Quarterly, 8*, 27–48.

Palmer, C.E., & Noble, D.N. (1984). Child snatching: Motivations, mechanisms and melodrama. *Journal of Family Issues, 5*(1), 27–45.

Pearson, J., Munson, P., & Thoennes, N. (1982). Legal change and child custody awards. *Journal of Family Issues, 3*, 5–24.

Risman, B.J. (1986). Can men "mother"? Life as a single father. *Family Relations, 35*(1), 95–102.

Robinson, B.E., & Barrett, R.L. (1986). *The developing father: Emerging roles in contemporary society.* New York: Guilford Press.

Rosenthal, K.M., & Keshet, H.F. (1981). *Fathers without partners: A study of fathers and the family after marital separation.* Totowa, NJ: Rowman and Littlefield.

Santrock, J.W., & Warshak, R. (1979). Father custody and social development in boys and girls. *Journal of Social Issues, 35*(4), 112–125.

Schlesinger, B. (1974). *One-parent families in Canada.* Toronto: University of Toronto Press.

Schlesinger, B. (1977). One parent families in Great Britain. *Family Coordinator, 26*, 139–141.

Schlesinger, B. (1978a). Single parent: A research review. *Children Today, 7*, 12–19, 37–39.

Schlesinger, B. (1978b). *The one-parent family: Perspectives and annotated bibliography.* Toronto: University of Toronto Press.

Schlesinger, B. (1985). *The one-parent family in the 1980's: Perspective and bibliography 1978–1984.* Toronto: University of Toronto Press.

Schwartz, S.F.G. (1984). Toward a presumption of joint custody. *Family Law Quarterly, 28*(2), 225–246.

Smith, R.M., & Smith, C.W. (1981). Child rearing and single-parent fathers. *Family Relations, 30*(3), 411–417.

Tedder, S.L., Libbee, K.M., & Scherman, A. (1981). A community support group for single custodial fathers. *Personal and Guidance Journal, 60*(2), 115–119.

U.S. Bureau of the Census. (1980). *Marital status and living arrangements: March 1980* (Current Population Reports, Series P-20, No. 365). Washington, DC: U.S. Government Printing Office.

U.S. Bureau of the Census. (1985a). *Statistical abstract of the United States: 1984.* Washington, DC: U.S. Government Printing Office.

U.S. Bureau of the Census. (1985b). *Household and family characteristics: March, 1984*

(Current Population Reports, Series P-20, No. 398). Washington, DC: U.S. Government Printing Office.

U.S. Department of Health & Human Services. (1975). *Handbook on child support enforcement*. Rockville, MD: Office of Child Support Enforcement.

Victor, I., & Winkler, W.A. (1977). *Fathers and custody*. New York: Hawthorn.

Weiss, R.S. (1979). Growing up a little faster: The experience of growing up in a single parent household. *Journal of Social Issues*, *35*(1), 97–111.

Weiss, R.S. (1984). The impact of marital dissolution on income and consumption in single-parent households. *Journal of Marriage and the Family*, *46*(1), 115–127.

CHAPTER 12

Visitation Fatherhood

JAMES W. LOEWEN

For the first time in history, more U.S. marriages are being dissolved by divorce than by death. More than half of all children born this year will live with only one parent during some or all of their growing-up years (Furstenberg, 1982). Despite the flurry of recent books on joint custody, sole custody with visitation is still by far the most common legal arrangement for separated or divorced parents, and by a ratio of 9 to 1, women still get custody, and men visitation. Within the next few years, as many as half of all fathers in this country can expect to experience the sorrows and satisfactions of the relationship with their children that we call visitation.

The conventional image of visitation fathering is provided by Ramos (1979):

> In most cases where there is a custodial parent, there is usually a visiting parent who spends roughly a day or two each week with the children, keeps in touch with them on other days, and contributes financially to their support. (p. 71)

In reality, however, most children of divorce rarely see their fathers. The modal pattern is that visitation is maintained for the first two years, then declines. Furstenberg (1982, 1983) found that fewer than half of a national sample of about 500 children had seen their father even once in the preceding 12 months, and fewer than one child in six saw their fathers as often as once a week. And when visitation declined, letters and phone calls generally did too. Child support was maintained better than visitation, but it too dropped off over time (Furstenberg & Spanier, 1984). Other researchers (Goode, 1956; Luepnitz, 1982) found that only 20–43% of fathers maintained regular visitation. Reviewing the research on custody issues following divorce, Maidment (1984) concluded, "For many noncustodial parents, divorce not only ends their marriage but also their participation as parents" (p. 238).

As late as 1973, social scientists knew very little about the effects of visitation on children or fathers, since most research on divorce had been done by interviewing custodial mothers. In the last 15 years, however, studies have included men and children as well (Anderson-Khleif 1982; Hetherington, 1979, 1980, 1981; Hetherington, Cox, & Cox, 1976; Rosenthal & Keshet, 1981; Wallerstein & Kelly, 1980;

My thanks to Peter Evans and Phyllis Rosser for their comments on this chapter.

Weiss, 1979), making it possible to address questions about visitation fathering with firsthand data, which is crucial in this sometimes emotionally charged area.

THE IMPORTANCE OF VISITATION FOR CHILDREN

Children are the big losers when visitation drops off. Daughters especially may be left with a deep, lifelong yearning for their fathers (Laiken, 1981; Tessman, 1978; Wallerstein & Kelly, 1980). Sons are left with a greater likelihood of becoming delinquent (Maidment, 1984). Both are subject to depression (Ramos, 1979). Intrinsic to non-visitation is the feeling of being rejected, with detrimental consequences for self-esteem. Whatever the real reasons for non-visitation, the child's natural inference is, "I must not be lovable, or Daddy would want to see me" (Maidment, 1984; Steinzor, 1969). As Wedermeyer (1984) put it:

> The withdrawal of the noncustodial parent has several very negative effects. The most critical effect is the child's sense of abandonment. Most emotional disturbances in children of divorce center around their anger at being left, or their sense of being unlovable because a parent did not love them enough to stay. (pp. 110–111)

In the past 15 years, researchers have looked at post-divorce families that maintained or did not maintain visitation (Anderson & Anderson, 1981; Francke, 1983; Hetherington, Cox, & Cox, 1982; Katkin, Bullington, & Levene, 1974; Oakland, 1984; Ware, 1982). Based on these studies, Maidment (1984) has concluded:

> Empirical studies are unanimous that one of the most important indicators of success is the quality of post-divorce relationships with *both* parents. Disruption of bonds with the absent parent as a result of divorce needs to be minimized. . . . In other words the principle of continuity, rather than suggesting a custodian, indicates that the courts' concern ought to be to ensure that the best possible custody and access arrangements are made so as to protect the child's relationship with both parents. (p. 215)

Conclusions from this recent research are consistent with findings from the earlier father-absence literature (reviewed in Biller, 1981; Lamb, 1981). Children from father-absent homes were found to be more likely to have problems in the areas of social relationships, sex-role development, and achievement, with boys from these homes more likely to become delinquent. However, in addition to other methodological weaknesses, most father-absence research did not consider the frequency of paternal visitation as a variable. Had it been considered, a much clearer picture of the effects of father absence might have been obtained. But even as it stands, the findings from the father-absence literature suggest that visitation should be extensive.

Children have consistently told researchers that they want contact with their fathers (Hetherington, et al., 1982; Laiken, 1981; Santrock, Warshak, & Elliot, 1982;

Tessman, 1978; Wallerstein & Kelly, 1980). Overall, based on their study of post-divorce family relationships, Hess and Camara (1979) concluded that "the child's relationship with the father without custody is of equal importance to his or her well-being and separate from the relationship with the custodial mother" (p. 94). Their conclusion is not surprising, considering the growing body of literature demonstrating the important role fathers play in children's development.

The father who maintains visitation is available as a resource to his children in the event of the death or major illness of their mother. Moreover, more than one-fifth of all children of divorce change their custodial parent at some point. Most shifts are to fathers, and are voluntary on the mother's part. These shifts usually stem from problems in the mother–child relationship (Furstenberg & Spanier, 1984). This alternative is seldom available to children of divorce whose fathers no longer see them. Fathers who maintain visitation can mitigate any negative patterns of child rearing on the part of the custodial parent by providing advice, alternative models of behavior, or simple relief. Maintaining visitation also helps children cope with the remarriage of their custodial parent (Hetherington, et al., 1982).

Finally, visitation fathers are also financial resources for their children. Researchers have focused national attention on the nonpayment of child support, which may be linked to custody and visitation. Parenthood is socially, not biologically, defined; for example, we don't expect child support from the biological parents of children given up for adoption. Visitation fathers who don't feel involved with the social process of parenting may feel that they need not be involved economically. Researchers have found that fathers who see their children weekly and are allowed to take an active part in the decisions that affect them have far better records of making their support payments (Bohannan, 1985; Rosenthal & Keshet, 1981). Conversely, Burgoyne and Clark (cited in Maidment, 1984) found that many mothers were prepared to forgo child support if it meant they were no longer inconvenienced by visits from their ex-partner. Most studies of child support have relied solely on interviews with custodial mothers; interviews with fathers might reveal a relationship between unhappiness with the visitation role and failure to maintain child support. If that relationship exists, then reforming visitation would be one way to increase payment of child support.

THE PLIGHT OF THE NONVISITING FATHER

As will be shown, frustration and pain are usually a part of visitation fathering. To avoid experiencing those feelings on a regular basis, many noncustodial fathers decrease their contact with their children. But this "solution" has emotional costs to fathers, as well as to children. Hetherington and colleagues (1982) found that fathers who had been highly involved, but coped with visitation by rarely seeing their children, continued to experience a great sense of loss and depression. Ambrose, Harper, and Pemberton (1983), in a study of divorced fathers, also found evidence of this continuing pain:

All except one of the no-contact fathers have developed some kind of a mental health problem since the divorce. . . . We were struck by the relationship between high anger levels and a failure to keep in contact with the children. Moreover the cost of not resolving these emotions often appears to have affected mental health and sometimes physical health as well. (p. 102)

The stress of nonvisitation spills over into other areas. Although it is difficult to distinguish cause and effect, fathers who don't maintain visitation move more often than fathers who do (Anderson-Khleif, 1982). A majority of Hetherington's visitation fathers felt less competent at work. Weston (cited in Ware, 1982) reported "a shocking sense of isolation" and "feelings of deprivation" that can last "for years after the divorce" (p. 59). These feelings, in extreme cases, have led to homelessness, suicide, homicide, amnesia, and even, in several instances, air piracy.[1]

In sum, non-visitation does not deal satisfactorily with the frustration of visitation. The sadness experienced by visitation fathers who don't see much of their children is in stark contrast to the exuberance of the 50 custodial fathers interviewed by McFadden (1974). Their exuberance suggests that there are better ways than abandonment to deal with the frustrations and sorrows of visitation.

VISITATION: PROBLEMS AND REMEDIES

Why do so many visitation fathers see their children so rarely? Economic factors don't explain it, since fathers in all strata above the lower working class maintain child support more consistently than visitation (Francke, 1983). Nor do the causes of the divorce, who initiated it, or details of the divorcing process predict which fathers maintain visitation (Furstenberg, 1983). Even more surprisingly, researchers have found no systematic relationship between prior parenting and parenting after divorce. According to Hetherington (1979), some fathers who had been relatively uninvolved became competent and concerned parents, while others who had been "intensely attached" found intermittent fathering painful, and withdrew from their children. Hetherington's fathers were more likely to maintain contact with sons than daughters, but not Furstenberg's. Age of child also played no consistent role. Some fathers saw their children oftener as the children grew older and could handle more of the logistics themselves; others, finding their teenagers' schedules already full, saw them less.

The key to understanding why fathers give up visitation apparently does not lie in these background variables but in the structure of visitation itself, which tends to elicit mostly negative reactions from fathers, including those who maintain it (Ambrose, et al., 1983). As one father told Anderson-Khleif (1982), "I hope you aren't thinking the frequency of visitation reflects how a father feels. I would like to see my children much more, but under these conditions of visitation it's impossible"

---

[1]Instances of such extreme reactions to nonvisitation are provided in Doyle (1976), Rosenthal and Keshet (1981), and Weiss (1979), as well as in a clipping file that I am maintaining on visitation, and in interviews I have recently conducted with caregivers for the homeless.

(p. 116). Wallerstein and Kelly (1980), based on their five-year study of divorced couples in California, concur that it is the institution, not whether it is the mother or the father who is the visiting parent, that is to blame for the falloff of visitation.

In order to understand why visitation for so many fathers occurs so rarely, and to suggest solutions, it is necessary to examine the visitation role and fathers' reactions to it. Studies of divorced fathers have identified five constellations of problems that explain why visitation is hard to maintain. These are: (1) expectations built into our culture; (2) conflict with or resistance from the custodial parent; (3) the fact that visitation is emotionally difficult; (4) the artificiality of the parent–child relationship imposed by the constraints of visitation; and (5) pressures from fathers' new commitments and relationships. The rest of this chapter will discuss the problems in each area, and consider possible resolutions and alternatives that may be available.

Cultural Expectations: The Initial Custody Decision

For men in our culture, divorce has traditionally meant that mothers' relationships with their children are unchanged, while fathers' relationships are drastically altered. These assumptions begin operating at or before the moment of separation, when it is assumed that the mother will get custody, and the father visitation. Some observers infer from the preponderance of male visitation that fathers *choose* visitation (Ramos, 1979); the fact that more than 9 out of 10 custody arrangements are worked out privately among the parents and their attorneys also implies choice. But in the conservative arena of family life, men and women tend to follow cultural templates, particularly in times of crises such as divorce, when new decisions about parenting must be made. These templates lead most parents to accept the traditional arrangement without really thinking about it. One of the fathers in Anderson-Khleif's (1982) interview study of 70 middle-income divorced couples stated the underlying premise: "I think we've all been buffaloed by society into the idea that women make better parents than men" (p. 128). Anderson-Khleif concludes that "women are under a great deal of social pressure to take custody of their children after divorce. . . . It is, indeed, possible that most women feel they have 'no choice'" (pp. 87, 90).

Men didn't always get visitation. Before the Civil War, children were seen as crucial to maintaining the economic interests of the family, and since men controlled those economic interests, children routinely went with their father when divorce occurred. Around the turn of the century, women's political rights improved, but their occupational options for the most part remained limited to teaching, nursing, being a secretary or maid, and caring for children. The culture rationalized women's exclusion from corporate boardrooms by "complimenting" them for what was said to be their superior ability to care for children. At that point, women won *preference* in divorce court (Amneus, 1979). The legal expression of this emphasis on motherhood was the "young and tender years" doctrine which, based on no empirical data, asserted that young children fared best with their mothers. "Young and tender" was gradually extended upward from 7 years to 12 and even 14.

Since the 1950s, states have converted their laws from "young and tender years" to the "best interests of the child" doctrine. But only for about the past 15 years have court decisions held that men can be the custodial parents of young children, including infants, without having to prove their ex-wives unfit. Mothers still win custody presumptively (Anderson-Khleif, 1982; Bohannan, 1985). For although the law is now formally equal, unless shown strong evidence to the contrary, many judges still cite the traditional division of labor to justify awarding custody to mothers, with fathers getting "customary" visitation—every other weekend, half of each holiday period, and four to eight weeks in the summer.

In addition, many lawyers still tell male clients they have little chance for sole or joint custody, perhaps because attorneys are not aware of the newest developments in domestic law, or because their own job is easier if their clients have low expectations (Francke, 1983; Solomon, 1977). Ambrose and colleagues (1983) found that "considerably more . . . men *would have* contested the custody issue had the lawyer not advised against such a course since in his (or her) view there would be little chance of winning" (p. 140).

Most fathers don't challenge the assumption that they can't win. Furthermore, a father who has not taken a primary role in caring for his children may doubt his competence as a parent, and may underestimate his own importance in his children's lives (Gatley & Koulack, 1979). In addition, the intractability of traditional parental roles in the culture, his ex-wife's assumption that she will have custody, a lack of support from his own relatives, a lack of alternative role models, and his lawyer's pessimism—any or all of these factors may lead a father to believe that mothers get custody.

Other emotions can cause men to make hasty decisions during pre-separation and separation, without considering their own or their children's long-term interests. They may feel such guilt about the break-up of their marriage that they let their spouses keep the house and children as atonement. They may be so angry or upset that they leave precipitously, just to get away. And of course, some fathers make an untroubled decision to play a minor role in their children's lives. Visitation lets them get on with their own lives, move to a new job, forget the mistakes of their marriage, avoid most child-care responsibility, or establish a new family. However, most custody decisions are made by default, along culturally traditional lines, without full realization of their implications for fathers and their children (Gatley & Koulack, 1979). Since the "default position" for fathers is visitation, men who remain passive while custody is being decided will almost certainly end up as visitation fathers.

Through the institution of visitation, the culture implies that fatherhood is not very important. The visitation father who rarely sees his children is merely following this implication to its conclusion. The implication that fathers don't matter can also get projected onto the children. Half of the men Wallerstein and Kelly (1980) interviewed feared rejection by their children. Most children don't want a changed relationship with either parent, but fathers often don't know this (Goldstein, 1982; Keshet & Rosenthal, 1978).

Even some self-help books counsel fathers to give up visitation when children don't want to visit, or when conflict looms with the custodial parent (Atkin & Rubin, 1976; Gardner, 1971). One book (Goldstein, Freud, & Solnit, 1973) went so far as to propose guidelines for visitation that allowed no recourse for fathers:

> Once it is determined who will be the custodial parent, it is that parent, not the court, who must decide under what conditions he or she wishes to raise the child. Thus, the noncustodial parent should have no legally enforceable right to visit the child. . . . (pp. 37–38)

Gradually, statements like this are going out of fashion. Slowly the cultural template is changing; slowly the law, too, is treating fatherhood more like motherhood. In many courtrooms, fathers who contest custody have a decent chance at winning. But the rate of change is slow and has been exaggerated. Observers overlook the vast gap that often separates fairness in the law from fairness in practice. The "best interest of the child" statutes did not inherently presume maternal custody, but judges typically did this in practice.

Statistics have been cited showing fathers winning custody in 38% of contested cases in Alameda County, California, 33% in Los Angeles County (Weitzman, 1985), and as high as 70% in other jurisdictions or samples (Chesler, 1986), suggesting that equality or even preference for fathers is at hand. However, since less than 5% of custody cases ever go to court, these statistics are based on tiny ns: for example, 13 cases in Alameda County, 15 in Los Angeles. The reality is that despite these father-won custody cases, the large majority of children of divorce end up in the custody of their mothers, owing in part to maternal presumption. In a survey of California divorce attorneys, Weitzman (1985) found that 98% "think an informal maternal presumption is still in effect" (p. 237). Eighty-one percent of her sample of 44 divorce court judges agreed.

What about joint custody? At least five states now presume joint custody, and a rash of joint custody books entered the bookstalls around 1980. But again, change has been exaggerated. It is important to distinguish laws that *presume* joint custody from laws that merely *allow* it. Moreover, the California joint custody law presumes joint *legal* custody, not joint *residential* custody; the typical arrangement actually resembles custody with visitation, but under a new name (Weitzman, 1985). Before major changes owing to joint custody can be proclaimed, two questions need to be addressed: Is the new joint custody real or only formal? A formal change is meaningful in itself but should not be mistaken for a change in actual custody patterns. And, are joint residential custody awards coming out of what would have previously been paternal custody awards (Kerpelman, 1983), so that joint residential custody is increasing at the expense of father custody, rather than mother custody? Recent studies suggest that the effects of legal changes on actual custody arrangements have been minimal (Arendell, 1986). Most fathers still do not get either sole or joint residential custody and do not see their children very often.

Relations with Custodial Mothers

Fathers who don't see their children frequently may also be meeting the expectations or wishes of their ex-wives (Bohannan, 1985; Goode, 1956; Maidment,

1984). Researchers have noted that from one-third to one-half of all custodial mothers resist visitation (Ambrose, et al., 1983; Anderson-Khleif, 1982; Furstenberg, 1983; Gatley & Koulack, 1979; Goldstein, 1982; Wallerstein & Kelly, 1980). A father's visitation is frequently affected by his ex-wife's perceptions of their respective parenting abilities, her view of the children's needs, and her unresolved feelings from the marriage and its break-up. In addition, since her weekly contact with the children decreases from 94 hours to 73 after divorce, owing to visitation and to her increased work outside the home, every bit of time she allows may strike her as a concession (Francke, 1983).

Complicating the custody/visitation relationship is the fact that custodial parents often do not perceive visitation in the same way as their ex-spouses. Wallerstein and Kelly (1980) found that women who interfered with visitation generally claimed to be supportive of their children's need to visit, and Anderson-Khleif (1982), who interviewed fathers as well as mothers, found that the same kind of "regular and reliable" visitation which mothers described with satisfaction was usually described by fathers in much less optimistic ways. A custodial mother's parental role customarily includes letting or not letting the children go places and do things; thus she may make decisions that interfere with visitation so easily as to be almost unnoticeable to her. Anderson-Khleif points out that custodial mothers can wield vastly unequal power "in terms of having the children with them on holidays and special events, by setting guidelines for routine visits, by setting down rules and limits, and by making final decisions on the extent of visitation allowed" (pp. 93–94). In all of this, she is encouraged by the rhetoric of sole custody, which implies the children are "hers," not "theirs."

Hostility between Ex-Spouses.

Although this power imbalance is not predicated on the existence of hostility between the ex-spouses, hostility is common (Anderson-Khleif, 1982; Hetherington, et al., 1982; Wallerstein & Kelly, 1980). When the relationship is hostile, Wallerstein and Kelly found that the details of visitation could become weapons the custodial parent used against the visitation parent:

> [These mothers'] irritations were expressed in their difficulties in accommodating the different schedules of the other parent . . . in forgotten appointments, in insistence on rigid schedules for the visits, in refusal to permit the visit if the father brought along an adult friend—in a thousand mischievous, mostly petty devices designed to humiliate the visiting parent and to deprecate him in the eyes of his children. (p. 125)

In this situation, a visitation father may bury his love for his children so that he can withdraw from this unequal power relationship and reduce his ex-wife's power to humiliate him. Anderson-Khleif (1982) concludes, "Just as women who try to collect child support often give up, fathers who cannot 'collect' their visitation rights give up. They just get worn down" (p. 109).

Visitation fathers can also undermine cooperative visitation with some maneuvers of their own. A father who perceives his ex-spouse as attempting to "oversee" his parenting may grow secretive to resist it. "Are you taking the kids to your parents this weekend?" "Uh, I don't know yet." His need to assert himself or to resist feeling controlled by his ex-wife may lead him to delay making plane reservations, not show up precisely when asked to, or not give adequate notice, even when he knows his plans. The custodial parent may tire of having to keep her own plans on hold until the last minute (Gatley & Koulack, 1979; Keshet & Rosenthal, 1978).

Avoiding Conflict and Promoting Cooperation

Avoiding power struggles is a key to successful visitation. Some divorced couples co-parent cordially, sharing information and ideas without struggling. Most do not. More often, when both parents stay involved with their children, they do what Ricci (1980) calls "parallel parenting," not co-parenting. A "pragmatic strategy which works for many divorced fathers," according to Anderson-Khleif (1982), is to "confine their contact [with their ex-wives] to the mechanics of passing the kids back and forth" (p. 110).

Of course, when relating has been whittled down to the mechanics of child transfer, even these can provide fertile ground for dispute (Keshet & Rosenthal, 1978). In addition, the unequal power relationship hampers communication. Men may fear asking for a visit because they don't want to risk a refusal, which would force them to recognize how little power they *do* have—thereby leading their ex-wives to infer that they are satisfied with existing visitation. Individual or group counseling can help visitation fathers improve their communication skills, and change any of their behaviors that may be undermining cooperative visitation.[2] If both parents are willing, divorce counselling can help them let go of unresolved marital issues, and learn parallel parenting skills.

A formal visitation agreement can also help visitation succeed. Visitation fathers are more likely than joint custody fathers to be back in court after divorce, but a specific agreement providing for extensive scheduled visitation is enforceable, and reduces the likelihood of re-litigation (Wheeler, 1980; Rosenthal & Keshet, 1981; Ware, 1982). Some fathers don't want to constrain themselves with schedules, perhaps believing they shouldn't need to specify when they can see their own children. However, although spontaneity is appealing, it rarely works in the long run. Schedules let fathers tell their children when they will see them next without having to clear it with mothers, and let mothers know what is happening without having to pry it from fathers. Moreover, nothing in a schedule prevents parents from arranging spontaneous visitation. A formal visitation agreement can provide a framework for spontaneity, if it occurs, and helps guarantee that the children have access to both parents, if it doesn't.

A detailed agreement can forestall other conflicts. For example, visitation fathers have reported problems getting school records, passports, social security numbers, and other documents; being informed about school functions and health problems; having a say about where their children attend school or church or what medical

---

[2]See Chapter 15 by Levant, and Chapter 17 by Schwebel, Fine, and Moreland, this volume, for a discussion of counseling and educational programs for noncustodial fathers.

treatments they receive; and obtaining consent for their children to fly unaccompanied on airlines. Court decisions have granted most of these rights to visitation fathers (Allers, 1982; Atlas, 1984), but suing to get them is harder than including them in a separation or divorce agreement in the first place. A good agreement also contains a mechanism to handle situations that cannot be foreseen at the time of separation, even including change of custody.

Because good visitation requires resources, fathers who maintain relationships with their children end up with many of the same expenses that live-in fathers have, including an extra bedroom for the children, a decent neighborhood, a yard, transportation, medical and dental bills, food, clothing, and recreation expenses (Anderson-Khleif, 1982). Therefore, Anderson-Khleif argues for divorce settlements that allow fathers enough money to maintain visitation. Although data show that women usually fare worse economically than men in divorce, divorce agreements that incorporate extensive visitation, and prorate child support to take longer visitation periods into account, can work to the benefit of custodial mothers, in comparison with the modal alternative of decreasing visitation and child support payments.

Researchers are virtually unanimous that visitation works best when it is frequent and routine (Furstenberg & Spanier, 1984; Tessman, 1978; Wallerstein & Kelly, 1980; Ware, 1982). Based on her extensive counseling of divorced couples, Ricci (1980) suggests two long weekends each month, beginning after school Thursday and ending Monday morning when the children leave for school. She found that when visitation includes three or four weekends each month, the custodial parent may resent her lack of play time with her children. Conversely, when visitation includes weekday school nights, the father is more involved with his children's homework and school. In addition to those weekends and a weekday supper, full visitation also includes Christmas, Thanksgiving, spring school vacations, and most of the summer.

The father who sees his children for the long weekends and other periods previously indicated may want to grant alternate Christmas or Thanksgiving days to the custodial parent, to help his children maintain their connections with their mother's extended family. However, many a visitation father asks for much less visitation, giving priority to his ex-spouse's desires, her extended family, and his own work schedule. He fails to realize that extensive visitation is required to build the common experiences that lead to unspoken rapport between father and children, as well as the children's sense of connectedness with their father's extended family.

The Emotional Strains of Visitation

Feelings of unfairness and anger are built into visitation even if the custodial parent never hampers visitation. As one father put it, "She's cooperative, but it's demeaning to have to ask to see my own children" (Sturner, 1983, p. 90). The visitation father is likely to be positive about seeing his children but negative about having to deal with his ex-spouse. A specific agreement with a visitation schedule helps deal with these feelings, but there are other emotions that make visitation hard to maintain.

A visitation father must learn to turn his emotions on and off. He may shower his children with attention and affection when he is with them, since he sees them so little; but as soon as the visitation ends, he must shut that part of himself off, because it is irrelevant to the role he now plays. Some visitation fathers cultivate a certain numbness, not wanting to answer friends' questions about their children, not wanting even to think about their children, because thinking about them can be painful. Ends of visits are especially hard. A father in Keshet and Rosenthal's (1978) sample said, "I hugged them at their mother's door when I was leaving. . . . I would hear them running down the steps calling for me. At those times I felt the agony of being separated for them and for me" (p. 15).

Another painful aspect of visitation is fathers' belief that they have little impact on how their children will turn out (Anderson-Khleif, 1982; Wedermeyer, 1984). Furstenberg (1982, 1983) found that only one visitation father in five felt he had great influence over his children; custodial mothers regarded even that as an overstatement. Rather than watch their children grow up as strangers, some fathers withdraw from the relationship altogether. Others express their ambivalence by making, then breaking, engagements with their children— the most common complaint of custodial mothers.

Rejection is another emotion that threatens visitation; fathers can be devastated by children who don't want to visit. A well-known "how-to" book counsels that children's wishes should be paramount: "I do not believe that a child should be made to see his [sic] father more often than he wants to" (Gardner, 1971, p. 101). But this advice ignores the father's rights and feelings. Just as children of intact families don't decide where to spend the weekend without parental input, neither should children of divorce. Visitation works best when everyone recognizes the father–child relationship as a given, as with the mother–child relationship. Divorced families that have violated this rule have usually seen the gradual erosion of the father–child relationship (Anderson-Khleif, 1982; Ricci, 1980).

Successful visitation depends on a father's ability to deal with his own feelings of sadness and powerlessness. Vocabulary can help a father deal with these feelings (Ricci, 1980). He can regard himself as "having a family," even when his children are not staying with him; his children are "home" at his house, not "visitors." Counsellors can also help fathers identify the psychic payoffs from their feelings of sadness and anger, so they can transcend those feelings and continue fathering their children. Fathers who cannot or do not maintain the homelike milieu and other practices suggested here can still be encouraged to feel good about the contact they *do* maintain, because involvement at whatever level is far more beneficial to child and father than dropping out.

Can interrupted visitation be resumed? From the children's side, after initial awkwardness and resentment, resumption is often surprisingly easy; researchers have found that children's attachment bonds persist despite periods of no contact. In Furstenberg's study (1983), almost half of the children with low paternal contact still felt extremely close to their fathers. Thus children are generally not "lost" to fathers—even fathers who haven't seen them for years (Maidment, 1984). Ricci (1980) offers specific suggestions for helping fathers resume visitation.

Making Visitation Less Artificial

Because visitation is wrenchingly different from parenting in marriage, the old norms from the intact family seem not to apply (Wallerstein & Kelly, 1980). Visitation has not really been institutionalized in our culture, so how are fathers to do it? As Wedermeyer (1984) put it, "Parents and children who see each other infrequently and only under visiting circumstances tend to lose the sense of intimacy they used to have" (pp. 109–110). Parental authority now feels strange. Do fathers discipline their children, or are they someone else's children? Most basic of all, what do they *do* with them, moment to moment?

Disneyland Daddy

In order to cover over this disturbing sense of strangeness and establish new parenting patterns in a new place (which may only be a motel), many fathers overplan. As Gatley and Koulack (1979) have explained:

> Separated fathers often feel that the limited amount of time they have with their children is precious and must be spent in ways specifically designed to ensure the maintenance of a loving relationship with their kids. . . . (p. 54)

The resulting flurry of activities has come to be called the "Disneyland Daddy" syndrome. Disneyland Daddies are always *doing*, when they need sometimes simply to *be*. Children get tired. They need periods of rest. So do fathers. Disneyland Daddyhood cannot be maintained, which may explain the drop-off in visitation noted by Furstenberg (1983) after the second year. In a downward spiral, intimacy decreases, so fathers plan more activities because they don't feel relaxed and intimate, which further reduces intimacy. The strain shows in these remarks Anderson-Kheif (1982) elicited from a divorced father: "You take an eight-year-old and try to entertain him all weekend and see how it is. . . . In a real father–child relationship, parents don't communicate with their children on a 24-hour basis" (pp. 116, 118). Another father told Anderson-Khleif:

> It's difficult. Very difficult. I'm going to part of the state I'm not familiar with. I don't know the swimming holes and so forth. . . . I'll be honest with you . . . at times I show up at noon and it's 3PM when I'm leaving. There's nothing to do. (p. 120)

In addition to artificiality, these quotations point to practical problems: where to meet, how to spend the time, what to talk about, how to afford transportation, where to find comfortable space to be a family. These problems begin with the first day of separation.

New Patterns for Starting Visitation

Even before departure, visitation fathers face the task of preparing their children for the impending separation. According to Goldstein (1982), *both* parents usually botch this job by not telling the children early enough and by reassuring instead of listening. Moreover, no matter what is said, the act of leaving implies to children that their father chose to leave (Atkin & Rubin, 1976). Some visitation fathers have found that to depart *with* their children, on the first visitation weekend, counters this implication and allows children and fathers to establish a new home together.

Rather than Disneyland Daddy activities, establishing a new home and basic routines meets children's needs (Fayerweather Street School [Divorce] Unit, 1981; Francke, 1983). Weiss (1980) describes a shift from the former to the latter pattern:

> The father who shopped, and cleaned the house, and lined up information about film times, because of his children, now becomes a much more relaxed parent who encourages the children to help him clean, gets their advice on the shopping, and may spend the time together reading side by side. (p. 139)

Such a routine shifts the center of attention from the child's interests—which movie the child might like—to the real needs of the family unit and reasserts a balance of authority that is more like regular parenting.

To have homelike visitation, fathers need to establish a homelike setting. Keshet and Rosenthal (1978) found that visitation fathers reported that it was helpful to keep a permanent supply of clothing, games, and other belongings for their children in their own house. A visitation father can feel petty insisting that toys or clothes he gives his children remain at his house when the children want to take them "home" to their mother's, but Gatley and Koulack (1979) suggest he insist anyway, for only thus does his house become their home, not a place they merely visit. And each child must have some space of his or her own, even if it is only a toy chest.

The location of the father's house can affect the quality of the visitation relationship. The father who lives near his ex-wife makes it easier for his children to see him, maintain peer relationships, and retrieve belongings without involving either parent. Francke (1983) reported that in one study, only the children who could ride their bicycles or walk between homes felt they saw each parent "almost enough" (p. 97). On the other hand, even when a father must locate in a different neighborhood or a different state, visitation can work well, if the father establishes a home in a neighborhood with peers and activities for his children. Then children don't just "visit" their father, they live in the milieu he has established. Although newly separated fathers often live with their own parents for a time in order to economize, visitation fathers are well-advised to make a more permanent choice in their first move if they can. Too often, fathers without custody move three to five times within the first five years after separation, with disastrous effects on visitation (Anderson-Khleif, 1982).

Rituals and Traditions that Enhance Visitation Fathering

Because visitation is not well-institutionalized in our society, rituals and traditions are particularly important to make it work. Rituals give people structured ways to behave in difficult situations. For example, a ritual hug reestablishes contact and gets everyone past the first awkward moment of a weekend. The hug becomes a tiny rite done every time, not something to be decided on each occasion. Other rituals can structure and make enjoyable long-distance car trips and phone conversations (Newman, 1981). Christmas, birthdays, and Father's Day can be stressful for visitation fathers, but special holiday traditions can remind children and their father that they form a family with continuity and meaning. So can such heirlooms as a photo book assembled by children and father together, a videotape of highlights of the weekend or summer, a wall poster to record children's heights, physical reminders of each child in the visitation home, and physical reminders of their father for their custodial home, such as his picture or a special object.

According to Keshet and Rosenthal (1978), visitation fathers often have difficulty in dealing with their children's emotional needs. They are likely to block communication from their children by offering false reassurance or by getting angry at their feelings. The father who tells his children everything will be all right may inadvertently make them feel their worries are not being taken seriously. Family traditions, such as a quiet time for conversation at bedtime or a weekly family council, can provide a structured safe arena in which to bring up these worries.

The Impact of New Commitments on Visitation

No father is only a father. Visitation fathers are also wage-earners, lovers, friends, colleagues, and often new husbands. For visitation to work, these roles must complement, not conflict with each other. Commitments in the visitation parent's new life sometimes take priority and can erode visitation. Wedermeyer (1984) observed:

> Seeing their children infrequently simply makes the children seem less important and less central to their lives. . . . Four days a month of seeing your children may not seem sufficiently important to refuse a job promotion which requires a move to another city or state. (pp. 109–110)

As men move on in their lives, their feelings of anger and frustration regarding their ex-spouses grow irrelevant and even harmful. New wives or lovers aren't enthralled by hearing about their predecessors, even negatively. Employers don't want employees distracted by lawsuits or emotions from their past. Thus new commitments exert not only time pressure but also psychological pressure on fathers to drop out.

Integrating Visitation and Other Roles

Successful long-term visitation must allow fathers to fulfill their other roles. Although visitation fathers may feel guilty about using child care—visits are all too short anyway—few visitation fathers have such flexible jobs that they can center wholly on their children for the summer or Christmas week, or even some week-ends. Thus, on these occasions, they must rely on day care or baby-sitters, or find ways to integrate child care and work (Atlas, 1984). Successful visitation fathers also introduce their children to their adult friends and extended families.

Visitation fathers are of two minds about integrating their children and their love life (Rosenthal & Keshet, 1981; Shepard & Goldman, 1979). Teenage children in particular can feel jealous or threatened by a new lover on the scene. On the other hand, children can infer that their father is ashamed of them or ashamed of sex if he keeps them from meeting someone he is involved with. Some fathers follow the practice of never having a friend stay overnight without letting their children know, thus avoiding late-night or next-morning surprises. As the relationship grows seri-ous, the father may find it a good idea to encourage activities that include the new lover and the children, sometimes with him absent.

Effects of Remarriage on Visitation

Most children want their parent to remarry (Santrock, et al., 1982). Half of all divorcees do in fact remarry within three years, and 80% remarry eventually (*Transitions*, 1985). The effects of remarriage on visitation seem to be mixed. Hetherington found that remarriage of the father usually signaled a sharp decline in visitation, especially with daughters, which sometimes indicated stepmother prob-lems (Francke, 1983, citing Hetherington). Kerpelman (1983), based on his exten-sive legal practice involving custody cases, has suggested that remarriage frequently triggers "harassment and attack" (p. 264) directed at visitation by the custodial par-ent (cf. Hetherington, et al., 1982; Maidment, 1984). On the other hand, Fursten-berg (1983) concluded that whereas in some cases remarriage aggravates tensions between ex-spouses, in others it helped them to set aside tensions and make peace with one other. He found that the nonresidential stepparent sometimes facilitated visitation; for example, child transfer arrangements were sometimes worked out be-tween the residential parent and nonresidential stepparent. In addition, he found that on average, remarriage of the visitation parent only slightly decreased visitation, was only slightly related to whether a father moved from the area where his children resided, and wasn't an important factor in whether child support was paid. This mild overall effect may have masked a larger impact in individual cases: remarriage sometimes led to fathers getting custody, and sometimes to markedly diminished visitation (cf. Hetherington, et al., 1982).

Why does remarriage sometimes hurt visitation? Visitation families suffer from all the strains of "blended" families. Is the new spouse just a spouse, or does she also have parental responsibilities? If she plays the role of parent, is she accorded parental authority? A visitation father, who may only recently have established his own role, may make a special effort to let his children know that he will continue to be their "real" parent (Rosenthal & Keshet, 1981), and thus put their needs during visitation ahead of those of his new wife. This can be painful to his wife, but since the problem is intermittent, it may not get brought up and resolved. If the new cou-ple has a new child, the visitation children may feel particularly intense sibling ri-valry; while they previously may have been center stage during visitation weekends, now the new infant demands attention. This problem usually eases as the new child grows older and can form relationships with the visitation siblings.

Relating to the father's former spouse is an added burden for the new couple. Among couples studied by Rosenthal and Keshet (1981), many new partners felt powerless to affect agreements between the former spouses, even though these agreements determined details of their daily lives. The noncustodial father in these new relationships reported frequent disagreements with their partners on matters involving the ex-wife.

BENEFITS FATHERS REALIZE FROM VISITATION

The artificiality of visitation, its problematic logistics regarding space, time, and role, and pressures from fathers' new commitments and relationships, conspire to make visitation difficult. Noncooperation or conflict between ex-spouses, which may involve resistance to visitation from custodial parents, can disrupt visitation both physically and psychologically. Perhaps most harmful of all to continued visitation is its emotional intensity, which can be difficult to communicate to those who haven't experienced it. The result: most visitation fathers play only peripheral roles in their children's lives by about the third year after divorce (Furstenberg, 1982; Furstenberg & Spanier, 1984).

Nonetheless, visitation isn't all sadness and strain for fathers. Benefits do flow from it, to the father as well as to his children, the custodial parent, and society as a whole. Although joint custody is better, extensive visitation helps fathers feel they are still a force in their children's lives (Little, 1982). Rosenthal and Keshet (1981) found that men who kept up visitation

> said they now felt closer to their children than they did before the separation. They attributed that closeness to the fact that they were now more likely to be alone with their children and the time spent together was more intense and meaningful. (pp. xii–xiii)

Extensive visitation gives fathers someone to live for, cook for, and do things for and with. As visitation fathers take care of their children, they also take care of themselves (Rosenthal & Keshet, 1981; Weiss, 1979). Maintaining visitation helps fathers stay in touch with their own feelings and challenges their values (Brandt, 1982). Visitation increases fathers' sense of purpose; some fathers feel a sense of exhilaration and even heroism, that they have persevered in relating to their children against the legal and cultural odds.

Fathers who maintain extensive visitation also receive affirmation and support from relatives, neighbors, and even strangers. Many women feel empathy with men struggling to balance occupational and parental roles, just as they have had to do. In turn, maintaining visitation can help fathers see ways that our traditional roles make fathering optional, equate parenting with motherhood, and shunt women away from many occupations. Thus visitation fathers who remain actively involved in parenting may feel that they are pioneers in breaking down society's sex-role stereotyping and increasing the value society places on child rearing.

DIRECTIONS FOR CHANGE

The literature indicates that extensive visitation is good for children's self-esteem, which leads to better outcomes on all kinds of behavioral indexes. Studies also show that maintaining visitation is good for fathers. Nonetheless, most divorced fathers see their children rarely, if at all.

A logical conclusion is that our society needs policies fostering contact between nonresident parents and their children. Four types of actions would be helpful. First, laws favoring joint custody can allow and encourage fathers to have equal access to children. Second, when visitation is chosen, agreements with extensive schedules and specific penalties for noncompliance can become a norm of the divorce process, enforced by the court. Third, counseling by professionals aware of the pain and problems of visitation can help fathers who have given up to restart and maintain visitation. Finally, every movement made by our society toward involving men in child care and women in the labor market makes it easier for divorced fathers to be meaningful parents.

REFERENCES

Allers, R.D. (1982). *Divorce, children, and the school*. Princeton, NJ: Princeton Book.

Ambrose, P., Harper, J., & Pemberton, R. (1983). *Surviving divorce: Men beyond marriage*. Totowa, NJ. Rowman and Allanheld.

Amneus, D. (1979). *Back to patriarchy*. New Rochelle, NY: Arlington House.

Anderson, H.W., & Anderson, G.S. (1981). *Mom and Dad are divorced, but I'm not*. Chicago: Nelson-Hall.

Anderson-Khleif, S. (1982). *Divorced but not disastrous*. Englewood Cliffs, NJ: Prentice-Hall.

Arendell, T. (1986). *Mothers and divorce*. Berkeley, CA: University of California Press.

Atkin, E., & Rubin, E. (1976). *Part time father*. New York: Vanguard.

Atlas, S. (1984). *The parents without partners sourcebook*. Philadelphia: Running Press.

Biller, H. (1981). Father absence, divorce, and personality development. In M.E. Lamb (Ed.), *The role of the father in child development*. New York: Wiley.

Bohannan, P. (1985). *All the happy families*. New York: McGraw-Hill.

Brandt, A. (1982, November). Father love. *Esquire*, pp. 81–89.

Chesler, P. (1986). *Mothers on trial*. New York: McGraw-Hill.

Doyle, R. (1976). *The rape of the male*. Forest Lake, MN: Poor Richard's Press.

Fayerweather Street School [Divorce] Unit. (1981). *The Kids' book of divorce*. Lexington, MA: Lewis.

Francke, L.B. (1983). *Growing up divorced*. New York: Simon & Schuster.

Furstenberg, F., Jr. (1982, August). *Parenting apart: Patterns of childrearing after divorce*. Presented at the annual meeting of the American Sociological Association, San Francisco.

Furstenberg, F., Jr. (1983). *Marital disruption and childcare*. Invited talk, Catholic University, Washington, DC

Furstenberg, F., Jr., & Spanier, G. (1984). *Recycling the family: Remarriage after divorce*. Beverly Hills: Sage.

Gardner, R. (1971). *The boys' and girls' book about divorce*. New York: Bantam.

Gatley, R., & Koulack, D. (1979). *Single father's handbook*. New York: Doubleday Anchor.

Goldstein, S. (1982). *Divorced parenting*. New York: Dutton.

Goldstein, J., Freud, A., & Solnit, A. (1973). *Beyond the best interests of the child*. New York: Free Press.

Goode, W. (1956). *After divorce*. Glencoe: Free Press. Retitled *Women in divorce*. Westport, CT: Greenwood, 1978.

Hess, R., & Camara, K. (1979). Post-divorce family relationships as mediating factors in the consequences of divorce for children. *Journal of Social Issues, 35*, 79–96.

Hetherington, E.M. (1979). Divorce: A child's perspective. *American Psychologist*, 851–858.

Hetherington, E.M. (1980). The effects of divorce on the social and cognitive development of children. In C. Baden (Ed.), *Children of divorce*. Boston: Wheelock College.

Hetherington, E.M. (1981). Children and divorce. In R. Henderson (Ed.), *Parent-child interaction: theory, research and prospects*. New York: Academy Press.

Hetherington, E.M., Cox, M., & Cox, R. (1976). Divorced fathers. *Family Coordinator, 25*, 417–428.

Hetherington, E.M., Cox, M., & Cox, R. (1982). Effects of divorce on parents and children. In M.E. Lamb (Ed.), *Nontraditional families: parenting and child development*. Hillsdale, N.J: Erlbaum.

Katkin, D., Bullington, B., & Levene, M. (1974). Above and beyond the best interests of the child. *Law and Society Review, 8*, 669–687.

Kerpelman, L. (1983). *Divorce: A guide for men*. South Bend, IN: Icarus.

Keshet, H., & Rosenthal, K. (1978). Fathering after marital separation. *Social Work, 23*(1), 11–18.

Laiken, D. (1981). *Daughters of divorce*. New York: Morrow.

Lamb, M. (1981). Fathers and child development: An integrative overview. In M.E. Lamb (Ed.), *The role of the father in child development*. New York: Wiley.

Little, M. (1982). *Family breakup*. San Francisco: Jossey-Bass.

Luepnitz, D. (1982). *Child custody*. Lexington: Heath.

Maidment, S. (1984). *Child custody and divorce*. London: Croom Helm.

McFadden, M. (1974). *Bachelor fatherhood*. New York: Walker.

Oakland, T. (1984). *Divorced fathers: Reconstructing a quality life*. New York: Human Sciences Press.

Newman, G. (1981). *101 ways to be a long-distance super-dad*. Mountain View, CA: Blossom Valley Press.

Ramos, S. (1979). *The complete book of child custody*. New York: Putnam.

Ricci, I. (1980). *Mom's house, Dad's house*. New York: Macmillan.

Rosenthal, K., & Keshet, H. (1981). *Fathers without partners: A study of fathers and the family after marital separation*. Totowa, NJ: Rowman and Littlefield.

Santrock, J.W., Warshak, R.A., & Elliot, G.W. (1982). Social development and parent-child interaction in father-custody and stepmother families. In M.E. Lamb (Ed.), *Nontraditional families: Parenting and child development*. Hillsdale, NJ: Erlbaum.

Shepard, M., & Goldman, G. (1979). *Divorced dads: Their kids, ex-wives, and new lives*. Radnor, PA: Chilton.

Solomon, P. (1977, October). The fathers' revolution in custody cases. *Trial*, *13*(10), 33–38.

Steinzor, B. (1969). *When parents divorce*. New York: Pantheon.

Sturner, W. (1983). *Love loops: A divorced father's personal journey*. New York: Libra.

Tessman, L. (1978). *Children of parting parents*. New York: Aronson.

Transitions (Coalition of Free Men). (1985). 83% of divorced men remarry. *5* (6), November–December.

Wallerstein, J., & Kelly, J. (1980). *Surviving the breakup: How parents and children cope with divorce*. New York: Basic.

Ware, C. (1982). *Sharing parenthood after divorce*. New York: Viking.

Wedermeyer, N. (1984). Child custody. In T. Oakland (Ed.), *Divorced fathers: Reconstructing a quality life*. New York: Human Sciences Press.

Wheeler, M. (1980). *Divided children: A legal guide for divorcing parents*. New York: Norton.

Weiss, R. (1979). *Going it alone*. New York: Basic.

Weiss, R. (1980). Growing up a little faster: The experience of children in a single-parent household. In C. Baden (Ed.), *Children of Divorce* (pp. 103–139). Boston: Wheelock College.

Weitzman, L. (1985). *The divorce revolution: The unexpected social and economic consequences for women and children in America*. New York: Free Press.

CHAPTER 13

Gay Fatherhood

FREDERICK W. BOZETT

It may seem to the reader that "homosexual" and "father" are opposite identities. The term "gay fatherhood" may bring to mind such questions as: Is it possible that a man who is homosexual is also a father? Why would a gay man become heterosexually married and have children? What effect does the father's homosexuality have upon the child, and on the father–child relationship? This chapter will attempt to answer those questions. It begins with a presentation of historical and statistical data on homosexuality and a discussion of gay men's identity development. The major portion of the chapter will then examine the ways that gay fathers manage both their gay and father identities in gay and nongay social contexts, and in the father–child relationship.

The content is derived primarily from my own research (Bozett, 1979a, 1979b; 1980, 1981a, 1981b, 1982, 1984a, 1984b, 1985a, 1985b, 1985c, 1987) and that of Miller (1978, 1979a, 1979b, 1983, 1986). My data were obtained through in-depth interviews of 18 gay men in the San Francisco Bay Area who had married and had children, with additional data obtained from my experiences as a participant–observer in a gay father support group over a four-year period.[1] An unstructured interview was used to gain insight into the lives of the subjects, as gay men, husbands, and fathers. The interviews were tape-recorded, transcribed, and analyzed using the constant comparative method of Glaser and Strauss (1967), in which transcripts are analyzed line by line, comparing every piece of data with every other piece. Conceptual categories emerge from the data, rather than being specified a priori, and through comparative data analysis, a core variable or key linkage emerges which connects the categories to one another. It is an inductive, qualitative strategy, intended to generate and suggest (but not test) properties and hypotheses about a general phenomenon. Miller's data were derived from a multiple-source snowball sample of 50 gay husbands and fathers in both the United States and Canada. Using a semistructured interview format, he encouraged each man to tell his own life history in his own time and in his own words. Miller used phase analysis (Lofland, 1971) to extract identity statements. He examined them for uniformities of behavior, regularities in change of identity over time, and

---

[1]Interviews from both my studies are housed in the Henry A. Murray Research Center, Radcliffe College.

commonalities in achieving identity congruence. Miller organized his data along a four-point continuum, representing the stages of identity development gay fathers typically experience.

PRELUDE

Historical Perspective

Homosexuality has been documented since the beginning of recorded history. It has not, however, always been considered a negative attribute. In some cultures, same-sex sexual interaction was accepted during certain periods of one's life (e.g., adolescence), while in others, same-sex sexual relations by married men were not considered abnormal. For example, in ancient Greece, homosexuality was acceptable for males from the age of 16 through their military training, until they were fully accepted as citizens, at which time they were to marry and have children. Later in life they were expected to take adolescents under their guidance and custody, thus repeating the cycle (Bullough, 1979). In many cultures the label "homosexual" was unknown. Without the label, a negative or positive connotation was impossible to apply. It is primarily in Western culture, where Judeo-Christian monotheism is most prevalent, that homosexuality is negatively labeled, and homosexually identified individuals are stigmatized. In fact, Altman (1982) maintains that homophobia, the irrational fear of homosexuality (Herek, 1984; Weinberg, 1972), appears to be espe cially virulent in the United States.

In isolated sectors of the United States there has been a lessening of pejorative attitudes toward homosexuality. The initial event that signaled the beginning of a social revolution for oppressed groups in the United States was the 1955 U.S. Supreme Court *Brown v. Board of Ed.* decision, which ruled that racially segregated public schools violated the equal protection clause of the 14th Amendment of the Constitution (*Brown v. Board of Ed.*, 1955). As a result, the Civil Rights Movement of the 1960s was born, and itinerant Mexican farm laborers, Native Americans, women, and Blacks began to seek equal rights. It was during this period that the Gay Rights Movement began, heralded by several nights in 1969 of retaliation by gays to police harrassment at the Stonewall Inn, a gay bar in Greenwich Village. Subsequently, many gays have collectively and publicly renounced society's condemnation, and laid claim to equal rights. They have organized around social and political issues, and many gay men and lesbians who had formerly kept their homosexuality hidden have avowed their gay identity with pride.

However, in spite of this increased visibility, as well as the commendable efforts of local, state, and national gay rights organizations, the oppression of gays continues to constitute a nationwide problem. For example, sexual acts in private by two consenting adults of the same sex is unlawful in many states. In 1985 in Atlanta, Georgia, a gay man was arrested in the privacy of his own home for engaging in sex with another man (Walter, 1985a). Because of the illegality of homosexual behavior, much of gay culture is thought to be semi-legal at best. Hence, police harrassment of homosexuals in gay settings such as bars is not uncommon. Men and women who are openly homosexual are barred from military service. There may also be job discrimination. For example, occupations that involve working with children, such as those of school teacher or child-care worker, are frequently denied to gays. Homosexuals remain the butt of jokes and physical violence, and public condemnation is not infrequent. For instance, in 1985 a candidate for mayor of Houston, Texas joked that one way to reduce the crisis of AIDS (acquired immune deficiency syndrome) would be to "shoot the queers" (Walter, 1985b). Moreover, disapproval of homosexuality by both Christian and non-Christian religions further alienates gays from mainstream society. More to the point of this chapter, within the judicial system, discrimination against gay parents is indisputable. According to Hitchens (1979/1980):

> Regardless of whether a parent has ever been involved in a court challenge, the threat of losing the custody of one's children—or being forced to choose between one's lover and a child—is an everyday reality for homosexual fathers and mothers. Gay parents are aware that their sexual orientation can all too easily be used against them by ex-spouses, family, or state authorities. Decisions about how to live, with whom to live, how to raise children, whether to "come out," and whether to become involved in political activities, all have potentially severe legal consequences bearing on the right to remain a parent. (pp. 93–94)

Hence, with injustice and inequity permeating the military, religious, educational, and legal institutions of the country, along with the overt ways in which the constitutional rights of gays are violated, gays, like nongays, internalize society's homophobia as they grow and develop. As adults, then, it is easily understood why so many gays experience varying degrees of self-hatred that is often exceptionally painful and difficult to exorcise.

During the 1970s, as the Women's Movement continued to gain momentum, the number of working women increased, and the divorce rate rose dramatically. Two main consequences of these trends are particularly relevant to gay fathers. First, many divorcees, both men and women, entered the gay world rather than the world of the formerly married (Hunt & Hunt, 1977). If the Gay Movement had not been visible, some of these individuals might have once again presented themselves as eligible heterosexuals. However, the visibility of gay lifestyles as a viable alternative was sufficiently compelling for persons whose orientation was toward same-sex partners to choose a homosexual lifestyle—difficult as that choice might have been, especially since many of them were also parents. The second consequence was that as more women left their traditional domain to enter the workforce, and as the number of single-parent (both mother and father) households increased, men began to reconsider the traditional mold that society had cast for them, particularly as family instrumentalist. The nurturing role had been neither expected nor necessarily desired of them, and most men had been living at the boundary of their family rather than at its heart (Colman & Colman, 1981). Prior to 1974, there was only a handful of substantive writings on the subject of fatherhood. Then in 1974, *The Father: His*

Role in Child Development by David Lynn was published, and two years later Michael Lamb published the first edition of *The Role of the Father in Child Development*. Since that time there has been a plethora of writings on fathers, fathering, and fatherhood.

Thus a confluence of sociohistorical events has affected the lives of gay fathers. Perceiving one's gay identity as positive, and living one's life as a gay person, has gradually gained some social respectability in limited, yet increasing, segments of the country. In addition, there has been a realization of the significance of the father to children's growth and development, coincident with many men's realization of their need to be expressive and nurturing. These factors have contributed to a growing awareness of the phenomenon of gay fathers. However, although there is research on married homosexual men (Bieber, 1969; Gochros, 1978; Humphreys, 1975; Humphreys & Miller, 1980; Maddox, 1982; Miller, 1978; Ponte, 1974; Ross, 1972; Saghir & Robins, 1973), and while lesbian mothers have had some recognition in the literature (Hall, 1978; Klein, 1973; Lewin & Lyons, 1982; Martin & Lyon, 1972), gay fathers, as a research topic, have thus far been all but ignored.

Although it is impossible to state with confidence the number of gay men and lesbians in the United States, it is estimated that there are approximately 23 million. This figure is based on statistics from the U.S. Bureau of the Census (1983) which report the nation's population at approximately 230 million, and on the studies by Kinsey, Pomeroy, and Martin (1948), Churchill (1971), and Kingdon (1979), who found that about 10% of the U.S. population is gay. In addition, it is estimated that 20% of gay men have been heterosexually married (Bell & Weinberg, 1978; Jay & Young, 1979; Spada, 1979). How many gay men have been married more than once, and how many of them have one or more biological or adopted children is unknown, although it is estimated that 25–50% of those who have been married are natural fathers (Bell & Weinberg, 1978; Miller, 1979a). According to Schulenburg (1985) there are over six million children of lesbian mothers and gay fathers in North America, while Peterson (1984) estimates there are upwards of 14 million. These numbers point to the importance of increasing our understanding of gay fatherhood.

Reasons for Marriage

There are multiple reasons why a gay man would enter into heterosexual marriage, many of which are shared by nongays (Bozett, 1985a; Ross, 1983). The man may be in love with a woman, or he may have the desire to be a father. While this affection may not have a strong sexual component, the affectional attraction for a particular woman, possibly (but not necessarily) coupled with the desire for children, may be sufficient motivation for some gay men to marry. Some men are looking for a stable lifestyle, which they may believe cannot be achieved in the gay world, or they may fear isolation and loneliness. Furthermore, there may be parental pressure to marry, especially if the man is a member of a culture in which the importance of family and children is central. In addition, the man may consider himself to be bisexual, he may think that a heterosexual relationship will rid him of his homosexuality, or he may seek marriage as a screen behind which it can be hidden. Moreover, the gay man who perceives homosexuality as pathological may consider marriage to be the only alternative to meet his intimacy needs. Also, the man may not be consciously aware that he is gay. This may be difficult for the reader to understand—how could a man who is in his twenties, the most common age for marriage, *not* know that he is gay? To answer that question requires a brief discussion of the process of acquiring a gay identity.

Gay Identity Development

In past decades, most of the literature on homosexuality has centered on its "cause." Researchers' efforts to identify the cause(s) were initially based on the notion that homosexuality, like disease, is detrimental to social well-being, and that identifying its cause would lead to effective prevention or treatment and cure. This application of a medical model is now considered specious, and in 1973 homosexuality was removed as a diagnostic category from the official manual of psychiatric disorders (Bayer, 1981).

It has been postulated that certain factors such as prenatal hormones, Oedipal conflicts, seduction, early same-sex experiences, and certain family characteristics—especially the dominant mother and weak or absent father constellation—singly or in combination contribute to the development of homosexuality in males (Weinberg & Bell, 1972). More recent theories, while not totally denying the possible significance of these factors, stress both the need to identify the way in which each factor interacts with other factors, and the meanings the interaction has for a given individual (Hart & Richardson, 1981). Two individuals can have identical experiences (e.g., homosexual sex at the age of 14), but the meaning and relative importance of the experience are different for each. This interactionist perspective explains how individuals vary in their developing awareness of their homosexuality. Since self-identification as gay is based on life experiences, self-concept, and other factors and their interactions, as well as the meanings ascribed to them, it can develop at any time in one's life; it is not a phenomenon that necessarily occurs by early adulthood.[2]

The term "coming out" is commonly used to refer to one's self-identification as gay. Although the term is variously defined, depending on the source, I use it to mean *defining the self as gay*, whether or not one has had a same-sex sexual experience, has told another person, or has experienced a gay social context. There are various levels of coming out: coming out to the self; coming out to others (which may or may not occur in a gay setting); and coming out publicly via mass media such as television, radio, or newspapers. In addition, since homosexuality is not outwardly visible, coming out is not a single event, but is one which takes place repeatedly over one's lifetime.

Unlike Black children who are socialized by their parents for both Black and non-Black society (Dank, 1971), most gay persons are reared in a heterosexual

---

[2]For a more extensive discussion of gay identity development, see Hart & Richardson (1981).

context—and in the United States, in a society that is notably homophobic. Both Bozett (1981a, 1981b) and Kus (1985) found that the task of most gay males is two-fold. The individual must rid himself of his own heterosexual expectations imposed on him by society and his childhood socialization, and he must also reject the negative stereotype of the homosexual, which he most likely has accepted as fact (introjected homophobia). This occurs as follows: Over time there is a gradual change in the meaning of the cognitive category (McCall & Simmons, 1966) of homosexual, by means of two primary mechanisms. First is participation in the gay social world, such as having gay sexual relationships, attending gay social functions, and reading gay literature. Through such participation, the man learns that there is little basis in reality for the socially held negative stereotype of gay persons and, as a consequence, he realizes that no change in his own behavior or affect is required for him to be accepted as gay by himself or other gays. Second is disclosure of his gay identity to others. Although disclosure is difficult because of the fear of rejection, stigmatization, and loss of friendship and significant others, actual rejection is rare. It seems that while gays as a collective are generally unacceptable, individually they are not. Hence, as a gay man comes out to an increasing number of persons and receives their approbation, he is gradually able to internalize their acceptance of him as gay, and to place himself in the cognitive category of gay. Cass (1979) identifies six stages of homosexual identity formation, from identity confusion and comparison (Stages 1 and 2), through identity tolerance (Stage 3), to identity acceptance, pride, and synthesis (Stages 4, 5, and 6). Critical to Cass' conceptualization is that identity "foreclosure" can occur at each stage, making progression to the next stage impossible.

THE GAY FATHER CAREER: THE HETEROSEXUAL CONNECTION

The term "career," as it will be discussed in this chapter, is used as a "heuristic device . . . for detailing the stages or sequential development of status passage" (Miller, 1978, p. 221). Careers can be objective (public) or subjective (private) (Lindesmith, Strauss, & Denzin, 1977). For gay fathers who ultimately identify themselves as gay, the gay-father career is both objective and subjective. Characteristically, the gay father proceeds through a series of identifiable public stages (the objective career) from dating, marrying, and becoming a father, to separating, divorcing, and living as a self-identified gay man. The subjective/private career occurs gradually, as the man alters his conception of himself from heterosexual to homosexual.

Prior to marriage, most but not all gay fathers have had gay sexual experiences. However, it seems that most of these men do not attach special significance to them, nor do they consider themselves to be homosexual (Bozett, 1982). They may justify gay sex as being therapeutic, since it relieves stress (Bozett, 1985a), or rationalize it in other ways, such as "I was just experimenting," "I was drunk," or "It's just for variety" (Hencken, 1984). Most gay fathers probably do not inform their future wives of their homosexual experiences, but some of them do. They may even reveal their physical attraction to men. These explanations are often couched in such a way as to indicate that such behaviors are all in the past. Yet it is not their intent to be deceptive. They believe what they say, that they can put their gay experiences and associated feelings behind them, and enter into a fully satisfying heterosexual lifestyle. Hence they marry.

Most of the men describe the first year or two of the marriage as quite satisfactory. At some point, however, many begin to have sexual fantasies about other men, especially during coitus with their wives, and eventually, they may begin to seek clandestine, impersonal sex with men in public restrooms, parks, or gay baths (Bozett, 1979a, 1982). This type of sexual liaison gradually increases in frequency, and, for most of these men, causes intense feelings of shame and guilt.[3] They feel torn between their sexual drive for men and their concern for their wife and children. They worry that their emerging gay feelings and behaviors will jeopardize the stability that they value in their heterosexual lifestyle. This was the case of a father whose first homosexual experience occurred two years after marriage and the birth of his son. He said:

> I was going through all sorts of guilt about being a bad father, and I felt, "Oh, I'm a terrible father; I can't hack it as a father." That was one of my biggest, worst fears. I didn't know how to be a gay father. I didn't think it was possible. Seemed like a contradiction of terms to me. I thought, "I can't." I was really hating myself for being a gay because I thought that it wouldn't work. I thought they were anathema. (Bozett, 1981a, p. 554)

Often, men who first begin having gay sex after marriage experience much greater feelings of shame and guilt than do men who have done so prior to as well as during the marriage (Bozett, 1981a). For the former, the duplicity of their behavior is much more difficult to tolerate. Even so, because of the intensity of the sexual drive, the behavior continues and may even increase in frequency. Elaborate excuses are developed to explain leaving the house at odd hours or arriving home late. Miller (1978, 1979b, 1986) refers to gay fathers at this stage as at the "covert behavior" point on the career continuum. Men in the "covert behavior" category attribute their behavior to nothing more than a genital urge; they consider themselves heterosexual, are isolated from the gay community, and cannot reconcile their homosexual behavior with their masculine self-concept. They may have sought counseling, viewing alternatives to marriage as severely limited, since the gay world is not perceived as a viable option.

However, as the man's career progresses he gradually meets other gay men in more social settings, and begins to realize that his negative stereotype of homosexuality is more fantasy than reality. He is gradually overturning his own negative stereotype of homosexuals, and is ultimately able to put himself in the cognitive category of gay, although he does not publicly identify himself as such. He may admit his homosexuality to other gays, while remaining marginal to the gay community.

---

[3]Most of the findings discussed in this chapter pre-date public awareness of acquired immune deficiency syndrome (AIDS). The AIDS phenomenon may have brought about changes in gay fathers' behaviors and feelings that as yet have not been measured.

Miller (1978, 1979b, 1986) identifies these men as at the "marginal involvement" point on the continuum. Men in this category are often self-employed, and tend to be upper-middle- to lower-upper-class. Their financial resources tend to be greater than those of fathers in the "covert behavior" category, so they may hire call boys or maintain a separate apartment for safe sexual encounters. Their homosexual behavior often induces strong feelings of guilt, which they may attempt to assuage by showering their wives and children with gifts. Although it is probably unsatisfying for most men to remain in one of these two unhappy states (Cory, 1951; Miller, 1978), it is the author's belief that most gay fathers do remain closeted in either the "covert behavior" or "marginal involvement" category. There are many reasons for this. One is their internalized homophobia; another is their honest affection for their family, especially their children; a third is their awareness that separation and divorce would seriously lower their standard of living. The appeal of their family, with the stability it provides, often overrides their desire to enter the unpredictable gay world voluntarily, and to take on a stigmatized identity.

On the other hand, many men do enter the gay world out of the necessity to be authentic, and to live their lives as the gay men they know themselves to be. Most men in my study reported that they reached a point where they could no longer tolerate the continual frustrations they had imposed on themselves by maintaining dual identities in dichotomous worlds. Over time, they may have become filled with anger at not being able to express themselves fully and openly as the men they knew themselves to be; finally they exploded, venting their hostility on their family. Typical of these men is the father who stated "I was becoming more and more frustrated and more unhappy with myself. My frustration would build up to anger and I'd stomp and bitch. Temper tantrums. And sometimes not even knowing why I was so uptight" (Bozett, 1982, p. 85). Resolution of their problems may seem impossible. During this time the entire family agonizes. The couple have grown apart, communication is almost nonexistent, sexual relations between the couple are rare to absent and, if marital therapy has been sought, it has not been effective. The marriage is failing and the family is disintegrating. It is at this time, when the situation becomes devastating for all concerned, that these men frequently will disclose their homosexual feelings and activities to their wives (Bozett, 1982).

However, not all families experience this kind of sharp conflict. Some couples experience a gradual distancing, quietly growing apart, having few if any common interests, with communication becoming sorely limited. When the man becomes sufficiently unhappy and dissatisfied with his life, and senses that he is only a facade of his real self, he is likely to disclose his homosexuality to his wife. Whether the disclosure is induced by the man's anger, or by the quiet dissatisfaction with his lifestyle and the conjugal relationship, appears to be determined by the extent of the man's sociosexual experiences in the gay world (Bozett, 1982). Men who have had only occasional, furtive, impersonal gay sexual relationships may feel more frustrated, harboring anger that is eventually directed toward their families. In contrast, men who have sought out sexual liaisons on a regular basis may feel less frustrated, and perhaps less angry (though no less dissatisfied) with their lifestyle arrangements.

Although reactions vary, it appears that wives who had been informed of their husband's homosexual inclinations before marriage react less negatively than do wives who had no forewarning. The latter women may demand that the man move out of the household immediately, or take other drastic measures, whereas wives who had former knowledge are often more understanding (Bozett, 1979a, 1982). There may be attempts to keep the marriage intact through counseling, menage-à-trois with the husband and another male partner, or allowing the husband to have one or more nights out with no questions asked. The wife may also read literature on homosexuality in order to better understand her husband's feelings and behavior (Bozett, 1981b). However, these attempts to salvage the marriage are almost always unsuccessful, and separation and divorce usually ensue.

The divorce is often very difficult emotionally. Although it may be easy to part from their wives, leaving their children is very painful for most of these men. As one father stated, "It was my feelings for my children, not Martha, but my children. That's the thing that was the most difficult. Martha I would have left in a minute, but my children I found very difficult to leave" (Bozett, 1985a, p. 336). However, not all men do separate from their children, since occasionally the wife will relinquish custody to the father. Also, some openly gay fathers have sought custody and have been successful (*A.v.A.*, 1973). Ten percent of the gay fathers in Wyers' study (1984) were custodial parents, which approximates the national norm of approximately 10% of children in single-parent households residing with their father (Hanson, 1985). Furthermore, it is often difficult for the man to leave his home and possessions in which he has considerable emotional and monetary investment.

Also, the man's homosexuality is not necessarily the only cause of the divorce. Most marriages deteriorate for at least several reasons (Hunt & Hunt, 1977), and these marriages are no exception. For example, in my research on gay fathers, one wife was having an extramarital affair and was the one to institute divorce proceedings, whereas two others left both their husband and children in order to independently pursue their own interests (Bozett, 1979a). Thus it is important to note that not all divorced gay fathers necessarily experience relief over ending the marriage (Wyers, 1984).

Although the man remains emotionally and often financially attached to his children, and possibly even to his wife (Weiss, 1975), he leaves his former life to enter the unpredictable gay world as a single man. A cognitive restructuring is evolving whereby the man is relatively accepting of his homosexuality, and is beginning to be able to place himself in the cognitive category of gay. He has yet, however, to integrate into his self-definition the cognitive category of gay father.

THE GAY FATHER CAREER: THE HOMOSEXUAL CONNECTION

The homosexual gay-father career begins when the man and his wife separate. Separation provides the man with the opportunity to seek gay relationships freely, and participate at will in the gay world. Although gay fathers with child custody are restricted by the daily obligations of parenthood, they are free to pursue a gay lifestyle within the boundaries imposed by their parental responsibilities.

From the two studies of gay fathers discussed here (Bozett, 1979a; Miller, 1978, 1983, 1986), it appears that gay fathers who embark on their homosexual career soon discover that social acceptance may not be as easy as it is for gays who are not fathers. This is because the subculture of the gay world these men often enter is that of the gay bar scene of cosmopolitan cities, which is generally frequented by young to middle-aged men with a singles-oriented lifestyle. Such men tend to be economically independent, to be able to spend their money without necessarily considering the needs of others, and to have no definitive commitments to another person. This independence allows many of them the option to move freely within and between cities. Similarly, these characteristics of the highly visible gay single world also exist for those fathers who enter the more covert gay world, where participants socialize primarily in private settings. Gay fathers, on the other hand, with or without child custody, do not usually have these kinds of freedoms. Younger children require their father's money and time regardless of custody arrangements, and adult children who live independently may still have occasional need for their father's assistance. The available data suggest that most gay fathers are concerned about the quality of their relationship with their children, and will do what is necessary to continue parenting them well, regardless of their children's ages (Bozett, 1980, 1981a; Miller, 1979a).

Gay men who have experienced neither fatherhood nor the commitment required in a marital relationship, often do not comprehend the meaning of children to the gay father. One gay father put it this way:

> For me, one of the most important aspects of my life is that I'm gay and another of the most important aspects is that I'm a father. And aside from a number of other interests, those are the things around which my life revolves. And I think, and I suspect this is true of many gay fathers, that there is a significant alienation from other gays because of the fact that you're a father. And I suspect that it arises from the idea of responsibility for another person. There is a tremendous restrictive, and I think almost a healthy restrictive, condition that arises from having to be responsible for another human being. And this marks you off from other gays. Because the primary mark of the gay world is that, essentially, people can be as unattached as they wish to be. And they can escape virtually every relationship they wish to escape from. And that makes my kind of life very different from the lives of most other gays. (Bozett, 1981a, p. 556)

Hence there is often conflict between the properties of the gay world and the requirements of the father role, which may make it more difficult for gay fathers to establish meaningful gay relationships. Another factor that may hinder the development of relationships is that the gay world is youth-oriented, and because most gay fathers are older, they may be less desirable even as an occasional sexual partner, solely because of their age.

Also, one obstacle that all fathers face is that many people who have never had children have a low tolerance for them (Veevers, 1975), and gays are no exception.

Although a gay man may desire a committed relationship, he may not envision a life with his partner's children as well. Thus having children can inhibit the gay father's success in developing a long-term relationship. In addition, the gay father experiences a process similar to the one he encountered when disclosing his homosexuality in the nongay world. Whereas in the nongay world he faced rejection by disclosing his gay identity, in the gay world he discovers that he may face rejection by disclosing that he is a father. Fadiman (1983) refers to this as a "double closet" (p. 82). The outcome in the gay world is that the father tends to distance himself from gay men who do not accept him as a father and who do not accept his children. It is important to gay fathers, especially custodial gay fathers, that their children be accepted by their close friends. If the children are adults and live independently, or if the father has little if any contact with his children, then other gay men's acceptance of his children is less important (Bozett, 1981a).

Acceptance of the man's children is crucial when a custodial gay father develops a couple relationship with a man who is not a father. My interview data suggest that gay male couple relationships tend to fail if the partner does not develop positive regard for the gay father's children, and if he is not willing to adopt at least some elements of the stepparent role. As in other types of stepfamily configurations, such relationships are often difficult to navigate and require patience and understanding by both the adults and children (Bozett, 1984b). Although there is no research evidence, it seems reasonable to assume that a custodial gay father who has established a lover relationship with another gay father has a greater chance of sustaining it over the long term.

Miller (1978, 1979b, 1986) divides gay fathers who separate from their families into two categories. In the first category are men at the "transformed participation" point on the career continuum; they usually do not live with their children, although they visit them regularly. Their older children often know they are gay, although it is not a topic generally discussed, since if the man's homosexuality were to become widely known he fears that his ex-wife might deny him visiting rights or that he might lose his job. In the second category are gay fathers at the "open endorsement" point on the continuum; they are proud of their gay identity and lifestyle, and their children, employers, and others are aware of their homosexuality. They may have custody of their children, with a high commitment to the parental role. Not uncommonly these men have a lover. If so, their lives center around a close circle of friends rather than gay social institutions.

The Gay-Father–Child Relationship

Disclosure of Gay Identity to Children

Although many gay fathers remain married and keep their homosexuality hidden (Harris & Turner, 1985–1986), many other gay fathers do disclose their gay identity to their children (Bozett, 1980). Most commonly they disclose because their gay identity is integral to their essence as a human being. It seems especially important for gay fathers, who may have burdened themselves for many years with a counterfeit heterosexual identity, to come out. As these men have progressed through various stages of identity redefinition, the homosexual identity becomes integrated into the self as a positive value. Hence the transformation of an attribute that was previously considered undesirable into one that is distinctly positive becomes cause for celebration. The burden of secrecy is lifted, and possibly for the first time the man feels free to be known by others as the person he knows himself to be. Don Clark (1977), a gay clinical psychologist and father, writes:

> Generally speaking, it is important for the gay person not to hide gay identity from offspring, because they are too close to keep in ignorance. To hide it is to give yourself the message that you are ashamed and that there is some cause for shame. To hide it is likely to give them the same message. And it is not such a good feeling to have a parent who is ashamed. (pp. 133–134)

Moreover, the father can integrate his children into facets of his life from which they have previously been excluded.

However, not all gay fathers do come out to their children, even though they may want to. One reason is because of the father's internalized homophobia. As one noncustodial 48-year-old father of four teenagers, who had had a lover for seven years, stated: "I don't want to say I'm gay, because I'm ashamed of it. And I shouldn't be after all this time, but if you want to come right down to it, I guess that's what it boils down to. That I'm ashamed of it" (Bozett, 1979a). Another reason is that if the former spouse found out she might be vindictive. One man reported to the author that he did not disclose to his daughter, since if his wife were to find out, he believed she might inform the board of education where he taught elementary school (Bozett, 1980).

Children's Reactions to Disclosures

Children are generally accepting of their gay fathers. In none of the reported research have children disowned their father because of his homosexuality. There are several explanations for this. Both Miller's (1979a) study and my own (Bozett, 1980) found that many children had been taught by their parents to accept social and personal variance in others. In some cases children had been introduced to the subject of homosexuality through reading about it, having informal discussions, and meeting family friends. Thus they learned to view the world in less prejudicial and conforming ways. Moreover, it is unlikely that children would perceive their fathers within the framework of the negative homosexual stereotype after years of having a positive father–child relationship (Bozett, 1980). A father's candor and honesty may also strengthen the father–child bond. In addition, the man's disclosure may help relieve family tensions since the children may be less likely to blame themselves for difficulties in the home (Miller, 1979a), and children's approbation may further promote the father's acceptance of himself as gay.

Children's acceptance of their father as gay can be manifested both through verbal responses and through behavior, such as attending gay events or accompanying their father to public gay social settings such as bars or restaurants. One father de-scribed his daughter's reaction to his disclosure this way:

> She said, "I thought you'd been fighting it all this time. I feel so relieved." And she reached over and grabbed my hand, and she just cried with great relief. She was feel-ing for me. Being compassionate with me—for my feelings. And it was just the most beautiful reunion. We held hands and talked for quite a while and it was very re-warding. Extremely rewarding. I didn't have to hold anything back. (Bozett, 1980, p. 177)

Another man reported that after coming out to his nine-year-old daughter she wrote a letter to Anita Bryant stating that if God did not like gays he would not have made them. Yet another father reported that after disclosing to his 25-year-old son, the young man reacted by bursting out crying.

> He's a very sensitive, emotional boy. And he just threw his arms around me and hugged me, and he cried and he cried, and I started to cry because I didn't know what was comin' off. And so finally he calmed down and I said, "What are you crying about?" And he said, "Because I'm a part of this culture that has suppressed you all these years." My stomach fell right down into my shoes. Can you imagine? He's so beautiful. And I assured him that he couldn't help it any more than I could help what I did or didn't do when I was bringing him up. And he has accepted it very well. (Bozett, 1980, p. 177)

Communication between father and child also seems frequently to improve after the father has come out to his children (Bozett, 1979b). As he becomes more com-fortable with his gay identity, a father is likely to be open and at ease in talking with his children, and his children are likely to respond in kind. For example, a 28-year-old son stated:

> Communication has been much better since he told me. Much better. Since then I've always felt much more comfortable in talking about anything. We would sit on week-ends and just talk from the time we got up in the morning until almost 9 or 10 o'clock at night. Just all day long, discussing my past, the problems that he was having then, talking back and forth. We were always very open to discussion. (Bozett, 1985c)

A 21-year-old daughter commented: "Through coming out of the closet my father has become more honest and more open about himself. He's more willing to accept that 'Hey, I've got flaws, too.' He's just basically more human now" (Bozett, 1985c).

However, the extent of children's acceptance does vary. One determining factor appears to be the father's own acceptance. In a survey by Schulenburg (1985), it was found that parents who were ashamed or confused about their homosexuality reported negative reactions from their children. Thus a positive response by children seems more likely when the fathers themselves are relatively accepting of their gay identity. Moreover, parents report that children who are told at an earlier age have fewer problems with acceptance than do children who are told later on (Schulenburg, 1985; Turner, Scadden, & Harris, 1985), which supports the belief of Berzon (1978) and Moses and Hawkins (1982) that gay parents should come out to children as early as possible. Foremost among the reasons advocated is that the longer one waits, the more likely it is that children will internalize society's antigay point of view, thus making it more difficult for a father to present a positive image of himself.

Furthermore, although most children are accepting, because homosexuality is so highly stigmatizing, it may be very difficult for children to manage the knowledge of their father's gay identity outside of the immediate family or gay social contexts. According to Moses and Hawkins (1982), children may be concerned that their home life is different from that of their peers, they may be embarrassed to be seen with their father in public, or they may fear that their friends will find out. Thus the fact that a gay father feels positive about his homosexuality is no guarantee that his children will, at least not in all social circumstances.

Children's Perspectives on Having a Gay Father

I conducted in-depth interviews of 19 children of gay fathers (Bozett, 1985b), asking them about their reactions to having a father who is gay. The children ranged in age from 14 to 35 years. There were 13 females and 6 males, and with 1 exception, they lived either in the environs of Oklahoma City or the San Francisco Bay area. Except for two sons who were gay, and one daughter who was bisexual, they all identified themselves as heterosexual. Their living arrangements varied: some lived with their father, some with their mother, and others lived independent from either parent. One of the gay sons lived with his lover.

The children's interviews were tape-recorded, transcribed, and analyzed according to the method of Glaser and Strauss (1967) described earlier. The findings, as previously stated, indicated that children whose fathers were more open about their homosexuality tended to feel closer and more genuine with their fathers than did children of more closeted fathers. However, the children of more open fathers also reported concern that they too would be viewed as gay. In order to avoid that possibility, they commonly employed social strategies to control the behavior of the father, the self, or others in relation to the father. Some of these strategies were in the behavioral realm. For example, a son might not allow his father to bring his lover to the son's party, although the father might be welcome to come alone. Or a daughter might, after her father's disclosure, refuse to be seen in public with him, since she was certain her father's homosexuality was readily evident. Or a son or daughter living with the father might not bring friends home, to prevent them from encountering the father and his lover.

Some children's attempts at social control were in the verbal realm—they used nondisclosure or disclosure as a means of handling their concerns about their father's gay identity. For example, a 15-year-old boy stated, "I don't tell anyone else because I'm afraid they'll think I'm gay." Other children might disclose their father's gay identity, in the belief that others were homophobic, that the father's homosexuality was obvious, and that people needed to be prepared in advance in order to be able to deal with it. Their disclosure implied, "My father is gay but I am not" (Bozett, 1985b).

Different factors influenced which controlling strategies children used, and the extent of their use (Bozett, 1984a, 1985b). One factor was whether or not the child identified or linked himself or herself with the father in some way because of some perceived similarity between them. Perhaps both were alcoholic, or overweight, or perhaps the child was also gay. If the father's homosexuality helped legitimize the child's own feelings of variance, the child tended to be more accepting of the father, and to use control strategies less. Another influencing factor was how overt the child perceived the father's homosexuality to be, with the degree of overtness depending on each child's stereotype of homosexuality, and the degree to which their father's behavior coincided with their stereotype. The more obtrusive the child perceived the father to be, the more control strategies the child utilized. An instance of this was the daughter who stated, "I don't invite him to any activities I think we might enjoy together 'cause I'm always afraid that we'll run into someone that I know. It is fairly obvious that he's gay. I am embarrassed by him and I resent that" (Bozett, 1985b). On the other hand, an adolescent boy reported, "I feel at ease when I'm in public with my dad. My dad does not act homosexual. He does not. And Walt (the father's lover) does not act like that" (Bozett, 1985b). Other influencing factors were the age of the children and their living arrangements, which were often directly related to age. Younger children had less control over their own, their father's, and others' actions than did older children. In particular, older children who lived on their own had far greater control regarding the activities they would participate in with their father than did their younger counterparts.

It should be noted, based on the research reported here (Bozett, 1979a, 1980; Miller, 1978, 1979a, 1983, 1986; Turner, et al., 1985) that gay fathers are usually sensitive to these concerns on the part of their children. They often attempt to avoid undue overt manifestations of their homosexuality and gay lifestyle. For example, one father doesn't march in gay day parades because he believes it would be too "up front" (Bozett, 1980), while other fathers may advise their children to refer to the father's lover as "uncle" or as a "housemate." Or the father and his lover may avoid even simple displays of affection, and gay artifacts such as newspapers may be hidden when the children's friends visit.

The Quality of Gay Father–Child Relationships

One study compared single-custodial gay and nongay fathers of children aged 12 or younger in their parenting role (Scallen, 1981). Findings indicated that the two groups did not differ significantly on the problem-solving dimension, on providing recreation, or in the encouragement of children's autonomy. However, gay fathers placed a greater emphasis on nurturance of their children, described themselves more positively as parents, placed less emphasis on the economic provider role, and were less traditional in their overall attitudes about parenting. Scallen concluded that sexual orientation did have a relationship to espoused paternal attitudes, and that the gay fathers in his study had a more substantial psychological investment in the paternal role.

Miller (1979a), in a study comparing covert gay fathers living with their wives with divorced gay fathers with custody who had come out to most of their significant others, found that the fathering of the covert men was of lower quality, because of the pull of their covert lives. They spent less time with their children, and father–child interaction appeared to be filled with tension. On the other hand, fathers with custody whose children knew they were gay, in addition to spending more time with their children (which might in part have been a consequence of single parenthood), were less authoritarian, used less physical punishment, and were more likely to report the desire to rear their children with nonsexist, egalitarian values.

Other findings suggest that gay fathers, with or without custody, often make special efforts to be exemplary in their father role (Bozett, 1979a; Turner, Scadden, & Harris, 1985). One reason may be that because society's sanctions against homosexual parenting are so intense, gay fathers feel the need to prove that society's homophobic viewpoints are erroneous. Another may represent an attempt to counteract some of the biases affecting decisions around custody and visitation. Although some progress has been made in lesbian mother-custody disputes (Schulenburg, 1985), the courts remain discriminatory toward gay fathers because of their homosexuality per se. In applying the "best interest" standard, a judge can decide that it is in the best interest of the child to be placed with the heterosexual parent, regardless of other factors in the case (Hitchens, 1979/1980). In addition, since some ex-wives express their vindictiveness by attempting to restrict legally the father's access to his children (Bozett, 1980), gay fathers may attempt to be exemplary fathers in order to prevent such problems.

Thus, based on the findings of Bozett (1980, 1981a) and Miller (1979a, b, 1986), it appears that gay fathers who have progressed to the latter stages of gay identity development achieve a sense of psychological well being that is not characteristic of their counterparts for whom identity foreclosure has occurred earlier. Children also seem to benefit directly from their fathers' completing the coming-out process. Hence while separation and divorce are very painful for the entire family, they are likely to be better than staying together, with the father enacting behaviors characteristic of men in the "covert behavior" or "marginal involvement" categories.

Children also talked about some of the advantages of having a gay father. Some felt that their fathers were more open than other fathers, which resulted in a closer father–child relationship. One daughter said that before her father came out she had only a father, but now she has a friend who also happens to be her father. Two other daughters explained that they thought their fathers were able to relate to them and understand their problems as women better than nongay fathers could. In addition, some children felt that they had learned to be more tolerant and open-minded about persons different from themselves.

The most common disadvantage children with gay fathers reported was that they considered the father's homosexuality to be responsible for the breakup of a cherished family unit. Several respondents discussed this with great emotion. For example a 33-year-old daughter stated:

> There's been so much that got taken away by my parent's divorce. I enjoyed the times I spent with my parents, and I had a lot of fun with them. It took that away. We don't have the house any more that we grew up in, and it was really a special house. It took away a lot of traditions. It took away a lot of innocence, I guess. The world just looked different. You couldn't trust it so much any more. Things weren't as they seemed. It took away a family. It broke up a unit of people, and over the years I'm learning that that's a really valuable thing to have. (Bozett, 1985c)

Also noteworthy is the fact that some children who were psychologically very close to their father, and reported great love and respect for him, did not necessarily approve of his homosexuality. Apparently, these children were able to separate their father's gay identity from his role as father. For example, one 28-year-old son stated "I perceive his lifestyle as wrong. I don't want to perceive what he's doing as wrong, really, but I just never have been able to change that perception" (Bozett, 1985c). Yet he also said, "I'm very proud of him, of the things he's accomplished. I look up to him a lot; his attitude toward life in general. I'm proud to have him as a father. And I love him very much" (Bozett, 1985c). A daughter who thought her father might "burn in hell" because of his homosexuality also explained that "If he wasn't gay, I'd say he was sent from heaven. That's how impressed I am with him. He's smart, he's successful, and he's also a very caring man" (Bozett, 1985c).

Children's Development of Sexual Identity

Studies of the children of lesbian mothers (Golombok, Spencer, & Rutter, 1983; Green, 1978; Hoeffer, 1979, 1981; Hotvedt & Mandel, 1982; Kirkpatrick, Smith, & Roy, 1981; Steckel, 1985, 1987; Weeks, Derdeyn, & Langman, 1975) have found no specific areas of sexual identity directly related to parental homosexuality. The findings of this research can be summed up by the statement of Green (1978): "Children being raised by transsexual or homosexual parents do not differ appreciably from children raised in more conventional family settings on macroscopic measures of sexual identity" (pp. 696–697). Although there are no reported studies of the development of sexual identity in children of gay fathers, there is no reason to assume that the findings would differ appreciably from those reported for the children of lesbian mothers, although certainly this is a much needed area of research.

In Miller's study of gay men (1979a), among the 27 daughters and 21 sons whose sexual orientation could be assessed, the fathers reported that one son and three daughters were gay. Among the 25 children in my earlier study of gay fathers (Bozett, 1979a), none of the fathers reported having a gay or lesbian child, although some of the children were not old enough for their sexual orientation to be determined. In my later study of 19 children of gay fathers (Bozett, 1985b), two sons reported being gay, and one daughter considered herself bisexual, while the remainder identified themselves as heterosexual. Hence the myth that homosexuality is communicable appears to have little empirical support. Heterosexual parenting does not ensure heterosexual children, and, likewise, second-generation homosexuals are rare (Miller, 1979a).

Moreover, there is some evidence that gay fathers attempt to develop "appropriate" gender identity and sex-role behaviors in their children. Harris and Turner

(1985/1986) found that the gay fathers in their study tended to encourage their children to play with sex-typed toys, and half of the gay fathers in a study by Turner and colleagues (1985) did so as well. Also, in my own study, it was not uncommon for gay fathers of both sons and daughters to express concern regarding the absence of a feminine influence in the household (Bozett, 1979b). Most of the fathers in the study by Turner and colleagues (1985) reported that they attempted to provide an opposite sex-role model for their children, primarily through contact with female friends. They reported that their children appeared to be developing normal sex-role identification, and that they considered their children's behaviors to be no different from other children of the same age and sex.

SUMMARY AND CONCLUSIONS

The purpose of this chapter has been to report what is known about gay fathers, although research is limited, and does not yet take into account, the effects of the AIDS phenomenon on gay fathers' feelings and behaviors. What we have learned thus far from existing research is that for many reasons, men who are gay do marry and have children. At some time during marriage, most of them begin having clandestine homosexual relations. For some men it is their first same-sex sexual encounter, but for most it is not. Most of the married gay men studied have tended to remain at this stage of the gay-father career, having occasional short-term, anonymous sexual relationships with men, and disclosing their homosexuality to few if any others, while at the same time attempting to achieve life satisfaction within the context of heterosexual married family life. Undoubtedly, there are some gay men for whom this arrangement is satisfactory. Likewise, there are others who find it unfulfilling, but who, for a variety of reasons, remain married.

On the other hand, there are gay fathers who are not content to live within the bounds of apparent heterosexuality. These men cannot tolerate the duplicity of their behavior, nor the deceit and guilt that the duality creates. Thus they admit their homosexuality to themselves, and often to their wives, children, and significant others. They organize their life so that the integration of a gay identity into their self-concept is made possible. Although there is the potential for losing the love of others after they disclose their homosexuality, as well as the possibility of being rejected by gays because of their father status, they generally discover that, contrary to their worst fears, most people are accepting of both identities, and that integration of them into their new lifestyle is possible. Thus they no longer need to conceal their gay or father identities from the people who are most important. Although they choose to live with an identity that is often stigmatized in this culture, the satisfaction derived from honestly portraying themselves as gay fathers appears to be worth the risk of occasional disparagement or discrimination. Their implementation of the father role in both quantity and quality appears to be little affected by their sexual orientation, per se. In addition, the father–child relationship tends to strengthen after the father discloses his homosexuality to his children.

As same-sex affectional preference becomes more acceptable, it is likely that fewer gay men will enter into matrimony. Even so, for a variety of reasons there will probably always be gay men who become fathers, either within or outside the confines of traditional marriage. It is anticipated that gays will become more tolerant and understanding of gay men who are fathers. Acceptance by both the nongay and gay communities will ease the integration of the father into both worlds, rather than requiring him to straddle both, while not permitting him to be a full member of either.

REFERENCES

A.v.A., 514 P.2d 358 (OR., 1973). (Cited in Walters, L.H., & Elam, A.W., 1985, The father and the law. *American Behavioral Scientist, 29*, 78–111).

Altman, D. (1982). *The homosexualization of America, the Americanization of the homosexual*. New York: St. Martin's.

Bayer, R. (1981). *Homosexuality and American psychiatry: The politics of diagnosis*. New York: Basic.

Bell, A.P., & Weinberg, M.S. (1978). *Homosexualities: A study of diversity among men and women*. New York: Simon & Schuster.

Berzon, B. (1978). Sharing your lesbian identity with your children. In G. Vida (Ed.), *Our right to love: A lesbian resource book*. Englewood Cliffs, NJ: Prentice-Hall.

Bieber, I. (1969). The married male homosexual. *Medical Aspects of Human Sexuality, 3*, 76, 81–82, 84.

Bozett, F.W. (1979a). Gay fathers: The convergence of a dichotomized identity through integrative sanctioning (Doctoral dissertation, University of California, San Francisco). *Dissertation Abstracts International, 40*(6), 2608–2609-B.

Bozett, F.W. (1979b). [Interviews of gay fathers]. Unpublished raw data.

Bozett, F.W. (1980). Gay fathers: How and why they disclose their homosexuality to their children. *Family Relations, 29*, 173–179.

Bozett, F.W. (1981a). Gay Fathers: Evolution of the gay-father identity. *American Journal of Orthopsychiatry, 51*, 552–559.

Bozett, F.W. (1981b). Gay fathers: Identity conflict resolution through integrative sanctioning. *Alternative lifestyles, 4*, 90–107.

Bozett, F.W. (1982). Heterogenous couples in heterosexual marriages: Gay men and straight women. *Journal of Marital and Family Therapy, 8*, 81–89.

Bozett, F.W. (1984a, October). *The children of gay fathers: Strategies for coping with identity variance*. Paper presented at the annual meeting of the National Council on Family Relations, San Francisco, CA.

Bozett, F.W. (1984b). Parenting concerns of gay fathers. *Topics in Clinical Nursing, 6*, 60–71.

Bozett, F.W. (1985a). Gay men as fathers. In S.M.H. Hanson and F.W. Bozett (Eds.), *Dimensions of fatherhood*. Beverly Hills, CA: Sage.

Bozett, F.W. (1985b, April). *Identity management: Social control of identity by children of gay fathers when they know their father is a homosexual*. Paper presented at the 9th annual Midwest Nursing Research Society conference, Chicago, IL.

Bozett, F.W. (1985c). [Interviews of children of gay fathers]. Unpublished raw data.

Bozett, F.W. (1987). *Gay and lesbian parents*. New York: Praeger.

Brown v. Board of Ed. of Topeka, KS, 349 U.S. 294 (1955).

Bullough, V. (1979). *Homosexuality: A history*. New York: New American Library.

Cass, V.C. (1979). Homosexual identity formation: A theoretical model. *Journal of Homosexuality*, *4*, 219–235.

Churchill, W. (1971). *Homosexual behavior among males: A cross-cultural and cross species investigation*. Englewood Cliffs, NJ: Prentice-Hall.

Clark, D. (1977). *Loving someone gay*. Millbrae, CA: Celestial Arts.

Colman, A., & Colman, L. (1981). *Earth father/Sky father*. Englewood Cliffs, NJ: Prentice-Hall.

Cory, D.W. (1951). *The Homosexual in America*. New York: Greenburg.

Dank, B.M. (1971). Coming out in the gay world. *Psychiatry*, *2*, 180–197.

Fadiman, A. (1983, May). The double closet. *Life*, pp. 76–78; 82–84; 86; 92; 96; 100.

Glaser, B., & Strauss, A. (1967). *The discovery of grounded theory*. Chicago: Aldine.

Gochros, H.L. (1978). Counseling gay husbands. *Journal of Sex Education and Therapy*, *4*, 6–10.

Golombok, S., Spencer, A., & Rutter, M. (1983). Children in lesbian and single-parent households: Psychosexual and psychiatric appraisal. *Journal of Child Psychology and Psychiatry and Allied Disciplines*, *24* (4), 551–572.

Green, R. (1978). Sexual identity of 37 children raised by homosexual or transexual parents. *American Journal of Psychiatry*, *135*, 692–697.

Hall, M. (1978). Lesbian families: Cultural and clinical issues. *Social Work*, *23*, 380–385.

Hanson, S. (1985). Single fathers with custody: A synthesis of the literature. In B. Schlesinger (Ed.), *The one-parent family in the 1980's*. Toronto: University of Toronto Press.

Harris, M.B., & Turner, P.H. (1985/1986). Gay and lesbian parents. *Journal of Homosexuality*, *12*, 101–113.

Hart, J., & Richardson, D. (1981). *The theory and practice of homosexuality*. London: Routledge & Kegan Paul.

Hencken, J.D. (1984). Conceptualizations of homosexual behavior which preclude homosexual self-labeling. *Journal of Homosexuality*, *9*, 53–63.

Herek, G.M. (1984). Beyond "homophobia": A social psychological perspective on attitudes towards lesbian and gay men. *Journal of Homosexuality*, *10*, 1–21.

Hitchens, D. (1979/1980). Social attitudes, legal standards, and personal trauma in child custody cases. *Journal of Homosexuality*, *5*, 80–95.

Hoeffer, B. (1979). *Lesbian and heterosexual single mother's influence on their children's acquisition of sex-role traits and behavior*. Unpublished doctoral dissertation, University of California, San Francisco.

Hoeffer, B. (1981). Children's acquisition of sex role behavior in lesbian mother families. *American Journal of Orthopsychiatry*, *51*, 536–544.

Hotvedt, M.E., & Mandel, J.B. (1982). Children of lesbian mothers. In W. Paul, J.D. Weinrich, J.C. Gonsiorek, & M.E. Hotvedt (Eds.), *Homosexuality: Social, psychological, and biological issues*. Beverly Hills, CA: Sage.

Humphreys, L. (1975). *Tearoom trade: Impersonal sex in public places*. Chicago: Aldine.

Humphreys, L., & Miller, B. (1980). Identities in the emerging gay culture. In J. Marmor (Ed.), *Homosexual behavior: A modern reappraisal*. New York: Basic.

Hunt, M., & Hunt, B. (1977). *The divorce experience*. New York: McGraw-Hill.

Jay, K., & Young, A. (1979). *The gay report*. New York: Summit.

Kingdon, M.A. (1979). Lesbians. *The Counseling Psychologist, 8*, 44–45.

Kinsey, A., Pomeroy, W., & Martin, C. (1948). *Sexual behavior in the human male*. Philadelphia: Saunders.

Kirkpatrick, M., Smith, C., & Roy, R. (1981). Lesbian mothers and their children: A comparative survey. *American Journal of Orthopsychiatry, 51*, 545–551.

Klein, C. (1973). *The single parent experience*. New York: Avon.

Kus, R. (1985). Stages of coming out: An ethnographic approach. *Western Journal of Nursing Research, 7*, 177–194.

Lamb, M. (Ed.) (1976). *The role of the father in child development*. New York: Wiley.

Lewin, E., & Lyons, T. (1982). Everything in its place: The coexistence of lesbianism and motherhood. In W. Paul, J.D. Weinrich, J.C. Gonsiorek, & M.E. Hotvedt (Eds.), *Homosexuality: Social, psychological, and biological issues*. Beverly Hills, CA: Sage.

Lindesmith, A.R., Strauss, A.L., & Denzin, N.K. (1977). *Social psychology*. New York: Holt, Rinehart & Winston.

Lofland, J. (1971). *Analyzing social settings*. Belmont, CA: Wadsworth.

Lynn, D. (1974). *The father: His role in child development*. Monterey, CA: Brooks/Cole.

Maddox, B. (1982). *Married and gay*. New York: Harcourt Brace Jovanovich.

Martin, D., & Lyon, P. (1972). *Lesbian/Woman*. New York: Bantam.

McCall, C., & Simmons, J. (1966). *Identities and interactions*. New York: Free Press.

Miller, B. (1978). Adult sexual resocialization: Adjustments toward a stigmatized identity. *Alternative Lifestyles, 1*, 207–234.

Miller, B. (1979a). Gay fathers and their children. *Family Coordinator, 28*, 544–552.

Miller, B. (1979b). Unpromised paternity: The life-styles of gay fathers. In M.P. Levine (Ed.), *Gay men*. New York: Harper and Row.

Miller, B. (1983). *Identity conflict and resolution: A social psychological model of gay familymen's adaptations*. Unpublished doctoral dissertation, The University of Alberta, Edmonton.

Miller, B. (1986). Identify resocialization in moral careers of gay husbands and fathers. In A. Davis (Ed.), *Papers in honor of Gordon Hirabayashi*. Edmonton, Canada: University of Alberta Press.

Moses, A.E., & Hawkins, R.O. (1982). *Counseling lesbian women and gay men: A life-issues approach*. St. Louis: Mosby.

Peterson, N. (1984, April 30). Coming to terms with gay parents. *USA Today*, p. 30.

Ponte, M. (1974). Life in a parking-lot: An ethnography of a homo-drive-in. In J. Jacobs (Ed.), *Deviance: Field studies and self-disclosures*. Palo Alto, CA: National.

Ross, H.L. (1972). Odd couples: Homosexuals in heterosexual marriages. *Sexual Behavior, 2*, 42–49.

Ross, M.W. (1983). *The married homosexual man*. London: Routledge & Kegan Paul.

Saghir, M., & Robins, E. (1973). *Male and female homosexuality*. Baltimore: Williams and Wilkins.

Scallen, R.M. (1981). An investigation of paternal attitudes and behaviors in homosexual and heterosexual fathers (Doctoral dissertation, California School of Professional Psychology, Los Angeles). *Dissertation Abstracts International*, *42*(9), 3809-B.

Schulenburg, J. (1985). *Gay parenting*. New York: Doubleday.

Spada, J. (1979). *The Spada report*. New York: New American Library.

Steckel, A. (1985). *Separation-individuation in children of lesbian and heterosexual couples*. Unpublished doctoral dissertation, Wright Institute, Berkeley, CA.

Steckel, A. (1987). Psychosocial development of children of lesbian mothers. In F.W. Bozett (Ed.), *Gay and lesbian parents*. New York: Praeger.

Turner, P.H., Scadden, L., & Harris, M.B. (1985, March). *Parenting in gay and lesbian families*. Paper presented at the meeting of the Future of Parenting symposium, Chicago, IL.

U.S. Government Printing Office (1983). Statistical abstracts of the U.S. 1984 U.S. Bureau of the Census (104th ed.). Washington, DC.

Veevers, J.E. (1975). The moral careers of voluntarily childless wives: Notes on the defense of a varient world view. *Family Coordinator*, *24*, 473–487.

Walter, D. (1985a, December 10). Supreme court: Historic test for Georgia sodomy law. *Advocate*, p. 15.

Walter, D. (1985b, December 10). Troubled times for Texas gays. *Advocate*, p. 11.

Weeks, R.B., Derdeyn, A.P., & Langman, M. (1975). Two cases of children of homosexuals. *Child Psychiatry and Human Development*, *6*, 26–32.

Weinberg, G. (1972). *Society and the healthy homosexual*. New York: Doubleday.

Weinberg, M.S., & Bell, A.P. (1972). *Homosexuality: An annotated bibliography*. New York: Harper & Row.

Weiss, R.S. (1975). The erosion of love and the persistence of attachment. In R.S. Weiss, *Marital separation*. New York: Basic.

Wyers, N.L. (1984). *Lesbian and gay spouses and parents: Homosexuality in the family*. Portland School of Social Work: Portland State University.

CHAPTER 14

The Role of Grandfathers in the Context of the Family

BARBARA J. TINSLEY and ROSS D. PARKE

I was so happy now that this little grandson would carry on my name, my father's name, this connection between all of us. It was a deep and mysterious feeling within me that I could never hope to put into words.

I had a fit when I became a grandfather. I still had two young ones at home whom I had to help through school. I was really mad. But after a week with the baby, well, she won my heart.

I'm a much better grandfather to my grandchildren than I was father to my own children. I learned from my mistakes.

The above quotes are from a survey of grandparents and grandchildren that provides a rich selection of anecdotal material about grandfathers (Kornhaber & Woodward, 1981, pp. 54, 59, 196). However, aside from many anecdotal accounts that exist, there is a dearth of studies that systematically examine the grandfather role and the influence of grandfathers on children and families. Although this situation is slowly changing, most recent studies address grandparents as a unit, or more often, investigate only grandmothers (Cherlin & Furstenberg, 1985; Feinman & Roberts, 1985; McGreal, 1984; Tinsley & Parke, 1984; Troll, 1979). This is reminiscent of the pattern set by traditional research on child rearing, in which only mothers were studied, and generalizations concerning parents were based on these findings. Only in the last 20 years have we considered fathers theoretically and empirically as a parenting influence (Lamb, 1981; Parke, 1979, 1981). Such is also the case with most of our initial research on grandparents; we know relatively little about the impact of grandmothers on children and families, but, with very few exceptions (Baranowski, 1985; Cath, 1982; Russell, 1985), we know even less about grandfathers.

The potential influence of grandfathers has increased historically due to several factors. As Hagestad (1982) has pointed out, increased life expectancy and more

Preparation of this chapter was supported by NICHD Grant HDO5951 and NICHD Training Grant HDO7205. We thank Rose Tenbrook and Karen McGuire for their assistance in the preparation of this manuscript.

closely spaced families (Glick, 1979; Neugarten & Moore, 1968) have produced greater "life overlaps" between parents and children, and given us multigenerational families, in which three or four generations of parents and children coexist (Troll, 1971; Troll, Miller, & Atchley, 1979). In our culture, men become grandparents at approximately 51–53 years of age, which leaves a 20–30 year potential period of grandparenthood (Troll, 1981). Although there is a general acceptance of the myth that intergenerational kin ties were more prevalent prior to industrialization, Hareven (1977) reminds us that "the opportunity for a meaningful period of overlap in the lives of grandparents and grandchildren is a twentieth-century phenomenon" (p. 62). There are, however, more grandmothers than grandfathers, due to disproportionate mortality rates between the sexes (Baranowski, 1985; Clavan, 1978).

At present, approximately 70% of older people in the United States have grandchildren (Atchley, 1980; Kahana & Kahana, 1971). Not only are grandfathers more available for interaction than in the past, but there is evidence of a significant amount of cross-generational contact. In spite of the geographic mobility of the U.S. population, the proportion of aged parents having contact with an adult child at least once a week is extremely high, varying from 77–83% over the years 1957 to 1975 (Shanas, 1979). Although it is not clear how many of these adult children are parents themselves, it is likely that these figures reflect a substantial degree of grandfather–grandchild contact as well. In an informal survey of 300 grandparents and grandchildren, Kornhaber and Woodward (1981) found a full continuum of involvement of grandparents with their grandchildren, ranging from close and regular contact (25%) to minimal or no contact (5%). Most grandparents fell in the middle range, with 70% reporting that they have only intermittent or irregular contact. However, though a significant percentage of grandfathers do not have the opportunity for regular face-to-face contact because of such factors as geographical separation, Litwak and Szeleniji (1969) have suggested that kinship systems maintain their viability by means of modern communication aids (e.g., telephone, rapid mail delivery, and transportation). Thus the form that grandfather relationships assume is at least partially dependent on contiguity and ease of access (Gilford & Black, 1972).

REASONS FOR THE NEGLECT OF GRANDFATHERS

Why have grandparent influences, and grandfather influences in particular, been conceptually ignored by social scientists? First, long-standing assumptions in developmental psychology about the primacy of the mother–child dyad led to the ignoring of other agents who could have an influence such as fathers, siblings, peers, and extended family members. In recent years, however, investigators have begun to challenge this view by exploring the role of fathers (Lamb, 1981; Parke, 1981; Parke & Tinsley, 1981), siblings (Dunn & Kendrick, 1982), and peers (Asher & Gottman, 1981). And now, with the growing awareness of the embeddedness of the family in a larger social environment, researchers are beginning to consider the role that extra-familial agents, including grandfathers, play in children's development (Feinman et al., 1985; Russell, 1985; Tinsley & Parke, 1984).

A second reason for the neglect of grandfathers was the absence in developmental research of a life span perspective, with its explicit recognition of the plasticity inherent in development. This led to a static view of adults in general, and of grandparents in particular. A life span perspective considers changes that may occur across the adult years, which may in turn affect the contributions grandfathers make to the family and to children's development.

Third, the limited extent to which grandfathers have been studied as influences on children's development is also a function of methodological limitations. There are difficulties associated with any research involving old people (Riegel, Riegel, & Meyer, 1967), such as their elevated morbidity and mortality rates compared to younger subjects. In addition, only recently have theoretical models and accompanying techniques of statistical analysis emerged to permit the meaningful analysis of units beyond the dyad. In grandparental research, while the grandparent–parent and grandparent–grandchild dyads are of interest, the interaction patterns among the three generations is of interest as well. This requires analyses of triads, and even larger groups of interactive agents (Parke, Power, & Gottman, 1979; Lewis & Feiring, 1981).

DO GRANDFATHERS HAVE DISTINCTIVE FAMILY ROLES?

One approach to investigating grandfathers is to determine the distinctiveness of their role by comparing them with grandmothers. Some theorists suggest that there is considerable overlap in the roles of grandmothers and grandfathers, while others emphasize the differences in the two roles. In an early and influential review, Cavan (1962) suggested that the grandparent role requires maternal behaviors on the part of men as well as women, describing men in the grandparent role as "slightly masculinized grandmothers." Relevant to this issue are Neugarten and Gutmann's (1968) and Gutmann's (1985) theories of later-life role reversal. Women in these models are portrayed as becoming more instrumental over the life span in contrast to men who are characterized as becoming more affective and interpersonally oriented as they age. But are grandfathers more affective, nurturant, and involved with caregiving than men at other stages of the life cycle?

Feldman and Nash, in an extensive series of studies, have demonstrated empirically that various stages in men's and women's life cycles, such as grandparenthood, can elicit differing degrees of expressiveness and autonomy (Abrahams, et al., 1978; Feldman & Nash, 1978, 1979; Feldman, Biringen, & Nash, 1981; Feldman, Nash, & Cutrona, 1977). Results from these studies indicate that grandfathers were more behaviorally responsive to unfamiliar infants in a waiting room situation than men at any other stage of life, except fathers of young children. Grandfathers approached and touched unfamiliar infants more often than other men (Abrahams, et al., 1978; Feldman & Nash, 1978, 1979). In a picture-preference measure, grandfathers also chose more pictures of babies as favorites than did fathers of adolescents or males with "empty nests" (Feldman & Nash, 1979). A third measure, the Bem Sex Role Inventory (BSRI), was also administered to subjects in the Feldman and

Nash studies: grandfathers described themselves as having more feminine characteristics than "empty-nest" fathers (Feldman & Nash, 1979), and compassion increased in a near linear manner for men from single adulthood to grandfatherhood. These studies indicate that the advent of grandfatherhood elicits greater interest in babies for men. However, the extent to which these shifts in male behaviors and attitudes actually affect the enactment of the grandfather role is unclear.

While there is other support for the nurturing aspect of grandparenthood, most researchers find that this characterizes grandmothers more than grandfathers. Neugarten and Weinstein (1964), in a classic study of grandparenting, interviewed 70 sets of non-live-in grandparents to determine their style of enactment of the role of grandparent. The grandparenting styles they identified included one that discriminated between grandfathers and grandmothers. Grandfathers never characterized themselves as parent surrogates for their grandchildren, whereas grandmothers reported that caring for their grandchildren was a substantial activity in their lives. Similarly, McGreal (1983, 1984), in an intensive study of 61 men and 71 women expecting a first grandchild, found that expectant grandmothers considered it more important than did expectant grandfathers that grandparents and grandchildren live near one another and interact on a daily basis. In addition, expectant grandfathers reported plans to help with the new infant less frequently than did expectant grandmothers. Subsequent interviews with these new grandparents indicated that grandfathers were much less likely to be involved in direct caregiving of the infants than were grandmothers (McGreal, 1985). However, Russell (1985), in a recent Australian study, did not find grandmother–grandfather differences in the extent to which they rated themselves as active participants in the rearing and disciplining of grandchildren, which suggests that there may be cross-cultural differences in the enactment of the grandparent roles.

Moreover, the characterization of grandfatherhood as a "maternal" role may be limited to the early years of grandparenthood, and the role may undergo shifts as the ages of the grandchildren change. Hagestad and Speicher (1981) suggest that the characterization of grandfatherhood as a maternal role, if accurate at all, describes grandfather–grandchild relationships during grandchildren's infancy and early childhood, and does not appear to be a very accurate description of interactions between grandfathers and adolescent grandchildren. More specifically, Hagestad and her colleagues found that grandfathers were active as advisors to their adolescent grandchildren in such areas as education, career choice, and financial matters (Hagestad, 1978; Hagestad & Speicher, 1981).

Other studies underscore the fact that grandfathers play a variety of distinctive family roles. Nahemow (1984) found that grandfathers in the African Baganda tribe function as storytellers and food collectors; 60% of the Bagandan schoolchildren reported that grandparents were funny and talkative, with this being most true of grandfathers. Neugarten and Weinstein (1964) reported that 6% of the grandfathers they interviewed described their style of grandparental functioning as a "reservoir of family wisdom," in contrast to only 1% of grandmothers who described themselves in this manner, and Russell (1985) reported similar grandfather–grandmother differences in his Australian sample. Our own recent research found that grandfathers were more likely than grandmothers to provide financial support either directly to their grandchildren or to their adult children (Tinsley & Parke, 1984). Finally, Russell (1985) found that grandfathers and grandmothers differed in the kinds of activities they engaged in with their grandchildren. Grandfathers engaged in more rough-and-tumble games than grandmothers, but were less likely to read, draw, or play with toys or educational games—differences that have also been found between mothers and fathers of young children (Parke & Tinsley, 1981).

Another indication of the different roles played by grandfathers and grandmothers comes from grandchildren's reports. Across several studies, grandchildren reported feeling closer to their grandmothers than to their grandfathers (Hagestad, 1982; Nahemow, 1984; Neugarten & Weinstein, 1964). When asked to name a favorite grandparent, grandchildren most often named the maternal grandmother (Baranowski, 1985; Hartshorne & Manaster, 1982; Kahana & Kahana, 1970), and least often the paternal grandfather.

On the basis of this limited information, it appears that grandfathers are not valued primarily for their caregiving and nurturance roles, as are grandmothers, but rather as companions, advisors, and perhaps financial providers. This suggests that greater care should be given to distinguishing grandfather–grandmother contributions in the study of grandparents' influence on children and families.

FACTORS INFLUENCING THE GRANDFATHER ROLE

A number of variables have been found to affect the extent of grandfathers' influence on families and children.

Sex of Grandchild

A major determinant of the quality of grandparent–grandchild relationships is the sex of the grandchild. It has been found consistently that same gender relationships tend to be closer intergenerationally (Aldous, 1985; Nahemow, 1984); that is, grandmothers tend to be closer to granddaughters, while grandfathers are more involved with their grandsons. In their study of three-generational relationships in families with young adult grandchildren in the United States, for example, Hagestad and Speicher (1981) found that grandfathers were much more active with their grandsons than they were with their granddaughters, especially when the grandsons were sons of sons. Nahemow (1984) reports the same finding in African Baganda grandfather–grandson relationships, suggesting that this may be a cross-culturally stable pattern. Especially in societies where roles and occupations are organized to some degree on the basis of gender, this same sex linkage is functional. Atchley (1980), for example, has maintained that grandmothers and granddaughters have a better opportunity to develop a relationship than do grandfathers and granddaughters because grandmothers who are housewives have roles that are more stable and compatible with that of their granddaughters. In other words, grandmothers' skills and knowledge are relevant to granddaughters, whereas grandfathers' knowledge and skills may be less useful for granddaughters, and perhaps even obsolete in the contemporary technological job structure. Similarly, Nahemow (1984) has discussed the "greater relevance" of the grandmother than the grandfather role, while acknowledging potential for change in this area, given current societal changes in women's roles.

Lineage

The effect of the grandparents' gender appears to be modified in its influence by lineage (paternal vs. maternal). Several researchers (Hoffman, 1979; Kahana & Kahana, 1970) have found that at least for school-aged and older grandchildren, there is more frequent contact and a closer relationship with maternal grandparents than with paternal grandparents. Kahana and Kahana (1970) found that children in the United States were least familiar with their paternal grandfathers, in comparison to their maternal grandfathers or either grandmother, although they clearly viewed their paternal grandfathers as meaningful figures. Similarly, Russell (1985) found that maternal grandfathers in Australian families spent more time alone with their grandchildren and more time baby-sitting along with their spouses than paternal grandfathers did. On the other hand, McGreal (1983) found a significant interaction between grandparent sex and lineage in her study of expectant grandparents. In response to interview items designed to determine their feelings about the grandchild as a vehicle for carrying on the family name and the blood line, maternal grandmothers and paternal grandfathers indicated stronger feelings of biological renewal. In a study of the Iteso tribe of Africa, Nahemow (1984) reported that children of school age felt closest to their paternal grandfathers. Perhaps the determinants of which lineage is important varies with the family structure of the society—namely, whether it has a matrilineal or patrilineal organization.

Age

The match between grandfathers' and grandchildren's age is also important to consider. Since advancing age is positively related to declining health, older grandfathers may be subject to more disease and disability, leaving them less likely to be energetic with their grandchildren. Neugarten and Weinstein (1964) found that older grandparents' styles were more distant and formal in comparison to those of younger grandparents. Moreover, younger grandchildren were judged more appealing to grandparents in studies by Kahana and Kahana (1971) and Clark (1969). Thus the same grandfather may behave very differently with individual grandchildren, depending on his age and health status with respect to each grandchild's age (Hagestad & Speicher, 1981).

Accessibility

Finally, parents often serve as important mediators of the relationship between grandparents and grandchildren; the grandfather's role is at least partially dependent on the extent to which parents make the grandchildren accessible to the grandfather. In effect, parents serve as gatekeepers between children and grandfathers. The parents' attitude concerning the significance of grandparenting for themselves and their child will determine, in large part, a variety of other aspects of the grandfather--grandchild relationship. Robertson (1975) has offered a useful set of dimensions along which this gatekeeping function can be organized: the form of contact, the location of interaction, the types of activities, and the frequency of contact. These factors, in turn, shape the nature of the grandfather--grandchild relationship.

GRANDFATHERS AND INFANTS: A STUDY OF EARLY INVOLVEMENT

Thus the literature, limited though it is, suggests that grandfathers may play a unique role in the lives of children and families. There is, however, very little information about how early this process begins, or what form it initially takes. There has been very little specific investigation of grandfathers' *early* influence in the lives of their grandchildren—how they may interact with and affect the socialization of their grandchildren during the first year of life. Accordingly, we undertook the following study to explore this early relationship and to obtain a greater understanding of grandparents' role in the socialization of their infant grandchildren.

Method

The study compared grandparent--infant and parent--infant interaction patterns in 30 families from a small midwestern metropolitan area (population; 100,000). We observed 30 grandmothers, 21 grandfathers, 30 mothers, and 30 fathers in individual 5-minute dyadic play sessions with 7-month-old infants in the parents' homes. Mothers, approximately half of whom were employed outside the home, ranged in age from 21–34 years (mean = 27). Fathers' ages ranged from 21–37 (mean = 29). Grandmothers' ages ranged from 42–65 years (mean = 53) and grandfathers' ranged from 36–68 (mean = 53).

In 18 families the grandparents were maternal, and in 12 families the grandparents were paternal. One set of grandparents had 34 other grandchildren, while the remaining grandparents had from 0–8. None of the grandparents functioned as daily caregivers for the infants, or lived in the same household with them. However, all grandparents lived within a 50-mile radius of their grandchild's residence. Of the grandmothers in the study, 23 were employed outside the home, and none of the grandmothers or grandfathers considered themselves retired from their careers.

Both parents and grandparents were present for the observation session. We began the visit with a brief description of the project, explaining that the purpose of the study was to understand better the role of grandparents in the lives of young infants. We then instructed each parent and grandparent to play with the infant individually for 5-minute periods, with toys provided by the experimenter. The order of the four adult--infant play sessions was randomly assigned by family.

The toys were presented to the infant on a blanket on the floor, and she or he was allowed one minute to explore them before the observation periods began. Toys included a clear musical ball with plastic animals inside, a rattle with a mirrored side, plastic keys on a ring, and a jack-in-the-box. Infants appeared to be very interested in the toys.

In general, the adults either sat near the infant on the blanket or carried the child around the room with one or two of the toys. For the most part, they seemed relaxed in the observational situation, and they sustained interaction with the infant during that time. During the 5-minute play sessions, we scored 14 categories of adult behaviors and 5 categories of infant behaviors using a 15-second time sampling technique. This required the observers to note during each 15-second interval the occurrence of predesignated behaviors, such as demonstrating with the toy, laughing, or physically restricting (see Table 14.1). We scored each behavior no more than once during a 15-second interval, wearing earplugs connected to a timing device inserted in a clipboard that produced a signal every 15 seconds. Thus, 20 15-second periods of adult–infant play were scored for each adult, making for a total of 80 intervals across four infant–adult pairs.

Immediately following each 5-minute play session, we scored both the adult and the infant global behavior categories (see Table 14.2). Global behavior was scored on a scale of 1 to 7, with 1 reflecting high social acceptability and 7 reflecting low social acceptability within each construct. Reliability between two coders for 40% of the observations, using Cohen's kappa statistic (Fleiss, Cohen, & Everitt, 1969), was .78 for the time sampling codes and .79 for the global codes. To analyze the data, we ran sets of $2 \times 2 \times 2$-way analyses of variance (generation by agent sex by infant sex). For present purposes we will report the results that pertained specifically to grandfathers (see Tinsley & Parke, in press, for a more detailed report of this study).

TABLE 14.1   Adult and Infant Time-Sampling Codes

Adult Codes	Infant Codes
Positive verbalization	Laugh/smile
Imitate verbalization	Vocalize
Laugh/smile	Fuss
Demonstrate/instruct with toy	Grasp/manipulate
Demonstrate/instruct without toy	Touch Caregiver
Rough and tumble play/rock bounce	
Present object	
Check/adjust	
Kiss	
Touch	
Assist	
Physical restrict	
Verbal restrict	
Physical + verbal restrict	

TABLE 14.2　Adult and Infant Global Codes

Adult Codes	Infant Codes
Responsive	Pleasant
Pleasant	Happy
Competent	Cute
Proximal	Hardy
Gentle	Easy
Playful	Predictable
Involved	Inquisitive
Exploratory	Secure
Persistent	Calm
Confident	Coordinated
Warm	Playful
Friendly	Alert
Interested	Attached
Attentive	Cuddly
Active	Consolable
Appropriate	Appealing
Accepting	Smiley
Instrumental	Responsive
Calm	Excitable
Smooth	Attentive
Controlling	
Easy	
Talkative	
Stimulatory	
Affectionate	
Attached	
Imaginative	
Flexible	
Consistent	
Relaxed	

Results

There were few significant differences between grandfathers and grandmothers or between grandfathers and parents on their time-sample behaviors. However, when infants were with their grandfathers, they laughed and smiled less, and fussed more, than when they were with their mothers, fathers, or grandmothers. Analyses of the global category data revealed similar differences between grandfathers and the other adults in terms of infants' behavior. Specifically, infants were rated by observers as being less cute, alert, and excitable when interacting with their grandfathers than with the other adults. Although these patterns suggest that grandfathers may be less competent interactive partners with infants, the many ways in which grandfathers were *similar* to parents and grandmothers in their behavior with infants on all other time sampling and global coding categories suggest that caution is necessary in interpreting these findings.

These effects are qualified by analyses of the impact of adult age. Grandparent age was divided into three categories: Younger (36–49); middle (50–56 for grand-fathers, 50–57 for grandmothers); and older (57–68 for grandfathers, 58–65 for grandmothers). Although there were few differences on the time-sampling behav-iors, there were significant effects for grandfather age on 80% of the global ratings. In general, grandfathers in the middle group were more involved, more playful, and more affectionate compared with both younger and older grandfathers, and infants behaved more positively with middle-group grandfathers than with grandfathers in the other two groups.

In addition, three composite global variables were constructed by combining cat-egories that were highly intercorrelated. The first, Competence, included the items Confident, Smooth, and Accepting. The second, Affect, included Warm, Inter-ested, Attached, Attentive, and Affectionate. The third, Style, included Playful, Responsive, and Stimulatory. Grandfathers in the middle age group were signifi-cantly higher on all three composite variables. In addition, the middle group of grandfathers were more emotionally expressive with male infants than either the youngest or oldest group. These age effects for grandfathers are especially interest-ing because there were few significant adult-age by infant-gender effects for grand-mothers or parents.

Discussion

For both the time-sampling and global behaviors, infants showed more positive be-haviors with their grandmothers, fathers, and mothers than with their grandfathers. These general findings are intuitively sensible: they suggest that infants interact most positively with their most frequent interactive partners. As suggested by the earlier review of the literature, grandmothers typically interact more with the infants than do grandfathers, especially in the caregiving context.

For grandfathers, however, age was a powerful modifier of interactive behavior. On the time-sampling, global, and global composite measures, the middle group of grandfathers (age 50–57) was significantly more active, responsive, and positive with infants than the youngest (age 36–49) and oldest (age 58–68) grandfathers. In addition, the infants themselves behaved more positively and responsively with the middle group of grandfathers. In fact, the positive interactive behavior of the infants and the middle group of grandfathers exceeded that of the mother–infant, father–infant and grandmother–infant pairs both qualitatively and quantitatively for many of the time-sampling and global-coding categories.

Although the n is small, these findings suggest the possibility that there may be an optimal match between grandfather age and grandchild age that offsets the fact that grandfathers have fewer contact opportunities with infants in comparison to those of grandmothers and parents. From a life span developmental perspective, the middle group of grandfathers could be viewed as having been optimally ready for grandparenthood, both physically and psychologically. Unlike the oldest group of grandfathers, they were less likely to be chronically tired, or to have been ill with age-related diseases. And, unlike the youngest grandfathers, they had completed the career-building portion of their lives and were prepared to devote more of their time to family-related endeavors. Moreover, the age of the middle group of grandfathers fits the normative age at which grandparenthood is most often reached; thus for these men, the role of grandfather was more age-appropriate than it was for the youngest and oldest groups of grandfathers. It is not clear why no comparable age-related patterns were revealed for grandmothers. One possible explanation is that the behaviors that contribute to the grandmother repertoire may be less sensitive to age variables, since women at any age appear to be capable of enacting these behaviors.

CONCLUSION AND FUTURE DIRECTIONS

It is clear that grandfathers play a unique and distinctive role in the extended family system. Grandfathers in their fifties can be very lively and enjoyable playmates for their infant grandchildren, sometimes eliciting more response than grandmothers and parents. The data suggest that to consider opposite-sex grandparents as interchangeable is not justifiable, and may, in fact, obscure important differences between grandmothers and grandfathers. A number of issues remain to be explored in future studies. With increasing life expectancy, the potential span of years spent as a grandfather becomes more extensive, and therefore more amenable to analyses of change over time. As reported earlier and illustrated by the present research, age of grandfather is associated with significant behavioral and attitudinal differences (Hagestad & Speicher, 1981; Neugarten & Weinstein, 1964). However, more research is needed on correlates of age, such as shifts in parenting and occupational roles. A grandfather who retires at 55 may have a very different relationship with his grandchildren than a man who stays on the job until age 70 (Troll, 1981).

Another consequence of increased life expectancy is the likelihood that a large number of older men are simultaneously grandfathers and great-grandfathers. According to one estimate (Shanas, 1980), 46% of all grandparents are also great-grandparents. Do men enact grandfather roles differently when they become great-grandfathers? Are there similarities in the styles of grandfathers and great-grandfathers? A more dynamic view of grandfatherhood, which recognizes the changing and multiple roles that men may play during their grandparenting career, would expand our view of men's parenting role in later years (Hagestad & Speicher, 1981).

The impact of social change on grandfathers merits consideration as well. Contemporary shifts in rates of divorce and remarriage will, by definition, yield a variety of new forms of grandparenting—for example, the step-grandparent and the multiple-grandparent family (Furstenberg, 1982; Troll, 1981). Researchers are only beginning to explore the roles and relationships that families develop with these new forms of extended kin.

Shifts in sex roles for contemporary men and women may have an impact on grandfathers as well. To the extent that men are assuming greater responsibility for the caregiving of their infants and young children, grandfathers may, in turn, begin to redefine the range of activities that are appropriate for their role. It will also be interesting to track the impact of heightened levels of child-care participation of current fathers on their future grandparenting behavior. Will these men become more nurturant, caregiving grandfathers than the grandfathers of today, and will grandchildren respond more positively to them? Longitudinal studies of the changing sex-role orientations and behaviors of men within the family context will help elucidate both the role of grandfathers and its impact on family members (Parke & Tinsley, 1984; Tinsley & Parke, 1984).

Another shift which may have implications for grandfathers is the increasing residential segregation of older people in retirement villages and nursing homes. Since many of these living situations are restrictive in terms of child visitors, and many of these new communities are geographically distant from the grandparental place of origin, there may be reduced intergenerational contact. This shift underscores that it is not simply adult children's career-necessitated mobility that affects contact between grandparents and grandchildren, but grandparents' mobility as well.

An understudied issue is the impact of grandparenthood on the grandparent's own development (Kivnick, 1982). Short-term longitudinal studies of the transition to grandparenthood would help answer questions about whether, for example, grandfathers and grandmothers react in similar ways to their new status. Does the impact vary with their current work status? Perhaps retired grandfathers experience grandparenthood with more enthusiasm than men who are still at work.

Clearly, there is no "average" grandfather. As with parental roles, we need to recognize the variation and diversity that characterize the ways in which the grandfather role is enacted, both within and across cultures. Better classification schemes for capturing this diversity are still needed. In addition, cross-cultural comparisons can help determine the effects of the culture in shaping the grandfather's role, and discover what, if any, universals there may be. The ways in which the grandfather's role is expressed, and the impact of the grandfather on both his adult children and his grandchildren, are only beginning to be understood. Systematic description and evaluation of that role and its impact within the family system are essential for a more complete model of family functioning.

REFERENCES

Abrahams, B., Feldman, S.S., & Nash, S.C. (1978). Sex role self-concept and sex role attitudes: Enduring personality characteristics or adaptations to changing life situations? *Developmental Psychology, 14*, 393–400.

Aldous, J. (1985). Parent-adult child relations as affected by the grandparent status. In V.L. Bengston & J.F. Robertson (Eds.), *Grandparenthood*. Beverly Hills, CA: Sage.

Asher, S.R., & Gottman, J.M. (Eds.). (1981). *The development of children's friendships*. Cambridge, MA: Cambridge University Press.

Atchley, R. (1980). *Social forces in later life*. Belmont, CA: Wadsworth.

Baranowski, M.D. (1985). Men as grandfathers. In S.M.H. Hanson & F.W. Bozett (Eds.), *Dimensions of fatherhood*. Beverly Hills, CA: Sage.

Cath, S.H. (1982). Vicissitudes of grandfatherhood: A miracle of revitalization? In S.H.

Cath, A.R. Gurwitt, & J.M. Ross (Eds.), *Father and child: Developmental and clinical perspectives*. Boston, MA: Little, Brown.

Cavan, R.S. (1962). Self and role adjustment during old age. In A.M. Rose (Ed.), *Human behavior and social process: An interactional approach*. Boston, MA: Houghton Mifflin.

Cherlin, A., & Furstenberg, F.F. (1985). Styles and strategies of grandparenting. In V.L. Bengston & J.F. Robertson (Eds.), *Grandparenthood*. Beverly Hills, CA: Sage.

Clark, M. (1969). Cultural values and dependency in later life. In R. Kalish (Ed.), *Dependencies of Old People*. Ann Arbor, MI: University of Michigan Institute of Gerontology.

Clavan, S. (1978). The impact of social class and social trends on the role of the grandparent. *Family Coordinator, 27*, 351–357.

Dunn, J., & Kendrick, C. (1982). *Siblings*. Cambridge, MA: Harvard University Press.

Feinman, S., & Roberts, D. (1985, April). *Infants' interaction with grandparents, relatives, and adult friends of the family*. Paper presented at the biennial meeting of the Society for Research in Child Development, Toronto.

Feldman, S.S., & Nash, S.C. (1978). Interest in babies during young adulthood. *Child Development, 49*, 617–622.

Feldman, S.S., & Nash, S.C. (1979). Sex differences in responsiveness to babies among mature adults. *Developmental Psychology, 15*, 430–436.

Feldman, S.S., Biringen, Z.C., & Nash, S.C. (1981). Fluctuations of sex-related self-attributions as a function of stage of family life cycle. *Developmental Psychology, 17*, 24–35.

Feldman, S.S., Nash, S.C., & Cutrona, C. (1977). The influence of age and sex on responsiveness to babies. *Developmental Psychology, 13*, 675–676.

Fleiss, J.L., Cohen, J., & Everitt, B.S. (1969). Large sample standard errors of Kappa and weighted Kappa. *Psychological Bulletin, 72*, 323–327.

Furstenberg, F.F. (1982). Remarriage and intergenerational relations. In R. Fogel, E. Hatfield, S. Kiesler, & J. March (Eds.), *Aging: Stability and Change in the Family*. New York: Academic.

Gilford, R., & Black, D. (1972, November). *The grandchild-grandparent dyad: Ritual or relationship?* Paper presented at the 25th Annual Meeting of the Gerontological Society, San Juan, Puerto Rico.

Glick, P.C. (1979). The future of the American family. *Current Population Reports*, Series P-23, No. 78.

Gutmann, D.L. (1985). The parental imperative revisited: Towards a developmental psychology of adulthood and later life. *Contributions to Human Development, 14*, 31–60.

Hagestad, G. (1978, August). *Patterns of communication and influence between grandparents and grandchildren in a changing society*. Paper presented at the World Congress of Sociology, Sweden.

Hagestad, G.O. (1982). Parent and child: Generations in the family. In T.M. Field, A. Huston, H.C. Quay, L. Troll, & G.E. Finley (Eds.), *Review of Human Development*. New York: Wiley.

Hagestad, G.O., & Speicher, J.L. (1981, April). *Grandparents and family influence: Views of three generations*. Paper presented at the biennial meeting of the Society for Research in Child Development, Boston.

Hareven, T.K. (1977). Family time and historical time. *Daedalus, 106*, 57–70.

Hartshorne, T.S., & Manaster, G.J. (1982). The relationship with grandparents: Contact, importance, role conception. *International Journal of Aging and Human Development, 15,* 233–245.

Hoffman, E. (1979). Young adults' relations with their grandparents: An exploratory study. *International Journal of Aging and Human Development, 10,* 299–310

Kahana, B., & Kahana, E. (1970). Grandparenthood from the perspective of the developing grandchild. *Developmental Psychology 3,* 98–105.

Kahana, E., & Kahana, B. (1971). Theoretical and research perspectives on grandparenthood. *Journal of Aging and Human Development, 2,*261–268.

Kivnick, H.Q. (1982). *The meaning of grandparenthood.* Ann Arbor, MI: UMI Research Press.

Kornhaber, A., & Woodward, K.L. (1981). *Grandparents/Grandchild: The vital connection.* Garden City, NY: Anchor Press.

Lamb, M.E. (Ed.). (1981). *The role of the father in child development* (2nd ed.). New York: Wiley.

Lewis, M., & Feiring, C. (1981). Direct and indirect interactions in social relationships. In L. Lipsett (Ed.), *Advances in Infancy Research* (Vol. 1). New York: Ablex.

Litwak, E., & Szeleniji, I. (1969). Primary group structures and their functions: Kin, neighbors, and friends. *American Sociological Review, 34,* 465–481.

McGreal, C.E. (1983, November). *Grandparenthood as a symbol: Expectations for the grandparental role.* Paper presented at the Gerontological Society of America, San Francisco.

McGreal, C.E. (1984, August). *Grandparental role meaning types.* Paper presented at the American Psychological Association, Toronto.

McGreal, C.E. (1985, April). *The grandparent-grandchild relationship during the neonatal period.* Paper presented at the biennial meeting of the Society for Research in Child Development, Toronto.

Nahemow, N.R. (1984). Grandparenthood in transition. In K.A. McCluskey & H.W. Reese (Eds.), *Life-span developmental psychology: Historical and generational effects.* New York: Academic.

Neugarten, B.L., & Gutmann, D.L. (1968). Age-sex roles and personality in middle age: A thematic apperception study. In B.L. Neugarten (Ed.), *Personality in middle and late life: Empirical studies.* New York: Atherton.

Neugarten, B.L., & Moore, J.W. (1968). The changing age status systems. In B.L. Neugarten (Ed.), *Middle Age and Aging.* Chicago, IL: University of Chicago Press.

Neugarten, B.L., & Weinstein, K.K. (1964). The changing American grandparent. *Journal of Marriage and the Family, 26,* 199–204.

Parke, R.D. (1979). Father-infant interaction. In J. Osofsky (Ed.), *Handbook of Infancy.* New York: Wiley.

Parke, R.D. (1981). *Fathers.* Cambridge, MA: Harvard University Press.

Parke, R.D., Power, T.G., & Gottman, J.M. (1979). Conceptualizing and quantifying influence patterns in the family triad. In M.E. Lamb, S.J. Suomi, & G.R. Stephenson (Eds.), *Social interaction analysis: Methodological issues.* Madison, WI: University of Wisconsin Press.

Parke, R.D., & Tinsley, B.R. (1981). The father's role in infancy: Determinants of involvement in caregiving and play. In M.E. Lamb (Ed.), *The Role of the Father in Child Development* (2nd ed.). New York: Wiley.

Parke, R.D., & Tinsley, B.R. (1984). Fatherhood: Historical and contemporary perspectives. In K.A. McCluskey & H.W. Reese (Ed.), *Life-Span Developmental Psychology: Historical and Generational Effects*. New York: Academic.

Riegel, K.R., Riegel, R.M., & Meyer, G.A. (1967). Study of the drop-out rates in longitudinal research on aging and the prediction of death. *Journal of Personality and Social Psychology, 5*, 342–348.

Robertson, J.F. (1975). Interaction in three generation families, parents as mediators: Toward a theoretical perspective. *International Journal of Aging and Human Development, 6*, 103–110.

Russell, G. (1985). Grandfathers: Making up for lost opportunities. In R.A. Lewis & R.E. Salt (Eds.), *Men in Families*. Beverly Hills, CA: Sage.

Shanas, E. (1979). Social myth as hypothesis: The case of the family relations of old people. *Gerontologist, 19*, 3–9.

Shanas, E. (1980). Older people and their families: The new pioneers. *Journal of Marriage and the Family, 42*, 9–15.

Tinsley, B.R., & Parke, R.D. (in press). Grandparents as interactive and social support agents for families with young infants. *International Journal of Aging and Human Development*.

Tinsley, B.R., & Parke, R.D. (1984). Grandparents as support and socialization agents. In M. Lewis (Ed.), *Beyond the Dyad*. New York: Plenum.

Troll, L.E. (1971). The family of later life: A decade review. *Journal of Marriage and the Family, 33*, 263–290.

Troll, L.E. (1979, August). *Grandparenting*. Paper presented at American Psychological Association, New York.

Troll, L.E. (1981). In L.W. Poon (Ed.), *Aging in the 1980's: Psychological Issues*. New York: American Psychological Association.

Troll, L.E., Miller, S.J., & Atchley, R.C. (1979). *Families in Later Life*. Belmont, CA: Wadsworth.

PART 4

Prevention and Intervention Programs for Men and Boys

CHAPTER 15

Education for Fatherhood

RONALD F. LEVANT

THE CHALLENGE FOR MEN IN THE 1980s

Up from Ozzie: Recent Changes in the Father's Role

Many men today can look back to their childhood and see Ozzie Nelson as one role model for fathering. Then there was Ward Cleaver, who always wore a tie and knew just the right thing to say to the Beaver. And of course Robert Young (before becoming Dr. Welby) was the father who knew best. Back in the 1950s, everyone had a gender-specific role to fill. Parenting children was a woman's domain, and fathers often missed the opportunity to have intimate relationships with their children.

Now both Ozzie and Ward are dead, and Robert Young was last seen selling coffee. The Beaver himself is a confused single parent on the Disney Channel. There have indeed been radical changes in the structure of the American family. Family roles are not clearly defined. Fathers are told they must work at communicating with their children, must develop new sensitivities, and must expand their notion of parenting. Ozzie never said anything about this.

It's not easy to see all of these changes in perspective. They include the development of more effective birth control methods in the late 1950s, followed by an explosion in the divorce rate beginning in the mid-1960s, and then the sharp increase in the employment of women in the 1970s. The most recent trend has been a restructuring of the father's role. Heralded in the popular 1979 film *Kramer vs. Kramer*, the initial focus was on fathers gaining custody of their children in an era in which women were vigorously challenging the "motherhood mandate." Dustin Hoffman portrayed with poignancy the struggles that some men were beginning to go through, as they confronted their limitations in such areas as maintaining a home and relating to their children, and as they made some painfully difficult choices regarding their careers.

Today, a brief eight years later, major changes are taking place. With regard to divorce and custody, mother custody is no longer the rule, and joint custody has become a frequent option. And there has been a rise in father custody.

With regard to intact families, a number of changes have occurred. Pleck's (1977) model for the "work-family role system" describes the reciprocal relationships between husbands' and wives' paid work. As wives increase their paid work, a reduction in their family work is required to avoid role overload, and a corresponding increase in husbands' family work is required to pick up the slack. In the middle and later 1960s, large-scale time budget studies indicated that husbands' participation in family work (both child care and housework) was quite low (1.0–1.6 hours/day) compared to that of their wives (7.6–8.0 hours/day for housewives and 4.0–5.3 hours/day for employed wives), and that husbands tended to increase their participation only slightly, if at all, in response to their wives employment (Robinson, 1977; Walker & Woods, 1976). By the middle 1970s, husbands' and wives' levels of time expenditure in family roles were found to be converging: husbands were spending more time (3.3 hours/day when their wives stayed at home, and 3.9 hours/day when their wives worked) and wives were spending less time (6.8 hours/day for housewives, and 4 hours/day for working wives) (Pleck, 1981a, 1981b).

There are several implications of these changes in time-use patterns. First, they reflect a greater degree of equity in men's and women's family and work roles. Although it may be that both men and women are now experiencing more role overload, women in general experience less role overload than previously relative to their husbands. Second, they reflect the increased level of men's psychological involvement with their families.

In the past it has been assumed that men's traditionally low level of participation in family work reflected a low degree of psychological involvement with their families. However, there are data that indicate that men's family roles are more significant psychologically than their paid work roles (Pleck, 1981b). These data include men's self-ratings of their psychological involvement in family and work (Erskine, 1973; Lein, Durham, Pratt, Schudson, Thomas, & Weiss, 1974; Pleck & Lang, 1978), and of the relative contributions of family and work experience to their sense of well-being (Andrews & Withey, 1976; Pleck & Lang, 1978).

This trend (that men experience their family role as more psychologically significant than their work role) is so far-reaching that its ramifying effects have yet to be fully appraised. In the family this trend is reflected in the current media attention devoted to the "new father," and is manifested in such life styles as shared-parenting and house husbanding. In the work place the effects are seen in such phenomena as:

Resistance to relocation. Employees on management tracks are increasingly refusing to relocate, citing family stability and rootedness as the reason.

Demands for child-care services. Initially a banner of the Women's Movement, this phenomenon came into being with the dramatic increase in women's employment. Currently, this is increasingly a concern of single and married fathers as well.

Paternity leave. A totally new concept, reflecting the importance that men place on being with their families during and shortly after the birth of their child.

Innovations in job design, including flexi-time, flexi-place, and job-sharing.[1]

---

[1]For further discussion of these trends, see Chapter 18, Catalyst, this volume.

Thus a growing number of men today are involved in reshaping their roles as fathers. They are doing so in most cases without the advantage of adequate role models, for our fathers were surely cut out of a different cloth.

Preparing the Next Generation for Fatherhood

To what extent will fathers today be adequate role models for their children? Beyond that, to what extent will we adequately prepare our children for the world of tomorrow?

Imbedded in these questions is a very crucial issue. Traditionally, fathers have served as gate-keepers of sorts. The research evidence indicates that traditional fathers have a potent influence on the sex-role socialization of both their sons and their daughters, and that fathers tend to reinforce sex role stereotypes of masculinity in their sons and femininity in their daughters (Block, 1979; Langlois & Downs, 1980; Osofsky & O'Connell, 1972; Radin, 1976).[2] A rather revealing portrait appeared in *Family Circle* magazine in 1979, in a story titled "Daddy's Home." As Daddy pulled into the driveway, his three children ran out to greet him. After hugging and kissing his two daughters, his son Jimmy wanted to be hugged and kissed. Daddy replied: "No, Jim, I hug and kiss all the girls. I shake hands with the men." Jimmy gets reorganized and offers a stiff, manly little hand to shake. (Baxter, 1979).

The available literature suggests that fathers traditionally have tended to encourage friendliness and interpersonal skills in interacting with daughters, while discouraging independence and task mastery. By the same token, fathers have traditionally tended to encourage their son's independence and task mastery, while discouraging their nurturance and emotional expressivity. This set of socialization behaviors is becoming dysfunctional in contemporary American society, as women increasingly enter the work force or adopt careers, and as men reexamine their views on masculinity, and think through alternative options for role behavior (Fasteau, 1975; Pleck, 1981c).

An unusually large challenge faces the current generation of fathers. First, it is now expected that fathers will learn a new role, one that departs radically from the role of their fathers, and one that involves skills such as sensitivity to children, nurturance, expressivity, and child management—skills that cannot be assumed to be part of men's existing repertoire. Traditionally, men have not been prepared for an extensive role in parenting, either through family socialization or formal education (Hill & Aldous, 1969). This lack of preparation poses difficulties for many men, which have been highlighted in recent popular and professional examinations of fathering after marital separation (Jaffrey, 1979; Keshet & Rosenthal, 1978). When there are no crises forcing them to develop an active parenting role, many men have chosen to stick to the traditional pattern (Eversoll, 1979), despite the fact that such a stance conflicts with contemporary social realities such as working

---

[2]For a more extensive discussion of this process, see Chapter 8, Bronstein on gender-role socialization, this volume.

mothers and greater acceptance of involved fathers (Hoffman, 1977), or with their idealized self-image (Anderson, 1977). Price-Bonham and Skeen (1979) have suggested that "fathers may be spending great amounts of time in their work role in order to avoid responsibilities of the father role because they lack the knowledge/skills to be comfortable in the role" (p. 58). A similar view has been put forth by Sawin and Parke (1979).

Second, in its fullest expression, the new father role is an ultimate act of pioneering, because not only must fathers learn to be different from their fathers, but they must also prepare the next generation to be different in the same way. A multigenerational transformational leap is thus required—one that involves not only conscious attitudes and behaviors, but also the deeper-lying, implicit, gut-level assumptions about what is appropriate for boys and what is appropriate for girls. Can girls be aggressive and competitive and at times self-absorbed and unfriendly? Can boys play with dolls and cook and bake and baby sit?

Clearly this second level of change is much more difficult than the first, and this difficulty shows up in studies such as Radin's (1982), where fathers who enacted nontraditional roles (such as role-sharing or house husbanding) still seemed to hold traditional assumptions about appropriate sex roles for their children. Thus although societal changes are pushing men in the direction of greater parenting involvement, other forces can help shape the extent and nature of that involvement, and the satisfaction men and their families derive from it. One such force is fatherhood education—the providing of parenting knowledge and training to males at various stages in the life cycle.

This chapter will describe some of the fatherhood educational programs that are currently emerging as needed instruments of change within the more general area of parenting education, programs that are tailored to fit the special needs and goals of present and future male parents.

EDUCATION FOR FATHERHOOD

Parent Education: General Background

Parent education has been defined as "purposive learning activity of parents who are attempting to change their method of interaction with their children for the purpose of encouraging positive behavior in their children" (Croake & Glover, 1977, p. 151). The first recorded parent education group in the United States was formed in 1815. Several such groups, or "maternal associations" were soon developed for the purpose of encouraging mothers to discuss their child-rearing concerns and promote the moral and religious development of their children. In 1888 the organization now known as the Child Study Association of America was founded and began to sponsor ongoing parent education groups (Croake & Glover, 1977).

By the middle of the twentieth century the parent education groups sponsored by the Child Study Association were based on Freudian psychology (especially the work of Anna Freud) and on child development research, such as was being conducted at the Gesell Institute (Cable, 1975). It was assumed that parental motives, thoughts, and feelings were more important than overt behavior (Brim, 1965), and these assumptions were reflected in the structure and format of the programs. The programs utilized a discussion group format in which the parents developed the agenda based on their interests and problems, and in which the group leaders attempted to provide support and advice (Auerbach, 1968). While these discussion groups varied in terms of the size of the group, the homogeneity of its members, and the length and number of meetings, they shared the following goals for parents: to be more loving and accepting of their children; to understand child development and the causes of children's behavior; to understand the effect of parents' behavior on children; to develop problem-solving skills; and to feel relaxed, secure, and natural in their parenting (Brim, 1965).

Pre-Parent Programs.

Pre-parent programs provide information on parenting for young people, in preparation for roles they are likely to assume some time in the future. Such programs have been developed by family life educators, and may be offered as part of an elementary, high school, or college curriculum. The Exploring Childhood curriculum, developed by the Educational Development Center (1977) in Cambridge, Massachusetts, is one of the better known programs. Designed for high school students, it integrates didactic instruction in child development with practical experiences in child care. An extensive evaluation of this program found gains in knowledge, attitudes, and behavior in child care, but many questions remain (Educational Development Center, 1976). In particular, de Lissovoy (1978) pointed out that such short-term gains do not ensure long-term preparation for parenthood. However, parts of the program (specifically, experiences in child care) might well prove to be relevant and important ways to help develop nurturance and expressivity in boys, as building blocks for their later parental roles.

New-Parent Programs.

New-parent programs consist of various forms of childbirth education classes offered in many local communities through prenatal clinics, maternity hospitals, the Red Cross, and the Childbirth Education Association. Usually led by nurses, a course typically includes information on the health needs of pregnant women, labor and delivery, and the care of the newborn infant. These classes are designed to help prepare women for the birth process. Whether or not they go beyond this, to help prospective parents cope with the developmental transition to parenthood, depends on the skills and awareness of the instructor. Prepared childbirth classes, especially the Lamaze Method (Bing, 1969), provide more systematic attention to the psychological needs of parents-to-be, helping them to come to terms with fears and anxieties, and to develop a concept of themselves as parents.

Child-Rearing Programs.

Child-rearing programs are those which are most commonly thought of as parent education, and which grew out of the initial discussion group approach discussed earlier.

In 1974 Tavormina reviewed the discussion group approach to parent education, and the research evaluating it. The initial evaluations, which ranged from parent testimonials and clinician's judgments to measures of change in self-reported parental attitudes, frequently found that changes in parent attitudes were not consistently associated with changes in children's behavior. (Friedman, 1969; Stearn, 1971; Swenson, 1970). And although Hereford's (1963) 4-year study reported changes in parent attitudes as a result of discussion groups, his results were not replicated in subsequent research. Furthermore, Chilman's (1973) review of parent education programs indicated that most discussion group programs failed to attract and hold many parents, especially those from a lower socioeconomic level. In a later review article, Tavormina (1980) criticized the discussion group approach to parent education for its lack of specificity, and pointed to the more recently developed didactic/-discussion and skills-training programs as the direction for the future.

Didactic/discussion groups differ from discussion groups in that more time is spent in a structured presentation of didactic material. The original didactic/-discussion groups were either Adlerian Parent Study groups or Ginott's parent groups. In the Adlerian group, parents read Dreikurs and Soltz's (1964) text, *Children: The Challenge*, from which they learned that children's misbehavior results from a sense of discouragement about being able to find a place in the family. They also learned to replace the authoritarian discipline techniques of reward and punishment with the democratic techniques of natural and logical consequences. Ginott's (1957) approach blended humanistic and psychodynamic concepts, and emphasized the importance of empathy and acceptance for interpersonal learning, for both parents and children. Recently, a spate of new didactic/discussion groups have appeared, and are described in several new texts and handbooks on parent education (Abidin, 1980; Arnold, 1978a; Fine, 1980; Lamb & Lamb, 1978). These new programs include a number of single-theory models, developed from systems theory (Arnold, 1978b; Benson, Berger & Mease, 1975), transactional analysis (James & James, 1978; Lamb & Lamb, 1978; and Sirridge, 1980), rational emotive therapy (Ellis, 1978; Lamb & Lamb, 1978), and reality therapy (Lamb & Lamb, 1978; McGuiness & Glasser, 1978). Numerous eclectic programs have also been developed, including: Developing the Productive Child (Gilmore & Gilmore, 1978); Becoming Us (Carnes & Laube, 1975); the Solution Oriented Approach to Problems, or SOAP Program (Lamb & Lamb, 1978); and Parenting Skills (Abidin, 1976). These didactic/discussion programs are for the most part fairly new; many have not yet developed a set of teaching materials or techniques, and most have not yet been evaluated. Three programs, by Benson and colleagues (1975), Gilmore and Gilmore (1978), and Abidin (1976), have been evaluated, and some empirical support for their effectiveness has been found.

Skills-training programs are available from a number of different theoretical perspectives. The client-centered programs include Parent Effectiveness Training (Gordon, 1970), Relationship Enhancement (Guerney, 1977), the Human Resource Development Program (Carkhuff & Bierman, 1970), and the Personal Developmental Program (Levant & Doyle, 1983). Behavioral Parent Training represents the behavioral approach, and Systematic Training for Effective Parenting (Dinkmeyer & McKay, 1976) represents an Adlerian approach. The various skills-training programs, while based on different theoretical foundations, share certain common elements, particularly the use of behavioral rehearsal as a skill-building technique. Whether through in-class role plays or out-of-class homework assignments, the emphasis is on participants trying out new behaviors in order to develop ease and effectiveness in relating to their children. Feedback is often given, either through group observation and discussion or video playback, which enables participants to refine their skills through a process of successive approximation. Considerable evaluative research on the skills-training programs has been done, and empirical support exists for the behavioral programs (Graziano, 1986) and the client-centered programs (Levant, 1986). More research is needed on the Adlerian model (Croake, 1983).

Educational Programs: A Focus on Fathering

Until very recently, parent education for fathers has been a badly neglected area. First, most popular parenting books endorse the traditional roles of father as breadwinner/chief disciplinarian and mother as nurturant caregiver. De Frain (1977), evaluating 53 popular parenting books on the market in the early 1970s, found only two that discussed the issue of "who shall bear the direct responsibility of rearing children" (p. 245). De Frain concluded that the vast majority of popular books explicitly or implicitly endorse sex-role stereotypes of parenthood. Cordell, Parke, and Sawin's (1980) finding that relatively few of the fathers in their study utilized the popular parenting literature becomes more understandable in this light; fathers are not likely to turn to books that do not in some way endorse their role as involved parents.

Second, parent education courses have, until quite recently, almost completely ignored fathers. A search of the reviews of the literature on parent education and training (Berkowitz & Graziano, 1972; Bernal & North, 1978; Croake & Glover, 1977; Johnson & Katz, 1973; O'Dell, 1974; Reisinger, Ora & Frangia, 1976; Tavormina, 1974) found not one study which focused on the training of fathers, or even indicated whether the "parent" group included fathers (Loiselle, 1980). Eversoll (1979) noted the lack of attention to the father's role in college-level parent education courses. Price-Bonham and Skeen (1979) interviewed 100 White and 60 Black fathers with regard to their perceptions and enactment of the father role, and found numerous signs indicating a great need for increased parent education for both groups. Among the signs were fathers' statements that they have discovered that fatherhood is a bigger job than they expected, that there is little to guide them in this role, and that they most often have relied on trial and error. In addition, the researchers found that there was an intergenerational transfer (often inappropriate) of discipline techniques learned in the families of origin.

In the past few years, this picture has begun to change. Attention to the father's role has become evident in all three fields of parent education—pre-parent programs, new-parent programs, and child-rearing programs. A number of these programs have been catalogued in the book *Fatherhood USA* (Klinman & Kohl, 1984), and some evaluative research studies have appeared in the literature.

Pre-Parent Programs.

Programs for boys and men are appearing in the traditional area of family-life education, which provides education for parenthood for young adults. In addition, there are two newer types of programs: child care classes for school-aged boys, and programs that encourage adult male involvement in the school setting.

Among the usual family-life education courses on the college and university level, courses designed specifically for fathers have begun to appear. Several are described in *Fatherhood USA* (Klinman & Kohl, 1984), and they show considerable variation. "Fatherhood: The Parental Role" is a semester course taught in the Department of Home Economics at the University of Akron, and is closest to the traditional model. Taught by a female instructor to an audience of young males, most of whom are not yet fathers, the course is largely didactic, and covers such topics as historical change in the father's role, the cultural impact of changing gender roles, and parent–child interaction; however students do learn some techniques for building positive parent–child relationships. On the other hand "Fathering in the 80's," at Napa Valley College in California, is taught by a male instructor to an audience of mostly new fathers, and provides information and support for men who are attempting to develop a nontraditional paternal role. Finally, some courses are tailored to the ethnicity of their students, such as "Child Development from a Male Perspective," which serves a largely Mexican-American population at Los Medanos Community College in California.

The concept of child-care classes for school-aged boys is based on the Exploring Childhood program described earlier. This concept has generated a lot of enthusiasm among educators but little commitment of financial resources, according to Klinman and Kohl (1984), who found few examples of this type of program. All were in private schools, and like the Exploring Childhood program, most were coeducational. However, several of those located use a variety of strategies to emphasize the value of nurturance for boys. For example, "Baby Care Training" offered to boys and girls (aged 10–14) at a nursery school, encourages the participation of boys through such strategies as involving adult males as guest lecturers (e.g., having a male firefighter teach safety and first aid). The course meets for eight weeks, during which the youngsters get one hour of course work and one hour of hands-on experience with feeding, comforting, diapering, and getting babies ready for naps. The course also includes practical information on how to become a "professional baby-sitter." In contrast, other programs have sought to encourage the participation of boys by offering the course only to them (at least initially), such as the after-school program at the Bank Street College of Education, and an "Infant Care Class for Boys" offered in a middle school in New York.

The third type of program focuses on the involvement of adult males in the school setting at the preschool and elementary levels. The purpose of such programs is to balance the preponderant presence of females as teachers in the early and middle childhood years, in order to provide children with the opportunity to interact with adult males (and vice versa), and to breakdown the sex-role stereotypes that exclude men from nurturant roles. Price-Bonham and Skeen (1979) have called attention to this need:

> School should be a place in which fathers are encouraged to observe and participate in their children's learning experiences. Fathers could be invited to talk about and/or demonstrate their work. . . . However, fathers should also be encouraged to engage in . . . "cuddly" and "fun" activities. If fathers are confined to "work related" activities, the instrumental role of males is reinforced while opportunities to practice nurturing are lost. (p. 58)

Klinman and Kohl (1984) have catalogued eight such programs, which include such efforts as hiring male teachers, inviting fathers to classes, and including fathers in home visits and parent-teacher conferences. They also have provided a set of "practical tips for encouraging father involvement in the schools" (pp. 59–61).

New-Parent Programs.

An indication of the increasing recognition of the father's role in the family is the development of education programs for new fathers. There are three types of such programs. The first involves the inclusion of fathers in traditional childbirth education classes. The second type extends through the preschool years, and involves fathers and their children in various activities. The third focuses on the growing number of teenage fathers, and aims at supporting the teenager's relationship to his young family.

It could be said that the "era of paternal re-discovery" (Lamb, 1979, p. 38) began with a reexamination of the father's role in infancy. After reviewing the cross-cultural, historical, comparative, and biological evidence, Parke and Sawin (1976) concluded that the father can certainly play an active and important role in infant development, and thus launched their participation in a large and growing literature on fathers and infants. It is probably no accident that there has been a major change in the role of the expectant father. This change was described by Klinman and Kohl (1984) as follows:

> No longer content to pace the hospital corridors during labor and delivery and then distribute self-congratulatory cigars, today's father is very likely to be an active participant in the birth of his children. In fact, a recent Gallup poll indicates that 80% of husbands are in the delivery room with their wives, up from just 27% about a decade ago. (p. 3)

Most hospitals and maternity centers now offer childbirth education courses to both expectant parents. Though the majority of these programs regard the father's role as supportive to the mother during the pregnancy and birth process, a growing number also attend to the developmental transition of the men themselves. Klinman and Kohl (1984) describe 25 such programs operating across the country; in addition, reports of such programs have begun to appear in the professional literature. Gregory (1981) described her experiences in setting up and running an expectant fathers' class in a village on the east coast of England. Barnhill, Rubenstein, and Rocklin (1979) described a one-session workshop developed for expectant fathers, which was offered as part of a prepared childbirth program for couples. The workshop, which was designed to ease fathers' transition to parenthood and to support their involvement with their children, provided expectant fathers with an opportunity to discuss stressful experiences during their wife's pregnancy, such as her morning sickness or crying episodes. Gearing (1978) described a more elaborate three-stage program, which included group sessions before, during, and after the birth of the first child. The first stage of the program focused on reducing the fathers' anxieties related to their wives' pregnancies, and on helping fathers develop concepts of their paternal roles. In addition, couples were advised to develop plans to spend time alone with each other after the baby was born. The second stage involved the actual process of birth, and encouraged fathers to remain with their wives during labor and delivery. Rooming-in, with the father staying overnight and sharing child care from the beginning, was described as optimal. The third stage consisted of group sessions on a less frequent basis, which served to support the father in his new role. Resnick, Resnick, Packer, and Wilson (1978) have developed a similar psycho-educational program for expectant and new fathers. The expectant fathers program is similar to Gearing's first stage, in which fathers discuss a variety of concerns and anxieties. For example, one father discussed his wife's plans to breast-feed in public, and worked through his feelings of disgust and anger. The new father program occurs after the birth, and fathers attend together with their infants. In the first half of each class, fathers and infants participate in structured exercises designed to establish a good relationship. In the second half, the men discuss their experiences as new fathers and receive support from the group, in a process similar to Gearing's third stage.

Preparation for fatherhood would seem to be an important activity. The available research literature indicates that developing a coherent father role (a pattern of behavior that meets fathers' needs and the needs of their wives and babies) is important for men's postpartum adjustment (Fein, 1976), and that father's lack of knowledge about parenting is predictive of high postpartum adjustment difficulty (Wente & Crockenberg, 1976). However, whether expectant father education is effective in facilitating postpartum adjustment has yet to be shown. The available research in this area is limited to evaluations of the effects of such prenatal interventions on fathers' behavior immediately after the baby's birth. For example, Miller and Bowen (1982) found that while fathers' presence during delivery increased certain attachment-type behaviors (visually inspecting and talking to their newborns), fathers' attendance at prenatal classes was not associated with any of the father behaviors observed.

The second type of new-parent program involves a continuation through the preschool years. For example, the psycho-educational program developed by Resnick and colleagues (1978) includes four sequential classes: "Your new baby and you" (birth to 6 months); "Your infant and you" (6–12 months); "Your toddler and you" (12–24 months); and "Your young child and you" (24–36 months). The classes, which are attended by both parents with their children, include a mixture of activities and discussion, a toy lending library, and consultation from nurses, nutrition-ists, pediatricians, home economists, and psychologists. Offered through university continuing education programs, the public school system, community mental health agencies, and health care clinics, the program has drawn its class members from several racial and socioeconomic groups. A similar program offered through com-munity colleges has been described by Charnley and Myre (1977).

As with prenatal classes, evaluative research has been very limited. Packer, Resnick, Resnick and Wilson (1978) reported that their psycho-educational pro-gram resulted in an enhancement of parents' ability to handle stress, as assessed by the Rosenweig Picture Frustration tests. Dickie and Gerber (1980) evaluated the ef-fects of a parent-training program designed to increase parental competence in re-sponding to their infants. Training was found to increase both parents' competence in the parent infant triad; an unexpected finding was that training induced fathers to take a more active role and mothers to take a less active role.

The third type of new-parent program focuses on teenage fathers, most of whom are unmarried. Recent research has helped correct the stereotyped view of the teen-age father as an irresponsible and uncaring person who absents himself from his family (Barret & Robinson, 1981; Pannor, Massarik, & Evans, 1971). Reports from innovative outreach programs indicate that the unwed teen father welcomes the op-portunity to talk about the situation, and has few available outlets for such discus-sion (Johnson, 1978). In recent years, educational and counseling programs for unwed teen fathers have been developed. Klinman and Kohl (1984) describe 15 such programs, eight of which are affiliated with the Ford Foundation funded Teen Father Collaboration Project, sponsored by the Bank Street College of Education (Langway, 1983). This latter effort links local agencies of various types, which of-fer a range of services to a diverse population. Services offered include individual and couples counseling, new-parent education, home visits, discussion groups, health care, and educational and vocational counseling. The latter service is key in interrupting the familiar pattern wherein the teen father compounds his first mistake (getting his girlfriend pregnant) with a second: dropping out of school and heading directly for a low paying job. An evaluation is in process in order to generate guide-lines and recommendations for more far-reaching efforts to serve this neglected population.

Child-Rearing Programs.

Equally encouraging is the growth of programs for fathers of older children and ado-lescents which have recently been developed, and in some cases evaluated. The pro-grams include discussion groups, didactic/discussion programs, and skills-training programs.

Discussion groups have been developed for fathers in general, single fathers, and stepfathers. On the whole, however, groups for fathers have been slow to develop and hard to keep going, largely because the very format of such groups conflicts with aspects of the male role: Men do not easily seek support or freely express their feelings. Nevertheless, such groups have emerged, sponsored formally by parent centers reaching out to fathers, and informally by groups of fathers themselves. Of these groups, those which have most often met with success have involved single fathers. Reasons for this include the severe stress associated with divorce, the increasing permission given to men to seek support, and discrimination against fathers in custody disputes (Hetherington, Cox, & Cox, 1976; Keshet & Rosenthal, 1978; Mendes, 1976; Orthner, Brown, & Ferguson, 1976; Woody, 1978).

As with parent education in general, didactic/discussion programs have been developed for fathers, and research reports have begun to appear in the literature. These programs combine discussion with didactic input. Most are atheoretical, although one program based on transactional analysis has been reported (Bredehoft & Clarke, 1982). This program ("Self-esteem: A Family Affair") was evaluated in a design which assessed both the effects of the program as compared to no treatment, and the effects of variations in attendance patterns (mothers only; mothers and fathers; mothers, fathers and adolescent child). Fathers who participated in the program showed gains in both adaptability and satisfaction with family cohesion on a self-report instrument; in addition, mothers and adolescents scored significantly higher on a self-concept scale when all three family members attended.

Kimmick (1975) evaluated a didactic/discussion program in two formats: lecture/discussion and seminar/role-play. The lecture/discussion approach was more effective in changing fathers' attitudes; however, the fathers preferred the seminar/role-play approach. Davis (1984) evaluated a program for fathers offered in the workplace. This program used filmed stimulus vignettes about family styles as the springboard for discussion. The five-session program was found to result in positive changes in fathers' self-reported attitudes and beliefs about child rearing and the fathers' role. Hill and MacFarlane (1971) reported a three-session program for farm laborers, also using films as the stimulus for discussion. They found that Black fathers seemed more comfortable in providing child care, which is what Price-Bonham and Skeen (1979) also found in their study of Black and White fathers' views of the father role. Steiner (1970) reported a four-session lecture/discussion program for fathers and teens, which seemed to open up communication channels. Finally, Lauritsen (1982) reported the field-testing of a taped program designed to increase "fathers' supportiveness toward their children and wives." The four-week program was offered to a group of Mormon fathers with generally favorable results.

The skills-training programs, which seek to enhance parenting skills through direct training, include both client-centered and behavioral approaches. The client-centered programs include Guerney's (1977) Relationship Enhancement Programs and Levant's Personal Development Program (Levant & Doyle, 1983), which will be discussed in more detail in the next section. With regard to the former approach, Stollack (1981) described the involvement of fathers in Filial Therapy, a Relationship Enhancement program in which parents are trained to be play-therapists for their emotionally disturbed children. Aggressive male children typically spend the early sessions with fathers engaged in competitive games and the expression of aggression. After five or six sessions there is often a change in the child's behavior, and the child might ask if he can sit on his father's lap. At this point the father requires support and encouragement to allow the child to sit in his lap and to feel comfortable while doing so. This usually turns a corner in the father–son relationship, and leads to the resolution of the problem. Although Filial Therapy has been subjected to rigorous evaluations, with positive results found for mothers and for children (Levant, 1986), no results have been reported specifically for fathers. The Parent–Adolescent Relationship Development Program, or PARD, (Grando & Ginsberg, 1976), which trains parents and their adolescent children in self-expressive and empathic-responding skills, grew out of the Filial Therapy Program. An evaluative study (Ginsberg, 1972) found that father–son pairs trained in a 10-week program improve significantly more than a no-treatment control group on the following variables: expressive and empathic communication skills, general communication patterns in the home, and quality of the father–son relationship. A quasi-replication, in which the results for control subjects who later elected to participate in the program were compared before and after their participation, confirmed the results of the primary study.

The behavioral approach, like Filial Therapy, involves the use of parent training as a method of treating emotionally disturbed children. The behavioral approach, known as Behavioral Parent Training (BPT), has wide variation in practice (Graziano, 1983), and has generally been offered to mothers. Several articles have appeared in recent years examining the issue of father involvement, with two studies finding no differences in mother–child interaction (Martin, 1977) or in children's classroom behavior (Firestone, Kelley, & Fike, 1980) attributable to fathers' participation in the programs. However, these findings should not be interpreted as indicating that father involvement is unimportant, given the very indirect relationship between the criterion measures (mother–child interaction, children's classroom behavior) and the likely effects of father involvement. Furthermore, a recent study found that fathers who did not attend the training sessions learned the skills from their wives anyway, and applied them effectively with their children (Reisinger, 1982). Hence, the findings by Martin (1977) and Firestone and colleagues (1980) of no differences between mothers-only and mother–father groups may reflect the fact that fathers learned and practiced the skills, whether they attended or not.

AN EXAMPLE FROM PRACTICE: THE FATHERHOOD COURSE AT BOSTON UNIVERSITY

The rest of this chapter describes a course that is part of the Fatherhood Project at Boston University, offered for married and single fathers who want to improve their relationships with their children. This Fatherhood Course, which meets one evening a week for eight weeks, teaches fathers' communication skills—particularly learning to listen and respond to their children's feelings, and to express their own feelings in a constructive manner. In addition, it teaches fathers about child development (stages and norms) and child management. The course uses a skill-training format, in which fathers role-play the particular skills in their own family situations, with videotape used to provide instant feedback. In addition, each father receives a workbook containing exercises that can be done at home with his children.

This approach to fostering father's communication skills comes from (1) the cognitive social development literature (Gilligan, 1982; Newberger, 1977; and Selman, 1980), which describes how social perspective-taking develops through a stagewise sequence; and, (2) the literature on the characteristics of effective relationships in counseling (Rogers, 1957) and parenting (Gordon, 1970), which highlight the importance of empathy. Both literatures are utilized to help fathers learn to take their child's perspective with increasing degrees of empathic sensitivity, and to balance their child's and their own perspective on particular issues.

Instruction in child development takes a novel approach, looking at the literature from the perspective of the father's role. Thus fathers learn about the important issues regarding the cognitive, social, emotional, and moral development of their children, such as how fathers may act as gatekeepers for their sons' and daughters' sex-role attitudes and behaviors. For example, observational studies with preschoolers indicate that fathers not only interact less frequently with their daughters, but that they treat them differently than their sons. From three years on, fathers tend to interact in expressive rather than instrumental ways with their daughters (Harrington, Block, & Block, 1975; Osofsky & O'Connell, 1972; see also Chapter 8, Bronstein, this volume), and when they do behave instrumentally with daughters, their behavior tends to be ineffective and confusing (Radin, 1976). In learning situations, fathers appear more concerned with making the task enjoyable than with facilitating their daughter's mastery of the task. In the Harrington and colleagues (1975) study, fathers sought to protect their daughters from failure, whereas in the Osofsky and O'Connell (1972) study, fathers either provided too much direction or withdrew completely, failing in either case to facilitate achievement or even to convey expectations that the child should seek mastery.

The format for the course is detailed in the Leader's Guide (Levant & Doyle, 1981a). The course is usually co-taught by the author (a father) and an advanced doctoral student in counseling psychology, who has had training in parent–child interaction and in leading structured groups, and who may or may not be a father himself. The first half of the course is on listening and responding to children, beginning with a session on nonverbal parental behaviors that can facilitate communication, such as staying at eye level with the child, and maintaining an open-body posture. In the next session fathers learn about listening and responding reflectively to the content of a child's message. In the third session, fathers learn about listening and responding empathically to a child's feelings. The fourth session is devoted to review, integration, and practice.

In the second half of the course, fathers work on speaking for themselves, beginning with a session in increasing their awareness of the thoughts and feelings that emerge while interacting with their children. Next comes a session on learning to express thoughts and feelings in a nondefensive, open manner. In the segment on acceptance, the fathers examine their own personal sensitivities, in order to become more accepting of their children's feelings and behavior. The final session is devoted to termination and includes a graduation ceremony.

The program includes didactic and experiential components. The format is as follows: (1) introduction and definition of a particular skill in a brief lecture; (2)

demonstration of the skill using videotaped and live examples, usually role-plays between the two instructors; (3) discrimination training, in which the instructors role-play parent–child situations, demonstrating varying degrees of skillfulness, and with the fathers rating and discussing the role-played examples; (4) practice of the skill in role-play exercises, using videotape for immediate feedback; and (5) consolidating and transferring the skill to the interaction with their children through homework assignments from the Father's Workbook (Levant & Doyle, 1981b). Fathers are expected to spend one hour per week on homework, including readings, paper-and-pencil exercises that progress from asking the fathers to discriminate between good and poor responses to asking them to formulate their own good responses, and interactional exercises. Homework assignments are discussed in class each week.

The program is designed to fit men's traditional learning styles. It is not held out as counseling, and men are not required to talk about their feelings. Instead, it is offered as an educational program, with an opportunity to develop skills. When men first walk into the room, hardware is immediately in evidence in the form of video equipment, which may provide a sense of familiarity, in terms of their traditional relationship to machines. Furthermore, they are told that we will teach them to be better fathers in a manner comfortable to them, in much the same ways they might have learned to play a sport, such as football or tennis.

The in-class role-plays in which the fathers participate serve several important functions. They are drawn from the discussion of the previous week's homework; in particular, from the interactional exercises between father and child. It is not uncommon that several fathers will have experienced difficulties in carrying out these exercises with their children, and it is also likely that these difficulties will reflect longer term problems in the father–child relationship. By selecting the role-plays in this manner, several purposes are served. For one thing, difficulties are attended to, so that hurdles are overcome and motivation remains high. It is highly possible in such short-term structured groups for unsatisfactory experiences with the homework to lead to discouragement, which can be expressed either in the form of dropping out of the group or participating at a pseudomutual level. For another, by focusing on the longer-term issues as they have emerged during the homework, an optimal balance between safety and depth is achieved. Ostensibly, we are working on the fathers' difficulties in learning the skills, but in the process, the fathers enact the difficulties in their relationships with their children, which then become available for modification. An additional benefit of focusing on such longer-term issues is that a climate of engagement and genuineness is created in the group.

In addition, the role-plays are performed in two different ways. At times we have the father role-play himself, while another participant plays the child. In these cases the goal is to have the father learn the skills and apply them to his interaction with his child. At other times the father role-plays his child. In these instances the intent is to help the father develop an appreciation of the child's point of view, and also to learn how his child experiences him. This latter learning can be quite profound in helping fathers modify their approach to their children.

The fathers who participate in the course come from all walks of life, from laborer to plumber to lawyer to stockbroker. Their ages have ranged from the late twenties to the mid-fifties, with their childrens' ages ranging from early infancy to young adulthood. About half the men are married and half divorced, with a few of them remarried and working out a reconstituted family. Those who are divorced have custody arrangements ranging from visitation to joint custody to sole custody.

Though the men are successful in the workplace and fulfill the "good provider" role, they experience dissatisfaction with their relationships with their children. Some speak with sadness of the distance in their relationships with their own fathers, or articulate a desire to not make some of the mistakes with their children that their fathers made with them. Others feel inadequate with their children, and marvel at how well their wives "do it." Some are very uncomfortable with feelings, both their own and their children's. Others get caught in the "anger trap," and become ensnared in unproductive repetitive patterns of testing and punishment.

Many assume that they know how to communicate with their children. Two fathers in particular, who thought their communication skills were adequate, were shocked to see videotaped replays of role-playing sessions. One saw himself towering over his child, the other talking from behind a newspaper. Another noted, "The idea that being a father is a learned skill never occurred to me."

About halfway through the course, after fathers have had some success at mastering the skills, some report that they are finding the skills useful not only with their children, but with their wives and others at the workplace as well. For example, one father said:

> I found the lessons in practicing communication particularly valuable. I would add the concept—the one most people miss—that communication is generally undervalued and completely misunderstood in our society. I think that people must feel as though they are doing fine, when in fact they are not dealing with the emotional level at all, in many cases.

And another observed:

> Like I said in the beginning, not only with family members, but I'm using the listening skills in my job. I'm taking those same skills that we developed, and applying them so that if I'm talking to an employee, and the employee is having a problem, I try to develop some trust with that person, establish eye contact, and respond to his statement by saying the statement back to let him know that I'm listening.

The Fatherhood Course has been evaluated (Levant & Doyle, 1983). Experimental group fathers, their wives, and one of their children were compared to control group families before and after training on several paper-and-pencil measures. Fathers' communication skills were assessed using the Sensitivity to Children Scale (in which fathers are presented with vignettes of children's behavior, and are asked to respond with written statements as to what they would say if the child depicted were their own) and the Porter Acceptance Scale, which measures parental acceptance of children's feelings. Fathers' and mothers' views of their actual and ideal families were assessed using the Family Concept Test, which measures family satisfaction, and congruence of husbands' and wives' perceptions. Children's perceptions of their fathers were assessed using the Kinetic Family Drawing Test, in which children were asked to draw a picture of their family doing something together.

The evaluation found that training resulted in an improvement in fathers' communication skills—specifically, a significant increase in overall sensitivity, a significant reduction in the use of undesirable responses, a trend toward increased use of desirable responses, and a trend toward increased acceptance of the child's expression of feelings. In addition, a complex pattern of findings of fathers' and mothers' real and ideal family concepts suggested that, as a result of the course, fathers underwent a cognitive restructuring, changing their views of the ideal family.

Changes were also seen in children's perceptions of their fathers, with significantly more experimental than control group children perceiving positive changes in their relationships. A telling example was the change in one boy's pre- and post-course Kinetic Family Drawing. Before the course began, the child drew a picture of a roller coaster, with the tracks filling 90% of the page. At the very top was a tiny little car. In the front seat was the boy, legs and arms akimbo, in the next seat was Mom and then Dad, and in the last seat was his brother, who appeared to be falling out of the car. After the course was over, the boy drew a picture of a spaceship running diagonally across the page, in which the cockpit filled about 40% of the page. Seated at the controls was Dad, and next to him, Mom. At opposite sides, looking out the window, were he and his brother. From a clinical perspective, this sequence of pictures suggests a remarkable transformation of family structure and emotional climate.

When the Fatherhood Project opened its door in September 1983, the focus was on men's roles in the family, and the only workshop offered was the Fatherhood Course. Since then, it has expanded, in recognition both of the stress and complexity of modern family life, and of the important interface between the family and the workplace. We now offer two new sets of services: (1) skills-training programs for fathers, single parents of both sexes, stepparents and their spouses, dual-earner co-parents, divorced parents with joint custody, and couples making the transition to parenthood; and, (2) consultation programs for industries focusing on the working parent, including lunchtime seminars and the design of parental benefits policies. Evaluative research for the skills-training programs is ongoing (Haffey & Levant, 1984; Levant & Doyle, 1983; Levant & Nelson, 1984; Levant & Tarshis, 1984), and a survey focusing on the corporate view of the working parent is nearing completion.

SUMMARY AND CONCLUSIONS

This chapter began with a consideration of tremendous changes that have taken place in men's and women's roles and in the structure of the American family in the past 25 years. These changes now offer up a challenge to contemporary fathers, to not only fashion a paternal role different from that of their fathers, but also to prepare their children for flexible adult roles that are not predetermined according to gender. To help fathers respond to this challenge, educational programs are needed both for the current generation of fathers, and for the next generation.

The field of parent education was reviewed, looking at its three areas of pre-parent, new-parent, and child-rearing education. Until very recently, parent education has been synonymous with mother education, but in recent years, new programs have been developed. In the pre-parent area, the traditional curriculum of family-life education has opened up, and courses have been developed for males at the college level. In addition, two new areas have developed: programs providing experiences in child care for school-aged boys, and programs fostering the involvement of men in preschool and elementary school settings. Both are aimed at providing boys with skills and experiences that will later facilitate their development of nurturing and expressive parental roles.

In the new-parent area, the traditional field of childbirth education has also opened up. Not only are men included in childbirth preparation classes in supportive roles, but also transition-to-parenthood experiences are provided for fathers-to-be. In addition, two new-parent program types have been developed: one offers interactive and play experiences, support, and resources to both parents and their children from birth through the preschool years; the second offers a range of support services to teenage fathers.

In the child-rearing area, there has also been considerable program-development activity. Discussion groups have been developed for fathers in general, for single fathers, and for stepfathers. Didactic/discussion formats have also been developed, usually from an atheoretical perspective. And skills-training programs from both the client-centered and behavioral schools have been opened up to include fathers. As an illustration of this latter type of education program, a particular model of a fatherhood skills-training course was described in detail.

All in all, this amounts to a high level of recent program-development activity, resulting in a broad range of programs that address contemporary changes in the father's role. Given the short period of time during which these programs have emerged, it is not surprising that very little research exists. No studies were located on the pre-parental programs, and only a few studies of a very limited nature were found in the new-parent area. More studies were located in the child-rearing area, but many of these were of an ad hoc nature, which neither referred to nor built on other work in this area. Clearly, the agenda for the future must include research, particularly research that evaluates the effects and effectiveness of these efforts to prepare the current and next generations of fathers.

REFERENCES

Abidin, R.D. (1976). *Parenting skills*. New York: Human Sciences Press.

Abidin, R.D. (Ed.). (1980). *Parent education and intervention handbook*. Springfield, IL: Thomas.

Anderson, C.L. (1977). Parenting and perceived sex roles of rural Iowa fathers. *Dissertation Abstracts International, 37*, 4177A. (University Microfilms No. 77–1011)

Andrews, F., & Withey, S. (1976). *Social indicators of well-being*. New York: Plenum.

Arnold, L.E. (Ed.). (1978a). *Helping parents help their children*. New York: Brunner/Mazel.

Arnold, L.E. (1978b). Helping parents beat the system. In L.E. Arnold (Ed.), *Helping parents help their children*. New York: Brunner/Mazel.

Auerbach, A.B. (1968). *Parents learn through discussion: Principles and practices of parent group education*. New York: Wiley.

Barnhill, L., Rubenstein, G., & Rocklin, N. (1979). From generation to generation: Fathers-to-be in transition. *Family Coordinator, 28*, 229–235.

Barret, R.L., & Robinson, B.E. (1981). Teenage fathers: A profile. *Personnel and Guidance Journal, 60*(4), 226–228.

Baxter, G. (November, 1979). Daddy's home. *Family Circle*.

Benson, L., Berger, M., & Mease, W. (1975). Family communication systems. *Small Group Behavior, 6*(1), 91–105.

Berkowitz, B.P., & Graziano, A.M. (1972). Training parents as behavior therapists: A review. *Behavior Research and Therapy, 10*, 297–317.

Bernal, M.E., & North, J.A. (1978). A survey of parents' training manuals. *Journal of Applied Behavior Analysis, 11*, 533–544.

Bing, E. (1969). *Six practical lessons for easier childbirth*. New York: Bantam.

Block, J. (1979). Another look at sex differentiation in the socialization behaviors of mothers and fathers. In F. Denmark (Ed.), *Psychology of Women: Future Directions of Research*. New York: Psychological Dimensions.

Bredehoft, D., & Clarke, J.I. (1982). *Family involvement in parent education classes: Who and how many should be involved?* Unpublished manuscript. Concordia College, St. Paul, MN.

Brim, O.G., Jr. (1965). *Education for child rearing*. New York: Free Press.

Cable, M. (1975). *The little darlings: A history of child rearing in America*. New York: Scribner.

Carkhuff, R.R., & Bierman, R. (1970). Training as a preferred mode of treatment of parents of emotionally disturbed children. *Journal of Counseling Psychology, 17*, 157–171.

Carnes, P.J., & Laube, H. (1975). Becoming us: An experiment on family learning and teaching. *Small Group Behavior, 6*(1), 106–119.

Charnley, L., & Myre, G. (1977). Parent-infant education. *Children Today, 6*(2), 18–21.

Chilman, C.S. (1973). Programs for disadvantaged parents. In B.M. Caldwell & H.N. Ricciuti (Eds.), *Review of child development research* (vol. 3). Chicago: University of Chicago Press.

Cordell, A.S., Parke, R.D., & Sawin, D.B. (1980). Fathers' views on fatherhood with special reference to infancy. *Family Relations, 26*, 331–338.

Croake, J.W. (1983). Adlerian parent education. *Counseling Psychologist, 11*(3), 65–71.

Croake, J.W., & Glover, K.E. (1977). A history and evaluation of parent education. *Family Coordinator, 26*(2), 151–158.

Davis, S.J. (1984). Fatherhood education in the workplace. *Dissertation Abstracts International, 45*, 1632A. (University Microfilms No. DA8420318).

De Frain, J. (1977). Sexism in parenting manuals. *Family Coordinator, 26*(3), 245–231.

de Lissovoy, V. (1978). Parent education: White elephant in the classroom? *Youth and Society, 9*(3), 315–338.

Dickie, J.R., & Gerber, S.C. (1980). Training in social competence. The effect on mothers, fathers, and infants. *Child Development, 51,* 1248–1251.

Dinkmeyer, D., & McKay, G.D. (1976). *Systematic training for effective parenting.* Circle Pines, MN: American Guidance Service.

Dreikurs, R., & Soltz, V. (1964). *Children: The challenge.* New York: Meredith.

Education Development Center (1976). *Exploring childhood: National field test. Summary of evaluation findings, year two.* Cambridge, MA: Educational Development Center.

Education Development Center (1977). *Exploring childhood: Program overview and catalogue of materials.* Cambridge, MA: Education Development Center.

Ellis, A. (1978). Rational-emotive guidance. In L.E. Arnold (Ed.), *Helping parents help their children.* New York: Brunner/Mazel.

Erskine, H. (1973). The polls: Hopes, tears and regrets. *Public Opinion Quarterly, 37,* 132–145.

Eversoll, D. (1979). The changing father role: Implications for parent education programs for today's youth. *Adolescence, 14,* 535–544.

Fasteau, M.F. (1975). *The male machine.* New York: Dell.

Fein, R.A. (1976). Men's entrance to parenthood. *Family Coordinator, 9,* 44–47.

Fine, M.J. (Ed.). (1980). *Handbook on parent education.* New York: Academic.

Firestone, P., Kelley, M.J., & Fike, S. (1980). Are fathers necessary in parent training groups? *Journal of Clinical Child Psychology, 9,* 44–47.

Friedman, S.T. (1969). Relation of parental attitudes toward child rearing and patterns of social behavior in middle childhood. *Psychological Reports, 24,* 575–579.

Gearing, J. (1978). Facilitating the birth process and father-child bonding. *Counseling Psychologist, 7*(4), 53–56.

Gilligan, C. (1982). *In a different voice.* Cambridge, MA: Harvard University Press.

Gilmore, J.V., & Gilmore, E.C. (1978). *A more productive child: Guidelines for parents.* Boston: Gilmore Institute.

Ginott, H.G. (1957). Parent education groups in a child guidance clinic. *Mental Hygiene, 41,* 82–86.

Ginsberg, B.G. (1972). Parent-adolescent relationship development. A therapeutic and preventive mental health program. *Dissertation Abstracts International, 33,* 426–427A. (University Microfilms No. 72–19, 306).

Gordon, T. (1970). *P.E.T.: Parent effectiveness training.* New York: Peter H. Wyden.

Grando, R., & Ginsberg, B.G. (1976). Communication in the father-son relationship. The parent-adolescent relationship development program. *The Family Coordinator, 25*(4), 465–474.

Graziano, A.M. (1986). Behavioral approaches to child and family systems. In R.F. Levant (Ed.), *Psychoeducational approaches to family therapy and counseling.* New York: Springer.

Gregory, S. (October, 1981). The father's class. *Nursing Times,* p. 28.

Guerney, B.G., Jr. (1977). *Relationship enhancement.* San Francisco: Jossey-Bass.

Haffey, N. & Levant, R.F. (1984). The differential effectiveness of two models of skills-training for working class-parents. *Family Relations, 33,* 209–216.

Harrington, D.M., Block, J.H., & Block, J. (1975, April). *Behavioral manifestations and parental correlates of intolerance of ambiguity in young children.* Paper presented at the Society for Research in Child Development. Denver.

Hereford, C.F. (1963). *Changing parental attitudes through group discussion*. Austin: University of Texas Press.

Hetherington, E.M., Cox, M., & Cox, R. (1976). Divorced fathers. *Family Coordinator*, 25(4), 417–428.

Hill, R., & Aldous, J. (1969). Socialization for marriage and parenthood. In D.A. Goslin (Ed.), *Handbook of socialization theory and research*. Chicago: Rand-McNally.

Hill, K.K., & MacFarlane, A. (1971). Family life education—for men. *Extension Service Review*, 42(10), 6–7.

Hoffman, L.W. (1977). Changes in family roles, socialization and sex differences. *American Psychologist*, 32, 644–658.

Jaffrey, S. (Producer) (1979). *Kramer vs. Kramer* [Film]. New York: Columbia Pictures.

James, M., & James, J. (1978). Games parents play. In L.E. Arnold (Ed.), *Helping parents help their children*. New York: Brunner/Mazel.

Johnson, C.A., & Katz, R.C. (1973). Using parents as change agents for their children: A review. *Journal of Child Psychology and Psychiatry*, 14, 181–200.

Johnson, S. (1978, March 15). Two pioneer programs help unwed teenage fathers cope. *New York Times*, p. 54.

Keshet, H.F., & Rosenthal, K.M. (1978). Fathering after marital separation. *Social Work*, 23, 11–18.

Kimmick, D.W. (1975). *Role-Playing and lecture-discussion in parent education: changing fathers' opinions about methods of child discipline*. Unpublished doctoral dissertation, Columbia University Teachers College.

Klinman, D.G., & Kohl R. (1984). *Fatherhood U.S.A.* New York: Garland.

Lamb, M.E. (1979). Paternal influences and the father's role: A personal perspective. *American Psychologist*, 34, 938–943.

Lamb, J., & Lamb, W.A. (1978). *Parent education and elementary counseling*. New York: Human Sciences Press.

Langlois, J.H., & Downs, A.C. (1980). Mothers, fathers, and peers as socialization agents of sex typed play behaviors in young children. *Child Development*, 51, 1217–1247.

Langway, L. (1983, October 24). A chance for young fathers. *Newsweek*,

Lauritsen, E.D. (1982). A program for increasing fathers' supportiveness toward children. *Dissertation Abstracts International*. 43, 1834B. (University Microfilms No. DA 8214774).

Lein, L., Durham, M., Pratt, M., Schudson, M., Thomas, R., & Weiss, H. (1974). *Work and family life* (Working Paper). Wellesley College Center for Research on Women.

Levant, R.F. (1986). Client-centered skills-training programs for the family. In R.F. Levant (Ed.), *Psychoeducational approaches to family therapy and counseling*. New York: Springer.

Levant, R.F., & Doyle, G.F. (1981a). *Parent education for fathers: A personal developmental program*. Leaders Guide. Unpublished manuscript, Boston University.

Levant, R.F., & Doyle, G.F. (1981b). *Parent education for fathers: A personal developmental program*. Parents workbook. Unpublished manuscript, Boston University.

Levant, R.F., & Doyle, G.F. (1983). An evaluation of a parent education program for fathers of school-aged children. *Family Relations*, 32, 29–37.

Levant, R.F., & Nelson, W. (1984). *Skills training for step-parents: A personal developmental program*. Unpublished manuscript, Boston University.

Levant, R.F., & Tarshis, E. (1984). *Skills training for single parents: A personal developmental program.* Unpublished manuscript, Boston University.

Loiselle, J.E. (1980). *A review of the role of fathers in parent training programs.* Unpublished manuscript, Boston University.

Martin, B. (1977). Brief family intervention: Effectiveness and importance of including the father. *Journal of Consulting and Clinical Psychology, 45*(6), 1002–1010.

McGuiness, T., & Glasser, W. (1978). Reality guidance. In L.E. Arnold (Ed.), *Helping parents help their children.* New York: Brunner/Mazel.

Mendes, H.A. (1976). Single fathers. *Family Coordinator, 25*(4), 439–444.

Miller, B.C., & Bowen, S.L. (1982). Father to newborn attachment behavior in relation to prenatal classes and presence at delivery. *Family Relations, 31*, 71–78.

Newberger, C.M. (1977). *Parental conceptions of children and child rearing. A structural-developmental analysis.* Unpublished doctoral dissertation, Harvard University.

O'Dell, S. (1974). Training parents in behavior modification. A review. *Psychological Bulletin, 4*, 418–433.

Orthner, D., Brown, T., & Ferguson, D. (1976). Single-parental fatherhood: the emerging life style. *Family Coordinator, 25*(4), 429–438.

Osofsky, J.D., & O'Connell, E.J. (1972). Parent-child interaction: Daughters' effects upon mothers' and fathers' behavior. *Developmental Psychology, 7*, 157–168.

Packer, A., Resnick, M., Resnick, J.L., & Wilson, J.M. (1978). An elementary school with parents and infants. *Young Children, 34*, 4–9.

Pannor, R., Massarik, F., & Evans, B. (1971). *The unmarried father.* New York: Springer.

Parke, R.D., & Sawin, D.B. (1976). The father's role of infancy: A re-evaluation. *Family Coordinator, 25*(4), 365–372.

Pleck, J.H. (1977). The work-family role system. *Social Problems. 24*, 417–427.

Pleck, J.H. (1981a). *Changing patterns of work and family roles* (working paper No. 81). Wellesley College Center for Research on Women.

Pleck, J.H. (1981b). Husband's paid work and family roles: Current research issues. In H.Z. Lopata (Ed.), *Research on the interweave of social roles of women and men* (vol. 3). New York: JAI Press.

Pleck, J.H. (1981c). *The myth of masculinity.* Cambridge, MA: MIT Press.

Pleck, J.H., & Lang, L. (1978). *Men's family role: Its nature and consequences* (Working Paper). Wellesley College Center for Research on Women.

Price-Bonham, S., & Skeen, P. (1979). A comparison of black and white fathers with implications for parent education. *Family Coordinator, 28*, 53–59.

Radin, N. (1976). The father and academic, cognitive, and intellectual development. In M.E. Lamb (Ed.), *The role of the father in child development.* New York: Wiley.

Radin, N. (1982). Primary care giving and role-sharing fathers. In M.E. Lamb (Ed.), *Nontraditional families: Parenting and child development.* Hillsdale, NJ: Erlbaum.

Reisinger, J.J. (1982). Unprogrammed learning of differential attention by fathers of oppositional children. *Journal of Behavior Therapy and Experimental Psychiatry, 13*(3), 203–208.

Reisinger, J.J., Ora, J.P., & Frangia, G.W. (1976). Parents as change agents for their children: A review. *Journal of Community Psychology, 4*, 103–123.

Resnick, J.L., Resnick, M.B., Packer, A.B., & Wilson, J. (1978). Fathering classes: A psychoeducational model. *Counseling Psychologist, 7*(4), 56–60.

Robinson, J. (1977). *How Americans use time: A social-psychological analysis*. New York: Praeger.

Rogers, C. (1957). The necessary and sufficient conditions of therapeutic personality change. *Journal of Consulting Psychology, 21*, 95–103.

Sawin, D.B., & Parke, R.D. (1979). Father's affectionate stimulation and caregiving behaviors with newborn infants. *Family Coordinator, 28*, 509–513.

Selman, R.L. (1980). *The growth of interpersonal understanding: Developmental and clinical analysis*. New York: Academic.

Sirridge, S.T. (1980). Transactional analysis: Promoting OK'ness. In M.J. Fine (Ed.), *Handbook on parent education*. New York: Academic.

Stearn, M.B. (1971). The relationship of parental effectiveness training to parent attitudes, parent behavior, and child self-esteem. *Dissertation Abstracts International, 32*, 1885–1886 B.

Steiner, G.J. (1970). Parent-teen education: an excercise in communication. *Family Coordinator, 19*, 213–218.

Stollack, G.G. (1981). Variations and extensions of filial therapy. *Family Process, 20*, 305–309.

Swenson, S.S. (1970). Changing expressed parent attitudes toward child-rearing practices and its effect on school adaptation and level of adjustment perceived by parents. *Dissertation Abstracts International, 31*, 2118–2119A.

Tavormina, J.B. (1974). Basic models of parent counseling: A critical review. *Psychological Bulletin, 81*, 827–835.

Tavormina, J.B. (1980). Evaluation and comparative studies of parent education. In R.R. Abidin (Ed.), *Parent education and intervention handbook*. Springfield, IL: Thomas.

Walker, K., & Woods, M. (1976). *Time use: A measure of household production of family goods and services*. Washington: American Home Economics Association.

Wente, A.S., & Crockenberg, S.B. (1976). Transition to fatherhood: Lamaze preparation, adjustment difficulty, and the husband-wife relationship. *Family Coordinator, 25*, 351–357.

Woody, R.II. (1978). Fathers with child custody. *Counseling Psychologist, 7*(4), 60–63.

CHAPTER 16

Working with Men Becoming Fathers: The Impact of a Couples Group Intervention

CAROLYN PAPE COWAN

Dear Ellen and Bill,
Sorry we didn't get back the questionnaires earlier. Helen started working in May. She was preoccupied with all of the changes in our life, and just did not feel she could answer all of your questions. We hope you can use our belated answers anyhow.

We do have a lot of problems. We are able to talk about our sexual problems, but talking has so far brought no change at all. At first, Helen was nothing but mother to Amy. Our relationship was restricted to providing care for Amy. There was nothing happening between us. (Sex every other week and more or less just because it was overdue.) Helen seemed to be perfectly happy with this state of affairs. The only problem was that I felt unhappy and frustrated, insisting on a lover relationship with Helen. At first it was amazing for me that I was not angry at Helen at all. Eventually I came to realize that I simply excused Helen's behavior because I was personally interested in having a close relationship with her. I didn't blame her because I didn't want to damage the positive feelings that still existed between us. It was easier to blame the baby.

At the moment, we're in some sort of deadlock situation; Helen knows as well as I do that we should try to develop a relationship that gives space and love for all three of us. She knows the dangers of her over-mothering, but she sees no way of changing. It might be that she only has energy to be emotionally involved with just one other person. Divorce is not yet the question, but it might come up sooner or later. For the moment, Helen hopes that Amy will become less and less demanding, leaving time and energy for my demands. I have serious doubts.

Please make sure to send us a copy of your study results.

Best wishes,
Gordon

This research is supported by NIMH grant RO1 MH-31109. The author gratefully acknowledges the collaboration of Philip A. Cowan, co-investigator of the longitudinal study, and major contributions by other members of the research team: Ellen T. Garrett, William S. Coysh, Harriet Curtis-Boles, and Abner J. Boles III, the other co-leaders of the intervention groups; Gertrude Heming, data manager; Dena Cowan and Barbara Epperson, data preparation and processing. Special thanks also to Hilde Burton for consultation on the clinical work of the project.

Gordon's[1] letter to a staff couple on our Becoming a Family project discusses conflicts that are common for men confronting the emotional demands of being husbands and becoming fathers. Yet, there are virtually no services or programs to help men with these relationship difficulties unless they feel in enough distress to seek counseling or therapy. Given recent findings that 15% of new parents separate or divorce by the time their first child is between three and four years old (Cowan, Cowan, Heming, Garrett, Coysh, Curtis-Boles, & Boles, 1985; Eiduson, 1981), it seems critical to understand more about what causes marital strain during family formation and to develop interventions that might buffer marital distress.

This chapter describes a group intervention developed at the University of California, Berkeley, and offered randomly to a sample of couples in a longitudinal study of partners becoming parents. Not childbirth preparation, and not groups about parenting, this intervention provided couples with a setting in which expectant fathers and their wives could explore their experience of change as individuals and as a couple during their transition to parenthood. Trained group leaders sought to help men and women address the stressful and potentially negative changes that appear to threaten marital satisfaction and stability for partners becoming parents (Belsky, Spanier, & Rovine, 1983; Cowan, et al., 1985; Grossman, Eichler, & Winickoff, 1980; LeMasters, 1957).

After a brief review of research on the transition to parenthood and interventions for new parents, this chapter describes the rationale, procedures, and early effects of this couples group intervention, which was designed to address both individual and marital change during family formation. In addition, it will present some new data concerning the longer-term effects of the intervention, and summarize what we have learned about fatherhood by working closely with men during family formation.

THE TRANSITION TO PARENTHOOD: A REVIEW

While becoming a parent is a joyous event for most men and women, this dramatic change in adult life is increasingly being described as a time of stress and potential crisis—by researchers, mental health professionals, and parents themselves. Early studies tended to be retrospective and to focus mostly on mothers, as if to suggest that we expect only women to be affected when partners become parents. This body of research documented a fair amount of negative change and stress, which different researchers attributed to mothers' changing sense of self (Rossi, 1968), traditional role arrangements (Hoffman, 1978), decreased quality of couple communication (Raush, Barry, Hertel, & Swain, 1973), or inadequate social support (Crockenberg, 1981).

Findings from a number of studies suggest that the birth of a first child tends to precipitate a crisis for the couple, with from 3–83% of couples in different studies reporting major strains in their lives during the family formation period (Hobbs, 1965; LeMasters, 1957). The most pervasive and consistent finding from a number

---

[1]Names of study participants have been changed to protect their privacy.

of newer longitudinal studies is that both husbands and wives report declining satisfaction with marriage as they move from life as a couple to becoming a family (Belsky, Spanier, & Rovine, 1983; Cowan, et al., 1985; Grossman, et al., 1980). The longitudinal data also show that the quality of the marriage before the baby is born is the best predictor of later marital quality and parents' well-being (Belsky, et al., 1983; Cowan, et al., 1985; Cowan, Cowan, & Heming, 1986; Feldman, 1987; Grossman, et al., 1980; Shereshefsky & Yarrow, 1973).

Men Becoming Fathers

Although a majority of studies of the transition to parenthood have focused on women, the few that focus on expectant fathers are informative about this stage of life for men (see Chapter 2, P. Cowan, this volume, for a discussion of studies of men becoming fathers). Several early studies in the psychoanalytic case study tradition suggested that becoming a father put some men at serious psychological risk by raising earlier unresolved conflicts (Wainright, 1966; Zilboorg, 1931). More recently, studies of parents not in treatment have found changes in expectant and new fathers, or in their relationships with their wives, that have implications for men's well-being as husbands and parents. Some of those changes are as follows:

> Most expectant fathers feel somewhat isolated as they attempt to maneuver the psychological changes of shifting perceptions of self, spouse, parents, and friends (May & Perrin, 1982).
>
> A substantial number of new fathers experience the blues or symptoms of depressed mood (Zaslow, Pedersen, Kramer, Cain, Suwalsky, & Fivel, 1981).
>
> When partners become parents, men take on a much smaller share of both housework and child care than either partner predicted. Both husbands' and wives' satisfaction with the couple's role arrangements declines between pregnancy and the second year of parenthood (Cowan & Cowan, 1987c; Cowan, et al., 1985).
>
> Communication between husbands and wives who have become parents is reduced in quantity and quality (Raush, Barry, Hertel, & Swain, 1974), and marital conflict and disagreement increases (Cowan, et al., 1985).
>
> Men who do not feel ready for or accepting of the birth of their first baby are more likely to have lower self-esteem, to report more symptoms of depression, and to have greater marital dissatisfaction when their babies are 18 months old (Heming, 1985).

These findings suggest that circular patterns emerge when stress is experienced by a parent, a child, or a couple; regardless of where the stress begins, it can be amplified in the relationships with other family members (Belsky, 1984; Clulow, 1982, 1985; Cowan & Cowan, 1983; Crockenberg, 1981; Nuckolls, Cassell, & Kaplan, 1972; Parke, 1979; Pedersen, Anderson, & Cain, 1977; Shereshefsky & Yarrow, 1973). The notion that there are links between parents' well-being and the development of their children is well-known to clinicians who work with families in distress (Haley, 1976; Minuchin, 1974; Satir, 1972). There have also been repeated findings of declining marital satisfaction and potential crisis for the parents during the period when parent–child relationships are beginning, and recommendations from both researchers and clinicians that interventions might buffer the stresses of this major life transition for all family members (Caplan, 1964; LeMasters, 1957; Rapoport, 1963; Rapoport, Rapoport, & Streilitz, 1977). Yet, we were unable to find a single study that both offered and systematically evaluated an intervention designed to address such marital change and stress when we first developed our intervention for expectant parents in 1975 (Cowan, Cowan, Coie, & Coie, 1978).

INTERVENTIONS FOR NEW PARENTS

Just as the early research examining family formation concentrated on women becoming mothers, interventions during pregnancy, childbirth, and the early parenting years have generally been addressed to mothers but not fathers in families with no prior identified physical or mental health risk. The content of these programs spans a wide range from exercise classes and preparation for childbirth to groups focused on parent support, baby care, and child development. While these programs are intended to be preventive or supportive by alleviating or buffering pain and distress during birth and early parenthood, almost none have evaluation components to assess their effectiveness in reaching those goals. Furthermore, none is designed to help women—or men—understand or work on the marital changes reported in the transition to parenthood research.

Prepared Childbirth

Although prepared childbirth classes have included fathers, they have not usually addressed men's reactions or adjustment, and have rarely evaluated the impact of the intervention on men or their wives. As May and Perrin (1982) point out, "most expectant fathers do not discuss their own emotional reactions with others (not even their spouses), and thus feel somewhat isolated as they make these adjustments" (p. 74), and "an expectant father who is having difficulty in adjustment to the pregnancy must himself be considered at risk for emotional disruption" (p. 83). In fact, Heming's (1985) analysis of risk in the families in our project shows that men who did not feel ready for or accepting of the birth of their first baby were more likely to have lower self-esteem, to report more symptoms of depression, and to have greater marital dissatisfaction when their babies were 18 months old. Since prepared childbirth classes end as the baby is due to be born, "prepared" mothers and fathers are virtually on their own to manage any concern or distress they experience during the rest of the transition to parenthood.

In one study that assessed the impact of prepared childbirth classes with postintervention telephone interviews, the authors reported positive effects of the intervention on men's and women's experience of the birth and their early adjustment to parenthood (Entwisle & Doering, 1981). In another study, Markman and Kadushin

(1987) found that couples who chose to attend prepared childbirth classes before giving birth reported fewer problems, less anxiety, and higher marital satisfaction at 8–10 weeks after birth than couples who had not chosen childbirth preparation. Since no prebirth information about the couples was reported in these studies, it is difficult to assess which effects may be attributable to the earlier state of the marriage and which may result from the intervention.

Support, Self-Help, and Parenting Groups

Support groups for parents have become very popular in the United States in the past decade, despite the fact that there are almost no systematic evaluations of their effectiveness. Most are addressed to mothers or are held at times when fathers would find it difficult to attend. Wandersman (1983) reviewed the available data on the impact of support groups for parents with infants. Despite the fact that participants often said that the groups had been helpful, Wandersman found few measurable positive effects on family adjustment or functioning.

The findings of one evaluation study of mothers' self-help groups (Reibstein in Lieberman, 1981) point to the importance of marital quality to new parents' well-being. Reibstein assessed women's support from their peers, husbands, and their own mothers, and used outcome measures of role strain, role dissatisfaction, and level of infant strain. When she compared women who had participated in support groups and a control group with no intervention, she found no significant differences in maternal adjustment. In fact, the correlations that were significant showed that the more women discussed and ventilated their feelings about the maternal role, the more likely they were to be distressed and to show strain. Lieberman (1981) discussed these unexpected trends:

> The findings on the role of peer groups was quite surprising. . . . What is most impressive in these data was the strong and consistent effect of the marital relationship on women's well-being. For those women whose husbands did not provide the needed resources, we could develop no evidence that suggested that other resources could substitute. (p. 773)

Interventions Using Mental Health Professionals

Bittman and Zalk (1978) describe groups for new fathers in which, with the help of a trained leader, men explored their roles as parents. Although the authors were enthusiastic about the success of these groups, there was no systematic evaluation of their effects. Thus we do not know whether men who participated in a fathers group experienced less strain and more satisfaction with themselves or their marriages after the intervention, or whether men's sharing of their negative experiences may have increased their experience of role strain or dissatisfaction, as it did for the mothers in Reibstein's (1981) study. In addition, since there was no control group without an intervention in this study, we cannot assess the comparative benefits of their work with fathers.

Shereshefsky and Yarrow (1973) developed an intervention using trained mental health professionals to work with individual expectant mothers; they offered several appointments to their husbands. In weekly sessions with a therapist from one of several different counseling orientations, each expectant mother was helped with "psychological preparation for the stresses of pregnancy, delivery, and parenthood" during the third trimester of pregnancy (p. 156). Perhaps the husbands recognized that the study's primary emphasis was on preparing women for becoming parents, for almost all of the men declined the offer of counseling appointments. However, the most significant predictor of women's adaptation to parenthood, for mothers in each group in the study, was the quality of the marital relationship.

An intervention for new parents was developed at the Tavistock Institute of Marital Studies in London, England (Clulow, 1982). Expectant couples at a number of London birth clinics were offered a series of six monthly couples group meetings, to help partners focus on their marriages in the last trimester of pregnancy and the first three months of parenthood. The groups were co-led by either a male-female team of mental health workers from the Institute of Marital Studies or female co-leaders who were nurses with the British Home Nurses Service that provides after-birth care for parents and babies. Like our Becoming a Family project, the British First Baby project was based on the assumption that parents' well-being and the state of their marriage might affect the quality of relationship that each parent developed with the child.

The results of the intervention were mixed. While some participants completed the series and reported that the discussions had helped their adjustment to parenthood, a number of couples did not return to the groups after the birth of their child. What Clulow found most disconcerting was that couples did not often use the groups to work on marital difficulties; in fact, he observed that when a couple felt different from others in their group, they were likely not to return to the group. Further, the leaders could not discern any positive effects of the group discussions on the couples' relationships. Yet, when the home nurses came to parents' homes after birth to check on the babies' health, they often heard hints or actual reports of marital tension. Because the couples' groups were not consistently well-attended and did not seem to stimulate talk of marital strain, Clulow seemed discouraged about the potential for a group intervention to assist partners with marital issues.

In sum, there is some evidence that the transition to parenthood can be stressful for men as well as for their wives. The finding that marital quality is a key to both men's and women's adjustment to parenthood and their later satisfaction with marriage is consistent across many studies. However, the effectiveness of interventions with new parents before or during the transition to parenthood is not yet clear. In general, the sparse data from inteventions with new and expectant parents have produced more questions than answers. Available studies suggest that the effects of support or self-help groups are equivocal at best; while parents often *say* that these interventions have been helpful, few positive short- or long-term effects on the participants have been demonstrated. Similarly, while mental health professionals have reported some positive effects in very small samples (Bittman & Zalk, 1978; Cowan, Cowan, Coie, & Coie, 1978; Shereshefsky & Yarrow, 1973), the impact of interventions addressing new parents' marital change and stress has not yet been adequately assessed. This was one major goal of our longitudinal study of couples becoming families.

THE BECOMING A FAMILY PROJECT

When it began, our study set out to address two major questions based on the findings of a small pilot study of couples becoming families (Cowan, et al., 1978): (1) How the transition to parenthood affects men, women, and marriage, and (2) Can a couples group intervention prevent the declines in parents' marital satisfaction reported in almost every study of the transition to parenthood? Results that address the first question have been presented elsewhere (Cowan, et al., 1985); however, because the changes in partners becoming parents are very relevant to the intervention we developed, I will summarize them briefly here.

From late pregnancy into the second year of parenthood, husbands and wives reported both positive and negative changes in themselves, and increasingly discrepant views of themselves and their marriage. These increasing differences in perception were accompanied by increased marital conflict and disagreement, and reports from husbands and wives of a greater sense of distance in the marriage. Furthermore, the greater partners' differences in perception, and the greater their increase in marital conflict, the greater their reported declines in satisfaction with the overall marriage from pregnancy to almost two years after giving birth (Cowan, et al., 1985). However, when we compared changes in couples who participated in our intervention with those of the other new parents in the study, we found significant differences in every one of the domains we studied. What follows here is a description of that intervention: its rationale, structure, process, and outcome—in particular for men as they made the transition to parenthood.

Design of the Study

Couples were sought from clinic and private obstetric-gynecology practices and a Bay Area-wide newsletter in the larger San Francisco Bay Area. Seventy-two couples were expecting a first baby and 24 couples had not yet decided whether to have children. One-third of the expectant couples were randomly chosen from the larger sample, and, at their initial interview, were offered the opportunity to participate in small weekly couples groups with trained couples as leaders. Of those offered a couples group, 85% accepted.[2] The other two-thirds of the expectant couples were randomly offered the opportunity of (1) completing questionnaires and being inter-

---

[2] The parents who declined said that the commitment of six months of weekly meetings was more than they could promise. Nevertheless, all but one agreed to complete our questionnaires and talk with us before and after giving birth. We continued to invite each third couple entering the study into the intervention groups, until there were 24 couples to fill six intervention groups. Data from couples who refused participation in the intervention groups were kept separate until we could establish whether their patterns differed from those of the other comparison couples.

viewed before and after having their babies, or (2) completing questionnaires and being interviewed after giving birth only. Of the nonintervention couples, 95% accepted participation in the study.

The husbands and wives ranged in age from 21–49 years; the mean age of the expectant fathers was 30 years and of mothers, 29 years. The length of their relationships when they joined the study ranged from 8 months to 12 years, with an average of 4 years. They lived in 28 different cities and towns within a 40-mile radius of the University of California, Berkeley. Their educational backgrounds spanned a range from high school to postgraduate degrees, and they held a wide variety of jobs; their family income levels ranged from working class to upper-middle-class. Of the partners studied, 15% were Black, Asian-American, or Hispanic, and 85% were Caucasian.

After the initial interview, and before the couples groups began, each husband and wife from the intervention sample completed a set of questionnaires alone at home, describing their lives as individuals and as couples. Their responses served as the pre-birth, pre-intervention assessment of each partner and couple. The other 72 couples in the study completed the same questionnaires.

The intervention groups, each of which consisted of four couples and a leader couple,[3] met weekly for six months—the last three months of pregnancy and the first three months of parenthood— with the babies becoming part of the groups as soon as they were born. The groups ended when the babies were about three months old, and every couple in the study was followed up separately with questionnaires and interviews when the babies were 6, 18, and 42 months old.

The theoretical model guiding the study led us to focus on five domains that we hypothesized would combine to determine couple-relationship quality (Cowan, et al., 1985). We designed the questionnaires and the intervention to focus on these domains, and assessed each one at every follow-up:

1. Each individual family member, including his or her self-esteem and adaptation
2. The marital relationship, including partners' mutual role arrangements and patterns of communication
3. The quality of each parent–child relationship
4. The intergenerational relationships with each family of origin
5. The balance between couples' life stress and social support from family, employment, and friendship networks.

The Intervention Structure and Why We Chose It

We chose a couples group format for a variety of reasons. First, a group might provide the kind of ongoing support that contemporary couples often lack as they create

---

[3]One of the 24 couples offered the intervention gave birth early, before their couples group had its first meeting. At the last minute, they declined to participate in the couples group, and that group went on with only three expectant couples and the leader couple.

new families far from parents and kin. We felt that groups composed of couples going through similar life experiences might normalize common strains and adjustments; by getting the idea that "we're all in the same boat," partners might come to
feel that the strain they are experiencing is normal at this stage of adult life (cf.
Lieberman, 1981), and might blame each other less for their distress. If we could
help family-making become more of a joint endeavor—not just during labor and
delivery, but in the months before and after as well—husbands and wives might not
feel so separated by their gender-linked roles once they became parents. Finally,
contemporary men generally have little access to settings in which they can share
their experiences about intimate family matters. In order to encourage men's involvement in talking about these aspects of their lives, our male staff members were
as involved as their wives were in recruiting, interviewing, and working with parents in the couples groups.

The groups met weekly during the transition to parenthood because we felt that
after partners anticipated becoming a family, it was important to have a forum for
exploring their actual experience and assessing their satisfaction with the reality of
their lives once the babies were born. We invited the babies to become part of the
group as soon as they were born so that parents would feel less pulled to stay with
their children on group evenings. This gave us the added benefit of having the "real-
life" tensions between parents' and babies' needs more available to work with in the
group.

The Group Leaders

Each group was led by one of three married staff couples. Five of the six leaders
were clinical psychologists[4] at the pre- or postdoctoral level and the sixth was a
businesswoman. The co-investigators of the longitudinal study, based on our experience in the pilot study intervention (Cowan, et al., 1978), trained the other two
couples. All leaders completed the study questionnaires, focusing on our own lives
as individuals and as couples. We then met weekly as a group over a 4-month period, using the semi-structured format we would be using with the intervention
groups. Monitoring our own feelings about self-disclosure, we explored aspects of
our individual and couple lives as they were evoked by the questionnaires and the
day-to-day events in our lives.

Six couples groups were conducted over a 2-year period. Once the intervention
groups began, supervision of the clinical work took place in our staff group on a
weekly and then bimonthly basis throughout the first and second years of the study.
Thus all staff couples monitored the process and progress of each group.

Group Structure

The couples groups were two-and-a-half hours long, and were held in evenings or
on weekends to be compatible with participants' work schedules. In completing the

---

[4]Only the co-investigators were parents when the study began. Later analyses established that there were
no significant leader effects.

study questionnaires at home, each partner had already begun to think about each aspect of family life. Their questionnaire responses served as a focus for the more structured part of each meeting. Over the six months of meeting together, men and women had a chance to make their expectations and experiences more explicit—to their partners and to other members of the group. In the first meetings, we began by focusing on each of the partners as individuals, and then, slowly over the next weeks, moved to talk of their lives as couples. On a questionnaire we call The Pie, for example, spouses described themselves by dividing a circle to show the main aspects of their life right now, based not on how much time each takes but on how large each aspect of the self feels. Our "Who Does What?" questionnaire, which asks about the couple's division of household tasks, family decisions, and baby care, helped couples begin to spell out their ideas about their role arrangements by focusing on "How it is now" and "How I'd like it to be."

As we talked about the various aspects of married life tapped by the questionnaires, both men and women began to appreciate how their perceptions and feelings about themselves, their division of family labor, and their style of handling conflict or showing caring affected them as individuals and as couples. As we ventured into new domains of life, they tied ideas from earlier group discussions to current issues. "You know, we agreed that it made sense for me to do most of the baby care in the first year. But I just realized that my resentment about Frank's getting to continue his work while I stay home has been affecting our arguments about handling the baby," one mother reported as we tried to understand the bickering she and her husband described. Group participants soon discovered how common it was for men and women to feel discrepancies between expectation and reality.

The unstructured part of each meeting was left open for group members to discuss questions or concerns about any part of their lives. During late pregnancy, several themes were common in each couples' group. Even though almost all were attending childbirth preparation classes together, both husbands and wives expressed concerns that didn't feel appropriate to raise in their childbirth classes. "Even though we've been practicing the exercises, I don't know if I'll feel really prepared when Jan's labor actually begins," Bob confessed. "This job of 'labor coach' feels like quite a responsibility, especially if there are any birth complications." "And I'm nervous about my mother coming to help when we bring the baby home," Jan added. "How do we accept her help and also get the privacy we need without hurting her feelings?" In each group, expectant mothers and fathers shared their worries and attempted to plan together how to meet the challenge of becoming families.

Most men did not know if they were eligible to take paternity leave. The few who were familiar with their company's policy worried about being seen as less serious workers if they cut back their usual work schedule. Wives commiserated about employers who suddenly seemed less eager about maternity leaves than their written policies dictated. Some reported being relegated to less important jobs as they revealed their plans for taking time off (see Chapter 18, Catalyst, this volume, for a discussion of these issues). These family/work dilemmas for men and women were problems for the couple as they tried to juggle their pictures of ideal family-making, their psychological and economic needs as a family, and the barriers in our culture for men and women who work when they have young children (Cowan & Cowan, 1987b). In every couples group, both men and women described racing nervously toward work or school project deadlines and the baby's due date.

Group Process

In the first few months of meetings, we talked about how the couples' lives were arranged now, and anticipated the changes that having a baby would bring. At first, some men seemed less comfortable than their wives about volunteering their questions, feelings, or worries, but with the leaders' encouragement, men in every group began to talk; they described their experience of the pregnancy, anxieties about managing the labor and delivery, and especially their pictures about becoming fathers. We were struck by how many men talked of wanting to be more involved with their children than their fathers had been with them. They wanted to be central figures in their sons' and daughters' lives and hoped that their children would feel able to talk with them about what was on their minds. Their wives seemed equally enthusiastic about having the rearing of the children more equally shared.

After several months of anticipation, couples began to give birth and bring their babies into the groups. Several couples did not miss a meeting in their eagerness to introduce their newborn and describe the details of their baby's birth. "Old hands" who'd been parents for weeks spontaneously brought dinners and words of wisdom for the newest ones. Men returned to the groups excited by their ability to handle long labors and difficult births; they extolled the strength their wives' had shown during labor and delivery, and said they were amazed by the intensity of their feelings for their newborns. The experienced men encouraged those who were about to become fathers: "You wonder and worry about whether you'll be ready when the time comes, and then, you just are," Dan related to Brian. "When the doctor told us it would have to be a Caesarian section, Janet and I just got in there and did it. It was amazing to see that little girl emerge. There's been no experience in my life to match it!" Every man and woman hung on the words of these birth stories, as parents began to call them. Throughout the weeks of sharing these intense experiences, we were continually impressed by how eagerly men who did not easily share intimate feelings began to talk of theirs. Slowly, groups of former strangers became trusted confidants.

In the most general sense, we conceptualized our role as leaders as one of encouraging partners to "have the experience they were having," as Dan Wile (1981) puts it, rather than to ignore unexpected or troubling feelings because they didn't feel entitled to them. After the babies were born, fathers talked more about their experiences of juggling their work outside the family, getting to know their babies, and trying to stay in touch with their wives. As each participant described his or her view of what was happening, we encouraged others to listen and share their reactions. We drew each partner out so that we could understand both points of view and explore the implications of their different perspectives for their relationship as a couple.

After meeting with couples in six different groups, it became quite clear that even the most compatible spouses had different views on many important aspects of their lives. Whether or not to pick up a crying baby drew varied intense reactions from group members; when we asked them to explain, men and women talked about patterns they did or did not want to repeat from their own growing up experiences. Most couples do not usually have the opportunity to hear these kinds of discussions between partners, and few have settings in which they can receive assistance in revealing, redefining, and negotiating what appear to be problematic differences. In each group, fathers and mothers were exposed to a range of ideas about how couples arrange lives and intimate family relationships. This may have been the most valuable lesson for the group participants.

In the last months of weekly discussions, the groups began to mirror the couples' lives at home. One father would describe his distress about having no time alone with his wife, and his wife and baby would begin crying. Another father would become absorbed in feeding or diapering his daughter, and we would all become distracted with him, focusing on the baby and unable to complete our thoughts. Many partners expressed surprise at how easily their needs as individuals and couples were relegated to the back burner as they tried to cope with the extraordinary demands of a newborn and the rest of life. "It's so difficult to finish a sentence!" one father said. "Just trying to do the laundry, bathe the baby, get dinner, and figure out how to manage our decreased income since she stopped working seems to take up all of our energy. We're like ships passing in the night." Others nodded with recognition of this new state of affairs. We encouraged partners to use the group to share their frustrations *and* their attempts at working them out. Our goal was to help couples keep track of their own needs as they took on the full-time job of parenting their infants.

Competence was often an unspoken issue for parents, especially for the men. Here our work in the couples' groups taught us about a delicate balance—between family and work and between husbands and wives. A father who had been at work all day might offer to hold his daughter to soothe or change her. Even though his wife was usually eager for him to become involved in the care of the baby, if he showed the slightest hesitation as he tried to make the baby comfortable, she was likely to move in. "She likes it better if you hold her this way," she might encourage. If their daughter fussed in the next few moments, he was likely to hand her back to his wife, saying to the baby, "Here, let's give you back to the expert." We began to see how these subtle shifts between parents and baby could lead spouses to take on more traditional roles than either intended (cf. Coysh, 1984). When we consider these subtle communications along with the powerful barriers in the outside world to men's family involvement (Cowan & Cowan, 1987b, c), the trends in our data of fathers being less involved in caring for their babies than they had predicted become even more understandable.

Marital Problems

When a couple used the protection of the group to work on a problem they couldn't resolve by themselves, we encouraged both spouses to describe their views of the situation. As Wile (1981) has suggested, based on his work with couples in distress, when partners ignore or bypass feelings they do not feel entitled to, it often creates more distance between them. It was common for husbands to say they were concerned about how the couple would get some time together, and for wives to feel misunderstood when they found it difficult to leave their babies in someone else's care. Finding that neither was alone in experiencing these pulls led some spouses to attribute their conflict more to the complexity of this time of life than to each other's stubborness.

In several cases, we saw a couple through a major crisis. Several months after their babies' births, mothers in two different couples' groups had to be hospitalized for serious physical illnesses. In both cases, frightened, anxious, and sometimes angry fathers were left to care for their infants with almost no preparation. We used the group setting to make sense of these dramatic events—for the couple in crisis and for the others. Group members rallied, spontaneously offering material and emotional support to the distressed parents and babies. In both groups, members suggested that the group go on meeting a little longer until the distressed couple was on a more even keel.

By the time each group in the project came to an end, almost every father and mother said that they felt close to some of the others with whom they had survived the first months of becoming a family. Many commented that they did not have other *couples* with whom they could talk in this way; few of their friends seemed able to sustain interest in their pressing concerns about how to handle a colicky baby or when to leave a newborn in someone else's care, and almost none felt able to discuss their marital concerns as they had begun to do in our groups. "The rest of the world wants to know how the baby is doing," one father commented, "but here we get to ask about us."

The Effects of the Intervention

There were certainly many anecdotal signs of the impact of the groups on parents: some men and women continued to visit with others they had met in their groups, and several families from our pilot study groups have remained friends since 1975. At the end of the 6-month intervention in the current study, participants of two of the six groups decided to go on meeting without the leaders. One group continued for four months, the other for almost a year. In both cases, the couples reported later, they decided to stop meeting regularly when one of the couples began to discuss serious marital difficulties. Without experienced leaders, it had been difficult for the group to know how to encourage the safe exploration of each others' marital problems.

From the participants' evaluations and our qualitative observations, we know that ongoing couples' groups with trained leaders can help partners anticipate change and discuss differences between spouses or between expectation and reality. With leaders who are trained to work with marital problems, a group for expectant and new-parent couples can provide a safe setting in which many new parents will feel able to explore both small and complex marital problems as they develop. Although these were not therapy groups, they appeared to function at times as safe containers for the sharing of complex and intense feelings. While it was gratifying to know that the couples felt the groups were helpful to their adjustment as families, we were anxious to see whether we could measure any effects of the intervention from the longitudinal questionnaire data describing parents' individual and marital change and satisfaction over time.

The findings reported next are based primarily on three-way analyses of variance and covariance (gender × time × condition) for 47 couples who became parents—23 who participated in an intervention group and 24 who completed pre- and post-birth questionnaires but did not participate in a group. We treated husbands' and wives' responses as related measures, and time as a within-subject variable. The comparison between 46 group participants and 48 men and women who did not participate in a group constitutes the third dimension of the analyses. The differences reported here were statistically significant with a probability of .05 or less.

Pregnancy to 18 Months After Birth

We found significant differences between intervention-group participants and parents in the comparison sample in almost every one of the five domains:

Sense of Self.

We measured each arc of The Pie in order to get a picture of men's and women's sense of themselves as they moved from being partners to becoming parents. Comparisons between "How it is now" and "How I'd like it to be" served as one satisfaction with self index, and the self-esteem subscale of the Adjective Checklist (Gough & Heilbrun, 1980) as another.

Whereas there were no significant differences between intervention and no-intervention fathers' changes in self-concept over time, differences in their wives' patterns suggested an impact on the couple. Over the transition to parenthood, mothers who had been in a couples group showed smaller declines in the "partner" or "lover" aspect of self than mothers without the intervention. Both subsamples of mothers showed similar declines in the "worker" or "student" aspects of self when the babies were six months old, but by 18 months postpartum, mothers who had been in the intervention showed a return to their pre-baby worker or student self, whereas mothers without the intervention showed pie pieces for work or study that were half the size of their pre-baby selves. It looks as if the intervention couples were less likely to move toward traditional work and family arrangements during the family formation period. Despite these differences in self-descriptions, there were no differences between the subsamples in *satisfaction with self* over the two years, during which self-esteem remained quite stable for men and women.

Partners' Role Arrangements.

These were measured on a 36-item "Who Does What?" scale (Cowan, et al., 1978) on which each partner described the couple's division of household, decision-making, and child-related tasks. Role satisfaction was inferred from the discrepancy between "How it is" and "How I'd like it to be" on this measure. Here too, it appears as if group participation had different effects on husbands and wives. When the babies were six months old, partners' style of dividing the baby care tasks was not different in the two subsamples, but fathers who had been in a couples' group were *less satisfied* with their involvement in the care of their babies than fathers without the intervention. By contrast, the wives from the intervention groups were *more satisfied* with the couple's division of labor than wives without the intervention. From the Ideal ratings, we could see that fathers who had been in a couples group wanted to be doing *more* housework and child care than they were.

From our discussions in the couples groups, it became very clear that men wanted to continue their involvement in outside-the-family work *and* become significantly involved in caring for their babies. Over the six months of meeting together, as fathers became painfully aware of what it takes to manage a demanding job and the day-to-day care of a household with a baby, their frustration rose. We think that fathers who were in our intervention groups probably talked more about reconciling these two aspects of their lives than most men do in the first year of new parenthood. While most mothers felt these work and family pulls too, their greater satisfaction with "Who does what?" may have reflected their appreciation that both partners were sharing a concern about running the household, raising their child, and keeping their relationship as a couple alive, even if they couldn't quite arrange the egalitarian division of labor they had planned.

One year later, when the babies were 18 months old, intervention fathers' satisfaction with "Who does what?" had remained stable, while fathers without the intervention showed a decline. At this point, fathers from the intervention groups were more satisfied than the comparison fathers with their involvement with the children. Here, we think, is the delicate balance in action. Perhaps the fact that their wives retained more of their "worker" and "lover" selves as well as their satisfaction with the couple's division of baby care helped men from the intervention subsample reconcile the discrepancies between what they had hoped to do and what the reality of their lives permitted. Some support for this idea comes from data showing that husbands and wives from the couples' groups began to have more similar perceptions of their division of baby care by 18 months after birth than spouses without the intervention.

Couple Communication.

Men from both samples reported similar increases in marital conflict and disagreement throughout the transition to parenthood. It is of interest, however, that men who had been in a couples group reported more conflict with their wives about two issues: the family division of labor, and the quality of time the couple spent together. While it is possible that the group discussions contributed to more arguments about these aspects of life, it is also possible that partners who had been in a couples group continued to talk more often about what disturbed them about their division of labor and how to get more time together. "We learned that we do better if we can talk about what is bothering us rather than sweeping it under the rug," one husband said, in answer to our question about the impact of being in a couples group. "Yes," his wife agreed, "because when you don't deal with them directly, those things tend to come out anyway."

While there were no differences in the two subsamples in reports of *positive* change in the sexual relationship from before to after birth, both husbands and wives from the intervention sample reported fewer *negative* changes in their sexual relationship than those without the intervention. This aspect of couple communication becomes very salient during the period of having a baby, and the protected setting of the couples groups seemed to make it possible for some couples to exchange information about this usually private aspect of married life. One couple would hesitantly mention the awkwardness of making love late in pregnancy or after giving birth, of attempting to arrange bodies that no longer fit together easily. Rueful laughter was often followed by squeals of "You too?" and relieved sighs from others in the group. This sharing of personal information was common in all of our groups; it clearly relieved tensions for some couples and answered questions for others. It may be that having married couples as co-leaders facilitated the sharing of intimate information (cf. Clulow, 1982). The reports of less negative change in the intervention couples are consistent with our impression that when group members shared their experiences of unexpected changes in their sexual relationship, the changes became normalized for many partners, who then said they felt less worried that something was wrong and more hopeful about things getting back to normal.

Marital Satisfaction.

Since most researchers who have examined marital satisfaction from before to after birth report moderate but significant declines (Awalt, 1981; Belsky, et al., 1983; Blum, 1983; Grossman, et al., 1980), we were most interested in examining any effects of the intervention on partners' feelings about their marriage. In our study, the marital satisfaction (Short Marital Adjustment Test; Locke & Wallace, 1959) of partners without the intervention declined from pregnancy to six months after birth, and dropped even more sharply from 6 to 18 months postpartum. For the intervention group participants, too, there was a decline from pregnancy to six months after birth, although their decline was less severe than that of the comparison couples. But from 6 to 18 months postpartum, parents from the intervention groups maintained their level of marital satisfaction, a period in which the no-intervention spouses became even more dissatisfied. Intervention participants' stable scores on marital satisfaction were maintained into the second year of parenthood despite the fact that their conflict had increased and their social support had begun to decrease. In her analyses of our data, Heming (1985) found that when initial levels of self-esteem, role satisfaction, and life stress were statistically controlled, there were still significant effects of the intervention, and the effects were stronger for men than for their wives.

Marital Stability after Two Years.

When all 96 couples in the longitudinal study were followed up two years after they joined the study, we learned that 10 couples had separated or filed for divorce. Four were from the subsample of 24 childless couples, and the other six were from the subsamples of 48 couples who became parents but had no intervention. By contrast, the marriages of all participants of the couples groups were still intact when the babies were 18 months old.

The Longer-Term Effects of the Intervention

We talked again with all of the couples four years after they joined the study, when the first children of the parent samples were three-and-a-half years old. We learned that one more couple in the no-intervention sample had separated, bringing the total to seven, or 15%. This figure is consistent with the findings of Eiduson and her colleagues (1981), in which 15% of the parents of three-year olds had separated or divorced after the birth of their first child. At this 42 months-after-birth follow-up, only one of the 23 (4%) intervention couples had separated. Thus the intervention couples were still more likely to be in intact marriages more than three years after the intervention ended. Although the numbers are too small to be statistically significant, the trend seems noteworthy.

There are many analyses to complete of the 42-month postpartum data to test our five-domain model and search for any longer-term effects of the intervention. At this point, several findings from our preliminary analyses suggest that there may be some intervention effects on parent–child relationships and on the developmental status of the children at three-and-a-half. The quality of parent–child interaction and the children's developmental level were assessed by different staff teams, each of whom were blind to other information about the family. In visits to our project playroom, fathers from the intervention groups were rated as warmer and less angry when they worked with their three-and-a-half year olds on challenging tasks than fathers from the comparison sample. Mothers who had participated in the intervention were rated as more creative than the comparison mothers as they worked with their children in our playroom. For the most part, our assessments of the children's coping styles and level of development at 42 months revealed few differences between the intervention and no-intervention samples, but one important difference favored the children of parents from the intervention groups. Using materials and assessments developed by Jeanne and Jack Block (1979), children of parents who had participated in the intervention groups were rated as more *ego resilient*—that is, more flexible and adaptable in approaching new tasks—than children of the couples who had had no intervention. Thus in addition to some longer-term marital differences between intervention and no-intervention couples, there were also some parent–child relationship and child outcome differences as well. Future analyses will explore intervention effects in each of the five domains of our model.

Evaluating the Results of the Intervention

Preventive Intervention.

It is clear that the groups did not prevent men from facing the typical changes and strains of new fatherhood. Anticipating a particular change and discussing discrepancies between expectations and reality did not prevent husbands from having tense middle-of-the-night discussions with their wives about their division of labor or whether to pick up the baby when it cried. But because extensive discussion had occurred in the groups prior to birth, disagreements between partners did not come as a shock to those fathers. They knew that other couples had had different opinions on a number of critical issues in their lives. Rather than conclude that one spouse or the other was wrong, participants tended to bring their differences back to the group for renewed consideration.

The group did not seem to affect basic aspects of men's behavior in their families. In general, fathers in the couples' groups did not become more involved in housework or caring for the baby in the first months of parenthood than fathers without the intervention. But by 18 months after birth, both men and women who had been in an intervention group were more *satisfied* with their role arrangements than parents without the intervention, even though group fathers had been less satisfied with their involvement one year earlier. One possible interpretation of these findings is that the groups function merely as a palliative to help parents feel more satisfied. Another possibility is that experiences in the group affected men's and women's *expectations* about their lives as parents and partners, leaving less discrepancy between what they expected and the reality of their lives (Belsky, 1984; Garrett, 1983; Parke, 1979).

Cognitive theories of stress and emotion (cf. Lazarus, 1984) seem relevant here too. They posit that our experience of stress is mediated by our cognitive appraisal of events. In this view, men's and women's evaluations of their stress as new parents could affect their ability to cope adaptively. Once group participants knew that their shifts were common to this time of life, they were less likely to view them as a commentary on their adequacy as a couple, and more likely to move to the next step of considering how they might make adjustments that would work for both spouses. This is where mental health professionals can play an essential role. By raising the question of what would be more satisfying for both parents, they can encourage couples to move beyond the realm of reacting to one of adaptive coping. There is some support for this idea in a pattern we noticed at our post-birth interviews with all couples in the study. Although partners in both subsamples often recounted difficulties or dilemmas they were experiencing, participants from the couples groups appeared to have a more optimistic attitude about it: "We haven't solved all the 'who does what?' issues yet," one father said, "but we're working on it." Many who had not been in a couples' group tended to report changes that seemed to be *happening to them*: for example, one father reported in answer to a question about changes in their relationship, "We're just not spending as much time together as we used to, and when we do, we find ourselves bickering a lot." The fact that all of the couples group marriages were still intact when the children were one-and-a-half, and that all but one couple were still together when the children were almost four, suggests that there may be a connection between group participation and a feeling of being able to do something about the less than satisfying aspects of marriage.

The Effects on Men and Marriage.

We have heard researchers and clinicians suggest that it is difficult to get men involved in a consideration of family issues. While a number of men in our study were skeptical at first, most became active and responsive participants. In the couples groups, fathers functioned as ongoing models for each other; as some men became involved in discussion and active caregiving of their newborns, others followed. As they diapered, fed, and soothed their infants, they talked about how to handle their children and keep their marriages vital, defying the stereotype of the uninvolved father. The structure and process of the group reinforced the attitude that regardless of the inequality of time spent with the baby, fathers and mothers were involved in a joint endeavor to remain partners as they created a new family.

By providing a setting in which both parents could continue to paint their pictures of life as a family, the intervention appears to have helped men become more satisfied with their own involvement in the care of the baby, with their sexual relationship, and with the overall marriage. It also appears to have made it possible for some couples to negotiate work and family balances that allowed mothers to retain more of the "worker" and "partner" aspects of themselves in the second year of parenthood. This balance between spouses may have contributed to the intervention couples' more sustained marital satisfaction and stability during their children's toddler years.

Short- and Long-term Effects

While the couples groups offered emotional support and a place to try new ideas, they may have also served as temporary disequilibrators to some parents. Despite the fact that group participants were vocal about the groups' helpfulness, the data from our postpartum follow-ups at six months suggest that participation in a couples group may actually contribute to increased dissatisfaction or distress initially. If our assessment of intervention effects had stopped at that point, we would not have seen any statistically significant differences in favor of the group members. Most of the measurable positive effects did not appear until more than a year after the groups ended.

From very different theoretical vantage points, Werner (1942) and Erikson (1968) propose that conflict, disequilibration, and temporary disorganization are *necessary* for individuals to proceed from one developmental stage to another. It may be that the positive effects of the intervention followed a period of disorganization, dissatisfaction, and some trial and error on the part of group parents. We know from our experience of leading the couples groups that when husbands or wives experienced unexpected change or dissatisfaction, they tended to feel disequilibrated and discouraged at first. We discussed these patterns often, especially in the early months of being a family. The fact that husbands and wives experienced their disappointments at different times in the transition may have helped keep the discouraged/renegotiate cycle in motion, especially in intervention couples who vowed to keep working on things after their groups ended.

The fact that the effects of the intervention were clearer at 18 and 42 months after the birth of the child than they were immediately after the intervention suggests that the groups helped parents face the initial strains of the transition, rather than ignore them as unacceptable, and eventually move on to create more satisfying patterns (see Chapter 2, P. Cowan, this volume, for a fuller discussion of this process). This delay in the positive effects of the intervention may be one reason why intervention studies with a one-time "outcome" measure—often quite soon after the intervention ends—find so few visible effects.

WHAT HAVE WE LEARNED ABOUT FATHERHOOD AND INTERVENTION?

From their responses to the questions in our interviews and the discussions in our couples groups, it is clear that men are quite comfortable thinking about and working on family issues. Although they often expressed more initial skepticism than their wives did about the need for the intervention, and took more coaxing to return their questionnaires, most fathers in our study eventually became vocal supporters of the couples groups. In the years since the intervention ended, a number of fathers have called asking for assistance in finding a counselor or therapist when they feel in difficulty; others have called when friends or relatives become pregnant, insisting that they would benefit from a similar group experience.

Breaking the Negative Cycle

Men who had low self-esteem during their wives' pregnancy tended to report more stress in the parent role two years later, if they had had no intervention. On the other hand, for fathers who participated in a couples' group, there was no link between their pre-parenthood self-esteem and later parenting stress. In addition, the more that men without the intervention experienced a decline in marital satisfaction, the more likely they were to experience low self-esteem, symptoms of depression, marital conflict, and parenting stress when their children were toddlers. Yet, none of these correlational patterns were found for men who had been in a couples group. We had suggested that status in one family domain would be related to the quality in others. What we have found is that although the model appears to capture how husbands and wives function during a major life transition, a preventive intervention can interfere with the spread of negative effects so that negative changes in one domain do not necessarily color a man's feelings about himself or about his relationships with his wife and child. We know from studies of marital therapy outcome (Gurman & Kniskern, 1978) that when both spouses are involved in working on the marriage, lower rates of marital dissolution occur. The intervention effects suggests that when expectant couples work with trained mental health professionals on marital strain and dissatisfaction during their transition from couple to family, they too experience less marital dissatisfaction and lower rates of marital dissolution.

Our finding of a 15% separation and divorce rate by the time the first child is three-and-a-half in no-intervention parents is consistent with data from Eiduson's (1982) study and seems to fit the timing of divorce in Santrock, Sitterle, and Warshak's study (Chapter 10, this volume). Given some suggestive data from a national survey showing that the time gap between family formation and family dissolution appears to be narrowing (Bumpass & Rindfuss, 1979), it appears as if contemporary marriages may be at greater risk for dissolution during family formation than were those of earlier cohorts. While the majority of marriages do stay intact during family formation, increased marital conflict and dissatisfaction are bound to have an impact on children's early development. It is time to move beyond the proliferation of risk studies, to create and evaluate systematically interventions designed to strengthen family relationships as early in the family-building process as possible. Men have shown their willingness to participate. Their children may ultimately reap the greatest benefits.

REFERENCES

Awalt, S.J. (1981). *Transition to parenthood: Predictors of individual and marital stability and change*. Unpublished doctoral dissertation, University of California, Berkeley.

Belsky, J. (1984, May). *The development of marriage and fathering across transitions*. Paper presented at NIH conference: Men's Transitions to Parenthood, Bethesda, Md.

Belsky, J., Spanier, G.B., & Rovine, M. (1983). Stability and change in marriage across the transition to parenthood. *Journal of Marriage & the Family, 45*, 567–577.

Bittman, S., & Zalk, S.R. (1978). *Expectant fathers*. New York: Hawthorne.

Block, J.H., & Block, J. (1979). The role of ego control and ego-resiliency in the organization of behavior. In W.A. Collins (Ed.), *Minnesota symposia in child psychology (vol. 13)*. Hillsdale, NJ: Erlbaum.

Blum, M.E. (1983). *A longitudinal study of transition to parenthood in primiparous couples*. Paper presented at the American Psychological Association Meetings, Anaheim, CA.

Bumpass, L., & Rindfuss, R.R. (1979). Children's experience of marital disruption. *American Journal of Sociology, 85*, 49–65.

Caplan, G. (1964). *Principles of preventive psychiatry*. New York: Basic.

Clulow, C.F. (1982). *To have and to hold: Marriage, the first baby and preparing couples for parenthood*. Aberdeen: Aberdeen University Press.

Clulow, C.F. (1985). *Marital therpapy: An inside view*. Aberdeen: Aberdeen University Press.

Cowan, C.P., & Cowan, P.A. (1987a). A preventive intervention for couples becoming parents. In C.Z.F. Bouykydis (Ed.), *Research on support for parents and infants in the first postnatal year*. Norwood, NJ: Ablex.

Cowan, C.P., & Cowan, P.A. (1987b). Men's involvement in parenthood: Identifying the antecedents and understanding the barriers. In P. Berman & F.A. Pedersen (Eds.), *Men's transitions to parenthood*. Hillsdale, NJ: Erlbaum.

Cowan, C.P., & Cowan, P.A. (1987c). Who does what when partners become parents? Men's involvement in the family. *Marriage and Family Review, 13, 1 & 2*.

Cowan, C.P., Cowan, P.A., Coie, L., & Coie, J.D. (1978). Becoming a family: The impact of a first child's birth on the couple's relationship. In W.B. Miller & L.F. Newman (Eds.), *The first child and family formation*. Chapel Hill, NC: Carolina Population Center.

Cowan, C.P., Cowan, P.A., Heming, G., Garrett, E.V., Coysh, W.S., Curtis-Boles, H., & Boles, A.J. (1985). Transitions to parenthood: His, hers, and theirs. *Journal of Family Issues, 6*, (4), 451–481.

Cowan, P.A., Cowan, C.P., & Heming, G. (1986). *Risks to the marriage when partners become parents: Implications for family development*. Paper presented to the American Psychiatric Association Meetings. Washington, DC.

Coysh, W.S. (1984). *Men's role in caring for their children: Predictive and concurrent correlates of father involvement*. Unpublished doctoral dissertation, University of California, Berkeley.

Crockenberg, S. (1981). Infant irritability, mother responsiveness, and social support influences on the security of infant-mother attachment. *Child Development, 52*, 857–865.

Eiduson, B.T. (1981, April). *Parent/child relationships in alternative families and socioemotional development of children at 3 years of age*. Paper presented at Society for Research in Child Development Meetings, Boston, MA.

Entwisle, D., & Doering, S. (1981). *The first birth: A family turning point*. Baltimore: Johns Hopkins University Press.

Erikson, E. (1968). *Identity, youth and crisis*. New York: Norton.

Feldman, S.S. (1987). Predicting strain in mothers and fathers of six-month-old infants: A short-term longitudianl study. In P. Berman & F.A. Pedersen (Eds.), *Men's transitions to parenthood*. Hillsdale, NJ: Erlbaum.

Garrett, E.T. (1983, August). *Women's experiences of early parenthood: Expectation vs. reality*. Paper presented at American Psychological Association Meetings, Anaheim, California.

Gough, H.G., & Heilbrun, A.B., Jr. (1980). *The Adjective Check List manual*. Palo Alto, CA: Consulting Psychologists Press.

Grossman, F., Eichler, L., & Winickoff, S., (1980). *Pregnancy, birth, and parenthood*. San Francisco: Jossey-Bass.

Gurman, A.S., & Kniskern, D.P. (1978). Deterioration in marital and family therapy: Empirical, clinical and conceptual issues. *Family Process, 17*, 3–20.

Haley, J. (1976). Toward a theory of pathological systems. In C. Zuk & I. Borszomenyi-Nagy (Eds.), *Family therapy and disturbed families*. Palo Alto: Science and Behavior Books.

Heming, G. (1985). *Predicting adaptation during the transition to parenthood*. Unpublished dissertation. University of California, Berkeley.

Hobbs, D.F., Jr. (1965). Parenthood as crisis: A third study. *Journal of Marriage and the Family, 27*, 367–372.

Hoffman, L.W. (1978). Effects of a first child on women's social role development. In W. Miller and L. Newman (Eds.), *The first child and family formation*. Chapel Hill, NC: Carolina Population Center.

Lazarus, R.S. (1984). On the primacy of cognition. *American Psychologist, 39*, 124–129.

LeMasters, E.E. (1957). Parenthood as crisis. *Marriage and Family Living, 19*, 352–355.

Lieberman, M.A. (1981). The effects of social support on responses to stress. In L. Goldberger & S. Breznitz (Eds.), *Handbook of stress*, 764–781. New York: Free Press.

Locke, H., & Wallace, K. (1959). Short marital adjustment and prediction tests: Their relia-bility and validity. *Marriage and Family Living, 21*, 251–255.

Markman, H.J., & Kadushin, F.S. (1987). *The preventive effects of Lamaze training for first-time parents: A longitudinal study*. Unpublished manuscript.

May, K.A., & Perrin, S.T. (1982). Prelude: Pregnancy and birth. In S.M.H. Hanson & F.W. Bozett, (Eds.), *Dimensions of Fatherhood*. Beverly Hills: Sage.

Minuchin, S. (1974). *Families and family therapy*. Cambridge: Harvard University Press.

Nuckolls, K.B., Cassel, J., & Kaplan, B.H. (1972). Psychological assets, life crises and the prognosis of pregnancy. *American Journal of Epidemiology, 95*, 431–441.

Parke, R.D. (1979). Perspectives on father-infant interaction. In J. Osofsky (Ed.), *Handbook of infant development*. New York: Wiley.

Pedersen, F.A., Anderson, B.J., & Cain, R.L. (1977). *An approach to understanding link-ages between the parent-infant and spouse relationships*. Paper presented at the Society for Research in Child Development, New Orleans, LA.

Rapoport, R. (1963). Normal crises, family structure and mental health. *Family Process, 1*, 68–80.

Rapoport, R., Rapoport, R.N., & Streilitz, A. (1977). *Fathers, mothers and society: To-wards new alliances*. New York: Basic.

Raush, H.L., Barry, W.A., Hertel, R.K., & Swain, M.A. (1974). *Communication, conflict and marriage*. San Francisco: Jossey-Bass.

Reibstein, A. (1981). Cited in Lieberman, M.A. The effects of social supports on responses to stress. In L. Goldberger and S. Brenitz (Eds.), *Handbook of stress*. New York: Free Press.

Rossi, A. (1968). Transition to parenthood. *Journal of Marriage and the Family, 30*, 26–39.

Satir, V. (1972). *Peoplemaking*. Palo Alto: Science and Behavior Books.

Shereshefsky, P.M., & Yarrow, L. (1973). *Psychological aspects of a first pregnancy and early postnatal adaptation*. New York: Raven.

Tinsley, B.R., & Parke, R.D. (1984). Grandparents as support and socialization agents. In M. Lewis (Ed.), *Beyond the dyad*. New York: Plenum.

Wainright, W.H. (1966). Fatherhood as a precipitant of mental illness. *American Journal of Psychiatry, 123*, 40–44.

Wandersman, L.P. (1983). An analysis of the effectiveness of parent-infant groups. *Journal of Prevention*.

Werner, H. (1942). *The comparative psychology of mental development*. New York: Follett.

Wile, D.B. (1981). *Couples therapy: A nontraditional approach*. New York: Wiley.

Zaslow, M., Pedersen, F., Kramer, E. Cain, R., Suwalsky, J., & Fivel, M. (1981, April). *Depressed mood in new fathers: Interview and behavioral correlates*. Paper presented at the Society for Research in Child Development, Boston, MA.

Zilboorg, G. (1931). Depressive reactions related to parenthood. *American Journal of Psy-chiatry, 88*, 927, 962.

CHAPTER 17

Clinical Work with Divorced and Widowed Fathers: The Adjusting Family Model

ANDREW I. SCHWEBEL, MARK FINE, and JOHN R. MORELAND

Assisted by Patrick Prindle

Fein's (1978) useful conceptual framework for understanding paternal behavior suggests that fathers have historically adopted one of three fathering roles: traditional, modern, or emergent. Differing from traditional fathers, whose primary activities center around the work world and who have little to do with the actual parenting of their children, modern fathers view successful child development as a main goal, primarily in the areas of appropriate sex-role identity, academic performance, and moral development. In contrast to both types, the emergent father participates more equally with his wife in child-care activities.

   We believe that the emergent father role has a number of advantages for fathers, their children, and their spouses. Not only can such fathers foster positive child development (Lamb, 1982; Radin, 1981; Radin & Sagi, 1982; Russell, 1982), but the process of being more expressive and nurturant can help men feel more satisfied as parents, and enrich their family relationships.

   Yet, current literature on fatherhood suggests that because men's repertoire of interpersonal and expressive behaviors has been unduly restricted by sex-role socialization, many may require considerable help in acquiring skills necessary for effective parenting. In addition, the fathers who in increasing numbers are engaging in nontraditional parenting activities may need assistance and support in maintaining positive levels of self-regard. As these men make greater commitments to the parenting process, their task is often made all the more difficult by the reactions of employers, colleagues, and peers.

   While fathers from intact families face many challenges in becoming effective parents, those experiencing the emotional turmoil of divorce or the death of a spouse have even greater difficulties. In this chapter we will examine three groups of single-parent fathers—widowers with custody of their children, divorced men with custody, and divorced men without custody—exploring the thesis that each must overcome both internal and external barriers if they are to engage in effective and satisfying parenting. We will describe our Adjusting Family Model (AFM), which outlines the stages a family passes through as it moves from a nuclear unit to one in transition, and then to one restabilized in a new form. The AFM also suggests a set of intervention strategies aimed at helping a family meet the problems it faces at each point.

The first part of this chapter will discuss the common and unique experiences of divorced, widowed, and single-parent fathers; the second part will review clinical and psycho-educational programs designed to help single-parent fathers engage more effectively and meaningfully in the parenting process.

IMPEDIMENTS TO EMERGENT FATHERING

It appears that there are at least three reasons why men are not adopting the emergent role in large numbers. First, men may believe they lack the requisite skills to become more competently involved with their children. Second, internalized conceptions of the male role may inhibit men's increased participation. Finally, there may be social and institutional pressures on men to continue to strive for achievement and to refrain from expanding their roles as fathers.

Father's Parenting Skills

Fathers have been found to be much less involved than mothers in giving care to infants (Clarke-Stewart, 1978; Kotelchuck, 1976; Pederson & Robson, 1969). However, there are data that suggest that fathers may in fact have equal potential for nurturance. Greenberg and Morris (1974) found that as early as three days postpartum, fathers experienced infant bonding, characterized by feelings of preoccupation, absorption, interest, and a desire to touch, hold, and interact with their babies. Similarly, Parke, O'Leary, and West (1972), Parke and Sawin (1976), and Sawin and Parke (1979) found that fathers were as involved as mothers in interacting with their newborns, noting that fathers were as responsive as mothers to their newborn's feeding distress signals and as competent in feeding them. Researchers have noted that while infants may prefer mothers to fathers during much of their first year, significant emotional bonds form between infants and their fathers (Kotelchuck, 1976; Lamb, 1976a, 1976b, 1977).

Differences in mothers' and fathers' parenting styles with young children (Clarke-Stewart, 1978; Weinraub & Frankel, 1977) seem to be due, at least in part, to factors other than competence. To illustrate, Golenkoff and Ames (1979) observed that fathers talked about half as much as mothers did in parent–child triads, but when parents were alone with their children, fathers talked the same amount of time to their children as did mothers. Skill performance differences in mothers' and fathers' interactions with older children (Berman, 1980) may be due to the fact that fathers, when their children are younger, do not relate in ways which allow them to acquire the more complex parenting behaviors required as offspring develop.

The Male Role and Implications for Fathering

Numerous authors (David & Brannon, 1975; Farrell, 1974; Goldberg, 1979; Nichols, 1975; Pleck & Sawyer, 1974; Tolson, 1979) have noted that men's conceptions of masculinity typically emphasize achievement and status, particularly in occupational settings; dominance and control over other people, including wives and children; nonemotionality, with an emphasis on rationality; and refraining from traditionally feminine activities, including child rearing. The role of the emergent father is clearly inconsistent with such a conception of masculinity, and the incongruity may be further exacerbated by life cycle issues. Specifically, at the time when men are likely to become parents, most are actively engaged in meeting the instrumental requirements of the male role by becoming established in the job or career (Gould, 1972; Levinson, 1978; Mayer, 1978).

Institutional Pressures Inhibiting Emergent Fathering

Men's internalized standards are a reflection of the institutionalized norms and expectations of work organizations. Mechanisms for career advancement serve to restrict those who, because of their parental responsibilities, do not demonstrate the expected level of commitment to work (Epstein, 1975; Shepard, 1977). Hood and Golden (1979) have described the detrimental effect that work settings can have on family relationships. For example, the seniority system, which is often the criterion for assigning an employee's work shift, is insensitive to the developmental needs of young families. Not surprisingly, Defrain (1979) found that flexible work schedules were the social change most desired by couples seeking to share child-care responsibilities equally.

EXPERIENCES OF SINGLE PARENT FATHERS

Although there are important differences among widowed, divorced custodial, and divorced noncustodial fathers, there are also a number of commonalities. First and foremost, the process of becoming a single-parent father is stressful, exacerbating the difficulties men have in becoming involved in the regular care of their children (Atkin & Rubin, 1976; Hetherington, Cox, & Cox, 1976; Moreland & Schwebel, 1981). Dreyfuss (1979) notes that beyond the pain men experience at marital separation or the death of a spouse, the loss of their home, their lifestyle, their hopes, and their dreams also causes distress. For example, Hetherington and colleagues (1976) found that noncustodial divorced fathers initially underwent major changes in self-esteem, and felt that their lives lacked structure. During the first year following divorce, these men experienced guilt feelings and depression to the extent that their occupational performance was adversely affected. Weiss (1975) found that the most distinguishing psychological characteristic of noncustodial fathers was the feeling of not being an integral part of the children's household. In contrast, for custodial fathers, even those with considerable prior child-care responsibilities, the role changes associated with increased household and child-care responsibilities have often been found to be frightening and anxiety-producing (Keshet & Rosenthal, 1978).

In addition to the shock, grief, outrage, and fear widowers initially experience as they are thrust into the single-parent role, these men are concerned about their children's well-being and adjustment. Widowers whose wives die suddenly assume the single-parent role without preparation, and have no opportunity either to anticipate and rehearse their new responsibilities or to prepare the children. On the other hand, when the death follows a long illness, widowers may have engaged with their children in anticipatory grief, and gradually assumed increasing responsibility for them. In this situation, family members may be able to ease their transition, as is often the case with divorce.

Following divorce, single-parent fathers often express concern about their changing relationships with their children. Weiss (1975) reports that many divorced fathers feel they have failed their children by leaving the home. These feelings are not restricted to noncustodial fathers. Keshet and Rosenthal (1978) found that even custodial fathers, regardless of which parent had initiated the divorce proceedings, felt as if they had failed their children, and feared the children would rather live with their mothers. In addition, although custodial fathers often report feeling close to their children following divorce (Beattie & Viney, 1981; Orthner, Brown, & Ferguson, 1976), they share a sense of guilt and regret with their noncustodial counterparts that they do not spend enough time with their children. For noncustodial fathers, the situation is often more extreme. Seagull and Seagull (1977) suggest that when noncustodial fathers no longer feel important to their children, they become less involved, with the result that their fears of losing their bond with their children become self-fulfilling prophecies.[1]

Significant interpersonal changes accompany a man's transition to single fatherhood. A number of investigations (Barry, 1979; Bartz & Witcher, 1978; Smith & Smith, 1981) have demonstrated that the members of single fathers' social networks tend to change from married friends to single parents. Mendes (1976) has suggested an explanation for this transition: that the absence of culturally specified role expectations for single fathers leads such men to seek to associate with others facing similar circumstances.

The Adjusting Family Model

The Adjusting Family Model (AFM) was developed to conceptualize how a nuclear family progresses from its own precrisis functioning state (healthy, in the ideal case) at any point in the child-rearing phase of the family cycle, through a stage of change (due to divorce or parental death), and then on to restabilize itself in a new family form. The AFM is based on the literature that views divorce as a dislocation in the family life cycle (e.g., Carter & McGoldrick, 1980, McPhee, 1984), and is informed by our own clinical observations of families experiencing major transitions.

The basic assumption underlying the AFM is that effective family functioning

[1] For a more extensive discussion of the problems of noncustodial fathers, see Chapter 12 by Loewen, this volume.

demands (1) mutuality among family members, defined as reciprocal sensitivity and responsiveness to each other's needs; (2) clear communication, without which intimacy and conflict resolution cannot be attained; and (3) explicit norms, and clear, certain consequences for their violation, making family life as predictable, comfortable, and nonthreatening as possible. We believe that these three characteristics are important in both intact families and single-parent homes. Our model further proposes that after a divorce, the members still constitute a family, but one which now exists in a new form, maintaining two homes, each headed by one parent. The stages of the AFM (see Table 17.1) are as follows:

TABLE 17.1   The Adjusting Family Model

	Intact: Stage 1	Deterioration: Stage 2	Transitional: Stage 3	Restabilized Single-Parent Family: Stage 4
Mutuality between parents	High	Decreased	Absent between divorced spouses.[a]	Circumscribed mutuality between ex-spouses.[a]
Mutuality between parent–child	Age-appropriate level; varies with parent–child dyad	Somewhat decreased	Struggle to rebuild in one parent unit(s)	Age appropriate level; varies with parent–child dyad
Communication between parents	Effective, explicit	Decreased in quality	Disrupted, often fuzzy, causing ineffective problem solving.[a]	Clear in regard to child-related issues.[a]
Communication between parent and child	Age-appropriate level; varies with parent–child dyad	Decreased in quality	Struggle to rebuild	Age appropriate level; varies with parent–child dyad
Norms	Clear	Tested by family members	Being redefined between divorced spouses; being reestablished between single parents and child	Clear
Consequences of violating norms in parental interactions	Predictable	Unpredictable, redefinition of consequences formed in reaction to violations	None, unless ex-spouse learns of behavior and seeks revenge.[a]	Predictable.[a]
Consequences of children violating family norms	Predictable	Possible inconsistencies in parents' reactions	Being redefined	Predictable

TABLE 17.1   *(continued)*

	Intact: Stage 1	Deterioration: Stage 2	Transitional: Stage 3	Restabilized Single-Parent Family: Stage 4
Appropriate interventions	None required. Personal, marital, or family enrichment possible	Individual, couple therapy, family mediation	Mutuality problems: divorce counseling, mediation, support-group membership. Communication problems: divorce counseling, mediation, skills training, particularly for fathers having difficulty in communication. Norm-breaking problems: behavior management skill training, parent-effectiveness courses	None required. Personal, marital, or family enrichment possible. If a new adult is introduced in home, short-term intervention might be useful.

[a]Not relevant for widowers.

Stage One: Effective Intact Family.

While clearly not all families undergoing transition begin as effective nuclear units, AFM uses this point as a baseline. Parental interactions in Stage 1 are characterized by mutuality, clear and explicit communication, and explicit norms concerning appropriate behavior, with predictable consequences for violations. Egocentrism (self-centeredness) in each of the married partners is low. Mutuality, communication, and norm-related concerns in parent–child relationships vary, chiefly depending on the youngster's level of maturity.

Stage Two: Family Deterioration.

Whether the cause is parental conflict, eventually leading to divorce, or repeated and/or lengthy hospitalizations during an illness, Stage Two couples experience a change in the quality of the three critical family characteristics. That is, the marriage partners experience less clear communication, more testing of norms, and less mutuality—although sometimes maternal illness increases a couple's intimacy. Parent–child interactions show decreases in mutuality, communication clarity, and norm clarity and enforcement. With the sudden death of a parent this stage may be omitted.

Stage Three: Family Transition.

Stage Three begins when the spouse dies, or, in divorce, when one parent physically departs from the home. The dynamics involved differ considerably, depending on what caused the family change. With divorce, each single-parent-headed family unit struggles to develop mutuality, clear communication, and explicit norms with associated contingencies for violations. Requirements, procedures, and conditions may vary between the two parent–child units. The ex-spouses must learn to accept that they do not have the ability to influence behaviors in the "other home." Widower-headed families face similar tasks, needing to reestablish mutuality, communication, norms, and contingencies. Their processes are often made more complex by the well-meaning intervention of extended family.

Stage Four: Family Resolution.

Stage Four begins when the family has achieved a new state of equilibrium, perhaps a year or two or longer after the parent's death or physical separation. In divorced families, two distinct, yet overlapping units have been created. Each interdependent unit is headed by a parent who shares responsibility for the children. For families headed by widowed fathers, resolution is accomplished through adequately coping with the major loss, and restoration of healthy levels of mutuality, clear communication, and explicit norms.

Adjusting Family Model Applied to Three Types of Single-Father Homes

Noncustodial Divorced Fathers.

Custody is not contested in over 90% of divorces involving children, but when it is, fathers win custody in approximately 35% of the cases (Lewis, 1978).[2] While fathers are awarded custody more often now than in the past (Tedder, Libbee, & Scherman, 1981), most divorced fathers are still noncustodial parents (Chapter 12, Loewen, this volume).

As Table 17.1 shows, the model Stage One family is assumed to have a satisfactory degree of mutuality, clear communication, and specification and enforcement of normative standards. Even in this stage, however, the seeds of difficulty are sown for future single fathers because most responsibility for expressive parenting is typically carried by mothers. The more parents have divided these responsibilities in gender-stereotypic ways, the less men will be equipped for the challenges they will face when intimacy with their children is threatened following divorce.

During Stage Two, marital conflict disrupts mutuality, family communication, and the family's definition of acceptable behavior. Families may remain in Stage Two for varying periods of time before they return to Stage One (either with or without intervention), or move to Stage Three.

Stage Three marks the actual physical separation, with the father or mother leav-

---

[2]Various percentages have been reported, depending on the sample studied. See Chapter 12 by Loewen, this volume, for further information on this issue.

ing the home. At this point, there is often a complete breakdown of mutuality between the two parents and disruptions of it between parents and children. Both parents become egocentric, finding themselves hesitant to cooperate and having intense feelings toward the other. The following is a typical example, as expressed by Dewey, a newly divorced father, at one of our parent skill-development workshop sessions:

> My ex-wife has nerve. Last Sunday night, just before I left my apartment to take Tommy home, Brenda calls and asks me to pick up a pack of cigarettes for her. I laughed and said, "We aren't married any more." She was mad but invited me in for coffee so we could plan Tommy's vacation. Before I left I asked Brenda to find out why Tommy had gotten so mad at me last Saturday night. Brenda refused and I was furious at the boy's mother.

Here, Dewey's egocentric-thinking prevented him from comprehending his ex-wife's hesitance to intervene on his behalf.

Hetherington and colleagues (1976) report that two months after the divorce, 60% of the contacts between the ex-spouses are characterized by conflicts, usually focused on issues of finances and child support, visitation, and child-rearing practices. Communication between parents and children is similarly disturbed. Father–child communication may be ineffective because fathers can no longer rely on wives to help them relate, because fathers may be preoccupied and emotionally unavailable, and/or because the father or the mother may be perceived by the children as requiring them to choose sides. With communication so impaired, conflict resolution and expression of intimacy in the father's household may be severely hampered.

Since each family unit establishes its own norms regarding appropriate behavior, the children may experience two sets of standards. When contrasted with fathers from intact homes, noncustodial divorced fathers have been found to make fewer maturity demands on their children, communicate less effectively with them, have less control, and be more inconsistent in their discipline (Hetherington, et al., 1976). Neal, a father in our psycho-educational training group for single parents, described the first month after his separation:

> I felt my relationship with the kids was shaky. I only saw them a few hours a week. I hated saying "no" to them over and over again, so I let them do pretty much what they pleased. Guess I thought they'd like me better that way. Instead, they seemed to get confused about what was okay when they were at my place and what wasn't. They kept doing wilder and wilder things.

Noncontingent permissiveness, in conjunction with fathers' inability to communicate with their children, usually gives rise to chaotic times between father and children, and to feelings of anger, resentment, and failure in fathers. Children's confusion about the appropriateness of behaviors and the lack of predictable consequences in their father's home, may be exacerbated by the involvement of a new significant other in the father's life. He may be lax when she is present, or she may fail to enforce house rules in an effort to win his youngsters' affection.

Noncustodial divorced fathers often have adjustment difficulties (Stewart, Schwebel, & Fine, 1986). Especially in the initial transition period (approximately two years), they appear to suffer from a pervasive sense of loss (Hetherington, et al., 1976; Wooley, 1979), lowered self-esteem (Hetherington, et al., 1976; Wallerstein & Kelly, 1980), and increased anxiety (Hetherington, et al., 1976; Keshet & Rosenthal, 1978). In some men, more serious adjustment problems develop, including sleep difficulties and poor work performance (Hetherington, et al., 1976).

Many noncustodial fathers who attempt to maintain close relationships with their children encounter difficulty (Atkin & Rubin, 1976; Dominic & Schlesinger, 1980), which can contribute to their concern about their own adequacy as parents. Further, a number experience strong feelings of guilt about breaking up the family unit, even if it was not their decision to divorce, and they attempt to "make it up" to their children by providing frequent gifts and constant entertainment (Dominic & Schlesinger, 1980). For example, during his every-other-weekend visits, one man in our program who had recently separated from his wife, was spending nearly a third of his income on gifts and entertainment for the children.

Both fathers and children may struggle during visits to develop new ways to relate. Because of the emotional upheaval associated with seeing children for only brief intervals, and noncustodial fathers' difficulties in communicating, many begin visiting their children less frequently as time passes (Dominic & Schlesinger, 1980; Hetherington, et al., 1976; Wooley, 1979). However, men who feel more competent in the role of father and have an easier time seeing their children, are better able to maintain an active involvement with them (Koch & Lowery, 1984; Tepp, 1983).

Table 17.1 shows that all members in families with noncustodial fathers can benefit from intervention at Stage Three, since there are adjustments to be made in each domain of family life. When families successfully adjust to the challenges of that stage, they enter Stage Four.

Custodial Divorced Fathers.

Pichitino (1983) estimates that there are between 1.0 and 1.5 million divorced custodial single fathers in the United States.[3] While the initial two stages of the AFM for these men are similar to those for their noncustodial counterparts, some evidence suggests that they may have been more involved with child-care activities during their marriages (Smith & Smith, 1981). Bartz and Witcher (1978) found that a majority of the custodial fathers in their study had been actively involved in raising their children before the divorce, and classified themselves as "atypical" in this regard. Also, Turner (1984) reports that fathers who contested and obtained custody at the time of the divorce had been more involved in parenting activities during their marriages than those who achieved custody after two years of contention.

Stage Three is less stressful for custodial than for noncustodial fathers. While

---

[3]For an extensive discussion of single parent custodial fathers, see the chapter by Hanson, this volume.

there are still problems in the areas of mutuality, clear communication, and designating norms for appropriate behavior, the presence of the children seems to have a positive effect on custodial fathers' general adjustment (Stewart, et al., 1986). Some problems may be exacerbated by the part-time entry into the family unit of the fathers' own mothers or other relatives who may try to assist during the early periods of adjustment. Also, while custodial fathers report that being a parent is richly rewarding (Bartz & Witchner, 1978; Grief, 1982; Keshet & Rosenthal, 1978; Orthner, et al., 1976), they often experience depression and anxiety. This, however, appears related to the loss of their spouse, and is not as pervasive or longstanding as the depressed and anxious feelings encountered by noncustodial fathers (Wooley, 1979).

Generally, custodial fathers feel capable, comfortable, and successful in their role, and eventually express pride and confidence in their ability to be a good, nurturant parent. They manage to handle household tasks (such as cooking, cleaning, shopping, and laundry) successfully, with minimal role strain or anxiety (Bartz & Witcher, 1978; Gasser & Taylor, 1976; Grief, 1982; Mendes, 1976; Schlesinger & Todres, 1976), frequently sharing these responsibilities with their children and, concomitantly, producing increased cohesion (Defrain & Eirick, 1981; Keshet & Rosenthal, 1978). In fact, one investigator (Ambert, 1982) reports that custodial fathers were more satisfied with their parental roles than were custodial mothers.

Turner's (1984) work suggests that Stage Three may be less stressful for fathers who either do not have to contest custody, or who achieve custody immediately following divorce. In the former instance, by avoiding the adversarial process, ex-spouses were able to maintain more amiable interactions, and thus were more able to progress efficiently, rebuilding satisfactory levels of mutuality, communication, and normative standards in their newly redefined relationship.

Widowed Fathers.

Although the death of a spouse has been identified as the most stressful life event on the Social Readjustment Rating Scale (Holmes & Rahe, 1967), there are relatively few empirical studies documenting the experiences of the many widowers in the United States with children under the age of 18 living at home. The following section presents some preliminary concepts, based on clinical experiences, concerning the developmental stages families experience when the wife/mother becomes terminally ill. First, however, it should be noted that the experiences of all members are affected by the family's place in its life cycle. The effects of a mother's terminal illness on a family will be very different if the children are very young, and needing extensive caregiving, or if they are in late adolescence, and are functioning more independently (see Herz, 1980; Vess, Moreland, & Schwebel, 1985a, 1985b, 1986).

For the present purposes, it is again assumed that the family is functioning effectively in Stage One. Stage Two begins when the wife/mother is diagnosed as seriously ill, and her treatment brings repeated or prolonged hospitalization and a decrease in her functional capacity. This, in turn, tends to decrease spousal mutuality. The support needed by the ill wife renders her less able to attend to her husband's needs and places extra demands for care and sensitivity on his shoulders. The disruptions in mutuality are particularly great when the seriousness of illness is denied by one or both spouses, when the wife feels guilty for being sick, or when the husband is angry at his spouse for her illness. Although spousal mutuality decreases, intimacy may actually increase as the two relate to each other on a more immediate and emotional level.

The extra demands placed on men during this stage are often overwhelming, rendering them incapable of discussing relevant, but stressful issues. As a result, many of their emotional needs remain unstated, and fears associated with the terminal illness remain unexpressed. This lack of clear and open communication hampers effective problem solving and planning, and exacerbates the stress experienced by all family members (Herz, 1980). Further, while the wife may be removed or protected from family functioning and problem solving even when she can still contribute, the father's preoccupation with his wife's illness and possible death may inhibit his ability to interact effectively with the children. During the last months of his wife's illness for example, Lee, a man in our program for widowers and men with terminally ill wives, was so burdened by passing moments of anger, fear, and anxiety, and by worries about his own competency, that he suppressed his feelings and became increasingly rigid in an attempt to maintain control of himself and the situation. A fellow group member attending his last meeting, recognized this, and told him:

> I know what it's like for you. I went through exactly the same thing, Lee. You think you have to hold everything in. . . . You think if you show any feelings the family will fall apart, just like a house of cards. What I did was retreat into my military days and run the family like I was the sergeant. Just recently I finally figured things out.

As often happens when one suppresses feelings to this degree, Lee had become increasingly out of touch with the needs of his children and those of his wife during her final days.

Hospitalization usually creates an increase in the involvement of the extended family in child-rearing activities. It is not uncommon for an in-law or other relative to move into the family home to help care for the children. The presence of another parental figure, coupled with lesser paternal involvement (the father may be at the hospital much of his non-work time), can produce inconsistency in the setting and the enforcing of rules, as well as in the quality and quantity of nurturing and caregiving the children experience. Children may test limits and seek structure, in reaction to the more frequent absence of both parents, the increased inconsistencies in parental monitoring of their behaviors, and the temporary introjection of extended family members into the home. Contributing further to family problems is the fact that the father, the children, and the ill spouse are typically engaged in periods of anticipatory grieving. These periods, which involve often unexpressed sadness and pessimism, may be offset by extended spells of greater optimism, hope, and energy. The cyclical nature of these emotions is draining for family members.

Stage Three begins with the death of the mother. This event tends to decrease mutuality in all family dyads. Another member of one of our widower's groups was so overtaken by his own distress and the duties ahead, that he failed completely to recognize and attend to his young children's irrational fears, which were obviously related to death. For example, his eight-year-old balked at eating in restaurants because she had to leave the family's pet dog at home, while the six-year-old consistently asked Martin to turn down the volume on the television because he was afraid of the music (Dad watched many mystery and adventure programs).

Disruptions also appear in family communication when fathers lack nurturant expressive skills. They are usually reluctant to share their own distress with the children and are often unable to facilitate their children's grieving. The unfortunate outcome is that all family members tend to have a host of feelings that go unexpressed and unexplored. At this point father–child communications are further hampered because fathers no longer have their wives to serve as an intermediary who knows about the children's experiences.

After the mourning period, when extended family members leave and the father becomes the sole limit-setter and dispenser of contingent reinforcement, confusion regarding appropriate behavior frequently continues. Sensing that the children may need to "act out" their grief in the form of uncooperative behavior, widowed fathers are often unsure about how to enforce limits. Thus as the youngsters balk or misbehave, the father may alternate between overreacting and ignoring, while feeling overwhelmed by the dual task of setting limits and being nurturant. This vacillation produces confusion in the children about the appropriateness of their behaviors.

Since Stage Three is a time when widowed fathers often feel immobilized and overwhelmed by business, household and child-care responsibilities, they need considerable support. While they typically receive short-term assistance from extended family, such involvement usually terminates after the initial adjustment has occurred. Fathers must develop plans and identify resources to meet their need for long-term, continued support. Since widowers did not choose to become a single parent, some argue that their circumstances are even more difficult than those of a divorced father who has to cope with an "ex" (Mendes, 1976; Nieto, 1982). On the other hand, Weiss (1979a, 1979b) has noted that widowed fathers received more social support than their divorced counterparts.

With or without psychological intervention, most widower-headed families progress to Stage Four, showing appropriate levels of mutuality, clear communication, and unambiguous standards for acceptable behavior. Follow-up contacts with men who participated in our groups has suggested that once families reach Stage Four, they remain stable until facing another challenge, such as integrating a new maternal figure into the family unit.

INTERVENTIONS WITH MEN ANTICIPATING OR EXPERIENCING SINGLE PARENTHOOD

Changes in family structure are a major source of stress for parents and children, who can easily feel overwhelmed by the seemingly monumental new tasks and responsibilities they face. The remainder of this chapter briefly describes the interventions we have found most effective with fathers and their families, as they progress through the stages of the Adjusting Family Model and cope with the changes precipitated by divorce or death.

Interventions at Stage Two: Individual, Couples, and Family Counseling

Stage Two families are characterized by the contemplation of the end of their nuclear family unit. When indicated, traditional individual, couples, or family therapy can be used, as well as psychologically oriented mediation.

Despite some important qualitative differences, therapy with individuals or couples about to initiate separation and divorce shares certain similarities with counseling with individuals or couples anticipating the mother's possible death. Husbands and wives in both types of families have anxieties about the future. Our response in each instance is to help identify fears and generate alternative ways of addressing them. In families in which the mother may die, we encourage the husband and wife to support each other emotionally as much as their current level of closeness and the mother's functional capacity allow. In families deciding to divorce, we encourage fathers and mothers to turn to other significant people in their lives for emotional support and nurturance, since one task confronting separating couples is to create new support systems.

For divorcing couples, shared concerns and responsibilities do not end with the separation. Continued active parenting by both parents is important for the children's psychological adjustment (Fine, Worley, & Schwebel, 1986; Moreland, Schwebel, Fine, & Vess, 1982, Wylder, 1982). For those families in which couples are willing and able to cooperate, we earlier suggested (Schwebel, Moreland, Steinkohl, Lentz, & Stewart, 1982) that counseling be available at this point, and that it be aimed at (1) reducing tension and creating an atmosphere in which bargaining can occur, and (2) helping fathers and mothers make their own plans with their children's needs in mind.

In the case of life-threatening illness, whether our initial contact is with the father or the couple, we generally focus attention on the formative years of the couple's relationship, and encourage the client(s) to identify the qualities which they initially found attractive in the other. Moving toward the present, we encourage discussion of each important event in their family's history, dwelling particularly on their major child-rearing experiences. While meaningful discussion of these topics often cannot occur until some of the immediate emotionality in the current situation has been addressed, such a focus often serves as a reminder to both adults that their spouse is someone with whom they have shared many positive, intimate times. Clients facing their wife's death find that such a review helps them summarize what they have accomplished together, and stimulates a degree of intimacy which has not recently been experienced, because of the all-consuming attention to the wife's health and her response to treatment. This renewed intimacy serves as a basis for confronting the guilt, anger, and anxiety surrounding possible death, and for more safely discussing fears and worries.

Besides promoting intimacy which, in turn, enhances family members' problem solving and improves their communication of feelings, we support anticipatory grieving, balancing it with the reality of the mother's current level of functioning, and her ability to contribute. Such balancing allows families to more thoughtfully consider whether to involve the mother in family business as fully as possible, or whether to "protect her" from how poorly things seem to be going so that she can "concentrate on getting well."

As the mother's illness progresses and the time of death approaches, increasing responsibility for child rearing must be assumed by the father. At this point, a man may begin to face serious questions such as, should the children be present at the death, how can he best help the children accept their mother's death, and what approaches will allow him to respond to the myriad of problems he expects to encounter with the children? If the mother becomes weak or requires lengthy hospitalization, and members of the extended family assume some responsibility for child care and home administration, counselors may find it useful to include these individuals in one or more treatment sessions.

As Stage Two nears its end, men can benefit from structured psycho-educational groups, such as those discussed under Stage Three interventions. However, most men who are preoccupied with the possibility of losing their wives are not receptive to invitations to attend these types of activities until after they enter Stage Three, and have begun to adjust to their changed circumstances. In entering Stage Three, both fathers and children come to experience in a very concrete way the unpredictability of family life.

Interventions at Stage Three: Mediation and Psycho-education

Mediation.

Mediation is a generic term describing techniques for resolving conflict, in which an outside party assists those experiencing an immobilizing difficulty. We have discussed the importance of the mediation process in helping ex-spouses achieve a state of circumscribed mutuality—that is, a level of reciprocal sensitivity and responsiveness to each other's needs as they pertain to their shared goal of rearing the children (Schwebel, et al., 1982). By reaching this point, parents can cooperate more effectively in child care, and allow their children to benefit optimally from life in each parent's household. More recently Schwebel, Schwebel, and Schwebel (1985) have described the Psychological Mediation Intervention model (PMI). Because PMI not only leads to the resolution of immediate issues, but also considers the types of psychological changes required of the participants to prevent similar future conflict, it lends itself well to work with custodial and noncustodial fathers and their ex-spouses. Through mediation, we help men compartmentalize the often intense and nonproductive emotions that may influence their contacts with their children's mother, by appealing to the "mature adult" portions of their personalities and underscoring the importance of a cooperative ex-spouse relationship.

The applications of PMI in Stage Three divorcing families are fairly obvious. Following the PMI session(s), we often encourage one or more post-divorce family therapy sessions to assist both parents and children in accepting new realities. During these sessions, we attempt to enable the family members to recognize that the family is not ending, but rather changing form. Mothers and fathers are supported in developing circumscribed mutuality, and reminded that their common concern for the children's well-being requires them to develop methods for communication and cooperation. When it is not possible to involve the ex-wife, teaching mediation principles to fathers and helping them modify the way they relate to their ex-spouses often goes a long way toward creating an atmosphere in which circumscribed mutuality can develop.

In a small portion of widower-headed families, we have discovered an important application of mediation. After a mother's death, extended family (often the maternal grandparents) frequently become involved in child-care activities. In the initial adjustment to the loss, as the intensity of grieving diminishes, some fathers feel that their role as a single parent has been undermined. Specifically, they may have different expectations for their children or favor different types of rewards or punishments than the grandparents, and may feel less able to resolve father–child conflicts while the grandparents are so centrally involved in the family. Maternal grandparents are often motivated not only by love and a desire to help, but also by a need to maintain contact with their daughter's children. When fathers attempt to decrease the maternal grandparents' involvement, intense emotions are often unleashed. Techniques used in PMI have been quite helpful to the parties in finding reasonable solutions.

Psycho-educational Interventions.

Proponents of psycho-educational interventions (Ivey & Authier, 1978, Moreland & Schwebel, 1981) view problems and frustrations in living as stemming from an individual's inability to clarify goals, to reconcile incongruities between attitudes and behaviors, and to learn new behaviors required by environmental demands. Some psycho-educational programs aim to teach fathers specific parenting skills, while others focus on consciousness-raising, attitude change, goal clarification, and the understanding of developmental differences in children's behaviors and reactions.[4]

A number of authors have identified the need for this type of intervention in working with single-parent fathers. For example, Orthner and colleagues (1976) propose seminars to help fathers improve their parenting skills. Keshet and Rosenthal (1978) emphasize the need for fathers to learn the basic interpersonal skills that are required for effective parenting. As a response to such suggestions, Tedder and colleagues (1981) describe one program for custodial divorced fathers; the five stages in their intervention are (1) an introduction to the purposes of the group, (2) the effects of divorce, (3) dating, (4) remarriage, and (5) homemaking. Similarly, Warren and Amara (1984) describe a parenting-after-divorce group which focuses on teaching specific skills to fathers.

Our psycho-educational interventions are based on the assumption that single-parent fathers, whether divorced or widowed, custodial or noncustodial, need assis-

[4]For a description of a range of such programs, see the chapter by Levant, this volume.

tance in becoming more aware of affective states, and of how to communicate effectively. In our work, we have found it necessary to first instruct men in how to identify their own and others' feelings, before they can fully master the skills taught in our communication training program. We have also found it useful to teach fathers behavioral management skills and problem-solving procedures, to help them become more consistent in defining and enforcing appropriate behaviors for their children in the home.

The core ingredients in our treatment package are: helping fathers to master target skills through the use of videotape models or written manuals, behavioral rehearsal during sessions structured around real life or simulated role plays, supervised feedback focusing on the parent's use of the target skills during behavioral rehearsal, and the use of home practice exercises between sessions. The microcounseling methodology of Ivey and Authier (1978), which suggests teaching clearly defined skills, one by one, and building social-skill competence in a cumulative manner, provided a model to guide our work.

While there are variations in the number and length of sessions in our psycho-educational programs, depending on the participants, our basic workshop consists of the following eight sessions, which have been led by doctoral students in a clinic or a hospital setting, and supervised by faculty members.[5]

Session One: Introduction and Capsulized Summary of the Literature.

Initially, we clarify goals and expectations for the workshop, and provide background material necessary to understand subsequent sessions. Naturally, the conceptual framework provided (primarily a review of the literature) varies, depending on whether the fathers are divorced with custody of their children, divorced without custody, or widowed.

Session Two: Identification of Feelings.

This meeting teaches men to become aware of their own feeling states as well as to increase their sensitivity to what their children or ex-spouses may be feeling. For example, when we ask noncustodial fathers to discuss their visit with their children during the past week, they are often not fully aware of the feelings that were aroused. They might say that the visit didn't go well, or that they have a bad feeling about it, but they are not able to identify whether the feeling is anger, anxiety, guilt, resentment, or sadness. We have found it particularly helpful to assist men in finding labels to describe various emotions.

Session Three: Active Listening.

We have found many elements of Gordon's (1970) Parent Effectiveness Training (PET) to be consistent with the views of emergent fatherhood previously discussed. We help men to demonstrate acceptance of their children, to listen actively, and to

---

[5]Professionals could undoubtedly train paraprofessionals, or individuals who have been through the experiences themselves, to conduct education and support programs effectively, such as the one we describe here.

encourage their children to share their feelings. We teach the notion of problem ownership, and the use of negotiated, noncompetitive, conflict resolution procedures.

Session Four: Advanced Communication Skills.

This session focuses on skills that build on the basic attending behaviors learned in previous sessions, including paraphrasing, summarization, confrontation, and self-disclosure. After instructing the men in these skills, we then have them try out the different techniques by role-playing situations that involve their children or ex-spouse. We videotape the role plays, and play them back, so that the men can have immediate feedback on their skill acquisition. If it seems useful, the leaders role-play situations first, before asking the men to do it.

Session Five and Six: Behavioral Management Principles.

We have made use of the parent training behavior therapy literature to teach fathers methods of increasing their children's compliance. For example, we first help fathers identify what household chores they feel their children should be involved in. Then we teach them how to draw up behavioral contracts with their children, involving the children in deciding what reinforcers should be contingent on the desired behaviors being performed. The wide range of available techniques are discussed by Moreland and colleagues (1982).

Session Seven: Problem-Solving Procedures.

Not only do fathers benefit from learning systematic ways of solving problems, but they can also teach certain principles to their youngsters, and apply them to produce cooperative family problem solving. This is Session Seven's focus. Discussion and role-playing build on previously assigned family homework. For example, we get fathers to identify a particular problem (such as what to do with the children when they visit), and then teach them techniques such as brainstorming possible solutions, evaluating the pluses and minuses of the different solutions, picking a solution, and developing an evaluation plan to determine how well the solution worked.

Session Eight: Follow-up.

To the extent possible, we reassemble the group approximately three months after Session Seven, in order to monitor fathers' progress.

While the preceding outline suggests an orderly flow of content and learning goals, one task confronting leaders is to respond immediately to the diverse expectations and emotional reactions the men bring with them to this experience. Many enter excited and eager to improve their relationships with their children. Others come feeling angry and at times depressed and hopeless, fearing that the legal system will alienate them from their children. And, there are usually a few men in the group who are so entangled with their ex-spouse, that they are at first only looking for a way to force her to do what they want. Group leaders must empathize with this range of feelings, while gently, or at times forcefully, nudging members to follow the goals and content prescribed. As the weeks pass, a spirit of cooperativeness and shared enterprise develops, with most men learning to enjoy the new horizons that are opening to them as their competence grows. Finally, while our clinical experience suggests that our program is effective, systematic research is needed to verify this observation, and to identify the active ingredients of the training.

One final point should be emphasized. While widowers and divorced men benefit equally from psycho-educational groups, we do not recommend having them in the same classes. Recently widowed men still in the process of grieving are often quite put off by the attitudes of some of the recently divorced men toward their ex-spouses.

CONCLUSIONS

Because of conceptions of the male sex role, specific parenting skill deficits, and the pressures and expectations of societal institutions, men who become single fathers are often ill-equipped to adapt effectively to their changing circumstances. The four-stage, developmental Adjusting Family Model provides a conceptual framework to help understand a family's transition to a single-father-headed unit, the kinds of problems such families face, and the type of psychotherapeutic and psycho-educational interventions that can be used at various points during the process. While literature can aid clinicians in planning interventions to benefit divorced and widowed men and their children, further research is needed to examine more closely the competencies and deficits of single-parent fathers with children at various ages and the relative effectiveness of alternative treatment options.

REFERENCES

Ambert, A.M. (1982). Differences in children's behavior toward custodial mothers and custodial fathers. *Journal of Marriage & the Family*, *44*(1), 73–86.

Atkin, E.L., & Rubin, E. (1976). *Part-time father*. New York: Vanguard.

Barry, A. (1979). A research project on successful single parent families. *American Journal of Family Therapy*, *7*, 65–73.

Bartz, K.W., & Witcher, W.C. (1978). When father gets custody. *Children Today*, *7*, 2–6.

Beattie, S., & Viney, L.L. (1981). Appraisal of lone parenthood after marital breakdown. *Journal of Personality Assessment*, *45*, 415–423.

Berman, P.W. (1980). Are women more responsive than men to the young? A review of developmental and situational variables. *Psychological Bulletin*, *88*, 668–695.

Carter, E.A., & McGoldrick, M. (1980). *The family life cycle: A framework for family therapy*. New York: Gardner.

Clark-Stewart, K.A. (1978). And daddy makes three: The father's impact on mother and young child. *Child Development*, *49*, 466–478.

David, D., & Brannon, R. (1975). *The forty-nine percent majority: The male sex role*. New York: Addison Wesley.

Defrain, J. (1979). Sexism in parenting manuals. *Family Coordinator*, *26*(3), 245–251.

Defrain, J., & Eirick, R. (1981). Coping as divorced single parents: A comparative study of fathers and mothers. *Family Relations*, *30*, 265–273.

Dominic, K.T., & Schlesinger, B. (1980). Weekend fathers: Family shadows. *Journal of Divorce*, *4*, 241–247.

Dreyfuss, E.A. (1979). Counseling the divorced father. *Journal of Marital and Family Therapy*, *5*, 79–95.

Epstein, C. (1975). Entering the male establishment: Sex-status limits on women's careers in the professions. In R. Unger & F. Denmark (Eds.), *Women: Dependent or independent variable*. New York: Psychological Dimension.

Farrell, W. (1974). *The liberated man*. New York: Random.

Fein, R.A. (1978). Research on fathering: Social policy and an emergent perspective. *Journal of Social Issues*, *34*, 122–131.

Fine, M.A., Worley, S.M., & Schwebel, A.I. (1986). The effects of divorce on parent-child relationships. *Journal of Social Behavior and Personality*, *1*, 451–463.

Gasser, R.D., & Taylor, C.M. (1976). Role adjustment of single parent fathers with dependent children. *Family Coordinator*, *25*, 397–401.

Goldberg, H. (1979). *The new male: From self-destruction to self care*. New York: Morrow.

Golenkoff, R., & Ames, G. (1979). A comparison of father's and mother's speech with their young children. *Child Development*, *50*(1), 28–32.

Gordon, T. (1970). *Parent effectiveness training*. New York: Wyden.

Gould, R. (1972). The phases of adult life: A study in developmental psychology. *American Journal of Psychiatry*, *126*, 33–43.

Greenberg, M., & Morris, N. (1974). Engrossment: The newborn's impact upon the father. *American Journal of Orthopsychiatry*, *44*, 520–531.

Greif, G.L. (1982). Dads raising kids. *Single Parent*, *25*, 9, 17–25.

Herz, F. (1980). The impact of death and serious illness on the family life cycle. In E.A. Carter & M. McGoldrick (Eds.), *The family life cycle: A framework for family therapy*. New York: Gardner.

Hetherington, E.M., Cox, M., & Cox, R. (1976). Divorced fathers. *Family Coordinator*, *25*, 417–428.

Holmes, T.H., & Rahe, R.H. (1967). The social readjustment rating scale. *Psychosomatic Medicine*, *11*, 213–218.

Hood, J., & Golden, S. (1979). Beating time/making time: The impact of work scheduling on men's family roles. *Family Coordinator*, *28*(4), 575–582.

Ivey, A., & Authier, J. (1978). *Microcounseling*. Springfield, IL: Thomas.

Keshet, H.F., & Rosenthal, K.M. (1978). Fathering after marital separation. *Social Work*, *23*, 11–18.

Koch, M.P., & Lowery, C.R. (1984). Visitation and the noncustodial father. *Journal of Divorce*, *8*(2), 47–65.

Kotelchuck, M. (1976). The infant's relationship to the father: Experimental evidence. In M. Lamb (Ed.), *The role of the father in child development*. New York: Wiley.

Lamb, M. (1976a). Effects of stress and cohort on mother and father-infant interaction. *Developmental Psychology*, *12*, 435–443.

Lamb, M. (1976b). Interactions between eight month-olds and their fathers and mothers. In M. Lamb (Ed.), *The role of the father in child development*. New York: Wiley.

Lamb, M. (1977). Father-infant and mother-infant interaction in the first year of life. *Child Development, 48*, 167–181.

Lamb, M. (1982). Generalization and inferences about causality in research on nontraditional families: A response to Radin, Sagi, and Russell. *Merrill-Palmer Quarterly, 28*(1), 157–161.

Levinson, D.J. (1978). *The seasons of a man's life*. New York: Knopf.

Lewis, K. (1978). Single-father families: Who they are and how they are. *Child Welfare, 57*, 643–651.

Mayer, N. (1978). *The male mid-life crisis*. New York: Doubleday.

McPhee, J.T. (1984). Ambiguity and change in the post-divorce family: Towards a model of divorce adjustment. *Journal of Divorce, 8*(2), 1–15.

Mendes, H.A. (1976). Single fathers. *Family Coordinator, 25*, 439–444.

Moreland, J., & Schwebel, A.I. (1981). A gender role transcendent perspective on fathering. *Counseling Psychologist, 9*(4), 45–54.

Moreland, J., Schwebel, A.I., Fine, M.A., & Vess, J.D. (1982). Postdivorce family therapy: Suggestions for professionals. *Professional Psychology, 13*(5), 639–646.

Nichols, J. (1975). *Men's liberation: A new definition of masculinity*. New York: Penguin.

Nieto, D.S. (1982). Aiding the single father. *Social Work, 27*(6), 473–478.

Orthner, D.K., Brown, T., & Ferguson, D. (1976). Single parent fatherhood: An emerging family life style. *Family Coordinator, 25*, 429–437.

Parke, R.D., O'Leary, S.E., & West, S. (1972). Mother-father-newborn interaction: Effects of maternal medication, labor, and sex of infant. *Proceedings of the American Psychological Association, 7*, 85–86.

Parke, R.D., & Sawin, D.B. (1976). The father's role in infancy evaluation. *Family Coordinator, 25*, 365–371.

Pedersen, F.A. & Robson, K.S. (1969). Father participation in infancy. *American Journal of Orthopsychiatry, 39*, 466–472.

Pichitino, J.P. (1983). Profile of the single father: A thematic integration of the literature. *Personnel and Guidance Journal, 61*(5), 295–300.

Pleck, J., & Sawyer, J. (Eds.) (1974). *Men and masculinity*. Englewood Cliffs, NJ: Prentice Hall.

Radin, N. (1981). Childrearing fathers in intact families: I. Some antecedents and consequents. *Merrill-Palmer Quarterly, 27*(4), 489–514.

Radin, N., & Sagi, A. (1982). Childrearing fathers in intact families in Israel and the USA. *Merrill-Palmer Quarterly, 28*(1), 111–136.

Russell, G. (1982). Highly participant Australian fathers: Some preliminary findings. *Merrill-Palmer Quarterly, 28*(1), 137–156.

Sawin, D., & Parke, R.D. (1979). Father's affectionate stimulation and care giving behaviors with newborn infants. *Family Coordinator, 28*(4), 509–513.

Schlesinger, B., & Todres, R. (1976). Motherless families: An increasing social pattern. *Child Welfare, 55*, 443–458.

Schwebel, A.I., Moreland, J., Steinkohl, R., Lentz, S., & Stewart, J. (1982). Research-based interventions with divorced families. *Personnel and Guidance Journal, 60*, 523–527.

Schwebel, R., Schwebel, A.I., & Schwebel, M. (1985). The psychological/mediation model. *Professional Psychology, 16*, 86–97.

Seagull, A.A., & Seagull, E.A.W. (1977). The noncustodial father's relationship to his child: Conflicts and solutions. *Journal of Clinical Child Psychology*, *6*, 11–15.

Shepard, H. (1977). Men in organizations: Some reflections. In A. Sargent (Ed.), *Beyond sex roles*. New York: West.

Smith, R.M., & Smith, C.W. (1981). Child rearing and single parenthood: A longitudinal perspective. *Family Relations*, *30*, 411–417.

Stewart, J.R., Schwebel, A.I., & Fine, M.A. (1986). The impact of custodial arrangement on the adjustment of recently divorced fathers. *Journal of Divorce*, *9*, 55–66.

Tedder, S.L., Libbee, K.M., & Scherman, A. (1981). A community support group for single custodial fathers. *Personnel and Guidance Journal*, *60*, 115–119.

Tepp, A.V. (1983). Divorced fathers: Predictors of continued paternal involvement. *American Journal of Psychiatry*, *140*, 11, 1465–1469.

Tolson, A. (1979). *The limits of masculinity*. New York: Harper & Row.

Turner, J.R. (1984). Divorced fathers who win contested custody of their children: An exploratory study. *American Journal of Orthopsychiatry*, *54*(3), 498–501.

Vess, J., Moreland, J.R., & Schwebel, A.I. (1985a). An empirical assessment of the effects of cancer on family role functioning. *Journal of Psychosocial Oncology*. *3*(1), 1–16.

Vess, J., Moreland, J.R., & Schwebel, A.I. (1985b). A follow-up study of role functioning and the psychological environment of families of cancer patients. *Journal of Psychosocial Oncology*, *3*(2), 1–14.

Vess, J., Moreland, J.R., & Schwebel, A.I. (1986). Understanding family role reallocation following a death: A theoretical perspective. *Omega*. *16*(2), 115–128.

Wallerstein, J., & Kelly, J. (1980) *Surviving the break-up: How children actually cope with divorce*. New York: Basic.

Warren, N.J., & Amara, I.A. (1984). Educational groups for single parents: The parenting after divorce programs. *Journal of Divorce*, *8*(2), 79–96.

Weinraub, M., & Frankel, J. (1977). Sex differences in parent-infant interaction during free play, departure and separation. *Child Development*, *48*, 1240–1249.

Weiss, R.S. (1975). *Marital separation*. New York: Basic.

Weiss, R.S. (1979a). *Going it alone*. New York: Basic.

Weiss, R.S. (1979b). Growing up a little faster: The experience of growing up in a single-parent household. *Journal of Social Issues*, *35*(4), 97–111.

Wooley, P. (1979). *The custody handbook*. New York: Summit.

Wylder, J. (1982). Including the divorced father in family therapy. *Social Work*, *27*(6), 479–482.

PART 5

Men's Changing Role in the Family: Directions for Research and Social Change

CHAPTER 18

Workplace Policies: New Options for Fathers

THE STAFF OF CATALYST

Both Daryl and Pam are working parents. Together they have two children, Cathy, 7, and Brian, 2½, and two full-time jobs. Daryl is a programmer with a high-tech firm; Pam was just promoted to senior financial analyst at a Fortune 500 manufacturing firm. Each commutes an hour each way to work, often works late, and does some traveling. They have a regular schedule of alternating days for bringing Brian to the child-care center, attending Cathy's school events, and doing household chores. Wednesday, before Daryl and Pam left for work, Cathy handed them a note (which she had received the week before and forgotten) informing parents that her school would be closed the next day due to a teacher's conference. On top of that, when they brought Brian to the child-care center, he screamed that he did not want to go inside. As they rushed off to work, each was thinking about Brian's apparent unhappiness, finding care for Cathy, and upcoming deadlines at work.

Daryl, with the memory of his son in tears still fresh in his mind, was tense. His firm had started offering seminars on work and family issues the previous year, and Daryl had been attending a series of three lunchtime seminars on "Fathers and Stages of Child Development." At the final session that day, Daryl related the morning's incident, and asked what an appropriate parental response to such behavior would be. He experienced tremendous relief when other working parents assured him that they had the same problem with their two-year-olds. The group together discussed ways to alleviate the separation feelings all young children express.

Pam, while finishing an important report before a late afternoon meeting, made phone calls to every sitter she knew. Finally, a college student who baby-sat for a colleague phoned to say that she had found a friend who could sit. Pam relaxed immediately, glanced over her report, and went to the meeting. Sometimes when an unexpected holiday or sick sitter has thrown the routine off schedule, Pam has had to take Cathy to work, leave her with an elderly neighbor, or have her stay at home alone—or else Daryl has had to take a personal day.

As new roles replace set roles of the past, and as employees and employers try to

Catalyst is a national research and advisory organization that helps corporations foster the career and leadership development of women. For more information, contact Margaret Meiers, Senior Associate, Career and Family Programs Catalyst, 250 Park Avenue South, New York, NY 10003.

adjust, each faces new challenges: for employees, how to perform well as both worker and family member, and for employers, how to manage human resources most effectively. A helpful tool for Daryl and Pam was their employers' offering work and family seminars. These seminars are one example of workplace policies which are creating new options for fathers.

Several societal changes account for the increased awareness of work-and-family issues. Men are beginning to play a more active role in their families, both because they seek personal satisfaction and psychological well-being from participating, and because they no longer have wives who will take complete care of the family. Today, many women are seriously committed to jobs outside the home, make a substantial contribution to family income, and often work through their childbearing years. In fact, only 9.8% of the population are married couples with children under 18 in which the husband is the sole wage earner, and 60% of married men who work have wives who also work full or part time (Bureau of Labor Statistics, 1985). Thus two-paycheck families are becoming the norm.

With both parents working, the gap in parenting means that, in some sense, men cannot avoid a larger role at home. Although the data on the involvement of fathers are recent, one sign of change came in a national survey by University of Michigan researchers (Radin & Goldsmith, 1983), from a representative sample of men queried in 1975 and again in 1981. The Michigan team found that during that six-year period, fathers had increased by 20 to 30% the time they spend in child care and housework. Fathers still spend only about a third as much time in child care as mothers do, but the important point is that their involvement is changing, and it is changing toward greater involvement. Another indication of change is the substantial increase in the number of divorced men who have taken custody of their children. In 10 years, from 1970 to 1980, the number of single-custodial fathers doubled, from 225,000 to 580,000. About one quarter of all families with children under the age of 18 are currently headed by single parents (U.S. Bureau of the Census, 1984), of which 1 in 10 is a father.

Two recent studies document the difficulties fathers and mothers are experiencing in combining the responsibilities of home and work. Emlen and Koren (1984), in their study of child-care needs of employees, found that 37% of fathers and 59% of mothers with children under 18 years reported some difficulty in balancing home and work. Googins and Burden (1987), studying stress associated with home and work responsibilities, found that men with high job–family role strain were just as likely as women to be depressed. These findings suggest that work and family stress will increase for fathers as they assume more family responsibilities.

The existence or lack of supportive workplace policies will have a significant effect on how successfully fathers can take a larger role in parenting and other family responsibilities. Yet, the workplace has been slow to respond to the changing picture of American life. In a recent survey (Mills, 1985), 90% of Fortune 500 chief executive officers estimated that 40–60% of their employees live in traditional families like their own. It is only innovative companies, adroit in adapting to the changing environment, who are now recognizing the need for providing progressive policies for working parents and providing new options, such as parental leave, relocation assistance, and employer-supported child care.

These new options were not created specifically for working fathers; they were designed for working parents and targeted, for the most part, at working mothers. How fathers use them depends on their knowledge of the options' existence, supervisors' support of use by fathers, family needs, and the personal motivation of the individual father.

In this chapter, we will examine the new workplace options, their use by fathers, and our perception of what the future holds for the continued development of supportive workplace policies for both men and women. The options fall into three general catagories: financial assistance, time flexibility, and employee services. Our material was obtained through several research projects, including surveys of human resource professionals in Fortune 1500 companies, focus-group discussions with personnel professionals and company employees, and interviews of child-care coordinators across the country.

FINANCIAL ASSISTANCE

Currently, there are two primary ways through which employers provide assistance for family expenses: dependent care assistance plans and flexible benefits plans with dependent-care options.

Dependent-Care Assistance

In 1981 the Economic Recovery Tax Act provided economic incentives for employers to help shoulder the financial burden of child care, through Dependent Care Assistance Programs. These programs permit employers to reimburse employees for their dependent-care costs, which generally include payments for care of children under the age of 15 and disabled dependents. The amount paid by an employer under the program does not have to be reported as taxable income on an employee's tax return, as it is considered a tax-free benefit. With the wage-earner role being shared by fathers and mothers, these pre-tax dollars savings become especially significant to the family budget. The employer, on the other hand, may deduct any reimbursement payment as an ordinary and necessary business expense. Dependent Care Assistance Programs may be offered to employees in a variety of ways. Options include:

—Establishing a child-care facility at the work site.
—Payment for dependent care to another facility providing the service, such as a community-based day care center.
—Direct reimbursement to employees for a portion of their dependent-care costs. The Polaroid Company in Cambridge, Massachusetts, for example,

uses a sliding fee scale for reimbursement, based on family income and family size, for families whose income falls below $25,000 a year.

—Reimbursement of dependent-care expenses through a third-party administration organization. One example of this approach is Community Coordinated Child Care of Central Florida, which processes payments on behalf of a number of local employers.

Flexible Benefits

Another way that employers can ease the financial burden of child rearing is through the company's benefits plan. Benefits packages were initially designed to meet the needs of a family where the man was employed outside the home, while the woman worked inside the home taking care of the children. However, when married women enter the work force, the traditional one-size-fits all benefits plan offered to two-career couples translates into duplicate insurance policies, duplicate medical policies, and so on.

The more progressive corporations have responded to this overlap by offering flexible benefits plans to their employees. In a flexible benefits plan, also known as cafeteria benefits, employees have a choice of what benefits they will receive from their employer. While the employer controls the cost of benefits, employees can select the kinds of benefits which most closely fit their individual life-styles and needs. Therefore, instead of a two-career couple wasting their benefits by, for example, duplicating insurance policies, the wife may choose the medical coverage for the entire family while the husband may choose to put his dollars into an optional account, which then provides reimbursement for such things as child care, certain legal expenses, and deductibles for medical or dental expenses.

TIME FLEXIBILITY

Another area in which employers are addressing the needs of working parents is time flexibility. Time may be made more available or flexible for an employee through alternative work schedules, and through family-oriented leave options such as parental leave. Clearly, traditional nine-to-five work cannot meet the scheduling needs of the entire employee population, especially working parents. Some flexibility, therefore, can allow employees more opportunity to balance work and family demands.

Alternative Work Schedules

Alternative work schedules are generally thought of for females, the elderly, and very young people. Such schedules are most often used by women; for example, women made up two-thirds of all part-time workers in 1985. The majority of part-time women are married, in contrast to the majority of part-time men who are single

(Bureau of Labor Statistics, 1985). However, as men become more family-oriented and want more time flexibility, these statistics may change.

Parental Leave

The time flexibility in the workplace most often talked about in relationship to men is parental leave. However, although parental leave has received a great deal of media attention, its availability is not yet widespread. Recently, Catalyst (1986b) conducted a study of parental leave policies, practices, and attitudes in a 10-page questionnaire that was sent to 1,462 of the nation's largest 1,000 industrial and 500 financial and service companies. Though less than one-third of the companies responded, the survey documented that a growing number of companies are offering unpaid parental leaves for men. Half of the respondents provided unpaid leave for women, and over a third (37%) also granted some unpaid leave time for men. The latter number contrasts sharply with the results of an earlier survey (Catalyst, 1981), in which 8.6% of the respondents reported offering some kind of "paternity benefits."

This change in policy seems to have been prompted by a concern over legal issues. While there are no laws requiring companies to offer these benefits to men, authorities agree that it is illegal to offer time off for new mothers and not for new fathers. Title VII of the Civil Rights Act, as well as the Pregnancy Discrimination Act (PDA), theoretically defend the rights of men to have the same parent benefits that women have, aside from disability leave for childbirth—and, in fact, Catalyst's survey (1986b) revealed that 88% of the companies that have altered their policies in the past five years have done so in response to the PDA. At present, although the issue has never come to court, several cases have been filed and settled without contest.

The survey also revealed that the amount of unpaid leaves available to men and women are comparable in length. (See Table 18.1.) Fully 65% of responding companies grant both men and women leave time of three months or less. The figures show a slight tendency to allow men one to four weeks of leave time and women one to three months, but the differences are not major. And yet, despite the increasing availability of paternity leaves, few fathers apply for leave. Men generally take a few days off from work upon the birth of a child, and describe their absence as vacation, personal days, or family crisis leave. What are the barriers that prevent men from taking parental leaves?

First, the availability of child-care leaves for fathers is usually not clearly com-

TABLE 18.1   Length of Unpaid Leave Companies Provide

	Females	Males
1–4 weeks	28.7%	36.0%
2–3 months	35.9%	29.0%
4–6 months	28.2%	25.4%
7 months–1 year	7.2%	9.6%

municated. Companies rarely use labels—such as paternity leave, or parental leave—that men will recognize. Results from the Catalyst survey (1986b) indicate that fully 90% of companies offering leaves for men call them personal leaves, and make no attempt to inform employees that they are available to new fathers. Consequently, many new fathers do not realize that they are eligible to take parental leaves. It should be mentioned, however, that some companies do clearly publicize the parental leave benefits offered to men. For example, General Foods Corporation distributes a child-care leave flyer to inform both new parents of the benefits they are entitled to, and Merck & Co., Inc. provides a parental leave kit for employees. Other companies such as Levi Strauss, Corning Glass Works, AT&T, and Proctor & Gamble also clearly communicate their parental leave policies.

A second reason men do not frequently take advantage of parental leave policies is their belief that doing so will have a negative impact on their careers. Catalyst's survey (1986b) corroborated these fears. When asked how much leave time was considered reasonable for men, 63% of all survey respondents replied "none," while 17% suggested a maximum of two weeks. Although many companies offer leaves to men, management often thought it unreasonable for men to take any time off for the purpose of parenting. Fully 41% of the companies that offered such leaves considered *no length of time reasonable, regardless of their written policy*.

Catalyst interviews with human resources managers corroborated the survey's findings. "If a man requested a leave for this purpose, his career would take a dive," said one manager at a major southern manufacturing company (Catalyst, 1986a, p. 132). Another manager, at a communications company in the northeast, reported that when a new father requested the three months leave time offered in company policy, he was told that such leaves were meant only for low-level employees, not for men who wanted to move ahead. Pleck (1986) reports a similar incident, in which a prospective father's union had negotiated for him to take a day off while his wife had a baby. He was granted the day, but only if the baby was born during his shift!

A third reason men seldom avail themselves of parental leave is that they frequently have little understanding of the role they might play as caregivers to a new baby. A Catalyst focus group conducted in Chicago with management-level employees provided insight into this phenomenon. One member, when asked during the structured discussion if he had considered taking a leave when his child was born, replied, "Why should I? How long could I work on the house?" (Catalyst, 1986a, p. 132). What this discussion clearly revealed is that men, who traditionally have been trained to provide the financial foundation for the family, have not been socialized to take nurturing responsibility for an infant. As a result, many do not conceive of that as their family role, and many may feel inadequate and unprepared in caring for a new baby.

A fourth reason may be that their wives' attitudes discourage men from taking parental leaves. Women, having dominated the domestic realm for generations, may have strong internalized role expectations that preclude their husbands' participation in infant care. Resistance may also come into play for some mothers when confronted with the prospect that their husbands may build bonds with infants that compete with their own.

Finally, the cost of taking a leave may be prohibitive for men. Often, the father commands a higher salary than his wife, and the cost of his unpaid time off while his wife resumes her career may be more than the family can afford. This financial concern may be tempered somewhat if a couple considers their respective careers to be of equal importance.

As paternity policies become more visible, and corporate culture begins to sanction them, more men may use them. In a recent series of telephone interviews with 25 professionals involved in workplace programs for parents (Catalyst, 1985a), one corporation's child-care coordinator noted, "Several years ago, I wasn't getting any requests for parental leave from men. Now, I get one or two a month" (p. 49). Still, the barriers that prevent men from taking advantage of parental leave policies continue to exist, even in countries where policies for fathers have been in effect for some time. For example, Sweden, which has the most liberal paternity leave policy in the Western world, has been offering paid leaves to both sexes since 1974. Yet, despite an intensive campaign to equalize opportunities, and a generous policy that gives up to 12 months of paid leave, Swedish fathers have only gradually taken advantage of this time. In 1983 the percentage of fathers taking paid leaves was 22%, with an average of 44 days taken by users (Pleck, 1986).

In Sweden, as in the United States, economic factors may also affect the willingness of men to take leave. In the public sector, the first nine months of leave are fully reimbursed, but in the private sector, they are reimbursed only 90%, up to a stipulated maximum. Also, as in the United States, men are more likely than women to hold professional jobs, and to be the primary financial providers for their families. In addition, the long-term career success of the father may be essential for the family, and he may not be able to afford to take time away from developing that career (Pleck, 1986). Lamb and Levine (1983), reporting on their study of Swedish parental leave, point out that, "Future prospects as an academic or as a trial lawyer, for example, may depend on continued visibility and professional activity. Thus although there may be little immediate financial cost for these people, the long-term costs may be substantial" (p. 49). And although Swedish law prohibits sanctions by employers against men who take parental leaves, managerial disapproval is hard to legislate against. A survey of 50 fathers who took one month or more of parental leave, and a small sample of employers in Goteborg, Sweden (Pleck, 1986), found that a substantial proportion of both groups report that employers view leave-taking fathers negatively, and may penalize them for it in many ways.

EMPLOYEE SERVICES

There are a number of services employers may provide to help men balance the responsibilities of home and career more effectively. Two examples of such services are relocation assistance and employer-supported child-care programs.

Relocation Assistance

Traditionally, employees and their families have packed their bags and moved when the company offered a relocation. And traditionally, men, who make up the majority of managerial employees, were those asked to transfer. Catalyst's study of corporations and two-career couples (1981) revealed that a majority of couples participating in the survey chose their current location primarily because of the husband's job opportunities. Although women are increasingly joining the managerial ranks and are being asked to relocate, of the 300,000–500,000 employees relocated annually by corporations (Catalyst, 1985b), 95% still are men, many of whom are fathers whose families move with them (Merrill Lynch Relocation Management Inc., 1987).

In the past several years, however, there have been significant changes in employee attitudes toward relocation. The Conference Board, a corporate research and advisory organization, has estimated a 24% refusal rate (Catalyst, 1983), which is a conservative estimate, given that many employees remove themselves from the selection process early, and that managers often do not report refusals to the relocation department for record keeping. Catalyst's relocation research (1983) indicates that this resistance to relocate is primarily due to a shift in loyalties; personal and family concerns today often outweigh employees' loyalties to their companies. In Catalyst's study of two-career couples (1981), human resource directors ranked reluctance of spouse and children to move as second on a list of the top five reasons why employees resist relocation. Many couples indicated they would move again only if the net gain for the family were irresistible, with the majority of husbands and wives claiming that their families were more important than their careers.

Corporate reactions to employees' refusal to relocate vary. Although managers today understand if an employee refuses a transfer because of children's needs, it is more acceptable for a man to express these concerns than a woman. Many women are still working to prove that family considerations do not interfere with or diminish their commitment to their careers. In a similar vein, because of traditional role expectations, it is more acceptable for women than men to refuse a transfer because of a spouse's career. Interestingly, it is more credible to the present generation of managers for men to cite fatherhood as a reason for refusing a transfer, than for them to bring up the issue of their spouse's employment.

In the past, companies provided only financial incentives to encourage employees to relocate. Today, because of the change in employees' attitudes about relocation, more and more companies are recognizing the additional need to address personal and family concerns if they want to achieve their relocation objectives. Catalyst's relocation research (1983) concluded that 80% of failed assignments result not from job-related or financial factors, but because of a lack of family or personal adjustment. In recognition that family adjustment is critical to the success of relocation, corporations and the relocation industry—third party firms which assist in home purchase and sale, realtors, consultants, and counselors—have developed human factors assistance programs to help families move and adjust more easily. Such programs are designed to help families work through feelings about moving, choose communities that are most comfortable for them, orient themselves to the new location, and learn how to help themselves during the adjustment process. One company, for example, has developed a kit for young children called "On the Move," which includes a T-shirt and tote bag with cartoon characters, stationery depicting some of the tasks involved in moving, and a coloring book and scrapbook to help children remember their old community and learn to become part of the new one. Other companies have developed new practices to involve spouses in the relocation process from the time of an initial offer. For example, the company's relocation administrator may call the spouse before the move to ask what assistance would be helpful. Or she or he may put the spouse in touch with a newcomer's group in the new location. Area consultants are hired by some companies to compile in-depth, personalized information for families about the new community—to help locate schools and child care, find activities that the family wants to be involved in, and generally ease the social transition into the new area. Such services are often used to assist employees in the relocation decision-making process, and are also included as incentives in employee recruitment.

Thus companies are trying to not only help employees (especially fathers) handle the relocation offer wisely and make the best decision for themselves and their family, but are also providing support once the move is accepted and in process. Both employees and companies benefit from this increasing sensitivity to the relocation process.

Employer-Supported Child-Care Programs

According to a recent report from the Work and Family Information Center of the Conference Board (1985), out of six million U.S. businesses of all sizes, only 2,500 gave support of any kind to employee child-care needs. There are many reasons for this low level of corporate involvement. One is that employees can't generally communicate problems related to their personal lives, especially if they are not certain that management is sensitive to the issue, or if they feel pressure to keep their home life separate from the workplace. Another is that men have not traditionally had to deal with the responsibilities of day-to-day child care, and thus have generally not been advocates for corporate change in this area. However, as men increasingly assume child-care responsibilities, particularly in dual-earner and single-father families, the absence of employer-supported child-care programs is likely to become an important workplace issue for them.

Employer support of employee's child-care needs can take many different forms, representing a wide range of involvement and cost. Some examples of services offered include child-care centers, child-care information, work and family seminars, and provisions for care of sick children.

Child-Care Centers

The most visible (though not the most common) form of employer-supported child care is the on-site or near-site child-care center. These work-site child-care models vary in their administrative oganization, in their relationship with the sponsoring company, and in the cost to the employee. Some are incorporated as separate, non-profit organizations, which may receive start-up and initial operating funds from the sponsoring company, and may include children from the surrounding community as well. Others operate as a separate division within a company for employees receiving salary and benefits from the company. Another arrangement is for the child-care center, usually on company property, to be run by a day care organization, management firm, or consultant, through a contractual arrangement with the company. In this type of arrangement, the center may be run exclusively for employees' children, or may only give preference to employees' children, while being open to the general public. In addition, the company will usually be responsible for the cost of renovating appropriate space, but may not be responsible for other child-care costs.

Having the center on the company site may increase participation by fathers. One corporation's care coordinator whom we polled (Catalyst, 1985a) described this phenomenon:

> If you've got a facility like we have where 80% of our employees are male, you're going to have more fathers involved because you're moving the home function close to the workplace. I have the opportunity to see how fathers use the center. It enables them to work later. The proximity to the workplace helps stressful situations. If the fathers know the child is nearby or if the child is sick, they can check on them. (pp. 26–27)

Another coordinator reported little difference between mothers and fathers in their use of the center:

> They both get caught in the same bind of having late meetings. I think mothers and fathers are both equally concerned about the quality of child care. We have 37 families at our center. Two families are headed by single fathers and at least 20 to 23 of the other families have fathers who are very actively involved. (p. 4)

Among the sample of coordinators of employer-supported child-care centers interviewed, the general perception was one of changing parental attitudes and responsibilities, resulting in increased participation by fathers. One coordinator pointed out:

> When the center started in 1979 it was used predominately by females. Currently, it is a 50/50 use by males and females. Some of the reasons fathers are using the center include being single parents, having custody during holidays or summer vacations, their wives working elsewhere, and an interest in educational quality. (pp. 45–46)

Child-Care Information Service (CCIS)

Working parents consistently lack an easily accessible source of information on work and family issues. Employers may choose to provide such information for employees, thereby increasing employee appreciation, and easing the burden of having two simultaneous full-time roles as parent and employee. Various types of CCISs have become increasingly popular across the country, partly because they are relatively low-cost and low-risk.

Many employers address employees' need for information and guidance in finding affordable, quality child care through a CCIS, with some companies employing someone in-house to provide this kind of information. In most cases, however, the employer contracts with an existing community organization to provide this service for its employees. The Gillette Company in Boston has paid for a phone system that enables its employees to have a direct access to the local Child Care Resource Center. Ameritrust in Cleveland has contracted with the Center for Human Services there for information services and to identify (and, if necessary, recruit) good child-care providers for employees' children. IBM has taken this process a step further by contracting with resource and referral agencies throughout the United States, in order to create a national network of child-care information for IBM employees. A CCIS is often the first step a company takes into the area of addressing work and family issues. It serves as an excellent needs assessment tool—a way to document accurately employee child-care needs over an extended period of time.

An increasingly popular form of corporate involvement with CCISs is to help develop family day-care systems, in which four or five children are cared for by a provider in her (or his) own home. Many parents prefer this setting for their infants and toddlers; in fact, 40% of all working parents send their children to family day-care homes, making it the most popular form of child care. Corporations have also begun to recognize that family care systems are less costly than centers, and also better able to accommodate the specific scheduling needs of a particular company's employees. American Express, for example, has contracted with a third party to recruit providers and increase the supply of child care, to benefit its own employees as well as the community at large. IBM, through a third party, contracts with resource and referral agencies across the country. One of their goals is to recruit family day-care providers for IBM employees living in communities where there is an inadequate supply of child care.

Corporate support of family day-care systems, in addition to increasing the availability of child care, also offers the possibility of upgrading the quality. For example, the Steelcase Corporation's CCIS established a family day-care system which offers free workshops and lends equipment such as cribs, high chairs, and car seats to providers who care for employees' children. It also works with local organizations to recruit family home providers, and has funded several child-care projects through its corporate foundation, to upgrade the quality of child care for the whole community.

Fathers are increasingly making use of CCISs. According to a Catalyst poll on workplace policies for fathers (1985a), in one company where 80% of the employees were male, the CCIS coordinator reported that the majority of the requests for child care were initiated by fathers. Fathers' participation has also increased with time. Another coordinator noted that "There seems to be more interest in the idea of dual responsibility. The usage of the resource and referral service by fathers is very high—50% of the parents I talk to are fathers. That wasn't the case when we started in 1977" (p. 22).

However, while fathers in two-career families find CCISs useful, the service is especially important to men who find themselves suddenly in charge of their children's needs due to death, divorce, hospitalization, or absence of a spouse who had been the primary caregiver for the children. CCISs are also helpful to fathers who have visitation or custody of children in the summer and/or during school vacations. This service offers them assistance in finding child care, referral to other family support organizations, and someone to talk to.

Work and Family Seminars

Work and family issues are important to employees, the company, and the larger community, because the majority of employees today are working parents in two-earner or single-parent families. Companies are coming to see that the work/family issue is directly tied to the economic health of the company and the society as a whole. Thus a growing number are offering work and family seminars, a series of meetings conducted at the workplace by a professional facilitator, focused on combining work and family responsibilities. At these sessions, employees discuss how family life influences work, how people deal with work/family conflicts, and how they can help each other and help themselves find solutions. Seminars vary from company to company in format, content, length, and number of participants, but all have one common goal: to address the work and family concerns of employees. Such seminars are receiving greater attention nationwide as companies discover their advantages, including cost-effectiveness, ease of implementation, flexibility, and alleviation of employees' tensions.

Seminar facilitators we interviewed (Catalyst, 1985a) estimated fathers' participation at these sessions to be between 10–20%. They viewed these fathers as being really involved with their children, with concerns ranging from topics such as CPR for infants and toddlers, and preventing child sexual abuse, to choosing child care, and living with a teenager. On the other hand, one seminar facilitator observed that "Most fathers were uncomfortable and didn't benefit from that feeling of 'not being alone' because they were in the minority" (p. 30), and another reported that men sometimes leave if there aren't many other men in the room.

Facilitators also talked about the parenting feelings fathers have that are different from those of mothers. For example, unlike women, men tend not to express guilt, which may be a reflection of the fact that they do not have to deal with an internalized societal message that children are primarily their responsibility. Men are more likely to express a sense of loss, in that they are missing out on many of their child's experiences, or voice concern that their child is not receiving the proper training or influences. The lack of societal supports for fathers taking a more active parenting role has also been identified. The following are some facilitators' impressions (Catalyst, 1985a):

> Management men were encountering child care problems, but were unwilling to share that information with their bosses. These fathers took vacation or sick days. They would not take business trips that they would have taken before they had children. They still took their briefcase home but opened it less often after they had kids. They hoped in 5 or 10 years that their bosses would be more sensitive. (p. 51)

To change things the silence has to change. More fathers need to be vocal so that policy makers can hear their concerns. The Catch-22 is that being vocal with your supervisor can lead to more stress; yet to help supervisors become more sensitive, policy has to be enacted and supervisors are key in bringing employee concerns to management's attention. (p. 55)

Some of the men have expressed the feeling that it is unusual for them to participate in seminars. Their manager may have had difficulty understanding why they would want to participate. As men have become more involved fathers, they often have felt unsupported by the larger society. If they're the only man in the pediatrician's office or at the park, they feel uncomfortable with that. It's a part of what men have to work through. Part of that is to admit to employers that it is important. One way of signaling that is to participate in work and family seminars. (p. 34)

Care for Sick Children

A company may also have special programs to aid parents with a sick child. Such programs are not common, but where they are available, they meet important needs for both mothers and fathers. Data are available from a midwest manufacturing company that recently initiated a program through which the company helps parents pay for a health care worker when their child is sick (Catalyst, 1985a). Utilization of this service is high—an average of 10 days of child illness per family per year —with users being 40% male and 60% female.

The program surveyed its parents to find out how they used the service, and how they allocated responsibility for the sick child. One interesting finding was that although most parents said their first choice was to stay home with the sick child, this is not what they actually did; 41% used the health care workers and only 22% stayed home. This seemed to be a self-imposed restriction on the part of the employee, with 68% expressing concern that the time off would jeopardize their careers. Supervisors agreed—but only if the time off was excessive. In terms of responsibility, 68% of the parents said they shared it, but on a day-to-day basis, the responsibility was taken by whichever parent had a more flexible schedule. In addition to this program, the company also offers employees five days a year of paid leave, which can be taken at any time for a family emergency. Men use these days, but according to the program's coordinator, not at the rate that women do. "I would say that 25% of the time, the men stay home. It depends on whose job is more critical that day. The woman still has the primary responsibility" (p. 39). Respondents to the survey were all professionals, and the results confirm a general tendency that seems to prevail in the area of child care. Responsibility is shared more equally when both parents are professionals than when one has a job of lower status.

CONCLUSION

In this chapter we have tried to present a picture of new and emerging trends in workplace policies that have already begun to affect the lives of fathers and their families. The findings presented are by no means conclusive, since to date, data are sketchy. We have reported some statistics and research results, and we have provided specific incidences of particular policy areas and their use. Our goal has been to show what policies are available, to indicate how and why many of them are being used less frequently by men than by women, and to suggest some ways in which these policies may increasingly become the focus of fathers' attention, as well as a source of support for their increased involvement in family life.

In their work lives, fathers are testing the waters of acceptance as they drop their toddler off at the corporate day-care center, skip a company party to take their daughter to the dentist, use a sick day to stay home with a feverish child, and (for the daring few), request a parental leave to share the early special moments of parenthood with their spouse. For some, the struggle has been worthwhile. For others, it has been fraught with problems. But, as in all periods of transition, the important questions may be less about how today's fathers are coping, and more about how tomorrow's fathers will fare. There can be little doubt that the trend for mothers *and* fathers to nurture their children, as well as to work outside the home, will continue to grow.

The new workplace policies described in this chapter, such as paternity leave, employer-supported child care, and flexible benefits, will have to become increasingly available in the private as well the public sector. Employed fathers as well as mothers will need the support these policies can provide. Many will expect to find them, and will increasingly, if necessary, demand programs, structures, and climates at the work site that foster their ability to be productive workers, while participating in the experience of helping their children grow and develop.

But providing policies to help fathers share child-care responsibilities, or even urging them to do so, does not solve all the problems. How will fathers feel about their new roles? Will they find joy in them, or mainly frustration and threats to their self-esteem? Will women remain burdened by guilt when they exchange some of their time as mothers for the opportunity to earn an income and be competent adults outside the home? Will men be penalized if they choose to relinquish the "married-to-the-company" approach to their careers?

Catalyst recently engaged in an experiment in which eight college campuses across the country used our materials in classrooms and in extracurricular settings to help students integrate their educational and career goals with their plans for personal relationships and family life. Among other things, students were asked to consider what it means to become a parent, and how to grapple with the changing roles of fathers and mothers in the workplace and in the home.

Pilot tests at three campuses have produced some interesting results. Pre-testing revealed that the students were essentially uninformed and unrealistic about what they expected from the workplace and family life. Both males and females thought they could have it all, and had little concept of how to manage time, share household chores, choose child-care options, or handle workplace cultures. However, at the end of these Catalyst-designed courses, both women and men showed some changes. Women students showed an increased desire to achieve and to share their talents with society, not just with family members. Men, on the other hand, indicated a growing desire for the opportunity to find intimacy, love, and the chance to nurture others. Moreover, both female and male students concluded by the end of these courses that it was the obligation not only of government, but of private industry, to offer policies that support the development of stable family life for all employees.

Thus it seems likely that this type of educational experience can make a difference in the way men think about themselves, their place in the world of work, and their role in the family configuration. One young male student wrote in his journal:

> When and if I do become a father I will definitely take an active role in the raising of my child. I was basically brought up by my mother with my father only playing an outside role. I don't think this is the best way to raise a child and I plan to put an end to this tradition which is really quite sexist. . . .

When this student becomes a worker and father, will his employer accommodate for his commitment? Enlightened attitudes, or even practical responses to circumstances are often costly, and being a pioneer father at work or at home may not be a simple task. Many questions remain about the way family life will develop in the next few decades, as well as about how the changing structure of work will affect the male and female employees of today and tomorrow. A factor shaping the direction and effects of these changes will be the responsiveness of the workplace in providing child-care policies that allow for maximum individual and family functioning.

REFERENCES

Bureau of Labor Statistics (1985, September 19). Labor force activity of mothers of young children continues at record pace. Washington, DC: U.S. Department of Labor.

Catalyst (1981). *Corporations and two-career families: Directions for the future*. New York: Catalyst.

Catalyst (1983). *Human factors in relocation*. New York: Catalyst.

Catalyst (1985a). *In-house report on workplace policies and fathers*. Unpublished manuscript. New York: Catalyst.

Catalyst (1985b). *No false moves: Audio cassette program and workbook*. New York: Catalyst.

Catalyst (1986a). *The corporate guide to parental leaves*. New York: Catalyst.

Catalyst (1986b). *Report on a national study of parental leaves*. New York: Catalyst.

The Conference Board (1985). *Corporate financial assistance for child care*. (Research Bulletin #177). (Available from The Conference Board, 845 3rd Avenue, New York, NY 10022.)

Emlen, A., & Koren, P. (1984). *Hard to find and difficult to manage: The effects of child care on the workplace. A report to employers*. Portland, OR: Portland State University.

Googins, B., & Burden, D. (1987). *Balancing job and home life responsibilities: Managing work and family stress in corporations*. Boston, MA: Boston University.

Lamb, M.E., & Levine, J.A. (1983). The Swedish parental insurance policy: An experiment in social engineering. In M.E. Lamb & A. Sagi (Ed.), *Fatherhood and family policy*. Hillsdale, NJ: Erlbaum.

Merrill Lynch Relocation Management Inc. (1987). *A study of employee relocation policies among major U.S. corporations*. White Plains, NY: Merrill Lynch Relocation Management Inc.

Mills, D.Q. (1985). *The new competitors*. New York: Wiley.

Pleck, J.H. (1986). Employment and fatherhood: Issues and innovative policies. In M.E. Lamb (Ed.), *The fathers' role: Applied perspectives*. New York: Wiley.

Radin, N., & Goldsmith, R. (1983, April). *Predictors of father involvement in childcare*. Paper presented at the meeting of the Society for Research in Child Development, Detroit, MI.

U.S. Bureau of the Census. (1984). *Current population report: Household and family characteristics* (Series P-20, No. 398). Washington, DC: U.S. Government Printing Office.

ADDITIONAL WORKPLACE RESOURCES

Adolf, B., & Rose, K. (1985). *The employers guide to child care: Developing programs for working parents*. New York: Praeger Special Studies.

Baden, R.K., Genser, A., Levine, J.A., & Scligson, M. (1982). *School-age Child care: An action manual*. Wellesley College Center for Research on Women. Dover, MA: Auburn House.

School-age child care: An action manual. Baden, R.K., Genser, A., Levine, J.A., & Seligson, M. (1982). Wellesley College Center for Research on Women. Dover, MA: Auburn House.

Bureau of National Affairs. (1986). *Work and Family: A Changing Dynamic*. (Available from BNA's Customer Service Center, 9435 Key West Avenue, Rockville, MD 20850.)

Burud and Associates. *U.S. directory of corporate child care assistance*. (1986). (Available from Burud and Associates Inc., 553 South Marengo, Suite 102, Pasadena, CA 91101.)

Burud, S.L., Aschbacher, P.R., & McCroskey, J. (1984). *Employer supported child care*. Dover, MA: Auburn House.

BusinessLink: The Report on management initiatives for working parents. (Newsletter available from Resources for Child Care Management, P.O. Box 669, Summit, NJ 07901.)

Catalyst (1983). *Child care information service: An option for employer support of child care*. New York: Catalyst.

Catalyst (1983). *Focus groups: A needs assessment approach to corporate child care policy*. New York: Catalyst.

Catalyst (1984). *Today's recruits and the campus-workplace gap*. New York: Catalyst.

Catalyst (1984). *The two-gender work force and corporate policy*. New York: Catalyst.

Catalyst (1984). *Work and family seminars: Corporations respond to employees' needs*. New York: Catalyst.

Catalyst (1985). *Commitment and the young recruit*. New York: Catalyst.

Catalyst (1985). *On-site child care: Pros and cons*. New York: Catalyst.

Catalyst (1986). *Communicating a parental leave*. New York: Catalyst.

Catalyst (1986). *Flexible benefits: How to set up a plan when your employees are complaining, your costs are rising, and you're too busy to think about it*. New York: Catalyst.

Catalyst (1986). *Leave policies for adoptive parents*. New York: Catalyst.

Catalyst (1986). *Memo to managers: Parental leave.* New York: Catalyst.

Catalyst (1986). *Moving ahead on child care.* New York: Catalyst.

Catalyst (1987). *Corporate child care options.* New York: Catalyst.

Charnov, E.L., Lamb, M.E., Levine, J.A., & Pleck, J.H. (Eds.). (1987). A biosocial perspective on paternal behavior and involvement. In J.B. Lancaster, J. Altmann, A. Rossi, & L. Sherrod (Eds.), *Parenting across the lifespan: Biosocial dimensions.* Chicago: De Gruyter Aldine.

Children's Defense Fund. *The child care handbook.* (1982). (Available from Children's Defense Fund, 1520 New Hampshire Avenue N.W., Washington, DC 20036.)

Children's Defense Fund. (1982). *Employed parents and their children: A data book.* (Available from Children's Defense Fund, 1520 New Hampshire Avenue N.W., Washington, DC 20036.)

Family Resource Coalition. (1984). *Business and the parent workforce: Profit and productivity.* (Available from Family Resource Coalition, 230 N. Michigan Avenue, Suite 1625, Chicago, IL 60601.)

Fernandez, J.P. (1986). *Child care and corporate productivity: Resolving family/work conflicts.* Lexington, MA: Lexington Books.

Fredericks, B., Hartman, R., Morgan, G., & Rodgers, F. (1986). *A little bit under the weather: A look at care for mildly ill children.* (Available from Work/Family Directions, 200 The Riverway, Boston, MA 02215.)

Friedman, D.E. (1986, March–April). Child care for employees' kids. *Harvard Business Review,* pp. 28–34.

Friedman, D.E. (1986). *Families and work: Managing related issues.* (Available from The Work and Family Information Center, The Conference Board, 845 3rd Avenue, New York, NY 10022.)

Galinsky, E. (1986). Family life and corporate policies. In T.B. Brazelton & M. Yogman (Eds.), *In support of families.* Boston, MA: Harvard University Press.

Gilbert, L.A. (1985). *Men in dual-career families: Current realities and future prospects.* Hillsdale, NJ: Erlbaum.

Greif, G.L. (1983). *Meeting the needs of single fathers raising children alone: Practice and policy implications.* Paper presented at the National Association of Social Workers Professional Symposium, Washington, DC.

Klinman, D.G., & Kohl, R. (1984). *Fatherhood U.S.A.: The first national guide to programs, services, and resources for and about fathers.* New York: Garland.

Lamb, M.E., & Sagi, A. (1983). *Fatherhood and family policy.* Hillsdale, NJ: Erlbaum.

Magid, R.Y. (1983). *Child care initiatives for working parents: Why employers get involved.* (Available from American Management Association's Membership Publications Division, 135 West 50th Street, New York, NY 10020.)

Men's lives: Changes and choices. (1984). (Available from Wellesley College Center for Research on Women, Wellesley, MA.)

Nardone, T.J. (1986, February). Part-time workers: Who are they? *Monthly Labor Review,* pp. 13–19.

National Association for the Education of Young Children. (1986). *Information kit on employer assisted child care.* (Available from National Association for the Education of Young Children, 1834 Connecticut Avenue, Washington, DC 20009.)

National Commission on Working Women. (1985). *Child care fact sheet: Working mothers and children*. (Available from National Commission on Working Women, 1325 G Street N.W., Lower Level, Washington, DC 20005.)

Nelson, E.T. (1986). *Parent Supported Services at the Workplace: What's Involved?* (Available from Prospect Hill Parents' and Children's Center, 200 Fifth Avenue, Waltham, MA 02154.)

New Ways to Work. (1983). *Job sharing for organizations*. (Available from New Ways to Work, 149 Ninth Street, San Francisco, CA 94103.)

Pleck, J.H. (1985). *Working wives/working husbands*. Beverly Hills, CA: Sage.

Rothberg, D.S., & Cook, B.E. (1985). *Part-time professiona;: How to pursue a career on a part-time basis*. Washington, DC: Acropolis Books.

CHAPTER 19

Fathers' Roles in the Family: Implications for Research, Intervention, and Change

CAROLYN PAPE COWAN and PHYLLIS BRONSTEIN

Our goal in this volume has been to describe recent research, educational programs, and clinical work with fathers who live in a variety of family forms, in order to understand better the kinds of changes contemporary men are making in their family roles. We hoped to define the challenges men face when they move beyond the traditional provider role and become more directly involved in the care and rearing of their children, and the implications of these changes for researchers, for professionals who work with parents, and for parents themselves.

A number of general conclusions have emerged from the studies of fathers in these chapters. The first is that there has been a marked shift in the focus of family research from an exclusive emphasis on mothers and children; there are now numerous investigations of fathers from varied backgrounds, in different family configurations, and at various stages of the family life cycle. The fact that chapters in this volume represent the quests of investigators in the fields of psychology, sociology, pediatrics, social work, and nursing illustrates the salience of knowledge about the changing role of fathers across academic disciplines. And, as we go beyond the practice of simply repeating the early studies of mothers and children with fathers and children, and begin to include data about both parents, their children, their marriage, their cultural background, and their families of origin, the findings point the way toward a more integrated understanding of the complexity of real family life and relationships. Although there is still much to be learned about men's roles in contemporary families, the search is clearly underway.

The contributors to this book, studying fathers in White, Black, Mexican, and Chicano families have examined both the stereotypes and realities of men in different cultures. In reports of clinical practice and in-depth interviews with fathers who are married, widowed, or divorced, with and without custody of their children, the authors have provided us with an expanded view of both the strengths and vulnerabilities of fathers today. Within each of these family forms, men appear to be working against the stereotype of the work-obsessed, authoritarian, or psychologically absent father, uninterested in his wife's welfare or his children's development. The fathers encountered in these pages are often open and nurturant, and are trying to develop close relationships with their children, while researchers and clinicians attempt to keep pace.

FATHER INVOLVEMENT

The chapters in this volume describe fathers whose involvement in their children's lives varies widely. Radin presents an intensive study of Michigan fathers who chose to be primary caregivers of their children, and summarizes similar studies by Pruett (1983, 1985) in Connecticut, Lamb and his colleagues' (Lamb, Frodi, Hwang, Frodi, & Steinberg, 1982) in Sweden, and Russell (1982) in Australia. Bozett (Chapter 13), Hanson (Chapter 11), Loewen (Chapter 12), Santrock, Sitterle, and Warshak (Chapter 10), and Schwebel, Fine and Moreland (Chapter 17) describe the challenges for fathers and stepfathers as they try to work out meaningful and satisfying relationships with their children after divorce or the death of the mother. In all of these families, we see that there is still a significant discrepancy between men's actual involvement and what men and women think men's role in modern families ought to be.

The gap between wanting change and making it happen begins very early in the family cycle. In the Cowans' study of California couples having babies in the 1980s (Chapters 1 and 16), both husbands and wives predicted that men would be more involved in the care of their babies than they actually became in the first year of parenthood. Although fathers began taking on more housework and care of the baby between the first and second year of family formation, almost all maintained their former level of involvement in work or study, whereas their wives made dramatic shifts in their life course—which is just what Daniels and Weingarten (Chapter 3) found in families formed on the eastern seaboard in the 1950s and 1970s. These differences in how men and women assume parental roles persist beyond the family formation period. Barnett and Baruch's fathers of five- and nine-year-olds in the Boston area (Chapter 5) were involved in their children's care, but they were not *responsible* for remembering, planning, or scheduling child-care tasks or home chores. Similarly, comparisons between stepfathers and mothers (Santrock, et al., Chapter 10), and between grandfathers and grandmothers (Tinsley & Parke, Chapter 14) revealed similar role differences between women's and men's interactions with children.

While discrepancies between men's and women's roles, and between expectation and reality, may not be news to researchers engaged in family studies, they do appear to affect husbands' and wives' feelings about themselves and their marriage by contributing to marital conflict, dissatisfaction, and instability. In the few families where men and their wives have reversed the usual child-rearing and employment rules, we see how difficult it has been to maintain them. Radin's (Chapter 9) four-year follow-up of her primary caregiver fathers demonstrated how short-lived this unusual arrangement of fathering tends to be when children are young. Of the 59 primary caregiver fathers in Michigan, only 25% had maintained that role four years later; similarly, of the 18 primary caregiving fathers in Russell's (1982) Australian sample, only 22% had maintained that role two years later. The data from fathers in Sweden (Lamb, et al., 1982) seem to corroborate this general trend: The average age of the Swedish children cared for primarily by their fathers was 2.8 years. Thus while it is clear that a small proportion of modern fathers have become centrally involved in the early care and rearing of their children, these arrangements do not necessarily hold throughout the preschool years.

On the other hand, it is important to distinguish between men's responsibility for the day-to-day care of the home and children and their influence in the family. From the reports of parents' shared decision making and observations of fathers in laboratory and home settings, it is clear that fathers, like mothers, set limits for their children when they are working or playing (McAdoo, Chapter 6; Yogman, Cooley, & Kindlon, Chapter 4), and actively teach them about the world and about relationships (Bozett, Chapter 13; Bronstein, Chapter 8; McAdoo, Chapter 6; and Mirande, Chapter 7). Bronstein (Chapter 8) discusses the likelihood that fathers have distinct influences on boys' and girls' ideas about growing up male or female, and what behaviors and self-perceptions are appropriate for their gender.

Although several chapters discuss factors that contribute to men's involvement in the family, we have only a glimmering of what helps them *stay* involved. One important factor is parents' feelings about their own experience of being fathered when they were young. Radin's work, along with that of Barnett and Baruch and the Cowans, demonstrates that data on *both* spouses' experience of being fathered sheds light on parents' determination to enable the father to become and remain involved in the caregiving of the children.

What does men's greater involvement in the family mean for men themselves, for their relationships with their wives, and for the early development of their children? Although the findings from families at different points in the family life cycle present a mixed picture at the moment, in general, the more time men spend with their children when they are young, the happier husbands and wives appear to be about his involvement in parenting. However, at this stage of the research, reports of the effects on the marriage are contradictory. In the Cowans' (Cowan & Cowan, 1987) study of new parents, the more men were involved in the care of their babies, the happier parents were with that arrangement and the marriage. In Barnett and Baruch's families with elementary school children (Chapter 5), more involved fathers felt more competent as parents than less involved men, but some were critical of their wives' management of time and the children. Although Parke (1981) suggests that a close relationship between father and child benefits the father as well as the child, because "fathers need their children too" (p. 132), data on child effects are still sparse. Both Radin and Pruett (1983) report that primary-caregiving fathers are generally pleased with their involvement, and their infants and toddlers appear to be developing well, sometimes ahead of their age mates. In the Cowans' study of couples with varied levels of father involvement (Cowan & Cowan, 1985), fathers who worked fewer than 40 hours a week, and thus had more time to interact with their preschoolers, had children who were adapting better to new tasks and challenges than children with fathers who worked more than full time; the fathers who worked fewer hours also reported fewer symptoms of ill health, lower parental stress, and higher self-esteem and marital satisfaction. In a recent study of family factors and 10-year-old children's school adjustment and academic performance, Bronstein and her colleagues (Bronstein, D'Ari, Pieniadz, Franco, Duncan, & Frankowski, 1987) found that the more fathers were involved with their fifth graders, the higher were their sons' and daughters' achievement scores. Future research on the effects of fathers' involvement in the family must examine the direction of these effects more fully.

A number of studies suggest that it is difficult for men to become more involved in the family: men are not socialized to take on nurturing roles; mothers may be ambivalent about encroachment in their former area of expertise; parenting programs and services have generally not been designed to include fathers; and employers and legislators are generally not enthusiastic about men using work time for family matters. Given the considerable obstacles to fathers moving into more active parent roles, it often takes a concerted effort on the part of both mothers and fathers to "make room for daddy." There is evidence that when women do overcome their understandable ambivalence about sharing the role of expert with the children, and when men override their doubts about their competence in this family domain, fathers are able to become centrally involved in their children's lives.

The barriers to fathers' involvement are especially salient when fathers face single parenthood after divorce or the death of a spouse, as chapters by Bozett (Chapter 13), Loewen (Chapter 12), Hanson (Chapter 11), and Schwebel, et al. demonstrate. And, despite the fact that Hanson and Catalyst (Chapter 18) provide evidence to suggest that many fathers are doing well with little institutional and community support, the need for education, support systems, and preventive interventions to impart parenting skills and ease family strain is obvious.

FATHERHOOD AS A GENERATOR OF MEN'S DEVELOPMENT

We need to know more about what becoming a father and being a father means to men. When women become parents they feel dramatic changes in their sense of themselves (McBride, 1976; Hancock, 1981; Rossi, 1968). While Levinson (1978) and Gould (1978) have certainly been interested in charting men's development, they have highlighted men's career changes, and played down their experiences of family relationships. It is important that we hear more from men about this major adult role, in order to understand the part that being a father plays in a man's own development. The early transition to parenthood research characterized the transition from partner to parent as a "crisis," pointing to the unexpected changes that occurred in men and women, especially in their relationship as a couple. One of the fathers in the Becoming a Family project couples groups (Chapter 16) taught us that the Chinese characters for crisis connote "danger" and "opportunity." It seems to us that becoming a father—or a new kind of father at this time in history—may contain the potential for both. As Philip Cowan points out (Chapter 2), we have a good deal of lore and belief about parenthood serving as a generator of development in men's and women's lives, but little systematic research devoted to charting that development. He proposes new criteria for thinking about and analyzing longitudinal data charting men's lives, to explore the hypothesis that becoming a father provides men with an opportunity for their own maturation.

EDUCATION AND INTERVENTION FOR FATHERHOOD

What have the findings from programs and interventions for fathers taught us about contemporary fatherhood? There seems to be some good news and some bad news. The good news concerns men's eagerness to become more involved in the parent role, often expressed as a desire to be more involved with their children than their own fathers were with them. Despite the barriers in the world around them, men from many backgrounds and in varied family configurations are becoming more active in caring for their children. At different points in the life cycle, boys and men are beginning to participate in classes and groups that focus on fatherhood. Expectant fathers are getting involved in preparation for childbirth and "coaching" their wives during their babies' births. This sets up the expectation for both parents that men will continue to have a central role in their babies' lives, although most men go back to their former work load soon after their babies are born. Nevertheless, when information and actual child-care options were made available to men in their workplace, 50% of the men in the companies surveyed by Catalyst in 1984 (Chapter 18) made use of these resources, a significant increase since their 1977 survey.

The bad news is in some ways old news: the process of shifting the balance of family roles is a slow and sometimes painful one. At this point in history, couples are essentially on their own to figure out how to resolve these critical and conflicting dilemmas—how to be devoted workers, to be there during their children's development, and to keep their marriages viable (cf., Lamb, Pleck, & Levine, 1986). Employers are skeptical about men taking work time for family matters. Schwebel and his colleagues (Chapter 17) point out that both men and women want more flexible work schedules so that they can share more of the child care responsibilities than their own parents did, but that men experience seniority systems as insensitive to the needs of young families, and feel that they suffer from the negative evaluations of their colleagues when they take more time for family responsibilities. Thus despite the fact that men and women say that their families are more important than their careers (Catalyst, 1981), policies in business and industry have not yet begun to reflect these priorities.

Since there is evidence from studies of families in the United States and Australia that more involved fathers are happier with themselves, show fewer symptoms of ill health, and have wives who report greater satisfaction with their marriages, it is important that families have assistance and support available as they attempt to negotiate marital, parenting, and work arrangements for the family's well-being. Pedersen (1985) suggested that if change in men's family roles is to be instituted effectively, interventions will need to be made at multiple points in the family system and maintained through a significant period of time (p. 499). The innovative programs and interventions that are outlined in this book are examples of ways that professionals have begun to work with men to ease their task of becoming more involved in their families as husbands and fathers.

A LIFE SPAN VIEW OF FATHERHOOD

In order for us to understand fully the changes that fathers are making today, we will need truly longitudinal studies of men in their family roles. Researchers have looked at fathers during the transition to fatherhood, during children's elementary school years, and after marital dissolution and remarriage. However, there have been very few studies of fathers of older children or of grandfathers. What are the special considerations and experiences of fathers of adolescents and young adults, and of fathers with empty nests? We need more of a three-generational view to understand both the nature of fatherhood, and the influences of particular patterns of fathering on children and on the rest of the family as well (Hanson & Bozett, 1985; Tinsley & Parke, this volume).

What then can we conclude is the nature of fatherhood today? It would seem to be a role in transition, from an older, traditional model of the hardworking but unavailable figure responsible for the family's economic welfare, to a parent who is personally and emotionally involved in the day-to-day rearing of his children. We can think of this changing perspective in terms of a kind of fatherhood family photo album. In the early pages, there would be pictures of the father as a young boy, being held by his mother, or playing with his brothers and sisters—with his own father absent from those pictures, perhaps in a snapshot by himself on another page. Later pages would show the father's own young family, mostly with pictures of his wife holding or feeding their baby, or reading to their toddler son—but also a shot of him tossing his son in the air, and another with his infant daughter asleep in a carrier close against his chest.

Still later pages might have photos of family vacations—or the father, now by himself, with occasional snapshots of his children taken during their every-other-weekend visits with him. There might be pictures of a different woman and another set of children, with the father in the picture, but standing a little aside from the family grouping. Most of the album, however, would not yet be filled. Patterns of fathering in this culture are changing dramatically. Since the traditional role of noninvolved provider is no longer the preferred model, men in their families have new challenges and choices. The contributors to this volume have presented what is known about those challenges and choices today. With continuing research on fathers, and systematic evaluations of programs, policies, and interventions addressed to fathers' concerns, we will be able to understand and help facilitate the evolution of new roles for the father and mother of tomorrow.

REFERENCES

Bronstein, P., D'Ari, A., Pieniadz, J., Franco, O., Duncan, P., & Frankowski, B. (1987, April). *Parenting behavior as a predictor of early adolescent school functioning.* Paper presented at the Society for Research in Child Development, Baltimore, MD.

Cowan, C.P., & Cowan, P.A. (1985, April). Parents' work patterns, couple and parent-child relationships, and early child development. Paper presented to Society for Research in Child Development, Toronto, CAN.

Cowan, C.P., & Cowan, P.A. (1987). Who does what when partners become parents: Men's involvement in the family. *Marriage and Family Review, Vol. 13,* 1 & 2.

Gould, R. (1978). *Transformations: Growth and change in adult life.* New York: Simon & Schuster.

Hancock, E. (1981). *Women's development in adult life.* Unpublished dissertation, Harvard University.

Hanson, S.M.H. & Bozett, F.W. (Eds.) (1985). *Dimensions of fatherhood.* Beverly Hills, CA: Sage.

Lamb, M.E., Frodi, A.M., Hwang, C.P., Frodi, M., & Steinberg, J. (1982). Mother- and father-infant interaction involving play and holding in traditional and nontraditional Swedish families. *Developmental Psychology, 18,* 215–221.

Lamb, M.E., Pleck, J.H., & Levine, J.A. (1986). Effects of paternal involvement on fathers and mothers. In R.A. Lewis & M.B. Sussman (Eds.), *Men's changing roles in the family.* New York: Haworth.

Levinson, D.J. (1978). *Season of a man's life.* New York: Knopf.

McBride, A.B. (1976). *Living with contradictions: A married feminist.* New York: Ballantine.

Parke, R. (1981). *Fathers.* Cambridge: Harvard University Press.

Pedersen, F.A. (1985). Research and the father: Where do we go from here? In S.M.H. Hanson & F.W. Bozett (Eds.), *Dimensions of fatherhood.* Beverly Hills, CA: Sage.

Pruett, K.D. (1983, April). *Two year follow-up of infants of primary-nurturing fathers in intact families.* Paper presented at the Second World Congress in Infant Psychiatry, Cannes, France.

Pruett, K.D. (1985). Oedipal configurations in young father-raised children. In A.J. Solnit, R.S. Eissler, & P.B. Neubauer (Eds.), *The psychoanalytic study of the child, Vol.40.* New Haven: Yale University Press.

Rossi, A. (1968). Transition to parenthood. *Journal of Marriage and the Family, 30,* 26–39.

Russell, G. (1982). Shared-caregiving families: An Australian study. In M.E. Lamb (Ed.), *Nontraditional families: Parenting and child development.* Hillsdale, NJ: Erlbaum.

Author Index

225, 228, 229, 230; (1979b), 214, 220,
221, 224, 229; (1983), 214, 223, 228;
(1986), 214, 221, 223, 224, 228, 229
Miller, B.C., & Bowen, S.L. (1982), 262
Miller, J.B. (1975), 28
Miller, W.B. (1958), 82
Mills, D.Q. (1985), 324
Minuchin, S. (1974), 279
Mirandé, A. (1985), 93; (1988), 343
Mitchell, G.D. (1969), 54
Montemayor, R. (1982), 68
Montiel, M. (1970), 94
Moos, R.H. (1974), 19, 30
Moreland, J., & Schwebel, A.I. (1981), 301,
313
Moreland, J., Schwebel, A.I., Fine, M.A., &
Vess, J.D. (1982), 311, 315
Mortimer, S., Hall, R., & Hall, R. (1976), 67
Moses, A.E., & Hawkins, R.O. (1982), 227
Moss, H.A. (1972), 120
Mowatt, M.H. (1972), 146
Moynihan, D.P. (1965), 82
Mrazek, D.A., Dowdney, L., Rutter, M.L., &
Quinton, D.L. (1982), 58
Myrdal, G. (1944), 80

Nahemow, N.R. (1984), 239, 240, 241
Nash, J. (1955), 66
National Commission on Working Women
(1983), 4
Neckerman, K.M., & Wilson, W.J. (1986), 81
Nelsen, E.A., & Maccoby, E.E. (1966), 140
Neugarten, B.L. (1968), 22
Neugarten, B.L., & Gutmann, D.L. (1968), 238
Neugarten, B.L., & Moore, J.W. (1968), 237
Neugarten, B.L., & Weinstein, K.K. (1964),
239, 240, 241, 246
Newberger, C.M. (1977), 266
Newman, G. (1981), 208
Newson, J., & Newson, E. (1963; 1968), 6,
108
Nichols, C.H. (1972), 80
Nichols, J. (1975), 301
Nieto, D.S. (1982), 310; (1983), 104
Noam, G. (1985), 23
Norton, A.J., & Glick, P.G. (1986), 190
Nuckolls, K.B., Cassell, J., & Kaplan, B.H.
(1972), 278

O'Dell, D. (1974), 259
Oakland, T. (1984), 196
Oppenheimer, V. (1974), 40
Orthner, D., & Bowen, G.L. (1985), 178, 179
Orthner, D., Brown, T., & Ferguson, D.

(1976), 168, 170, 180, 181, 184, 264, 302,
308, 313
Orthner, D., & Lewis, K. (1979), 166, 167,
181
Oshman, H., & Manosevitz, M. (1976), 148
Osofsky, H. (1982), 13
Osofsky, J.D., & O'Connell, E.J. (1972), 88,
111, 255, 266
Osofsky, J.D., & Osofsky, H.J. (1985), 15

Packer, A., Resnick, M., Resnick, J.L., &
Wilson, J.M. (1978), 263
Palmer, C.E., & Noble, D.N. (1984), 167, 186
Pannor, R., Massarik, F., & Evans, B. (1971),
263
Paredes, A. (1967), 94; (1977), 104
Parens, H. (1975), 22
Parke, R. (1979), 62, 110, 236, 237, 278, 293;
(1981), 29, 343
Parke, R.D., Grossman, K., & Tinsley, B.R.
(1981), 109
Parke, R.D., & O'Leary, S.E. (1976), 108,
109, 110
Parke, R.D., O'Leary, S.E., & West, S.
(1972), 57, 108, 109, 300
Parke, R.D., Power, T.G., & Gottman, J.M.
(1979), 238
Parke, R.D., & Sawin, D.B. (1975), 7, 55, 62,
108, 109, 110; (1976), 261, 300; (1980),
109, 110
Parke, R.D., & Tinsley, B.R. (1981), 237, 240;
(1982), 15; (1984), 247
Parsons, T. (1951), 28; (1955), 66
Parsons, T., & Bales, R.F. (1955), 112
Pasley, K., & Ihinger-Tallman, M. (1984), 146
Patterson, G.R. (1980), 88
Paz, O. (1961), 94
Pearson, J., Munson, P., & Theonnes, N.
(1982), 185, 186
Pedersen (1985), 345
Pedersen, F.A., Anderson, B., & Cain, R.
(1977), 278; (1980), 109
Pederson, F.A., & Robson, K.S. (1969), 6, 56,
108, 109, 300
Pedersen, F., Yarrow, L.J., Anderson, B.J., &
Cain, R. (1979), 62
Pedersen, F., Zaslow, M., Suwalsky, J., &
Cain, R. (1982), 61
Perrucci, C., Potter, H.R., & Rhoads, D.L.
(1978), 67
Peterson, N. (1984), 217
Pettigrew, T.F. (1964), 82
Phillips, C.R.N. (1978), 45
Piaget, J. (1967), 30

Piaget, J., & Inhelder, B. (1967), 26
Pichitino, J.P. (1983), 307
Pleck, J.H. (1977), 253; (1981), 67, 93; (1981a), 42, 254; (1981b), 41, 254; (1981c), 255; (1983), 67, 68, 70, 74, 75; (1986), 328, 329
Pleck, J.H., & Brannon, R. (1978), 93
Pleck, J.H., & Lang, L. (1978), 254
Pleck, J., & Sawyer, J. (1974), 301
Ponte, M. (1974), 217
Power, T.G., & Parke, R.D. (1979), 57; (1981), 109, 110, 112; (1982), 7; (1983), 109
Price–Bonham, S., & Skeen, P. (1979), 85, 86, 256, 259, 261, 264
Pruett, K.D. (1983), 137, 138, 342; (1985), 129, 139, 141, 342

Radin, N. (1972), 86, 87; (1976), 140, 255, 266; (1981), 61, 68, 119, 120, 128, 137, 140, 141, 299; (1982), 128, 137, 139, 140, 141, 256; (1985), 68; (1986), 140; (1988), 42, 342, 343
Radin, N., & Goldsmith, R. (1983), 130, 324; (1985), 5, 127, 130
Radin, N., & Russell, G. (1983), 127
Radin, N., & Sagi, A. (1982), 128, 137, 140, 141, 299
Ramirez, R. (1979), 103
Ramos, S. (1962), 94, 102; (1979), 195, 196, 199
Rapoport, R. (1963), 13, 279
Rapoport, R., Rapoport, R.N., & Streilitz, A. (1977), 15, 279
Raush, H.L., Barry, W.A., Hertel, R.K., & Swain, M.A. (1973), 277; (1974), 278
Rebelsky, F., & Hanks, C. (1971), 109
Redican, W.K. (1976), 54
Reibstein, A. (1981), 280
Reisinger, J.J. (1982), 265
Reisinger, Ora, & Frangia (1976), 259
Rendina, I., & Dickerscheid, J.D. (1976), 57, 109, 110
Resnick, J.L., Resnick, M.B., Packer, A.B., & Wilson, J. (1978), 262
Ricci, I. (1980), 203, 204, 205, 206
Richards, M., Dunn, J.F., & Antonis, B. (1977), 109
Riegel, K.R., Riegel, R.M., & Meyer, G.A. (1967), 238
Risman, B.J. (1986), 174, 176, 178, 179, 180, 181
Rivara, F., Sweeney, P., & Henderson, B. (1986), 83

Robertson, J.F. (1975), 242
Robinson, B.E. (1984), 144, 146, 147, 150
Robinson, B.E., & Barrett, R.L. (1986), 181, 185
Robinson, J. (1977), 254
Robson, I., & Moss, H. (1970), 55
Rodholm, M. (1981), 55
Rogers, C. (1957), 266
Rosenberg, M. (1979), 25
Rosenthal, K., & Keshet, H. (1981), 171, 172, 195, 209, 210
Ross, H.L. (1972), 217
Ross, J.M. (1975), 54
Ross, M.W. (1983), 217
Rossi, A. (1968), 15, 17, 277, 344
Rotter, J. (1966), 25
Rubel, A.J. (1966), 97, 100, 104
Ruddick, S. (1980), 41
Russell, C. (1974), 15
Russell, G. (1982), 66, 109, 127, 128, 129, 133, 133, 138, 139, 342; (1985), 236, 237, 239, 240, 241, 299, 342
Russell, G., & Radin, N. (1983), 67, 75
Rypma, C.B. (1976), 54

Saghir, M., & Robins, E. (1973), 217
Sagi, A. (1982), 128, 137, 141
Sanchez, A.F. (1979), 102
Santrock, J. (1972), 148
Santrock, J.W., & Sitterle, K.A. (1987), 146, 161
Santrock, J.W., Sitterle, K.A., & Warshak, R. (1988), 296, 342
Sanfrock, J., & Warshak, R. (1979), 7, 151, 167, 177, 181, 182, 183
Santrock, J.W., Warshak, R.A., & Elliot, G.W. (1982), 150, 151, 196, 209
Santrock, J.W., Warshak, R., Lindbergh, C., & Meadows, L. (1982), 147, 148, 149
Satir. V. (1972), 279
Sawin, D.B., & Parke, R.D. (1979), 256, 300
Scallen, R.M. (1981), 228
Scarpitti, F.R., Murray, E., Dinitz, S., & Reckless, W.C. (1960), 82
Schaffer, H.R., & Emerson, P.E. (1964), 6, 108
Schlesinger, B. (1974), 167; (1977), 167; (1978a), 167; (1978b), 167, 179; (1985), 167, 178, 179
Schlesinger, B., & Todres, R. (1976), 308
Schulenburg, J. (1985), 217, 227, 229
Schwartz, S.F.G. (1984), 186
Schwebel, A.I., Fine, M.A., & Moreland, J. (1988), 38, 188, 342, 344, 345

Subject Index

and communication with children, 310
divorced, 299
research need for, 316
stress in, 308
and daughters,
  behavior with, 115, 116, 118
  and cognitive achievement, 111
  encouragement of vocal behavior, 110
  social interaction with, 111
decision making by, 130
education of, 132
employment policies, 285–86 (See also, Employment)
homosexual, 214
  career development, 219–20, 222–23
  child relations, 226, 228–30
  children of, acceptance by gays, 224
  children's reactions to, 223–24, 225, 226–28
  and children's sexual identity, 230–31
  closeted, 221
  and gay relationships, 223
  marriage, 217–18
  parenting, 223, 229
  restrictions due to children, 223
and household tasks, 68–69, 71, 324
involvement, 6, 7, 20
  barriers to, 344
  in child care, 66, 71, 76
  determinents of, 73
  effects on family, 342–44, 345–46
  employment, 61–62, 67, 70, 74
  family structure, 67, 70, 73, 75
  level of, 70–73
  marital relationship, 61, 76, 277, 281–82
  and maternal employment, 61, 66–67, 73, 74
  maternal illness, 61
  mother's feelings, 61
  and newborns, 53, 55, 56–57, 61, 286, 287, 289–90, 342
  with preschoolers & older children, 111
  research on, 76
  sex-role attitudes, 67, 68, 70, 73, 74, 75
  socialization, 67, 68, 70, 73
  socioeconomic status, 67, 70, 75
  well–being, 75–76
Israeli, 128, 137
in the media, 3
Mexican, 113, 114, 115, 117
noncustodial, 302, 307
  and communication with children, 307
  problems of, 6, 307
nonvisitation, 198–99
nurturance by, 128, 132, 135, 137, 140

parenting skills, 300
perception of parents, 135
with preschoolers & older children, type of play, 111, 118
  verbal dominance, 111
as primary caregivers, 127, 128, 129, 130, 131–32, 133, 136, 137, 139, 141
  age of, 135
  education, 135
and psychological control, 115
research on, 6, 108
roles, 180
  emergent, 299
  in fostering autonomy, 57–58, 61
  inhibitions on, 301
  interpersonal behavior, 299
  nontraditional, 299
  traditional, 141, 299
  in transition, 341, 346
single, 166–67, 178–79, 324
  adoption, 167
  demographic characteristics of, 178, 179
  differences among, 301–2
  divorced, 166–67, 299
  homemaking, 181
  income support, 181
  and nurturance, 181–82
  problems of, 184, 301–2
  research on, 166–67, 177, 190
  social support for, 182–83, 187–88
  socio-economic status, 179, 187
  strengths of, 184–85
  visitation, 183, 195
socialization of, 190
and sons,
  behavior with, 110, 118
  and cognitive achievement, 111
  controlling and directive of, 110, 111, 115
  encouragement of exploration, 110
  instructive of, 115–16
  as role models, 119–20
as "superdads," 3
Swedish, 127, 129
widowed, 167, 299, 308–10
  and intervention, 310, 313
Flexible hours, 132, 138, 326–27
  child-care responsibilities, 138, 139, 301
Freedman's Bureau, 81

Gay identity, development of, 218
Gay men, before marriage, 219–20
  marriage and anger, 221
  married, sex with men, 220
  separation and divorce, 221, 222